4/24   £3

THE LOST PRIME MINISTER

The Dilke Family Crest

Pencil drawing of Dilke by W. Strang, 1908

THE
LOST PRIME MINISTER

———

A LIFE OF SIR CHARLES DILKE

DAVID NICHOLLS

THE HAMBLEDON PRESS
LONDON   AND   RIO GRANDE

Published by The Hambledon Press 1995

102 Gloucester Avenue, London NW1 8HX (U.K.)
P.O. Box 162, Rio Grande, Ohio 45674 (U.S.A.)

ISBN 1 85285 125 2

A description of this book is available from the British
Library and from the Library of Congress

Typeset, printed on acid-free paper and bound in
Great Britain by Cambridge University Press

Contents

Illustrations

(Between Pages 162 and 163)

Text Illustrations

Acknowledgements

The author and the publisher are most grateful to the following for permission to reproduce illustrations: Birmingham Library Services, pl. 7; the British Library, p. 194, pls 3, 4, 5, 10, 12, 14, 15, 16, 19; the Master and Fellows of Churchill College, Cambridge, pls 13, 18, 19; the Cooperative Union Library, Manchester, p. 7; Manchester Central Library, pl. 21; the National Portrait Gallery, pls 6, 8, 9.

Preface

Sir Charles Dilke was one of the most prominent nineteenth-century radicals. Hitherto, he has been the subject of two biographies. By comparison, other leading radicals, such as Cobden, Bright and Chamberlain, have been paid much greater attention by historians, while lesser figures, such as Henry Labouchere, have received at least as much as Dilke. An official two-volume *Life*, by Gertrude Tuckwell and Stephen Gwynn, was published in 1917. Tuckwell was the niece of Dilke's second wife and determined to portray her uncle in the most favourable possible light. To this end, she excised materials from the Dilke Papers (a process sanctioned by Dilke in his will appointing her his literary executrix), and at the same time used them in a way that distorted the overall picture of his life and career. The resultant hagiography almost totally ignored the scandal that ruined him. A contemporary diarist observed when the biography came out 'that Dilke only cared for beds and blue-books, and that in this book the beds were left out'.[1]

This omission was made good by Roy Jenkins in his 1958 biography, *Sir Charles Dilke: A Victorian Tragedy*. The two years covered by the divorce case occupy two-fifths of his narrative. However, as Jenkins himself admitted, his account remained dependent on the Dilke Papers. His biography contained little that was new on Dilke's political career nor, reflecting the time at which it was produced, did it have much to say by way of assessment of his contribution to the overall trajectory of nineteenth-century radicalism.

The need for a thoroughly researched and up-to-date biography is illustrated by the entry on Dilke in a recent dictionary of modern British radicals. It is suffused with serious omissions and questionable interpretations.[2] Among the latter is the assertion that the second half of the 1870s was an 'uneventful' period of Dilke's life yet that he was being considered as a possible future Prime Minister by the end of that decade; an apparent contradiction which is not satisfactorily explained. Furthermore, Dilke's radicalism during the 1870s 'may properly be questioned', and only under Chamberlain's influence did he move 'quickly leftward in an ideological sense'. After 1886 he 'sank into semi-obscurity', and on returning to the Commons 'took little part in its proceedings', adopting an 'apathetic position' on such questions as the Boer War and tariff reform. I offer a substantively different assessment of all these aspects of Dilke's life, reinterpreting his major achievements and providing information on the events which appear, on the evidence of this dictionary-entry, to have passed from historical memory.

To this end, I have consulted a large number of primary sources, most of them untapped by Dilke's earlier biographers. This has been especially necessary given the extent to which his own papers were doctored and mutilated. Such censorship was not simply, or even primarily, the work of Gertrude Tuckwell but a process which Dilke had begun himself, and one which cast his character in a bad light at the time of the divorce scandal. He admitted that he never kept any letter which he did not intend to use in compiling his own personal Memoir.[3] He appears to have believed that only a person's public life should be public property. The rest was private. To this end, he not only carefully pruned his own papers but he also burnt letters in his possession concerning John Keats's relationship with Fanny Brawne. He sometimes bought letters solely for the purpose of destroying them. When one vendor reproved him for this and waxed lyrical upon the importance of rescuing 'from destruction, every such relic of great men' and of cherishing all they had written, Dilke scribbled across the letter: 'A specimen of the folly of not burning letters.'[4]

In addition to the Dilke Papers themselves, therefore, considerable use has been made of other private collections and of the voluminous documentation of Dilke's public speeches and writings. He was an assiduous parliamentarian and his speeches in the House of Commons and in the country are a valuable source. Above all, he was a prolific writer. While previous biographers have made good use of the several books he wrote, his numerous pamphlets and the essays he contributed to a wide range of periodicals have been less well used. These sources, which are listed in full at the end of this book, permit a more complete assessment of his life than anything hitherto. In particular, apart from the additional and corrective information which they provide, they allow a clearer picture of Dilke's radicalism to emerge and thereby make it easier to situate his politics within, and to assess his contribution to, the English radical tradition.

Without any apparent trace of irony or evidence that he was thinking of his own fortunes at the hands of posterity, Dilke remarked, upon the success of Greville's *Memoirs*, that it made one think that 'the art of *biography consists* solely *in the reviving of forgotten* scandals'.[5] At the risk of failing in that art, the emphasis in the present biography will not be upon the intimate details of the *cause célèbre* of Dilke's own life, which Jenkins described so fully. I have, however, made use of the evidence assembled at Cambridge by the historian Stephen Roskill, who was descended from both parties to the case by virtue of the marriage of Dilke's brother, Ashton, to Virginia Crawford's sister, Maye. In the wake of Jenkins's account of the scandal, and from a strong feeling that it had done less than justice to his great aunt's part in the story, Roskill accumulated papers belonging to the Crawford side of the family that permit some new reflections on the case. Notwithstanding, Dilke deserves much more from history than to be remembered primarily as the central player in a sordid sex-scandal. It ended his chances of becoming Prime Minister and thereby reduced his political effectiveness. Although important for this and for the light which the scandal throws upon Victorian social mores, Dilke accomplished many things in spite of it. The focus of the present book will therefore be upon his political ambitions and achievements, and above all upon an assessment of his contribution to the progress of radicalism as it unfolded during his political life.

Historians owe a huge debt to librarians and archivists. I have nothing but admiration for the courtesy and help which they invariably continue to provide, despite the ever increasing pressures upon their time and resources. I would particularly like to thank the staff of the following institutions: Birmingham University Library; the Bodleian Library, Oxford; the British Library at Bloomsbury and Colindale; the British Library of Political and Economic Science; the Churchill Archives Centre at Cambridge University; the Cooperative Union Library, Manchester; the Liverpool Record Office, Liverpool Libraries and Information Services; Manchester Central Reference Library; Manchester Metro-politan University Library; the Museum of Labour History, Manchester; the National Army Museum, London; the Public Record Office, Chancery Lane; the Library of University College, London; and the Library of the University of Kent.

I am grateful to several of these for granting me permission to use the private papers in their possession listed in the bibliography at the end of this book. I also wish to thank the following for their kindness in allowing me to use and to quote from private papers for which they own the copyright: the British Library; the Trustees of the Chatsworth Settlement; Lord Derby; Sir John Dilke; the Hon. Mrs E. A. Gascoigne; the Master and Fellows of Churchill College, Cambridge; Lord Monk Bretton; Mr John W. Roskill; Mr Nicholas Roskill; Baron Simon of Glaisdale; and Mr W. K. Stead. I beg the indulgence of any owner of copyright material whom I have unsuccessfully or unwittingly failed to trace.

Manchester Metropolitan University granted me study leave during 1992–93 and 1993–94 which expedited the completion of this book. One of my students, Patricia Harrington, assisted me with a useful bibliographical search undertaken as part of an undergraduate project. The Registrar of Wills kindly supplied me with a copy of the will of Sir Charles Dilke.

Writing a book of this sort inevitably incurs some special debts. The late Professor F. S. L. Lyons first suggested the subject to me many years ago. I will never forget the gentle and humane way in which he managed my early and jejune researches. Latterly, I owe thanks to Professor John Saville for his stimulating and constructive comments on a first draft of the biography and for encouraging me to complete it. I am grateful also for the painstaking care with which Mr Martin Sheppard of Hambledon Press has supervised its production. As always, my greatest debt is to Carol. Needless to say, any errors that remain are entirely my own.

In the notes throughout this book, the place of publication is London unless otherwise stated.

Abbreviations

BP	Battersea Papers
CP	Carlingford Papers
C-BP	Campbell-Bannerman Papers
CRA	Congo Reform Association
CWD	Papers of Sir Charles Wentworth Dilke, 3rd baronet
DP	Papers of Sir Charles Wentworth Dilke, 2nd baronet
DFM	*Dean Forest Mercury*
EHP	Edward Hamilton Papers
FH	Frederic Harrison Papers
GP	Granville Papers
G. & T.	S. Gwynn & G. M. Tuckwell, *The Life of Sir Charles W. Dilke* (2 vols, 1917)
HGP	Herbert Gladstone Papers
IP	Iddesleigh Papers
JBP	John Burns Papers
JC	Joseph Chamberlain Papers
LCC	London County Council
LGB	Local Government Board
LHJ/LHP	Lewis Harcourt's Journal/Lord Harcourt Papers
LTRA	Land Tenure Reform Association
MBP	Monk Bretton Papers
MFGB	Miners' Federation of Great Britain
MP	Miscellaneous Papers (correpondence of Hepworth Dixon)
NEL	National Education League
NLF	National Liberal Federation
PD(3)	*Parliamentary Debates*, third series
PD(4)	*Parliamentary Debates*, fourth series
PD(5)	*Parliamentary Debates*, fifth series

PP   *Parliamentary Papers*
REND   Roskill-Enthoven-Dilke Papers
RP   Ripon Papers
STED   William T. Stead Papers
SWP   Spenser Wilkinson Papers
TUC   Trades Union Congress
WEG   William Ewart Gladstone Papers
WHP   William Harcourt Papers

In
Memory
of
Mark and Paul

who never had the chance to
make their own history

Introduction

Sir Charles Dilke's name has recently been in the newspapers again, but for the wrong reasons. Under the lurid headline, CABINET MINISTER'S THREE-IN-A-BED ROMP, the former Conservative Minister Kenneth Baker used the spate of scandals that have rocked his party as an opportunity to resurrect in the pages of the *Daily Express* the salacious details of the Dilke-Crawford divorce case of 1886.[1] Only by a careful reading of Baker's text was it possible to discern that the events he described might never have actually taken place.

The calumny of Mrs Crawford's accusation continues to haunt Dilke's reputation and to overshadow his achievements, which were by no means insignificant. He was one of the most advanced reformers of his day who was regarded by many of his contemporaries as a future Prime Minister. He was a prolific and successful author who published a best-selling travelogue at the youthful age of twenty-five. He had an almost unparalleled knowledge of foreign, imperial and defence questions and was able to influence government policy both as a Minister and from the backbenches. He represented Chelsea and the Forest of Dean, each for eighteen years, during which time he was responsible for legislation which democratised the constitution and for social reforms which improved the lives of working men and women. He formed an alliance with the other leading radical of the day, Joseph Chamberlain, which for a while seemed likely to transform Victorian Liberalism. The story of Dilke's life therefore is one of much more than passing or prurient interest. It offers a fascinating insight into the High Politics of the late nineteenth century, especially the relationship between aristocratic Whigs and middle-class radicals, which cannot be ignored by anyone wishing to understand the history and changing fortunes of the Liberal Party. His reforming instincts and legislative initiatives, and his empathy with labour and feminist issues, are indicative of the potential for a radicalised Liberal Party to survive into the era of modern politics. While, therefore, the continuing fascination with the mystery surrounding his private life is perfectly comprehensible, it should not be allowed to distract or detract from his public record.

To understand Dilke's political career, it is necessary to know something about the historical context in which he operated. He was part of a reforming tradition in English politics known as 'radicalism'. It is rare to find evidence that radicals ever gave much thought as to why they were called 'radical'. In the early nineteenth century the epithet was used as a term of abuse denoting, as Sir Walter Scott wrote in 1819, 'a set of blackguards'. However, as is often the case, the intended victims took up the title and, in the words of one of them, the Benthamite Thomas Perronet Thompson, began to 'glory in the designation'.[2] The noun 'radical' was usually reserved for those individuals who believed in advanced reform, particularly parliamentary reform. As time went on, it was increasingly used indiscriminately to describe any root-and-branch reformer. It came, therefore, to be applied to individuals of very different background and outlook from across the political spectrum (such as the Whig Lord Durham, the Tory Richard Oastler and the Chartist Bronterre O'Brien).

As a result, historians have, in general, despaired of finding any consistency or coherence in nineteenth-century radicalism. Indeed, it has been pronounced 'practically useless' as an analytical concept.[3] It might appear that the most that can be said about the English radical tradition is that it has embraced all classes and given rise to an eclectic programme of reforms driven by humanitarianism. This view of radicalism as sentimentalist, untheoretical and idealist is echoed in F. D. Roosevelt's famous definition of a radical as 'a man with both feet firmly planted in the air'.

Despite the contradictions and inconsistencies surrounding the use of the term 'radicalism', I believe that there are sufficient policies and practices shared by English reformers to justify retaining it as an explanatory concept.[4] The development of radicalism as an ideology of reform is, in fact, best understood in the context of the progress of British capitalism. During the eighteenth century British economy and society had expanded dramatically. The countryside was transformed by the rapid enclosure of land and the organisation of the agrarian economy on capitalist lines. The successful prosecution of commercial wars led to increased trade, the expansion of the British Empire, a massive accumulation of capital and the consolidation of a mercantile elite whose power-base was the City of London. Surplus capital was invested in improving transport, especially by building roads, canals and, later, railways, and in

new technological processes that marked the beginnings of industrialisation. Among the social changes that accompanied this economic
progress were the substantial growth in the population of England and
Wales (from around 7,000,000 in 1750 to 18,000,000 in 1850), its
displacement from the countryside into towns and cities, and the rise in the
political awareness and activity of the middle and working classes.

The political system was placed under great stress by these changes.
Following the constitutional settlement of 1689, which confirmed parliament's supremacy over the Crown, a ruling bloc consisting of landed
gentlemen and wealthy merchants had consolidated its grip on the levers
of political power: by extending the life of parliament to seven years; by
monopolising parliamentary seats through the control of elections; and by
protecting its privileges, sinecures and rewards through such measures as
the Place and Pension Bills. The outcome was a closed, oligarchic system
which William Cobbett later disparagingly christened 'Old Corruption'.
The new social groups spawned by the growth of the economy came
increasingly to challenge these political arrangements. An emerging
'middling class', consisting of the lesser merchants, tradesmen and
craftsmen, especially in London, joined forces with the politically-excluded
Tory gentry of the country at large to demand reform. They turned for
ideological inspiration to the seventeenth-century Commonwealth tradition and formulated a radical programme (essentially peace, retrenchment and parliamentary reform) designed to prise open the closed political
system. The most sustained of these early campaigns were those led by
John Wilkes in London and by the Rev. Christopher Wyvill in Yorkshire.
They would almost certainly have succeeded in reforming parliament in
the late eighteenth century but for the alarm generated by the revolutionary upheavals in France, which inaugurated a period of reaction.
Faced with a politicised artisanal class, most middle-class radicals drew
back for the time being from their confrontation with Old Corruption.

Pressure for reform was renewed after the Napoleonic Wars and, for a
while, serious social conflict seemed possible. That prospect was reduced,
however, by the compromise of 1832, when the aristocracy conceded a
limited measure of enfranchisement to a section of the middle class. The
Reform Act of that year set a pattern for political relations between the old
and the new wealth which persisted for much of the next half century: a
predominantly landed parliament prepared to enact, in the face of
organised pressure, reforms that were vital to the interests of the middle
classes. For as long as the aristocracy dominated parliament, the pressure-
group was one of the most important organisational forms employed by
middle-class reformers to bring about change. Important among the

concessions extracted by such tactics prior to 1850 were the New Poor Law, the reform of the municipal corporations, the reduction of the newspaper taxes, the repeal of the Corn Laws and the freeing of trade generally. The generic terms 'radicals' and 'radicalism' were used with increasing frequency to describe the protagonists of these reforms and their multi-faceted programme. Among the supporters of radical reform were the politically excluded; those with religious grievances, especially the large body of Nonconformists who felt discriminated against; the newly wealthy, such as the manufacturers of northern England, who wanted legislation to catch up with and reflect economic progress; members of the rising professions, some of whom gave a theoretical voice to radicalism and helped to articulate the general discontents of the middle class; and the so-called 'crotcheteers', individuals who regarded the government as an obstacle to some cherished objective, such as currency reform (Thomas Attwood), improved educational provision (Davenport Hill), or abolition of the civil list (Whittle Harvey).

Radicalism, therefore, was an important lubricant of nineteenth-century class relations. It provided a language and a programme by which excluded sections of the middle class sought a political influence commensurate with their new-found economic power. At the same time, conflict was constrained by a common interest on the part of the aristocracy and the middle classes in the continued expansion of capitalism, and a recognition on both sides therefore of the desirability of compromise. Class and political divisions were in any case being blurred by the gradual intermingling of old and new wealth. Investment by landowners in mining, industry and the new railways, the purchase of landed estates by manufacturers, and the absence of social barriers restricting intermarriage between landed, commercial and manufacturing families were among the developments helping to consolidate British capitalism. A concern for social order was an additional factor in this class equation, cautioning middle-class reformers against intemperate action and imprudent demands.

The capacity for compromise paved the way for a political alignment between the middle-class radicals and a section of the aristocracy, the Whigs, who were sensitive to the need for an accommodation. Although generalisations are difficult, it is broadly the case that the Whigs were representative of a wider range of interests, and more inclined to embrace the new wealth and incorporate it into the political institutions of the state, than were the Tories. Several of their leaders, such as Charles James Fox at the end of the eighteenth century and Henry Brougham at the time of the Reform Bill crisis, had been sympathetic towards radical aspirations.

The Whigs had shown a willingness to defend minority rights, displayed tolerance over religious differences by granting religious freedoms to Nonconformists, and were prepared to concede reforms to the manufacturing centres when pressed. It was upon this foundation that the Liberal Party was to be built in the second half of the nineteenth century, as a coalition designed to overcome sectional interests and to harmonise them in pursuit of a consensual creed.

Middle-class radicals like Richard Cobden and John Bright hoped that the working class might also be incorporated into this liberal consensus. Their criticism of the corrupt political system was shared by leaders of the working class. The middle-class radicals recognised the usefulness of mobilising working-class support behind their own campaigns to extract concessions from the aristocracy. As Cobden put it at the time of the Corn Law agitation, working-class support would be 'something in our *rear* to frighten the aristocracy'.[5] A common interest in reform therefore provided a platform for cooperation between classes whose relationship in other respects (for example, in the workplace) was potentially antagonistic. In addition, by condemning the landed aristocracy's unearned income from rent and by praising the productive labour of the working class, James Mill, David Ricardo and other middle-class political economists strove to introduce a moral dimension into their theories which would influence working-class behaviour.

These ideas were supplemented with religious and family values disseminated by the middle-class entrepreneurs who controlled the burgeoning press. The educative importance of the press had been recognised by middle-class radicals from the time of the Wilkite movement in the 1760s. Newspapers, pamphlets and periodicals were important in informing and mobilising public opinion. Political pamphlets were often short, cheap and acidly polemical. In the well-known case of the *North Briton*, Number 45, Wilkes had successfully challenged the government's attempts to muzzle a critical press by resorting to general warrants to arrest persons suspected of treasonable and seditious libel. Later, as juries proved less than willing to find publishers guilty of libel, the government introduced exorbitant newspaper taxes as an alternative means of curbing the influence of the press, until forced in 1836 to reduce them by the combined efforts of middle- and working-class radicals. The provincial press and reforming periodicals, like the *Westminster Review* (the journal of the Philosophic Radicals), grew in importance in step with the growing wealth of the middle classes themselves. Radicals well understood the importance of the written word. Cobden, for example, was a prolific pamphleteer as well as a regular contributor to newspapers which supported the Anti-Corn Law League.

The attempt by the middle class to influence and to shape public opinion was by no means a smooth and untroubled process. Working-class radicals, especially in the Chartist era, were resistant to many elements of classical political economy and developed their own ideological agenda. Feargus O'Connor, Bronterre O'Brien, George Julian Harney and other of the 'Physical Force' Chartists felt betrayed by the compromise of 1832. Francis Place observed of the reactions of the working class to the Reform Act: 'The consequence ... was the total abandonment of all reliance upon the middle class to an extent which never before was entertained by them.'[6] Place had been born into poverty and had served on the committeee of the workingmen's London Corresponding Society in the 1790s. He had established a successful tailoring business and had afterwards gravitated towards the middle-class circle of Philosophic Radicals associated with Bentham and the Mills. His background led him to encourage cooperation between the middle- and working-classes and left him well qualified to understand and to judge the seriousness of the breach in harmonious class relations brought about by the Reform Act. A period of heightened class awareness and distinct class organisation and activity followed 1832, lasting until the middle of the century and dominated by the campaigns for the People's Charter and for the repeal of the Corn Laws. Attempts at cross-fertilisation between these two great class-based movements were for the most part unsuccessful. O'Connor summed up working-class suspicions of middle-class attempts at reconciliation in this period when he remarked of the Anti-Corn Law Leaguers: 'They offer you the minimum necessary to gain their ends.'[7]

However, middle-class radicals never lost sight of the desirability of cultivating working-class support. One of them, Joseph Sturge of Birmingham, organised a conference at the height of Chartist activity in 1842 aimed at reuniting the middle- and working-classes behind his Complete Suffrage Union. As Chartism subsided, Cobden, Bright and other of the Manchester School radicals, alarmed by rising military expenditure and a belligerent foreign policy (which culminated in the Crimean War), tried to win the working class over to their pacifist programme. They failed.[8] The bases for compromise in the 1850s and 1860s came instead from other sections of the middle class: Christian Socialists, Oxbridge liberals and Positivist intellectuals. An improvement in middle- and working-class relations was assisted by a common sympathy for continental nationalist movements. Oxbridge radicals such as Henry Fawcett and Leslie Stephen also displayed concern about the persistence of poverty in England, while Positivists like Frederic Harrison and E. S. Beesly developed economic arguments that justified trade unionism. Together they helped to promote a willingness among a new generation of middle-class radicals, which included Dilke, to moderate some of the harsher tenets of classical political economy. The outcome was the renewed class cooperation that led to a further instalment of parliamentary reform in 1867.[9]

It is against this background that Dilke's career must be seen. In many respects he was a typical radical. He was an unequivocal supporter of greater parliamentary and local democracy. He was critical of the persistent influence of the landed aristocracy. He believed in economical government. He espoused policies, such as education and land reform, that were shared by most other middle-class radicals. He adopted methods familiar to the middle-class radical tradition. He used his pen to disseminate his views in a wide array of books, pamphlets and newspapers. He joined pressure-groups that agitated for radical reforms, including the National Education League, the Commons Preservation Society, the Land Tenure Reform Association and the Aborigines Protection Society. He was in favour of a programme of reforms that would be attractive to the working class and thereby sustain a consensual liberalism. In other respects, however, he departed from the mainstream of middle-class radicalism. He was a believer in strong defence and in the pursuit of an active foreign and imperial policy. He was a republican. Above all, he went further than most towards embracing collectivist and social policies, especially in the later stages of his life.

Many of these characteristics of Dilke's radicalism were a product of his metropolitan upbringing: He came from the uppermost rank of London's middle class. The term middle class was used by contemporaries, and is used by historians, to include a wide diversity of occupations and considerable disparities of income. At one extreme there were, for example, clerks and shopkeepers earning around £150 a year; at the other (and including Dilke whose own fortune came from publishing and from investments) were manufacturers, bankers and shipowners with incomes in excess of £5,000 per annum. The middle classes did not therefore form an homogeneous bloc. There was competition between capitalists for a share of the market and some sharp regional differences (for example between Manchester and Birmingham in the 1830s and 1840s) over economic policy. Despite all this, the middle classes were united by a common sense of identity, a shared consciousness, a standard of living that was at the least reasonably comfortable and secure and, above all, by a sense of difference from the aristocracy and the working classes.

The source of Dilke's income and his class background therefore distinguished him from the landed aristocrats and in part accounted for his political differences with them. At the same time, his great wealth set limits to those differences. Dilke was a radical reformer not a revolutionary nor, even in his later life when he worked closely with trade unionists and Labour politicians, a socialist. The interpenetration of landed and commercial wealth had gone further in London than elsewhere in the country. Dilke counted landed gentlemen among his ancestors and was related to the Fetherstone Dilkes, a Warwickshire landed family. His father had earned a baronetcy for services to the monarchy. In the course of his life, Dilke owned several large houses, kept many servants, received lucrative dividends from Australian landholdings, and moved easily in upper-class circles.

The dynamic but uneven development of the economy had lent a regional dimension to radicalism. London's importance as a centre of commercial capitalism had provided the context for the Wilkite movement. Later, the spread of industry had seen Birmingham, Manchester and other cities emerge as centres of important provincial radical organisations and leaders. Dilke's emergence onto the political scene in 1868 coincided with the diminution of the influence of the Manchester School and the revival of cooperative class relations, especially in London. Despite the decline there after 1832 of parliamentary radicalism, London remained the most important centre of an extra-parliamentary radicalism that embraced working-class activists and middle-class intellectuals. Dilke's contact in the late 1860s with working-class radicals, like George Odger, with the working-class clubs in his Chelsea constituency, like the Eleusis, and his friendship with middle-class republicans and trade union sympathisers, such as Harrison, were important early experiences.

Dilke's enthusiasm for cultivating close relations with the working-class radicals in the immediate post-Reform period led to an involvement with republicanism which made him a household name in the early 1870s, but which did not endear him to the political establishment. He was afterwards much more circumspect but it took him the best part of that decade, and a calculated attention to the less controversial area of foreign policy where his erudition was welcomed by the Liberal hierarchy, before he was able to regain the respect of the House and to establish himself as a political frontrunner. Despite this new-found caution, his interest in the welfare of London's working class, and his receptiveness to working-class radicalism, persisted throughout his life.

There was a heavy concentration in London of members of the new professions, including administrators, civil servants and men of letters. From this stratum of the middle class came many of its leading ideologues. Dilke's radicalism was partly a product of his education at the hands of several committed Benthamites: especially his paternal grandfather, who had known Bentham, and his Cambridge tutors, Fawcett and Stephen. On entering politics, however, he struck up an intellectually rewarding friendship with one of the leading lights of the London intelligentsia, the philosopher John Stuart Mill, which lasted until Mill's death in 1873. As a result of their association, Dilke came to play a prominent part in the Political Economy Club and was drawn into the critical debates over Benthamite individualism and the role of the state that were then preoccupying its members. Mill's elaboration there of collectivist ideas anticipated the evolution of liberal thought and the practice of the Liberal Party. His arguments persuaded Dilke, who was afterwards in the vanguard of attempts to move the Liberal Party towards more interventionist policies.

There was, within Dilke's wider family, a tradition of naval service and this, together with London's importance as a centre of commercial capitalism and Chelsea's military history, shaped his political interests and made his radicalism unusual. Dilke loved to travel – he went round the world twice, in 1866–67 and 1875 – and he was a voracious reader of international news. These factors, together with his exceptional memory, accounted for his refined knowledge of foreign, imperial and defence affairs. His expertise here not only enabled him to recover from the setback caused by his flirtation with the republican movement, it led as well to his first government appointment, in 1880, as Under-Secretary at the Foreign Office.

Dilke was never a Little Englander or 'peace-at-any-price' radical, differing sharply in this regard from the Manchester School and from colleagues with whom, on the domestic planks in the radical programme, he was in close agreement. Cobden in particular had hoped that free trade would lead to universal peace: he had pressed for international relations to be structured around the principles of arbitration, disarmament and non-intervention. His proposals were welcomed by many Nonconformists, especially Quakers, who hoped that they might become the principles guiding Liberal foreign policy. Although Dilke worked hard in 1880–81 to renew Cobden's commercial treaty with France, he was not primarily motivated by Cobden's idealism. He had a more pragmatic approach to international relations, judging most policy initiatives by their importance, as he perceived it, to British interests. In this regard, his nefarious part in bringing about armed intervention in Egypt in 1882, when looked at in conjunction with the resignation of John Bright, is a symbolic moment in the history of middle-class radical attitudes to empire, denoting the decisive failure of Cobdenite internationalism and the eclipse of the 'peace' element of the old middle-class radical programme. Dilke's biography therefore throws light upon the break with the pacifism of the Manchester School by many middle-class radicals in the last quarter of the nineteenth century, and upon the alignment of aristocrats, financiers and industrialists behind a more committed overseas policy.

Although unorthodox with regard to 'peace', when it came to 'reform' and 'retrenchment', the other parts of the traditional radical triad, Dilke was much more conventional. Unlike Cobden and Bright, his name is not linked with any major reform measure. Yet it deserves to be. When he entered the cabinet in 1882 parliamentary reform was still the central plank in the middle-class radical programme, despite the concessions of 1832 and 1867. The Reform Acts of those years had focused primarily on the progressive extension of the male franchise, a process that was largely completed by the Third Reform Act of 1884. As yet, however, the equalisation of constituencies, which had been one of the six points of the People's Charter and which was important as a means of equalising the value of each vote, had been virtually ignored. The Redistribution of Seats Act of 1885, which remedied this neglect, and which was therefore one of the most important milestones in the nineteenth century on the road to democratic government, was Dilke's achievement. Acknowledgement should also be made of his role in reforming the local state, which was as important to middle-class progress as reform of the central state. Significant parts of a draft local government scheme, which he produced during his short spell in the cabinet as President of the Local Government Board from 1882–85, were revived in the landmark Local Government Acts of 1888 and 1894.

In conformity with the main thrust of the radical tradition, the democratisation of central and local government was perceived by the middle-class radicals as part of a broader struggle to achieve political supremacy. This in turn entailed wresting control of the Liberal Party from the aristocratic Whigs. Dilke's biography throws light upon these internal party dynamics and upon the evolution of the coalition underpinning Liberalism. His political career was in fact almost co-terminous with the effective life of the Liberal Party, which had been formed in 1859 less than a decade before he entered parliament and which, within a few years of his death, had irrevocably split and had lost office never to regain it. The bid by the middle-class radicals for political ascendancy did not automatically entail the splitting up of the party, but they did want a shift in the balance of power within it. They aimed to make the party reflect what they believed to be the true strength of middle-class feeling in the country. The strategy of Dilke's close friend and ally, Joseph Chamberlain, was to cultivate support at the constituency level through the caucus and the press. Dilke, by contrast, concentrated on organising radical groupings in parliament and anticipated ultimate victory by way of a gradual accretion of central power through the occupation of key cabinet positions.

In the summer of 1885, with elections scheduled to be held under the new democratic arrangements, these different but complementary stra-tegic emphases appeared to be on the verge of yielding success. At that moment, however, fate intervened and abruptly dashed the expectations of the radicals. The twelve months from July 1885 to July 1886 were a period of personal tragedy for Dilke and political tragedy for the Liberal Party. The first tragedy impacted upon the second. Dilke's exclusion from the central councils of the party, through his involvement in the Crawford divorce scandal, affected the course of the debate over Irish Home Rule. He was perhaps the only politician who could have brought about an accommodation within the reforming wing of the Liberal Party – capable, as he would have been, of mediating between Gladstone and Chamberlain, had his influence not been diminished.

In the pharisaical reaction to the scandal, Dilke was at first denigrated by many contemporaries – including leading politicians – and then ig-nored by them when they came to write their memoirs. His historical reputation has suffered from this, but so too have accounts of late nineteenth-century radicalism. Chamberlain is usually regarded by historians as the major radical of the Gladstone administration, an interpretation seemingly confirmed by his persistent political influence after 1886.[10] By contrast, Dilke is often perceived as a minor player, at best little more than Chamberlain's lieutenant, whereas this biography will suggest that he was the more advanced of the two radicals on most of the reform issues of the day. Furthermore, there is good reason to believe that, but for the scandal, he and not Chamberlain would have led any radical-dominated government after Gladstone's retirement. His sudden exclusion from the centre of politics therefore contributed significantly to radical weakness and demands greater attention than it has hitherto received.[11]

The general neglect in historical writing of key elements of Dilke's radicalism is particularly apparent when his career after the divorce scandal is examined. Roy Jenkins's blunt assertion, that 'the great controversies of education, licensing, the Lloyd George budget, and even the constitutional struggle itself drew forth few pronouncements' from him, is incorrect.[12] These and other aspects of his later political life, such as his opposition to tariff reform and his prominent stand against the Aliens Bill and the inception of the colour bar in South Africa, have never received from historians the recognition they deserve. This is perhaps because of the inevitable tendency to associate power with office. Dilke achieved as much, in different ways, from the backbenches as he did from within the cabinet. His obituarist in the *Manchester Guardian*, in a rare acknowledgement of his achievements after 1886, wrote: 'We are not sure that he did not do better work after his fall than before... The possible splendours of his life ended with his official downfall; its usefulness to humanity lasted till its close.'[13]

The *Manchester Guardian*'s appraisal is borne out by a consideration of the emphases in Dilke's politics after 1886, which came about partly as a result of the ostracism that attended the scandal and partly through the influence upon him of his second wife, Emilia Strong Pattison. The first led him to produce some of his most effective writings on foreign affairs and defence, while the second saw him move progressively closer to the labour movement. In the last phase of his life he attempted to push radicalism beyond its traditional concerns with peace, retrenchment and reform, towards more interventionist policies on military and social questions: an unusual combination which made him one of the most independent and respected, but at times also one of the most isolated, men in the House of Commons. In 1894 he was offered the leadership of the Independent Labour Party but felt obliged to refuse it because of his belief in strong defence. All the same, he continued to cultivate close links with the trade union and labour movements and these aspects of his later life are interesting for the light which they throw upon the character of the emergent Labour Party and upon the fortunes of the moribund Liberal Party.

The Liberal Party was being squeezed, as Leonard Hobhouse perceptively observed in the year Dilke died, between 'the upper grindstone of plutocratic imperialism, and the nether grindstone of social democracy'.[14] To have survived, it would have had to come to terms with the new working-class electorate and the requirements of the labour movement. This did not entail embracing socialism, as the subsequent history of the Labour Party has demonstrated. What might have happened had Dilke succeeded Gladstone as party leader and Prime Minister remains one of those tantalising imponderables with which history is strewn. The Liberal Party might have retained the services of the Chamberlainite radicals and it might also have avoided the effete interregnum of Rosebery and

Harcourt. It might also have embraced the new liberalism earlier, and with a little more enthusiasm, thereby quietening the disaffection that prompted the establishment of a separate party.

Dilke's place within the radical tradition and among the front rank of reformers should not, however, rest upon speculation about what might have been but upon a balanced estimate of his political strengths and weaknesses. In spite of his private misfortunes, his achievements were considerable. His contribution to English democracy and to social progress deserves to be commemorated. My aim therefore has been to provide a clear account of his personal and political history, set in the context of the evolving radical tradition, and to avoid judging his life by its unfulfilled promise. Even so, it is impossible for a biographer who has lived with his subject for so long not to feel a tinge of regret that the 'Lost Prime Minister' was unable to press his policies from that position of greater power which he once seemed destined to hold.

Chapter 1

The Formation of a Radical

On a wall of Sir Charles Dilke's Chelsea home there hung a portrait of Sir Thomas Wentworth, the sixteenth-century aristocrat and politician. Dilke was flattered when his visitors remarked upon the striking resemblance that the Victorian statesman bore in middle age to his Tudor forbear. Indeed, for a professed radical and republican he displayed a rather unhealthy fascination with his noble ancestry and devoted a great deal of time and energy to uncovering its roots.

He succeeded in tracing his lineage back to the late middle ages, when the Dilke clan owned land at Ashton-under-Lyne in Lancashire.[1] By the sixteenth century the Dilkes had become wealthy landed gentry with estates in Warwickshire, and in 1589 Sir Thomas Dilke acquired Maxstoke Castle. The Dilke and Wentworth branches of the family came together in the seventeenth century when Fisher Dilke, a fanatical Puritan, married Sybil Wentworth. The latter was the sister of Sir Peter Wentworth, a member of Cromwell's Council of State. He never married and left his property to his nephew on condition that he and his descendants took the name Wentworth. Charles Dilke's great grandfather and the first-born sons of the next four generations were all christened Charles Wentworth. In order to distinguish between them, the family had an understandable predilection for nicknames, but to avoid confusion here the subject of this biography will be referred to as Charles, his grandfather as Mr Dilke, and his father as Wentworth Dilke.[2]

Charles Dilke came from a background of great wealth and privilege. He was born at 76 Sloane Street, Chelsea, on 4 September 1843. His mother, Mary Chatfield, was the daughter of an Indian Army captain. Her health was never good and she died shortly after her son's tenth birthday. She indirectly influenced his future by entrusting his upbringing to her father-in-law rather than to her husband.

Charles's paternal grandfather, Mr Dilke, was born in the first year of the French Revolution. He worked as a clerk in the Admiralty, but developed a talent for literary reviewing which introduced him to a circle of friends that included John Keats, Thomas Hood and Charles Lamb. He married Maria Dover Walker, the daughter of a Yorkshire yeoman, and their only child, Dilke's father, was born in 1810. In 1830 Mr Dilke purchased the *Athenaeum*, founded two years earlier by James Silk Buckingham, and it was largely through his rigorous editorship that the journal flourished. He turned round its fortunes by halving its price and giving it a reputation for independent and trenchant literary criticism. In 1836 the Navy Pay Office was abolished and he retired on a pension. For a while in the late 1840s he was manager of the radical *Daily News*, working in collaboration with Charles Dickens. In 1849 he participated in the setting up of *Notes and Queries* which, with the *Athenaeum*, passed in later years into the hands of his grandson.

In 1850 Mr Dilke's wife died and three years later he gave up his own house in Lower Grosvenor Place, made over all his money to his son and went to live permanently at Sloane Street. The self-made scholar and friend of the *literati* had held high ambitions for Wentworth and was disappointed when he failed to fulfil them. He now transfered the hopes and expectations of his twilight years to his grandson. The two became close companions. It was partly in order to console the old widower and partly because of Charles's poor health that Mary Dilke was prepared to leave much of her son's early education to his grandfather. At first glance, the attentive and personal nature of this education is reminiscent of that bestowed by James Mill, another Benthamite of Mr Dilke's generation, on John Stuart Mill, which led to the latter's nervous breakdown. Fortunately, Charles was not subjected to the same sort of hot-house utilitarian instruction and his imaginative faculties were never neglected. On the contrary, it was the sort of education any boy might wish for. Travel, observation and conversation were its organising principles. Mr Dilke took Charles to every cathedral town in England and to other places of historic interest. No more stimulating or pleasurable method could have been devised for introducing a child to the history, geography and architecture of his country: Charles's fondness for this period of his childhood is evidenced in the preservation among his papers of his sketches of buildings and monuments made on these journeys. In 1854 language was added to the curriculum when Mr Dilke took his grandson on his first trip to France. Charles inherited from his grandfather his ambition, his left-wing radicalism, his appetite for work, his passion for literature and his intellectual arrogance.

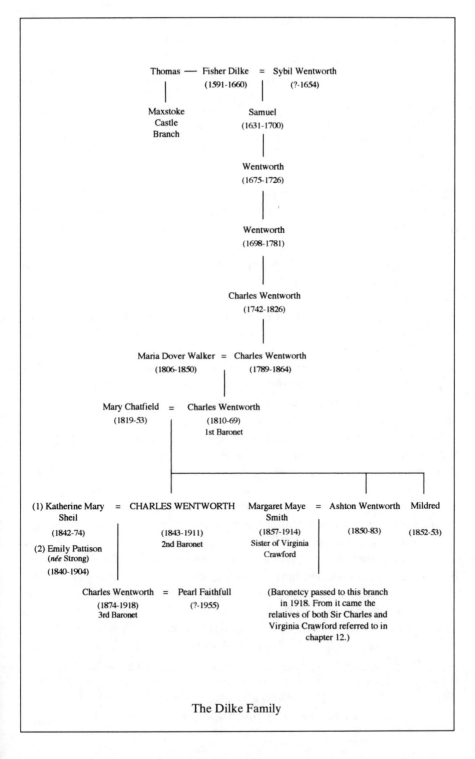

Thomas —— Fisher Dilke = Sybil Wentworth
(1591-1660)   (?-1654)

Maxstoke   Samuel
Castle   (1631-1700)
Branch

Wentworth
(1675-1726)

Wentworth
(1698-1781)

Charles Wentworth
(1742-1826)

Maria Dover Walker = Charles Wentworth
(1806-1850)   (1789-1864)

Mary Chatfield = Charles Wentworth
(1819-53)   (1810-69)
                    1st Baronet

(1) Katherine Mary = CHARLES WENTWORTH   Margaret Maye = Ashton Wentworth   Mildred
      Sheil   Smith
   (1842-74)   (1843-1911)   (1857-1914)   (1850-83)   (1852-53)
(2) Emily Pattison   2nd Baronet   Sister of Virginia
  (*née* Strong)   Crawford
   (1840-1904)

Charles Wentworth = Pearl Faithfull   (Baronetcy passed to this branch
   (1874-1918)   (?-1955)   in 1918. From it came the
   3rd Baronet   relatives of both Sir Charles and
                                        Virginia Crawford referred to in
                                               chapter 12.)

The Dilke Family

When composing his Memoir in later life, Dilke recalled that his grandfather 'completely overshadowed' his father:

> My father loved my grandfather deeply, but my grandfather was greatly disappointed in him, and always a little hard towards him; while my father suffered through life under a constant sense of his inferiority. He suffered also later from the fact that, while his elder son was the grandfather's and not the father's boy, his younger son was as completely under my influence in most matters as I was under the influence of my grandfather.[3]

This 'younger son', Ashton, was born in 1850. Two years later Mary gave birth to a daughter, Mildred, who did not survive for more than a few months. Her own health went into decline after the delivery of this third child and she died in September 1853.

Dilke was a harsh judge of his father, whose life was by no means devoid of achievement. He was educated at Westminster School, until the age of sixteen, and then in Florence before going up to Trinity Hall, Cambridge. As a young man he enjoyed the luxury and indolence made possible by his family's substantial wealth, preferring swimming, shooting and opera to academic work. Upon his marriage in 1840 to Mary, he took out a long lease on 76 Sloane Street and proceeded to populate it with his new wife's relations, including her grandmother, mother and unmarried niece. Perhaps they compensated in some way for the lack of love shown towards him by his own immediate family.

Sloane Street had been constructed in the late eighteenth century as a fashionable thoroughfare linking Sloane Square and Knightsbridge. Jane Austen had been one of its early residents. Number 76 was a tall and extensive five-storey building. Occupation of such a property was a sign not just of Wentworth's wealth but also perhaps of his entrepreneurial aspirations and upward mobility. He certainly now began to apply himself more earnestly to his business affairs, revealing an acumen not altogether inferior to either of the generations between which Charles had so disparagingly sandwiched him. He established two profitable periodicals, the *Gardeners' Chronicle* and the *Agricultural Gazette*, was chairman of the council of the Society of Arts, and succeeded in reviving the Royal Horticultural Society. He next turned his accomplished hands to the organisation of the Great Exhibition of 1851, thereafter acting as British representative at further industrial exhibitions held overseas during the following decade. This work brought him into contact with many distinguished people at home and abroad, to whom the young Charles was frequently introduced. He was rewarded with a baronetcy by Queen

Victoria for his services as one of the five royal commissioners for the exhibition of 1862.

Charles was slighting about these achievements. Perhaps he was, as one who came to know him quite well said, a *poltron révolté*, consciously rebelling against what he thought were his father's sycophantic labours on behalf of the monarchy.[4] Even the love of sport which he inherited from his father forged no bond between them: when he abandoned shooting (for humanitarian reasons) on going to Cambridge, it was a cause of some friction, for Wentworth Dilke was extremely fond of the pastime and had rented an estate at Alice Holt, near Farnham, to indulge it. Dilke got rid of the property – a mere shooting-place he called it – when his father died. Besides, such a traditionally aristocratic pursuit was hardly fitting for an up-and-coming radical.

Dilke's earliest recollections were of seeing the Duke of Wellington ride through the streets of London at the time of the Chartist demonstration in 1848, of reading NO POPERY scrawled on the walls in 1851, and in that same year attending a meeting at which the great Hungarian revolutionary, Louis Kossuth, spoke. At the Great Exhibition he encountered Wellington once more, but on this occasion the Iron Duke was almost crushed by the throng. By his almost daily visits to the exhibition in the company of his father, he was introduced to many of the leading personalities of the day, including the Queen herself. He later wrote of his

memories from about 1851 of the bright eyes of little Louis Blanc, of Milner Gibson's pleasant smile, of Bowring's silver locks, of Thackeray's tall stooping figure, of Dickens's goatee, of Paxton's white hat, of Barry Cornwall and his wife, of Robert Stephenson the engineer, to whom I wanted to be bound apprentice, of Browning (then known as Mrs Browning's husband) ...

and so on. Through his father's business and his grandfather's literary contacts, and in view of his later travels, the sweeping claim made in the Memoir – 'I have known everyone worth knowing from 1850 to my death ...' – is less exaggerated that it might seem.[5]

At the age of ten he began regular theatre-going, which became such a passion that it was over-indulged and had burnt itself out by the time he went to university. In later life, one idiosyncrasy was his habit of leaving the theatre after the first act of a play.

In 1855 Wentworth took his family to Paris for five months in connection with his exhibition work, during which time Charles perfected his fluency in the French language. The highlight of the visit was his attendance at a ball at the Hôtel de Ville given by the Emperor and Empress in honour of Queen Victoria. However, his most abiding memory was of watching the military displays in the Place Vendôme. On a holiday to Paris in the summer of 1860, the future republican found himself hob-nobbing with French royalty. He got to know King Jerome, the last surviving brother of Napoleon Bonaparte, who captivated the imagination of the young man with his reminiscences, and he lost his heart from afar to the beautiful wife of the Duc de Morny. His first visit on his own was during the Christmas of 1860, when he travelled to Paris in a terrific snowstorm. He afterwards returned regularly to France; corresponded in French with his brother; and allowed his latent Francophile sympathies to come fully to the surface after the fall of Napoleon III.

The interesting but somewhat desultory education which Dilke was receiving from his grandfather was supplemented from 1853 with rather more formal lessons in classics and mathematics administered by a local curate. Because of a nervous disposition, he was only 'half attached to a day school' in 1856, and then did not attend regularly for health reasons. The result was a stifling of his mental development:

> I was nervous, &, therefore, in some things a backward child, because my nervousness led to my being forbidden for some years to read and work, ... & during this long period of forced leisure I was set to music and drawing, with the result that I took none of the ordinary boy's interest in politics & never formed an opinion upon a political question until the breaking-out of the American Civil War when I was nineteen ... Even in this question, however, I only followed my grandfather's lead ....[6]

In truth, Dilke had been pampered and overprotected, and he emerged from childhood vain and weak. At university sporting activity was to improve his physical strength and new friends helped to reduce, if not entirely cure him of, his vanity.

He went up to his father's old college, Trinity Hall, Cambridge in 1862. He was there at a time of great intellectual ferment as a group of young liberal academics at both Oxford and Cambridge sought to influence the direction of political reform. Trinity Hall had acquired a reputation for its prowess in rowing and law and was strongly imbued with the influence of two men, both of them radicals: Leslie Stephen, a practitioner of muscular Christianity, and the Benthamite intellectual Henry Fawcett. Stephen, who was Dilke's tutor, believed that cultivating the body was as important as cultivating the mind, and this pedagogy rubbed off on Dilke who worked at his examinations fanatically and yet found ample time to devote to rowing. He won a place in the Trinity Hall crew and recorded its achievements with obvious relish, but on the advice of his doctor declined an offer to row number seven in the university boat. He rowed at Henley in June 1863 and went head of the river in the Trinity Hall boat in May

76, Sloane Street. S.W. 12ᵈ apl.

My dear Sir,

The Mc Arthur spoke to me about the plan some time ago. Pictures has much influence there. I have always declined to contest seats for the next election or for any bye election — While thinking it probable that the time will come when I may wish to stand. The offer of seats, &

A letter with sample of Dilke's handwriting
(*Cooperative Union Library, Manchester*)

1864, on both occasions watched by an admiring grandfather. He was already fond of walking, having made the journey from London to Brighton in a single day in 1861, and went on to win a walking race while at Cambridge. He also joined the Volunteers and there are passages among his letters of this period which anticipate his writings on military subjects a generation later.[7]

Fawcett had been blinded in a shooting accident at the age of twenty-five and was not therefore a sporting, but was certainly an intellectual, mentor. His strong anti-aristocratic radicalism and his commitment to representative government undoubtedly rubbed off on Dilke. Fawcett was extremely rigid in his attachment to the received ideas of Benthamism. He believed in the superiority of intellect over emotion and in the importance of education, especially of mathematics, in honing the reasoning faculties. It was only later, when Dilke came to know John Stuart Mill, that he managed to shake himself free of Fawcett's inflexible individualism. Fawcett was soon to enter parliament and he and his pupil were to be colleagues in Gladstone's second administration.

The discipline brought to both mind and body in the educational philosophy of Dilke's Trinity Hall tutors was in harmony with his own dogged determination to prepare for a life of public usefulness. He even gave up alcohol the better to concentrate on his education; and when his father cautioned him on the distractions of rowing he was indignant:

> I am very sorry to see by your letter of this morning that you have taken it into your head that I am not reading hard. I can assure you, on the contrary, that I read harder than any freshman except Osborn, who takes no exercise whatever; and that I have made the rowing men very dissatisfied by reading all day three days a week. On the other three, I never read less than six hours besides four hours of lectures and papers. I have not missed reading a single evening yet, since I have been here ... .[8]

His protestations were soon supported by proof of his ability, for at the end of his first year he won a scholarship in mathematics. In a characteristically calculated manner he then abandoned mathematics in favour of law, on the grounds that it would be 'more congenial ... and more useful to me in after life'. This brought him into competition with George Shee, an Irish Roman Catholic, with whom he developed a rival's friendship and who had the advantage of one year's extra study of the subject. All the same he was determined to show Shee that he was destined by nature to beat him. Another friend at university was H. D. Warr, a clergyman's son, to whom he became particularly close in 1863. Warr, critical of the mechanical manner in which Dilke pursued both study and sport, chided him in letters which, though they often contained sound advice, were censorious and puritanical in tone. When Dilke later drifted away, Warr reacted by publishing one of the few damning criticisms of his first book.[9] A rowing companion at Cambridge, D. F. Steavenson, later a judge, was to become a lifelong friend.

Dilke's intellectual development at university can be gauged from his reading and academic interests. In addition to his prescribed studies, he read the works of More, Bolingbroke and the contemporary French socialists Proudhon, Cabet and Blanc, and wrote essays on comparative psychology, the association of ideas, the originality of the anti-selfish affections and the influence of language on thought. His foray into European, especially French, social theory may have raised in his mind for the first time doubts about the limitations of orthodox political theory. Much additional reading was done in preparation for the college English prizes of 1864 and 1865. The first was on Sir Robert Walpole and the second on Pope's couplet, 'For forms of Government let fools contest/ Whate'er is best administered is best'. For the latter, he spent September 1864 in the British Museum reading 'all the Utopias' and as many books on political theory as possible. His 'favourite' books and writers in 1864 proved to be Shakespeare, the Bible, J. S. Mill (*Political Economy; On Liberty; Dissertations*), Longfellow (*Evangeline; Miles Standish*), Homer, Tennyson, Plato (*Republic*), Sir Philip Sidney (*Arcadia*), Helvétius, Victor Hugo (*Les Misérables*), and William Godwin (*Political Justice*),[10] – a somewhat eclectic list but one leaning heavily towards classic radical texts. By hard labour he beat Shee in the examinations, won the essay prizes and emerged at the end of his third year as Senior Legalist, the highest distinction open to him. His capacity for sustained work and an excellent memory made up for what he lacked in terms of an original or powerful intellect.

It was at Cambridge also that Dilke took his first steps in public speaking. With his usual thoroughness he participated in the affairs of the debating union and, on 5 November 1862, excitedly informed his grandfather that his first speech was soon to come off. When the debate was suddenly abandoned, the old man coaxed his grandson with advice to write upon the subject instead: '*Till a man can write he cannot speak.*'[11] A year later, Dilke took his seat as vice-president of the Union, and opened a debate on coinage, weights and measures, arguing that the greatest trading nation in the world had the worst system. At the time he favoured the French metric system, but on coming across the notes for this speech years later, he wrote in the margin, 'I took the wrong side'.[12] Despite his professed radicalism, and as an early indication of his apostasy when it came to foreign affairs, he supported in a Union debate the naval policy of

Palmerston against that of Cobden, and admired Bismarck's handling of the Schleswig-Holstein affair. Indeed, he remarked, 'I was certainly more pro-German than was Palmerston who was not pro-anything except pro-English.'[13] In other respects, too, his speeches at the Union anticipated his later radicalism: support for electoral reform; for the establishment of a Greek republic; for the North in the American Civil War; and condemnation of the barbaric methods employed by Governor Eyre to curb the black revolt in Jamaica. His speech on parliamentary reform, for example, although somewhat verbose, revealed that he was already a thoroughgoing democrat. In it, he warned that the attempt 'to keep the great mass of the people from all political power' was 'as idle as the attempt of Canute's courtiers to check the tide'. The 'advent to power of the mass of the people' was inevitable, and 'the longer we delay to prepare for it, – the worse it will be when it comes'.[14]

His energies on behalf of the Union were such that he received the unprecedented honour of being elected vice-president and president twice, having stayed on at the university for an extra two terms, ostensibly to read moral science, but in practice in order to see forward the erection of a new Union building which he had helped to get underway.[15] He developed at Cambridge the technique of writing down the heads of his arguments, a practice which led him later in life to carry with him into the House of Commons long strips of paper from which he would draw the points of his speech. He was never to be an inspired extempore speaker, but he was always to be well-prepared.

Mr Dilke followed his grandson's progress with the solicitude one would expect from someone with such high expectations and vicarious ambition. He carefully scrutinised Charles's examination results and advised and encouraged him in his studies. 'After all and above all', he wrote to Cambridge, 'remember that the highest honors [*sic*] of the University require only a certain amount of knowledge of a few given subjects, but that the *honors of life* require a great deal more... I desire only to acknowledge that I have a dear and good grandson who is ever *in my thoughts* as in my heart.'[16]

Meanwhile, Dilke continued to widen his experience of the world. He spent the long vacation of 1863 travelling through Germany, Holland and Belgium with his father, and in August went to Jersey and Guernsey and then on to France alone. The following summer he was suddenly summoned by telegram from Cambridge to Alice Holt where his grandfather was dying. Dilke described the death-bed scene in poignant terms – how his grandfather had clung to life until he arrived; how he made one last early birthday gift, the money for a stop-watch which Dilke badly wanted; and how he died telling Dilke that he had fulfilled his every hope. 'What a blessing that boy has been to my old age!' he had declared.[17]

His death was a great blow to Dilke, whose recurring sense of loss was reflected in a poem which he wrote two years later. It was, he tells us, 'a history of my affection for my grandfather, for the hero was undoubtedly myself. I dwelt upon "his mother who was dead", enlarging on the fact of my having no mother as partly explaining my relation to my grandfather, and my difficulty in standing up against certain weaknesses of nature such as "the fatal gift of facile tears".' This piece of alliteration, along with a few extracts preserved among his private papers, justify Dilke's own judgement that he showed 'a total want of cultivated power of writing verse'. He believed that his grandfather's influence remained with him to some degree throughout his life.[18]

After the funeral, he went on a walking-tour of Devon. In 1865 he gained valuable experience by canvassing for his father, who was successfully elected to parliament for Wallingford. The summer was spent with Warr in Guernsey, and alone again in France.

Dilke's physical weakness as a child, his upbringing amongst adults rather than children, the death of his mother and the cold relationship with his father had left their marks on his personality. In recording his reasons for not attending school regularly, he concluded that 'there was nothing the matter with me except a very nervous turn of mind, over-excitable and overstrained by the slightest circumstance. This lasted until I was 18, when it suddenly disappeared and left me strong and well ....'[19] But it never completely disappeared. There were to be moments of crisis in his life, notably in 1874 and 1885, when the mental turmoil resurfaced. Just as he had found a substitute for his mother's love in the affection of his grandfather, he was later to demonstrate an over-dependent and self-sacrificing relationship with his fellow radical, Joseph Chamberlain. There was some truth in his admission that he was not jealous of political rivals, though it was said 'half in jest half earnest'.[20] More seriously, his childhood experiences appear to have left him at times of personal stress with a strong craving for female companionship – a dependency that would eventually prove his undoing.

The adult world in which he grew up had the effect of making Dilke at ease in society, and a great conversationalist with catholic interests, an attribute facilitated by a memory which was, in T. P. O'Connor's colourful phrase, as 'retentive as a rat-trap'.[21] It had also made him, as he later recognised, something of a prig. His treatment of his father and brother in the 1850s and 1860s was condescending and arrogant. For example, in

1866 he pompously told Ashton that he was going to 'explain my views about you and yr. future', and then went on to detail his own future:

> My aim in life is to be of the greatest use I can to the world at large, not because that is my duty, but because that is the course which will make my life happiest – i.e. my motives are *selfish* – in the *wide* and unusual sense of that word. I believe that, on account of my temperament and education, I can be most useful as a statesman, and as a writer. I have therefore educated myself with a view to getting such power as to make me able at all events to teach men my views, whether or not they follow them.[22]

He was later to make light of his youthful arrogance, but it never entirely left him.

The fact that his early contacts were not with children of his own age but with his immediate family and their adult acquaintances was to be important in other ways. In later life his friends were amazed to find that such a knowledgeable and serious statesman could revel like a child in the sports in which he indulged, and they would reflect upon his 'boyish' laughter, his love of pranks, and his almost childlike fondness for cats and other animals. After one particularly raucous beano, following a successful day on the river at Cambridge, he was deprived by the college authorities of the scholarship he had won in his first year.

Dilke was brought up in the Anglican faith, but throughout his adult life he oscillated between belief and scepticism. The two poles had their counterparts in his family background. While his mother and maternal grandmother were devout, the male side of the family, father and grandfather, were not regular churchgoers. Dilke was attracted and repelled by the two extremes. His mother's very last letter exhorted him to remember that her 'dearest wish' was that he 'might grow up a *good* man'. Never, she told him '*under any circumstances* neglect saying your prayers at night and giving thanks to God for all his daily goodness to you. You will have troubles, dear boy, as all the world have, but never set your grief as a barrier between you and your hea enly father ... .'[23]

His mother's pious influence had begun to wane by the time he went up to Cambridge. In 1863 he ceased to attend Holy Communion and entered a period of agnosticism that lasted until 1874. He spoke at the Union against the system of enforced attendance at chapel, and felt so strongly upon the subject and on that of university tests, that he afterwards took his master's degree as a 'non-declarant', thereby forfeiting the full rights of his degree, one of which was to sit in Senate as an examiner for the law tripos.[24]

Nevertheless, even during the periods of scepticism, Dilke retained 'an unbounded admiration' for Christ's teaching. This was an essential ingredient of his radicalism, and he stressed at all times its moral matrix.

He believed in the practical application of the principles of Christianity to the affairs of mankind, and in later life attributed the spread of reform and the amelioration of social conditions to the dissemination of Bible education.[25] His devout upbringing was therefore fundamental, for it familiarised and inspired him with a moral philosophy upon which he built his theory of radicalism. Something of its influence upon him can be gleaned from a frank and very private note passed to Chamberlain at a cabinet meeting in February 1885:

> I never talked to you on these matters. I never talk to anyone about them. I was brought up in the Church by a very devout mother and afterwards grandmother. I never broke with the church in which I was married, and wh. from my love of church music (chiefly) I always attended frequently tho not regularly. I'm really a Positivist more than anything else but I think they are asses! I don't keep Sunday, but I often attend church. I always try to make as little fuss about doing so as possible – as I hate things being said about it one way or the other. I have a very strong belief in Christ's moral teaching and a good deal of what is called religious feeling ... I agree with you about the afterwards. But the teaching ought to have a great effect on the present. It has some on me.[26]

The intellectual formation of many middle-class radicals was shaped by Dissent, and the consonance of Anglicanism and radicalism in Dilke's case perhaps accounts for why he never got closely involved in some of the traditional Dissenting radical campaigns, such as disestablishment and temperance. However, there is no doubt that throughout his life he was to draw profound moral inspiration from Christianity, even during the periods when his faith was shaken.

But this is to anticipate. In 1866, when he left Cambridge, Dilke seemed to have perfectly prepared himself for the career which he (and his grandfather) had carefully mapped out. Cambridge had added significantly to his education. His speaking and writing abilities had improved, his arrogance had moderated, and his exploits on the Cam had contributed to a marked improvement in his health and fitness. Moreover, despite a predisposition towards radicalism inherited from his grandfather, it was only at Cambridge, with his wide reading in political theory, that his political opinions began to take shape. He was now ready to embark on the grandest of grand tours in order to complete his education prior to entering upon the prominent career in politics for which he believed he was destined.

Chapter 2

Greater Britain

By the time Dilke had left university, he had given a great deal of thought to the radical tradition and had even begun to take notes for a projected *History of Radicalism*, a book which, he said, 'I shd. be all my life slowly writing and improving'.[1] He did not keep the notes, but he later described his intentions. He had read the major political theorists, especially those of the Enlightenment, and sketched out a plan which he hoped to flesh out on his travels by including information on the 'communistic experiments' tried in the United States. However, his interest in producing a travelogue meant that the *History of Radicalism* never went beyond a sketch: 'It began with a definition of Radicalism as going to the root of things which naturally led to the doctrine of the perfectibility of man, and, quoting the gospels freely, I attempted to prove the essential Radicalism of Christ's teaching.' The early chapters were to be historical and largely concerned with religious reformers, but

> When I came to Radicalism of the time present I discussed it under various heads, of which the first was Great Britain, the second the British colonies, & the third the United States, showing ... the predominance which colonial questions were already assuming in my mind. In the last part of the sketch of the book I dealt strongly with the political Radicalism of the future.[2]

That this mammoth project was never completed is regrettable for it would not only have told us much about radicalism but, more interestingly, it would have told us a great deal about Dilke's perception of radicalism. As it is, his synopsis of the proposed book demonstrates the extent to which his wide reading at Cambridge and his innate Christian principles were coming together to shape his own radical convictions. It also makes clear the extent to which one area remained underdeveloped in this intellectual progress – namely, the contribution which a first-hand knowledge of colonial practices would make towards rounding off his political education.

The Grand Tour of Europe which had completed the education of the eighteenth-century gentleman was no longer sufficient for his Victorian counterpart. With the spread of the British Empire, nothing less than a circumnavigation of the globe would do. Accordingly, Dilke began to formulate plans for a tour of what he later called Greater Britain. With hardly a break after leaving university he found himself, in June 1866, aboard the S.S. *Saratoga* bound from Liverpool for the United States.

The embers of passion stirred up by the Civil War were still glowing fiercely when he first set foot in the New World in the summer of 1866. Sunken ships littered the river beds, forts and earthworks were everywhere to be seen, unemployed and disabled soldiers lounged around the bars and black children dug up bullets for old lead. Dilke landed at Norfolk, Virginia, travelled on to Richmond, the former Confederate capital, and moved up the eastern seaboard to Canada, visiting *en route* Washington (where he sat in on a meeting of the Congress), New York (which he thought vulgar), and Boston. Of these eastern cities he found the last, because of its intellectual climate, by far the most congenial. There he met 'a group of men undoubtedly, on the whole, the most distinguished then collected at any city in the world', including Ralph Waldo Emerson, Wendell Holmes, Asa Gray, James Russell Lowell and Henry Longfellow.[3] He visited Harvard University, where he found academic abuses as commonplace as in England. He counselled the rowing men on their technique but, in true Trinity Hall fashion, observed that in general brain was being developed at the expense of brawn.

From Quebec he travelled via Buffalo, Cincinnati and Pittsburgh to Chicago. The State University of Michigan was, in his view, probably 'the most democratic school in the world', though he disliked its over-competitive ethos.[4] At St Louis, a town ravaged by cholera where prisoners were being released in return for their burying the dead, he met up with Hepworth Dixon, the editor of the family journal the *Athenaeum*, who was travelling to Salt Lake City to study the Mormon community.

Suspecting that his father would forbid a world tour, Dilke kept him in ignorance of his intention to travel beyond North America. Only when he had reached Leavenworth in Kansas did he condescend to enlighten him. From there he wrote of his plans to proceed to Australia and, with characteristic arrogance, asked his father to send money and 'such introductions as you can get'. 'If they don't turn up,' he went on, 'I shall start a shaker colony, or a newspaper, or row people ashore from the emigrant ships.'[5] In view of the tone of this letter and the fact that Dilke

GREATER BRITAIN:

A RECORD OF TRAVEL

IN

ENGLISH-SPEAKING COUNTRIES

DURING

1866 AND 1867.

BY

SIR CHARLES WENTWORTH DILKE, BART., M.P.

WITH ILLUSTRATIONS.

THIRD EDITION.

London:

MACMILLAN AND CO.

1869.

Title-page of *Greater Britain* (1868; 3rd edition, 1869)

had been less than open with him, Wentworth Dilke might have been forgiven had he chosen to abandon his son to these pursuits.

From Leavenworth, Dilke and Dixon travelled on to Denver. The transcontinental railway was not yet completed and at Manhattan, just west of Kansas City, they had to give up the comparative luxury of the train for the stagecoach. The next four days of the journey were the most uncomfortable and potentially the most dangerous of the whole expedition. In addition to the constant threat of an Indian attack, they had to ride shotgun for the U.S. postal service, paying for the dubious privilege of sharing the already cramped conditions of their coach, 'our fort upon wheels', with forty bags of mail. The risk of being scalped, Dilke sardonically observed, was enough to temper his initial sympathy for the noble Indian. Indian attacks on the trading-posts meant that the party was provisioned only upon insufficient and irregular helpings of buffalo and prairie dog, though the latter proved to be 'wholesome nourishment, and fit for kings'.[6] Short on both food and sleep, Dilke was decidedly jaded by the time he reached Denver, but he soon bucked up in the cooler and more refreshing mountain climate. His vanity recovered along with his spirits. When the Governor of Colorado offered to name a peak in the Rocky Mountains after him if he would settle there, Dilke, convinced of his own destiny, replied that 'unless he would carry a constitutional amendment allowing a foreign-born subject to be President of the United States, he would not receive my services'.[7]

Five more days of travel saw the party in Salt Lake City, where they interviewed Brigham Young and others about Mormonism. Dilke discovered that it was fruitless trying to dissuade his hosts from polygamy, and simply recorded his view that the practice was degrading to women.[8] He and Dixon then parted company, the former carrying on to California while the latter returned eastwards. After travelling for a further five days and nights across the rough terrain of Nevada, Dilke came to Virginia City. He described the social mores of this 'Wild West' gold-rush town where, through every saloon bar, 'the diggers can be seen tossing the whisky down their throats with a scowl of resolve, as though they were committing suicide – which, indeed, except in the point of speed, is probably the case'.[9] From there, the going became easier. At Placerville he caught the train to Sacramento, after which his transcontinental journey was completed by river boat to San Francisco. Here he dined in the Chinese quarter and visited the gambling dens.

From California, Dilke embarked on the Pacific leg of the journey to New Zealand. The 7,000 mile voyage, with brief stops at Acapulco, Panama and Pitcairn Island, took twenty-nine days. To pass the time, he

Illustrations from *Greater Britain*
based on sketches by Dilke: America

gave free rein once more to his limited poetical talent and, though he wisely destroyed much of what he wrote, he retained the manuscript of 'an opéra bouffe of which the prologue was spoken by myself in the character of Neptune', entitled *Oparo, or the Enchanting Isle*. Whatever its shortcomings as verse, it served its immediate purpose of entertaining his fellow passengers.[10] He was also able to 'indulge' himself by reading novels and was particularly impressed by a certain Miss Evans (George Eliot), 'the best *indirect describer* of character, & the wittiest observer of human nature that has lived in England since Shakespeare....'[11] He arrived in New Zealand in November. Its government he pronounced costly and inefficient. While he predicted a 'brilliant' future for the Pacific it would be led, he believed, not by New Zealand but by Japan or Vancouver.[12] From there he went on to Sydney, Australia, arriving in time for the midsummer meeting of the Jockey Club, held on New Year's Day.

Dilke found Australia in every possible way different from New Zealand. He visited Melbourne, which possessed 'the finest climate in the world for healthy men',[13] Tasmania, where he observed and was impressed by the operation of the secret ballot, and Adelaide. At the very moment that England was juggling with the franchise, he thought it timely to describe, in a letter home to his father, the democratic experiment in Victoria:

> the most interesting place I have been in, since it probably presents an accurate view 'in little' of the state of society wh. will exist in England after manhood suffrage is carried, but before the nation as a whole has become fully democratic... Democracy – like Mormonism – would be nothing if found among Frenchmen or niggers, but is at first sight very terrible when it wears an English broadcloth suit, and smiles on you, from between a pair of rosy Yorkshire cheeks.
>
> The moral of all this sermon is that while I *worship* my ideal of a perfect democracy, & *admire* the American & French democracies – wh. approach ideal without reaching it, I am *displeased* at the sight of a democracy as yet so imperfect as is that of Australia.[14]

One by-product of democracy, he observed lightly, was that 'women dress with great expense and care, the men with none whatever'.[15] In the end, however, he found himself disappointed that Australia lacked the potential for future greatness that he had once held out for her. This willingness to modify or abandon preconceived opinions was evidence that travel did not, in Dilke's case, narrow the mind.

After a brief stopover in Western Australia, the last main part of his journey was spent in Ceylon and India, through which he travelled extensively, visiting most of the major cities. Having reached the North-West Frontier and convinced himself that the natural terrain was an insurmountable barrier to any Russian invasion, especially if Afghan independence and friendship were maintained, he sailed down the Indus to Karachi, then on to Bombay. Of the dangers of the climate for Englishmen he advised: 'If a man wears a flannel belt and thick clothes when he travels by night, and drinks hot tea, he need not fear India.'[16] Britain, he decided, had not made too bad a fist of governing India in view of the enormous cultural differences. For the Indians were by nature a caste people: 'Just as in England the people are too democratic for the Government, in India the Government is too democratic for the people.'[17]

He returned home via Egypt, where the Suez Canal was nearing completion. He cynically but prophetically remarked that, were it to prove a success, the French would only find that they had 'spent millions upon digging a canal for England's use'. His preference was for the overland route to India through Turkey and he advocated construction of a railway along the Euphrates valley – 'the Direct Route to India is one of the most pressing of the questions of the day'. He was no doubt glad to leave Alexandria, which surpassed 'Cologne for smells, Benares for pests, Saratoga for gaming, Paris itself for vice'.[18] From Egypt, he travelled to Italy and then to London, which he reached in June 1867, twelve months after having first set sail.

Dilke had set out on the voyage with the intention of recording his impressions for posterity. Ideas flooded his head. He would write 'a work such as that of De Tocqueville wd. have become had he seen Australia, and seen America *now*'; or 'a work on International Law: In two parts'. He contemplated writing 'a book on Political Economy viewed in a *modern* and *practical* light – with great stress laid on Emigration, Facility of Communications'; and he continued to accumulate notes for his *History of Radicalism*. But only the last of his dreams was to materialise – a book on 'The English World' which would 'consider the effect on the English race of the presence of Chinese, Irish and German populations by its side' in America and Australia.[19]

Publication of his adventures was delayed by bouts of malaria and typhoid contracted in Ceylon. Correction of the proofs had to be left to his father and, in consequence, the first edition contained a number of errors. The book, now entitled *Greater Britain*, eventually appeared in March 1868. It proved to be a phenomenal success, selling 10,000 copies of the English edition in its first year, as well as pirated editions in America and an abridged Russian translation, and it continued to sell steadily for the rest of Dilke's life.

Historians have rarely done justice to *Greater Britain*.[20] It has been treated, along with J. R. Seeley's *The Expansion of England* (1883), and the essays of J. A. Froude, as a seminal text in the transformation of public feeling about the value of the empire at a time of growing economic rivalry, which prepared the way for the new imperialism of the last quarter of the century. In the wake of the Manchester School's diatribes against an empire cemented by blood and Disraeli's castigation of the 'wretched colonies', Dilke certainly portrayed the empire in a new light. However, reducing *Greater Britain* to the status of a key text in the evolution of British imperialism distorts and obscures its wider significance as a statement of the new, post-Reform Act radicalism.

The popularity of a book of almost 600 pages can only be understood as deriving from its appeal on a multiplicity of levels. First, and perhaps most important in accounting for its wide readership, it is a well-crafted travel-guide. Dilke had a sharp eye and a keen ear. His descriptions are leavened with anecdotes and epigrams, snatches of conversation, and pen-and-ink illustrations. The whole is written in a confident and knowledgeable style that belied the author's youth. He is never shy to express an opinion, on almost any subject. There is something in the book for everyone – the anthropologist, the natural historian, the etymologist, the geo-politician, the student of religion. For those interested in the world's cuisine, he sampled Chinese food in San Francisco, curries in India, and appended the menu for a typical Maori dinner just in case anyone in the south of England cared to imitate it.[21] The populist appeal of the book rested above all on its narrative of adventure and danger: it must have given vicarious pleasure to the many thousands of its readers who had little or no chance of undertaking a similar journey.

Secondly, the book afforded the aspiring politician a platform upon which to expound and disseminate his radical views. Attendance at a Fenian meeting in the United States prompted a discourse on Irish land reform. India, by contrast, led him to his first excursion into print on the subject of military reform, though it was to be another twenty years before he took up again seriously the plan sketched here for a separation of the home and Indian armies. It was Australia, however, that drew from him his most detailed thoughts on social questions. He naturally approved the progress of colonial democracy but found that it had done nothing to improve the wages and conditions of women. He was obviously not yet familiar with the refutations of the classical wage-fund theory which were just then beginning to appear, for it shaped his analysis of labour questions, particularly the effects of immigration on wage-costs. He believed that capital-labour relations were 'anti-democratic' and, in an interesting echo of Marx's contemporaneous observations on primitive communism, argued for a return to the cooperative relations of production that had existed in early societies – 'it is the mission of the English race to apply the ancient principle to manufactures'.[22] Finally, his visit to the penal colony

Illustrations from *Greater Britain*
based on sketches by Dilke: Australia

of Western Australia was the cue for a denunciation of transportation as a system that fulfilled none of the necessary criteria for punishment, being neither 'equable', 'reformatory', 'deterrent' nor 'cheap'.[23]

Dilke therefore regarded the areas of English settlement as laboratories for social experiments. His experiences confirmed him in his democratic and egalitarian opinions, which were particularly apparent in his strong sympathy for women's rights and his distaste for slavery. Throughout his career he supported domestic reforms with examples drawn from colonial practices, and this methodology later became the organising framework for the *Problems of Greater Britain.*

The third dimension of the book, and the one which has attracted the attention of historians, concerns his analysis of colonial relations. Dilke's main contribution to the evolution of British thought about the empire lay in the distinction which he made between 'colonies' and 'dependencies'. The colonies were the areas of white settlement, such as Canada, Australia and New Zealand, where transplanted Anglo-Saxons were refining, with local but not crucially significant variations, the economic, social and political institutions that were characteristic of their race.

In assessing the mother country's relations with these colonies, Dilke disposed of four traditional arguments for their retention: that they contributed to Britain's needs in terms of defence, trade, emigration and prestige. In so doing, he endorsed the counter-arguments of mid century separatist writers, such as Goldwin Smith.[24] Defence of the colonies was a burden on the English taxpayer and in most cases would probably prove ineffective in wartime. Moreover, in the event of a European war, Australia and Canada were unlikely to be of much assistance, having no interest themselves in the affairs of countries like Luxembourg and, not one of Dilke's better predictions, Serbia.[25] The determination of the colonies to protect their infant economies by tariffs on British goods meant that the economic relationship was one-sided and to Britain's detriment. Dilke was a free trader by conviction, but he nevertheless treated the protective policies of the colonies in a sympathetic way, recognising the part such policies played in their overall economic development. If he could not quite bring himself to abandon his faith in the Cobdenite cosmology of a world united in peace and harmony by free trade, he nevertheless recognised that its time was not yet ripe. 'A country in which Free Trade principles have been carried to their utmost logical development must be cosmopolitan and nationless', he wrote, 'and for such a state of things to exist universally without danger to civilisation the world is not yet prepared.'[26] There was no reason to believe that the attraction of the colonies as emigration fields would diminish with independence – indeed, the experience of America proved quite the opposite. Finally, he was contemptuous of the argument that an empire conferred prestige on a nation. On the contrary, history taught that extended empires were a source of weakness. Britain's future depended on encouraging the 'citizenship of the greater Saxondom' and in this process, colonial independence would, paradoxically, 'bring us a step nearer to the virtual confederation of the English race'.[27]

The colonial burden did not lead Dilke, like Goldwin Smith and other writers before him, inevitably and inexorably towards advocating separation. The colonies should remain within the empire if they wished to. Independence for Australia was not advisable until confederation had been accomplished. If, however, confederation led on to independence, then Britain should not resist but welcome it. The case of Canada was totally different, for Britain's presence there was a source of friction with the United States. Canada would in any case be peopled one day by Americans and, in the interest of Anglo-American relations, should therefore be merged with the United States. Moreover, trade with Canada, far from following the flag, would improve rather once the flag was taken down: 'Common institutions, common freedom, and common tongue have ... far more to do with trade than union has ... ', and in this regard, America was 'a truer colony of Britain' than Canada.[28] In many respects, Dilke's views on the white colonies anticipated the Commonwealth ideas of the twentieth century rather than the imperialist ideas of the late nineteenth with which they are more familiarly associated.

Turning to the dependencies, Dilke found that they were not at all ripe for independence. They were the parts of the empire, such as India, Ceylon and the Crown Colonies, where the climate was unsuitable for permanent white settlement and where, therefore, the indigenous population was destined to remain numerically preponderant. The Indian Mutiny, less than a decade before Dilke's journey, had profoundly influenced British views on empire, and he was among the first to popularise a case for the retention of India and to articulate the bases upon which its government should proceed. In the short term at least, the British occupation was necessary to prevent anarchy, and in the longer term to prepare India and the other dependencies for self-government. In the case of India, this would be later rather than sooner, 'but history teaches us to believe that the time will come when the Indians will be fit for freedom'.[29] In the meantime, it was incumbent on Britain to assist the transition to eventual independence by a programme of reforms. Indians should be given experience of government and civil service, and educated in the English language in order to unify the nation. A continuing British presence was also justified in other countries, such as Afghanistan, where nationalism remained underdeveloped.

In defending the retention of dependencies, Dilke acknowledged the argument advanced by the Manchester School radicals that such acquisitions had a corrupting influence on the British ruling class, as, for example, in John Bright's caustic description of empire as a 'gigantic system of outdoor relief' maintained for the benefit of the aristocracy. In Dilke's opinion, the corrupting effects of such accretions of power were counterbalanced by the benefits brought to these countries by British civilisation. Moreover, the ties were mutually beneficial: 'Whether... dependencies pay or do not pay their actual cost, their retention stands on a wholly different footing to that of the colonies. Were we to leave Australia or the Cape, we should continue to be the chief customers of those countries: were we to leave India or Ceylon, they would have no customers at all; for, falling into anarchy, they would cease at once to export their goods to us and consume our manufactures.'[30] It was convenient to his argument for Dilke to forget the destruction wrought upon the Indian economy, and especially upon textile manufacturing, by the early British occupation. Yet in his belief in a responsible trusteeship for undeveloped areas of the empire he was ahead of his time, for the problem was rarely considered by either the separatists of the mid, or the imperialists of the late, nineteenth century.[31]

Greater Britain played a role in preparing British public opinion for the shift from informal to formal imperialism. However, Dilke's support for formal imperialism, though a departure from Cobdenism, went no further than this defence of the need to retain the dependencies for just so long as it took to modernise them. It is important to make this clear in view of the way in which his name has been linked with imperialism and his book portrayed as a precursor of the grand partition of the globe. In fact, in *Greater Britain* Dilke wrote against any further state-orchestrated territorial expansion. Britain should not follow the example of France which, he wrote mockingly, had the 'singular habit of everywhere annexing countries ... except the only ones that are of value'.[32] Climate ruled out the colonisation of tropical Africa. While he was prepared to swallow the corrupting influence of British rule in the dependencies for the sake of civilisation, he was not prepared to see it augmented unnecessarily by further annexations, even where the climate was more temperate.[33] Besides, annexation was not necessary. Because of the 'energy and adventure' of the Anglo-Saxon race, English civilisation was 'destined to overspread the temperate world'. Indeed, if gold were to be discovered in Japan, he averred, it 'would be English in five years'.[34] If this is imperialism, it is an imperialism of race and civilisation and not imperialism as it is conventionally understood, that is as a stage in capitalist political economy or as a form of territorial aggrandisement. Dilke believed in the inevitability of the colonisation of the temperate world by the Anglo-Saxon race, but it was a colonisation prompted by the energy of the people and not by the interests of the state, and he was none too worried as to which of the Anglo-Saxon nations provided the settlers.

This emphasis on the importance of race over nation state and territorial possession is the keystone of *Greater Britain*. In the preface, 'in which the title is justified & explained', and which many years later he described as the 'best piece of work' of his life,[35] he analysed the spirit which motivated his writing:

> The idea which in all the length of my travels has been at once my fellow and my guide – a key wherewith to unlock the hidden things of strange new lands – is a conception, however imperfect, of the grandeur of our race, already girdling the earth, which it is destined, perhaps, eventually to overspread.

For Dilke 'Greater Britain' meant more than just the British Empire, to which many later commentators applied the term and which he considered a contraction of his original conception. Although he applied it to an area of the world settled by the Anglo-Saxon race, it was not in essence a geo-political or territorial concept at all but one based upon a cultural, psychological and social Darwinian interpretation of race. The theme of the inevitable Anglicisation of the globe suffuses the book:

> The first thing that strikes the Englishman just landed in New York is the apparent Latinization of the English in America; but before he leaves the country, he comes to see that this is at most a local fact, and that the true moral of America is the vigour of the English race – the defeat of the cheaper by the dearer peoples, the victory of the man whose food costs four shillings a day over the man whose food costs four pence. Excluding the Atlantic cities, the English in America are absorbing the Germans and the Celts, destroying the Red Indians, and checking the advance of the Chinese. The Anglo-Saxon is the only extirpating race on earth ....
>
> America is becoming, not English merely, but world- embracing in the variety of its type; and, as the English element has given language and history to that land, America offers the English race the moral directorship of the globe, by ruling mankind through Saxon institutions and the English tongue. Through America, England is speaking to the world ....
>
> The ultimate future of any one section of our race, however, is of little moment by the side of its triumph as a whole, but the power of English laws and English principles of government is not merely an English question – its continuance is essential to the freedom of mankind.[36]

Dilke had no doubts whatsoever that race determined character. The Russians were: 'Drunken, dirty, ignorant, and corrupt'. The Singhalese of

Ceylon were 'not merely lazy, they are a cowardly, effeminate, and revengeful race', whereas their Kandian neighbours were 'energetic and warlike'. India was populated by 'naked barbarians, plunged in the densest ignorance and superstition, and safe only from extermination because the European cannot dwell permanently in the climate of their land'. The Irish in New York were responsible for the corruption that dogged the city, while 'a fog of unenterprise' hung over Quebec where French influence had left it locked in the middle ages. American Indians were incapable of civilisation and would always revert to type. Of the non-white races, only the Chinese impressed Dilke by their hard work and endeavour, but even they were destined only to work for the English. 'Nature', he added, 'seems to intend the English for a race of officers, to direct and guide the cheap labour of the Eastern peoples.'[37]

Dilke's pronouncements were delivered in a detached and objective style, as empirical observations on the human races that would stand comparison with Charles Darwin's classification of other species, and which were subject to the same evolutionary laws. Just as the English fly, 'the best possible fly of the whole world', was destined to 'beat down and exterminate, or else starve out' the native Maori fly of New Zealand, so it was with man: 'Both old inhabitants and interlopers have to maintain a struggle which at once crushes and starves out of life every weakly plant, man, or insect, and fortifies the race by continual buffetings.'[38] In the evolution of mankind, the fittest races would survive and others would be wiped out, but in that process civilisation as a whole would progress.

Nor did Dilke flatter the English in his description of their racial characteristics. They had, he said, 'a strong disposition towards cruelty', and he disliked the 'antipathy' they exhibited towards other races. He was censorious of the racial prejudice shown by Americans towards both 'negroes' and 'yellow men'. The empire had been built by the 'scum and outcasts' of a race that was, after all, extirpating:

> If I leave the Pacific with a diminished belief in *its* future – I leave – on the other hand – the new homes of the English race, – America & Australasia with a greater belief than I ever before possessed in its destined predominance over all other races – to the destruction, I fear, of all that is picturesque, beautiful or poetic in the world.[39]

Doubts about the eventual triumph of the English race sometimes seeped through Dilke's prose and contradicted its generally confident tone. After visiting New York, where the Irish were 'beating down the English', he was uncertain for a moment whether the United States was destined to be Celtic or Saxon. He was unsure also about the effects of miscegenation. In Colorado the mixture of Celtic and Saxon blood had produced 'a generous and noble manhood'. Elsewhere, he claimed that where a conquering race married into a conquered race, 'it ends by being absorbed, and the mixed breed gradually becomes pure again in the type of the more numerous race'. He also wondered at one point whether the Englishman could, in the end, manage to thrive in the hot and dry climates of America and Australia without 'mist and damp [to] preserve the juices of his frame'. Finally, it was by no means certain that in the competition between the dearer and the cheaper races, it would be the former that would triumph. 'One race' would eventually 'inhabit the whole earth', but there was no divine guarantee that it would be Anglo-Saxon. The spread of steam power was 'correcting' differences in the price of labour and making all races equally competitive, and the cheaper race might therefore 'extinguish' the dearer. Here Dilke's belief in the ineluctable laws of the market clashed with his attachment to social Darwinism, but he did not pause to examine the contradiction further. Indeed, doubts such as these were only fleeting. The mood of the book is one of great confidence in the future of the English race. Already England and America together were more than a match for the rest of the world. By 1970, he prophesied, the Anglo-Saxon race would number 300,000,000, by the side of which the French, Spanish, Italians and Russians would be mere pygmies.[40] In this confidence, Dilke echoed contemporary attitudes to race, which had developed alongside increasing contact overseas and which rested upon an innate feeling of English superiority, but one coupled also with a sense of duty, obligation and destiny. As Nancy Stepan has observed, most of the mid-century students of race were not consciously racist, but 'people of humane outlook, opponents of slavery, decent individuals who would have been shocked by any charge that they were racists'. They believed that a scientific understanding of race would assist rather than hinder a resolution of the problems of human society.[41] Their message was on the whole reformist not reactionary.

The incorporation of *Greater Britain* into the literature of the new imperialism has tended to obscure its radical thesis. A belief in the intrinsic democratic character of the Anglo-Saxon race had a long pedigree in English radicalism. Dilke was simply among the first to give it an imperial dimension. This is not to deny the significance of the appropriation by imperialists of Dilke's views on race and their pejorative use of his term 'Greater Britain'. Unlike Seeley and other of the imperialist writers with whom he is frequently bracketed, however, Dilke did not advocate the expansion of empire, and had his programme been implemented it would have meant a contraction of the empire in the short term and its complete abandonment in the long. Nor do his views on race contain the sort of dogma and racial hatred that was soon to appear in the writings of proto-fascists like Houston Stewart Chamberlain and some of the continental imperialists, though the extent to which they were influenced by *Greater Britain* is uncertain. The book sits uneasily on a cusp in the history of bourgeois thought between classical liberalism and the new statist and imperialist ideologies. It is both a part and a product of this transitional moment and contains elements from both sides of the ideological divide. In this way, Dilke's writings on the differences between races anticipated the later period when such views were deformed by an explicit race hatred. Race now became the basis for an ideology of dominance and aggression, integrally linked to nationalism, whereas for Dilke, race transcended nationalism.[42] This problem of how to read the text is amplified by the (perhaps deliberate) ambiguity of its title, suggesting as it does both a geo-political and a moral expansion. There is no doubt that when read as a whole the latter interpretation preponderates. Focusing only upon the book's racial and imperial dimensions distorts its fundamentally radical message. Dilke's analysis may be intrinsically flawed, and his theory of race shot through with contradictions, but his book is not *au fond* about racial domination but about the progress of freedom and civilisation.

The prestige which the publication of *Greater Britain* brought its young writer far outweighed the not insubstantial financial gain. Reviews of the book were generally highly favourable: the cleverness and originality of its author were widely acknowledged. It also marked the beginnings of a highly-valued friendship with John Stuart Mill. Charles had written to his father from Ottawa in August 1866, asking him to save newspaper clippings of any speeches made by Mill during his absence.[43] He was therefore no doubt doubly delighted to receive the following warm praise from the elderly philosopher:

> It is long since any book connected with practical politics has been published in which I build such high hopes of the future usefulness and distinction of the writer, shewing, as it does, that he not only possesses a most unusual amount of real knowledge on many of the principal questions of the future, but a mind strongly predisposed to what are (at least in my opinion) the most advanced and enlightened views of them.[44]

By the side of this, the few criticisms – of Dilke's proposals concerning Indian government and of his theories of race and climate – appeared perfunctory. As soon as Mill returned from his retreat at Avignon he invited Dilke to his London home.[45] The older man appears to have derived as much benefit from the friendship as his new-found disciple. The two were to correspond on many of the leading subjects of the day and to cooperate in the causes of free education, land reform and women's suffrage.

Meanwhile, Dilke had been taking steps to advance his political career. He had been disappointed with the limited terms of the Reform Act of 1867. The observation of colonial institutions in Australia, and 'the rampant toryism' he had met with in India, had made him 'much more of a thoroughgoing democrat'. He had therefore advised his father to vote against the second reading of Disraeli's bill: 'The only thing I want reform for – is to get a house of commons that will pass certain democratic measures, & this bill wd. do nothing of the kind.'[46] Disraeli's tactic, and his 'aim throughout his life', was to court working-class support in order to give the seal of popular approval to the *status quo*.[47] At the same time, he thought that the act would lead to the disappearance of the Whigs and leave only two parties, the Conservatives and the Radicals. This in turn would be 'the prelude to the *death of party*', which pleased Dilke, for he considered 'party-govt. a very rough & illogical kind of forerunner of better things'.[48]

The act created a new two-member parliamentary borough for Chelsea, Dilke's birthplace, and when a general election was called for the autumn of 1868, he was naturally interested in becoming its first representative. George Odger, the working-class leader of the London Trades Council, agreed to stand down in his favour. Chelsea itself was only a small part of a constituency which extended as far north as Kensal Green and as far south as Fulham, and included within its bounds a cross-section of society from the fashionable circles of Kensington to the slums of Hammersmith. With a registered electorate of 30,000, it provided a big challenge to a youth of twenty-four fighting his first electoral campaign.

Dilke brought to the contest his characteristic vigour and thoroughness. He spoke often and at length in the different areas of the constituency but, in trying to be moderate in order to please his father and the general Liberal voter, his speeches ended up, in his own judgement, 'more timid than were my opinions, and present few features of interest'.[49] Of the three main planks in his platform, Irish disestablishment was of immediate but passing importance, while army reform and parliamentary reform were subjects with which his name was to become familiarly linked but which caused little excitement in 1868 – except within the Dilke household. In reply to remonstrances from his father, Dilke wrote:

> If I read yr. words rightly – you speak of my being 'too extreme'. Well, I'm a radical I know – still I have for yr. sake done everything I can to speak moderately. For my own part – though I shd. immensely like to be in P[arliamen]t, still I shd. feel terribly hampered there, if I went in as anything except a radical. Now I have spoken against

Fenianism, in spite of my immense sympathy for it...[the letter is torn and a part missing]...radicalism is too much a thing of nature with me for me to throw it off by any effort of mine. If you think it a waste of money for me to contest Chelsea, I will cheerfully throw the thing up, and turn to any pursuit you please.[50]

The last sentence was gestural rather than serious, but it served its purpose of quelling the paternal wrath.

Dilke's spade-work during 1867 and 1868 paid dividends. When the poll was taken in Chelsea on 18 November, he was returned with the largest share of the vote: Dilke (L), 7,374; Hoare (L), 7,183; Russell (C), 4,177; Freake (C), 3,929. He could pride himself on the achievement not just of winning, for the constituency was strongly Liberal at that time, but of heading the poll over the experienced Sir Henry Hoare, twenty years his senior and a former MP for Windsor. Their opponents were by no means nonentities. W. H. Russell was the correspondent of *The Times*, famous for his graphic descriptions of the Crimean War, and C. F. Freake was a building contractor whose local reputation rested upon the fact that he had constructed the Cromwell Road.

Dilke had shown great organisational skill. He later claimed that he had invented a caucus ahead of Birmingham.[51] Liberal affairs in Chelsea had been managed by five men, 'when they happened to work together', and of the five, 'four were Tories in their hearts'. He replaced this *ad hoc* body with a Liberal association and an elected council 'representative of every section of the party, and containing every well known and active Liberal and Radical in the borough'. The latter drew support from the four west London radical clubs – the Eleusis, Cobden, Progressive and Hammersmith – and liaised with local working-class bodies and promoted the electoral registration of the new working-class voters. To this end, and for canvassing the Liberal vote, voluntary as well as paid agents were used, a relatively novel development, though one necessitated by the size of some of the new constituencies. However, his claim to have pioneered this type of organisation is exaggerated. The Birmingham Electoral Association, formed in order to get around the minority clause in the Reform Act,[52] had arisen out of a spirit of cooperation between the middle and working classes that had been there since at least the 1840s. Dilke's achievement, rather, was to establish the only popular Liberal association in London. Such pioneering organisation, by its involvement of the working class, paved the way for the emergence of London radicalism in the late 1880s as the most advanced sector of British Liberalism.[53]

Dilke was to be Chelsea's Member of Parliament for the next eighteen years, albeit with an increasingly tenuous hold on the seat. These problems, however, lay ahead. In 1868, with the election victory secured, he left for a short visit to Paris and Toulon, returning in December to take his place in the House. He appeared to have all the advantages necessary for establishing a satisfactory niche for himself in fashionable society. He was young, rich, a well-publicised writer, a bachelor of natural charm and fairly handsome mien, and now, following his election, a member of the most select club in the land. A promising political future beckoned. Yet within three years of entering parliament he had, almost perversely, jeopardised this future and dissipated many of his natural advantages. In his determination to demonstrate his independence and radicalism, he embarked on a series of clashes with the Liberal leadership which culminated in a campaign that seriously damaged his chances of political advancement.

Chapter 3

Radical Politics

The general election, on the wider franchise introduced in 1867, had given the Liberals an overwhelming victory and the first clear majority for any party since the *débâcle* over the Corn Laws in 1846. Over a third of MPs had been elected for the first time, and it was thought by some that a new departure in politics was at hand. Dilke reflected with pleasure that Gladstone, who had been returned for Greenwich following a setback in South-West Lancashire, 'is much more likely to become a democratic leader now that he sits for a big town'.[1] His optimism was only slightly checked by the Prime Minister's choice of a cabinet which, with too many peers, was behind the average opinion of the party.[2] In truth, for a radical its composition was not very encouraging. Seven of its fifteen members were peers. Lords Clarendon and Granville held the Foreign and Colonial Offices respectively. Of the commoners in the government, John Bright at the Board of Trade was the only radical and, by this stage, something of a spent force. At the Exchequer was Robert Lowe, the arch-Adullamite who had been at the forefront of the opposition to the Reform Bill. Gladstone, for his part, had announced that his personal mission was to pacify Ireland, a mission that was to preoccupy overmuch of his remaining thirty years.

Dilke's enthusiasm, therefore, quickly evaporated and he found himself in opposition to the government on a wide range of issues. Many of his early interventions were indicative of a growing restlessness and a deepening independence. His father, who had been defeated at the general election, was a loyal Liberal and did not approve. Charles was not to be shaken:

I don't mean to let either you or Glyn [the Liberal Chief Whip] frighten me into supporting the government when I think they are wrong, but I vote for them when I am at all doubtful – for instance – I voted with them against Graves on halfpenny postage which was a very tight fit for my conscience.[3]

Dilke's maiden speech on 9 March 1869 was a plea for a more efficient system of electoral registration. Characteristically, he had chosen a technically complex issue upon which to make his debut. After the Second Reform Act approximately one third of the adult male population was entitled to vote. However, the period of residential qualification necessary for registration, in theory one year but in practice over two due to the time involved in compiling the registers, effectively debarred many working men, especially lodgers, from voting. Both parties exploited the intricate registration requirements by employing agents to issue objections. It is impossible to estimate how many working men were disfranchised in this way, but one historian has suggested one million per annum.[4] Hence, although Dilke had chosen a dry subject for his first speech, it was an issue that was of crucial importance to working-class democracy. This early plunging into electoral law afterwards stood him in good stead, for it gave him an unrivalled understanding of the registration and rating systems which he was able to draw upon later in framing parliamentary and local government reform legislation.[5]

Likewise, his knowledge of foreign electoral procedures, acquired on the world tour, was recognised when he was called to give evidence to a Select Committee on Parliamentary and Municipal Elections, chaired by Lord Hartington, the Whig leader and heir to the Devonshire title and estates. It was particularly interested in hearing his views on the secret-ballot systems of Victoria and New South Wales. The most contentious proposal in the Secret Ballot Bill that arose out of its report concerned the numbering of ballot papers to allow for a scrutiny of votes. Dilke was opposed to this on the grounds that it would be seen by the electorate as undermining the principle of secrecy. His view prevailed in the Commons, but the Lords reinserted the scrutiny provisions and they have remained in force ever since.[6]

On another electoral issue he made one of his most effective early interventions. In 1869 he and Jacob Bright were responsible for the granting of the municipal franchise to women. It became the basis upon which many suffragists wished to see the parliamentary franchise modelled. Dilke urged this himself when he addressed a public meeting organised by the London Society for Women's Suffrage in July 1869, the first on the subject to be held in the capital.[7]

He had barely had time to enter his name in the annals of parliamentary debate before he was summoned to St Petersburg, where his father, who had gone there with Ashton on exhibition work, was critically ill with influenza. He arrived too late. He had never been close to his father, but he was distressed at having to sort out the arrangements for bringing his body back to England, and it was some months before he recovered sufficiently to resume an active interest in politics. The interim was spent in Russia, a country which fascinated him by its promise of future greatness and which he revisited several times in the next three years. He travelled as far east as Siberia, met a number of the leading politicians, including reformers such as Alexander Herzen, began to learn the language, and planned a book on Russia as a sequel to *Greater Britain*.

It was never completed, apparently because it was beaten into the field by an account written by his friend, Hepworth Dixon. Dixon had already published ahead of Dilke a narrative of their American journey together – *The New America* – which lacked the sparkle of *Greater Britain* but which took some of the edge off the latter by its prior appearance. When Dixon repeated the manoeuvre, Dilke clearly felt he had overstepped the mark and asked his editor to 'resign' from the *Athenaeum*. He does not appear to have borne much of a grudge for, at the same time as sacking Dixon, he agreed to give the latter a clear run by delaying publication of his own book for one year.[8] By the time the year had elapsed he had obviously lost interest in the project. The hundreds of pages of notes for the book, many on scraps of paper, were passed to his brother Ashton, who by then had left Trinity Hall without taking his degree in order to travel in Russia and study its language and people. Ashton, too, never completed the intended study, but the residue of the manuscript which resides among his papers reveals a prophetic grasp of Russia's latent power.[9]

From Dilke's notes, it is clear that he hoped to repeat the formula that had made *Greater Britain* such a success, blending a travel guide with economic, political and social observations. Chapters were planned on, *inter alia*, the aristocracy, the peasantry, the universities and the political parties. There are notes on the price of vodka and drunkenness, on the effects of serf emancipation, on Russian bureaucracy, and on the judiciary and criminal procedure. On scraps of paper he scribbled down shrewd observations of the sort that had lit up the pages of *Greater Britain*. While the Russians 'make bad leaders, they are splendid rank & file'. 'In St Petersburg the spy *corps* may not exist – but everybody is a spy on all.' 'Even now it is impossible not to feel the influence of the spy in the conversation of a Petersburg drawing room.' Russia has the advantage of 'a compact *village* life. This keeps the school at every child's door.' 'The Rn. students have no clubs, no gymnasia, no games, no duels, no meetings, no kind of life in common.' 'One is tempted sometimes to think that the

Russians are an Asiatic people, "playing at being" Europeans.' And so on.

At twenty-five Dilke succeeded to the baronetcy and to the by no means meagre family fortune. His grandfather's shrewd business acumen had made the *Athenaeum* and *Notes and Queries* lucrative enterprises, while the *Agricultural Gazette* and the *Gardener's Chronicle*, established by his father, yielded quite handsome profits. The family wealth, which stood in the region of £100,000, was invested in these journals and in various properties, securities and trusts. This assured Dilke an annual income in the 1870s which fluctuated around £7,000. As a well-placed member of the Victorian upper middle class, he had no real financial worries. Yet, although he always lived comfortably, an obsession with waste forbade him from living extravagantly, while a morbid fear of disaster led him to hoard gold reserves and to economise on such things as clothes and underclothes whenever he thought he might overspend his annual budget. This financial neurosis was not the product of miserliness. Indeed, Wentworth Dilke had left two-thirds of his property to Charles and the rest to Ashton, but Dilke equalised their inheritances by handing over one-sixth of his own to his brother when he came of age.[10]

Dilke owned three-quarters of the shares in the *Athenaeum* in 1869. He purchased the rest shortly afterwards. He initially attempted to edit the journal himself, following Dixon's 'resignation', but soon abandoned the task. Nevertheless, for a month or so each year he took over while the editor was on holiday, and he was a regular contributor to its columns, reviewing books on history, travel, art, poetry and archaeology. He also purchased the remaining shares in *Notes and Queries* for £2,500 in 1872 and later wrote for it. He never sought to use either journal for political purposes. His contributions were generally submitted under a pseudonymn or simply under the initial 'D'.[11]

Dilke resumed his political activities at the start of the 1870 session. The Prime Minister had recently read *Greater Britain*, been much impressed by it, and now honoured its author by asking him to second the address on the Queen's Speech. Perhaps Gladstone hoped by this to muzzle the independent radical, but if so he had miscalculated. When parliament assembled on 8 February, Dilke spoke with studied moderation but could not refrain from warning the government that, if they failed to carry the reform of education promised in the address, battle would be joined 'until the reproach of ignorance' was banished from the land.[12]

Elementary education in 1870 was rudimentary. For most of the century the propertied classes had been at best indifferent and at worst hostile towards educating the masses. Schoolbuildings were inadequate for their purpose, a staff of trained teachers was virtually non-existent, and the niggardly system of payment-by-results, introduced in 1862, was failing to produce a work force sufficiently skilled and educated to meet the requirements of an expanding industrial society. An inspector of schools described the system as 'an ingenious instrument for arresting the mental growth of the child, and deadening all his higher faculties'.[13] Faced with accelerating international competition, a number of manufacturers, mainly from the Midlands, belatedly began to perceive education as a means of reopening the rapidly closing gap between Britain and its economic rivals. Moreover, the Reform Act had pushed education to the front of the agenda, not so much because the new voters demanded it, but rather because of an heightened awareness of its socialising importance in the changed political circumstances. It had become imperative to educate the new 'masters'.

The man charged with the task was the MP for Bradford and Gladstone's vice-president for education, W. E. Forster, a long-standing proponent of reform. Two schemes were pressed upon him which embodied the respective interests of Anglicans and Nonconformists and which were symptomatic of the bitter sectarian rivalries that framed the whole education debate. On the one hand, the voluntaryist National Education Union urged him to buttress the existing system by increasing the state grant to church schools. On the other, the radical National Education League demanded a root-and-branch reform establishing free, compulsory, non-sectarian education. Forster inclined to the former. He proposed to allow the church schools a period of grace (originally one year but reduced to six months by the House) in which to remedy the shortcomings in education, after which the state would step in to establish board schools, financed out of the rates, wherever deficiencies remained. This patchwork policy Forster called 'filling in the gaps'.

Nonconformists were outraged by the bill and turned to the NEL as a pressure group through which to orchestrate a nation-wide campaign against it. The league sprang from an organisation originally formed in Birmingham to promote rate-aided education, and when it became a national body, early in 1869, it retained its Birmingham leaders, George Dixon as chairman, Joseph Chamberlain as vice-chairman and Jesse Collings as secretary. Dilke became chairman of its London branch. From the introduction of the Education Bill, he 'ceased to be a steady supporter of the Government'. On 9 March he and Chamberlain were the spokesmen for a deputation, numbering nearly 500, which protested to Gladstone and Forster at Downing Street.[14] In this way, the education crisis introduced Chamberlain to Dilke, led to their first joint action and prefigured a radical alliance that, ten years later, was to become as politically potent as the Cobden-Bright partnership of the previous generation.

Dilke's secular stand on the bill's religious clauses, however, found him at odds with the NEL. Forster had proposed to allow each school board to decide the kind of religious instruction to be provided, subject to a conscience clause. Nonconformists feared that the clause would prove ineffective and that, where Anglicans were in a majority on the boards, the new schools would be little better than church schools, though financed out of Nonconformist pockets. They urged Forster instead to allow only non-sectarian Bible-reading in the schools. Dilke was adamantly against this proposal on the grounds that it was unfair to Roman Catholics, Jews and secularists, and he drafted a manifesto in the name of the London branch to condemn it. Perhaps his agnosticism at this time explains his more extreme position. He was certainly to moderate later, but for the moment he urged the league not to compromise. To no avail. The objections of the NEL were fully met by the Cowper-Temple amendment, which outlawed religious teaching that was distinctive of any one denomination. In Dilke's view, this merely turned an Anglican settlement into a Protestant settlement. He therefore took 'the extreme and logical line' of voting against it – the only Liberal MP to do so – on the grounds that it offended all non-Protestants; and he resigned as chairman of the league's London branch.

Dilke's manifesto had also drawn attention to the implications for Nonconformists of clause 25 of the bill, which empowered school boards to send children to denominational schools at the expense of the ratepayer, and which was therefore a form of 'endowment in disguise'.[15] The league failed to recognise the significance of this clause until after the bill had become law, when it became the focal point of its opposition.

During the bill's passage through the House, Dilke supported amendments that would have made school attendance compulsory and religious teaching dependent upon voluntary funds.[16] Compulsion was left to the discretion of the local authorities, a half-hearted step which he roundly condemned. He did manage to get two valuable changes to the provisions governing school-board elections, introducing the ballot and enacting a ratepayer franchise in rural areas. The ballot amendment was accepted by Forster but attracted extreme hostility from the Conservative benches. In a diatribe on Tory obstruction made many years later, Dilke recalled the circumstances of his success. They had, he said, sat up all night and his amendment was only carried 'at twenty-five minutes to six in the morning – when everyone had gone away except the Speaker and myself'.[17] The Lords subsequently restricted its operation to London. Nevertheless,

Dilke's amendments made the school boards into the most democratically elected of all local bodies.

As an opponent of the act and a supporter of free and compulsory education, it was impossible for Dilke to remain independent of the NEL for long. By November 1871 Chamberlain was inviting him to become chairman of a Chelsea branch. His letter spoke of a fear of '"impracticables" – men who would break up the best organisation in the world rather than bate one jot of their prejudices or principles' – an ironical sentiment in view of Chamberlain's later career.[18] Dilke's predictions regarding permissive compulsion had proved correct. 'Is not the compulsory part of the Education [*sic*] a dead letter?' he asked Chamberlain in August 1872. 'Is it *worked in reality* anywhere, or are all towns in the same melancholy position as London?'[19]

The education controversy confirmed Dilke in his assessment of the essential conservatism of the Liberal administration, pushed him deeper into opposition, and led him into attempts to organise an independent radical grouping. He conducted his attacks on the government from the corner seat below the gangway, which soon became his almost by prescriptive right. His early political associates included George Trevelyan, with whom he was to cooperate throughout the seventies in the cause of parliamentary reform, Edmond Fitzmaurice, a friend from Cambridge days, and Henry Fawcett. Above all, he struck up a close relationship with William Vernon Harcourt during the education debates. Nicknamed 'Jumbo' on account of his bulky physique, Harcourt was a curious mixture of radical and patrician Whig. His tastes were of the eighteenth century. He once declared that he would have liked to have been a member of Walpole's cabinet. He was a bluff, swashbuckling character who could be boisterously humorous and warm-hearted to his friends, but he was also short-tempered and prone to use strong and colourful language.[20]

There was no organised Radical Party in parliament, only a collection of around twenty advanced reformers, together with a further sixty or so who were radical on a more limited range of issues. A common opposition to Old Corruption and support for political democracy were the unifying forces that drew them together, though even here there were many nuances of opinion. A determination to introduce some semblance of order and discipline into the serried radical ranks, therefore, led Dilke to take the lead in setting up the Radical Club in 1870. The founder members included Mill, John Morley, Frank Hill, Leonard Courtney, Henry Sigwick, McCullagh Torrens, Fawcett and Dilke himself, who was its first secretary.

It appears to have grown out of the Political Economy Club, to which Dilke had been elected in May 1869 at Mill's instigation, a month after they had first met. Dilke put Mill's proposal of him down to the fact that he was 'somewhat heterodox', a reference to his doubts about classical theory and his sympathy with what he called Mill's 'semi-socialist' position. In this regard, the club was the scene of clashes between the collectivist ideas of Mill and the entrenched individualism of Fawcett. Dilke was placed in a curious position by this duel between his former teacher and his new friend, but it was with little hesitation that he came down upon the side of the latter, though this did not stop him from trying, albeit unsuccessfully, to get Millicent Fawcett elected as the first woman member of the club.[21] He was greatly influenced by the advance in Mill's ideas at this time. In 1897 he wrote a valedictory article arguing that 'the most remarkable development' in Mill's political activities occurred in the last five years of his life, and 'produced a result more valuable than the mere theorising of his earlier years'.[22] All the same, while Dilke derived much benefit from this relationship, he was not always in full agreement with Mill – notably upon such questions as the ballot and London government reform – and he recorded that he 'finally came to march even in front of Mill', a fact which is evident from many of his later activities. He was, after all, of a new generation of radicals. He felt deeply Mill's death in 1873 – 'I loved him greatly' he confessed – though he derived some consolation from the fact that he possessed the only portrait (by G. F. Watts) for which the philosopher ever sat, and, rather more curiously, from the fact that 76 Sloane Street was the last house at which Mill had dined out.[23]

The Radical Club, like the Political Economy Club, was primarily just another debating society. It was to consist of twenty backbench MPs and twenty influential figures from outside parliament, in an attempt to bring together the respective qualities of academic theorists and practical politicians. It aimed to meet once a week during the parliamentary session to debate a paper on a current issue prepared by one of its members and to canvass a radical programme. It was not a great success. Some of its distinguished members were to be defeated at the general election of 1874, thus upsetting the balance between its parliamentary and non-parliamentary clientele, while a decision at the outset to allow women to attend meant that the less eminent wives of many members could not be kept out. Above all, many of its best members, such as Mill, were not as assiduous in attendance as others less desirable.[24] It mirrored, therefore, the enormous divisions among radicals in the 1870s and the theoretical and impractical nature of much of their thought. In the words of the positivist thinker Frederic Harrison, the club epitomised 'the inherently metaphysical and impotent nature of modern Radicalism'.[25] Issues like the Franco-Prussian War, education and republicanism produced no common agreement. Chamberlain for one recognised that radicalism would never advance very far on the backs of intellectual debating clubs of this sort.

All the same it provided a forum for Dilke to cooperate with like-minded individuals and in particular with Mill, with whom he now combined on the women's issue and the land question. In May 1870 he took the former campaign forward when, in tandem once more with Jacob Bright, he seconded the Women's Disabilities Bill. In doing so he ridiculed the stereotypical arguments produced by opponents of women's suffrage – arguments which appear absurd to modern ears but which were maintained with great sobriety by the Victorian patriarchs – for example, that women would be hindered from going to the poll by the roughness and rudeness of men; that they would not use the vote if it was granted to them; that they were already 'represented' by men; and that the vote was the thin end of a wedge leading to women in parliament.[26] One of his counter-arguments – namely, that a woman could be the monarch but was ranked with lunatics and criminals in being excluded from the right to vote – failed to amuse Queen Victoria. Her response to the debate highlighted the scale of the task confronting reformers like Dilke. 'The Queen is most anxious', she wrote, 'to enlist everyone who can speak or write to join in checking this mad, wicked folly of "Women's Rights", with all its attendant horrors, on which her poor feeble sex is bent, forgetting every sense of womanly feeling and propriety.'[27]

Hitherto, Dilke's oratory in the House had been undistinguished, but his speech of 4 May was cogently argued and turned votes. The motion was carried by a majority of thirty-three, the only occasion before 1897 that the House divided in favour of enfranchising women. The bill was subsequently mangled by amendments and finally killed by Gladstone's opposition to it.

Mill, who had championed women's suffrage in parliament before his defeat at the 1868 general election, advised Dilke against merging 'the women's question in that of universal suffrage', on the grounds that it would weaken the women's cause for years to come.[28] For the time being Dilke recognised the expediency of Mill's recommendation, though he eventually swung behind the tactic of going for universal adult suffrage rather than incremental reform.

Dilke also aligned himself with Mill on the question of land reform. The Land Tenure Reform Association grew, under the latter's inspiration, out of the Radical Club, and for a while Dilke was its secretary. It included among its members Odger,[29] Morley, Fawcett, Thorold Rogers, Frederic Harrison, Peter Taylor and Alfred Russel Wallace, who was later to establish the Land Nationalisation Society.

During the course of 1870 land was, according to Dilke, 'the chief of all the questions' with which he had to deal, and it involved him in several riotous meetings.[30] The excitement engendered by the land question may be difficult to comprehend today and therefore requires some explanation. The first point to understand is that the attention paid to land reform by middle-class radicals was not an anachronism or a distraction from urban problems. Rather, it was held to lie at the root of all social issues and was perceived as a crucial way of ameliorating urban problems by reversing the population drift from the countryside to the towns and by tackling the ownership of lucrative ground rents. Moreover, it was as much a political as an economic or social issue. Control of the land lay at the heart of the power-struggle between the middle class and the aristocracy. Middle-class radicals pilloried the landowners as the main obstruction to their cherished reforms and as the major obstacles to social progress. To deprive the aristocrats of their land would be to weaken their powers of obstruction. The radicals pressed for removal of restrictions on the sale of land ('free land') to break up the landed monopoly and improve agricultural efficiency. They focused upon the legal arrangements, such as primogeniture and strict family settlement, by which the landed class secured their estates against changes in ownership. Mill had sought to treat land as a special kind of property (natural not man-made, and a scarce commodity essential to sustaining life) to which the traditional liberal defence of individual rights of ownership did not apply. This departure from conventional liberal analysis held out the possibility of closer cooperation with working-class radicals, who were looking for more positive state intervention on socio-economic questions. Under pressure from a number of left radicals, Mill broadened the LTRA's programme to include taxation of the unearned increment on land. By this he meant the profits derived from the inflated value of land, and only created by developments that were entirely independent of the work of the owners, such as railway building and the expansion of towns. Landowners would be offered the chance to sell their land at its *agricultural value*. Labourers would be settled on the land thus acquired, but they would own it privately, not by virtue of a lease from the state. Dilke took this message to the country in a series of speeches in which he emphasised the extent to which the LTRA's programme now went beyond that of the Manchester School. He recognised that the traditional Cobdenite emphasis upon the freeing up of the trade in land by legal reforms would not in itself lead to a more equitable distribution of land and would not therefore have much attraction for the working classes.[31]

This more radical line does not appear to have gained much support from the middle class at large. Mill's distinction with regard to landed property was probably too fine for the majority who, as owners of property themselves, drew back from attacks on private property of any sort. Despite the rhetoric about peasant proprietorship, therefore, most of them believed that it would be owners of capital like themselves rather than landless labourers who would be able to benefit from free trade in land. Faced with the much more radically redistributive proposals of a working-class organisation like the Land and Labour League or of land nationalisers like Wallace, they preferred to concentrate on freeing up the market in land by the abolition of legal restraints, hiding this economic self-interest behind a moral critique that emphasised the landowners' parasitic dependence on unearned income.

Land reform was nevertheless presented by middle-class radicals as an issue of mutual interest to the working class and as a basis for inter-class cooperation. This was especially evident in the campaign to save common land from further enclosure. Enclosure was regarded by many radicals as a particularly pernicious example of the ways in which the aristocracy manipulated the law to secure their control of the land, and as an attack on the ancient rights of the poor. It had prompted the establishment in the mid sixties of the Commons Preservation Society. Inspired by George Shaw Lefevre, the CPS achieved an immediate success with the passing in 1866 of an act to safeguard the metropolitan commons. The society remained in existence to see that the provisions of the act were implemented and to try and extend them to other cities. Dilke became its chairman in 1870, and was involved in the course of the next decade in resisting several attempts to enclose urban open spaces, especially in and around London.[32]

Dilke's first two sessions in parliament had seen him move rapidly to the left of the Liberal Party, a process hastened by the death of his father and by the education controversy. His dissatisfaction with the Liberal hierarchy and his impatience with the slow pace of reform had led him into association with a small coterie of the most advanced middle-class radicals. However, even they blanched at the campaign which he now embarked upon. In terms of his future political prospects, his involvement with republicanism bordered upon the wilful and reckless. It led many contemporaries to question the soundness of his judgement.

This cartoon illustrates Dilke's partial political recovery
by 1877. He was among the prominent Opposition spokesmen
on foreign policy – seen here (on the left) flagellating a
member of the government with Eastern Questions – but
he is still depicted wearing the republican cap of liberty.

Punch, 24 February 1877

Chapter 4

Republicanism

There had been a vigorous but fluctuating anti-monarchical and republican tradition in English politics since the Civil War and it had, at various times, influenced both middle- and working-class radicalism. It had been present in the Chartist movement, and had attracted supporters among those sympathetic to American and French republicanism and to the several European republican and nationalist movements of the 1850s and 1860s. The parliamentary agitation of 1871–72 proved to be republicanism's climacteric moment, when it was finally evacuated from the body politic and seemingly wiped (apart from in Ireland) from the public memory.

The movement had its origins in the economic slump that followed the financial crisis of 1866. By 1869 over one million people were in receipt of poor relief. The crisis was particularly acute in London, where high unemployment was compounded by an influx of hungry migrants from the countryside. Dissatisfaction among the working classes was fuelled by a sense that the demonstrations for a democratic constitution had been ill-rewarded by the Reform Act of 1867. Disillusioned with 'constitutional monarchy', they espoused the ideal of a republican assembly to which every class would send its own delegates. The workingmen's Eleusis Club, situated in Dilke's constituency, became a centre of republican debate.

The declaration of the French Republic on 4 September 1870, following the setbacks in the Franco-Prussian War, gave a further impetus to the movement. London's working class turned out to urge recognition of the provisional government at a series of large demonstrations held during the autumn and winter. It was only now that middle-class radicals entered the fray. Positivist intellectuals like Frederic Harrison and Professor E. S. Beesly wrote passionate vindications of the revolution, and the issue of monarchical extravagance was taken to the country by Charles Bradlaugh in a series of lectures (shortly to be published as *The Impeachment of the House of Brunswick*). The isolation of Queen Victoria's court from the performance of official duties, the association of her eldest son with the unsavoury Mordaunt divorce scandal, and the economic burden of the civil list in such circumstances were the central elements in middle-class radical criticism. This dove-tailed with working-class republican sentiment that castigated the royals for shaking their 'begging-box' at a time when honest labourers were deprived of gainful employment and were compelled to suffer the humiliations of pauperism, charity and poor relief.

During the course of 1870, Dilke witnessed at first hand the republican movements in France and Spain. He spent the Easter vacation in Spain where he met Emilio Castelar, a leading republican and, he decided, 'the greatest orator in the world'.[1] With the outbreak of the Franco-Prussian War in July, he seized the opportunity to play a part in the overthrow of Napoleon III, whom he despised as a despot and a warmonger, by assigning himself to the Prussian ambulance corps. He was joined by Auberon Herbert, an engaging young companion whom he described as 'physically brave, and politically the bravest, though not politically the strongest man of our times',[2] and by Henry Winterbotham, later an under-secretary at the Home Office.

En route to join the invading Prussian army, they were arrested as French spies. Dilke later recounted the escapades that followed their release:

> Among our adventures was ... [that] of our being lost in the Vosges, and nearly coming to be murdered by some French peasants, who in the night tried to force their way into the village school in which we had barricaded ourselves. Another adventure was our being nearly starved at Pont-à-Mousson, where at last we managed to buy a bit of the King of Prussia's lunch at the kitchen of the inn on the market-place at which it was being cooked ....[3]

He witnessed the major battles of the war – Metz, Worth, Wissembourg, Phalsbourg, Mars-la-Tour and Gravelotte – and he found the experience useful in shaping his opinions on army reform. He wrote later of these experiences:

> War is really even more ridiculous than it is terrible:– how terrible, only those who have seen it know ... I was glad to have seen the beginning of the invasion. At no other time could I have gained a real knowledge of that which every politician ought to know, – the working of that vast and cumbersome machine – the transport system of a modern army.[4]

He missed the decisive battle at Sedan, having resigned his post and returned to London, but on hearing the news he left at once for Paris.

With the proclamation of the French Republic on his twenty-seventh birthday, and prodded by the overbearing attitude which success had bred in the Prussians, Dilke's latent Francophile sympathies quickly resurfaced and he defected to the French cause. In the company of Henry Labouchere, the radical secularist and former MP who was reporting on events for the *Daily News*, he watched the scenes in Paris as the change in government took place. He met many of the prominent republicans, such as Louis Blanc. As the leaders of the revolution chalked up the names of the provisional government on a column of the Chamber, he drew the moral 'on a day of revolution always have a bit of chalk'. He stayed until Paris was almost encircled by the Prussian army before leaving for Geneva on 16 September.

During the autumn he was in Russia, where he stayed with the mayor of Moscow and was introduced to the Tsar, Alexander II, and to his son, the future Alexander III. The war continued to fascinate him and by January 1871 he was back in France. On this occasion he heard Léon Gambetta address a crowd at Lille and thought it the 'finest oratorical display' he ever heard. He developed a strong admiration for Gambetta and was soon to become his close friend. He crossed the Channel several times to buy provisions in Dover, some of which he gave to his friends when the siege of Paris was lifted on 29 January. He witnessed the fighting at Bapaume and the siege of Longwy before returning home.

Evidence of his increasing independence and isolation was provided during this brief return to national politics. At the opening of parliament, he opposed the £30,000 dowry and the £6,000 annuity voted to Princess Louise for her marriage to the Marquis of Lorne. He and Peter Taylor, the radical MP for Leicester, acted as tellers in a division which brought only one other dissentient into their lobby – Fawcett. A month later, on 30 March, he flew in the face of Liberal opinion by moving a resolution condemning the weakness of the government in accepting Russia's demand for a conference to revise the Treaty of Paris and thereby to justify her flagrant violation of the clauses excluding her from the Black Sea. Dilke had never been a partisan of Black Sea neutralisation but he recognised the danger involved in allowing one nation to violate a treaty upon the sanctity of which the peace of Europe depended.[5] The speech displayed to the House his grasp of foreign affairs but it did not endear him to the Liberal leadership. Gladstone treated it as one of censure on the government and, for this reason, Dilke decided not to press for a vote. He afterwards regretted this. ' ... I ought to have divided', he wrote, 'even if I had been in a minority of one, for the proposal to withdraw my motion brought a hornets' nest about my ears, and was a Parliamentary mistake'.[6] He completed his apostasy by opposing Lowe's proposal to include a tax on matches in his budget. The radicals regarded it as a tax on the poor and the Chancellor was forced to withdraw it.

Meanwhile, events in France had taken a dramatic turn. At the end of February fighting had broken out between the National Guard and government troops, and the Paris Commune was proclaimed in March. Dilke returned to France in early April, accompanied by his brother, and was nearly hit during the fighting by a stray bullet, which he kept as a memento. He described with some amusement how the National Guard would leave off fighting to go home for dinner. 'Indeed', he added, 'many would in the morning take the omnibus to the battlefield, and fight, and take the omnibus back home again to dine and sleep.'[7]

On 6 April he had an interview at Versailles with the Duc de Broglie, later Prime Minister but at that time Foreign Minister in Thiers' government, and thought him pompous and silly. From there he went on to St-Germain and then to the Prussian headquarters at St-Denis. After virtually skirting the whole of Paris he was finally admitted to the city through the Belleville-Villette drawbridge. On 7 April he and Ashton were almost killed when a shell burst near them. A few days later he returned to London and to his parliamentary duties. He was back again in Paris at the end of May in time to witness the last days of the Commune, which was suppressed by the French army at a cost of 20,000 lives.

Fired with an enthusiasm generated by the events he had witnessed, Dilke returned to political life in England sporting a red tie,[8] and declaring his theoretical preference for free government unhampered by monarchical and aristocratic restrictions. He was extremely proud of his anti-monarchical pedigree, and was always delighted to find evidence of republicanism in the family genes. In later life, he contributed to the *Dictionary of National Biography* the entries on the brothers Paul and Peter Wentworth, ardent Elizabethan Puritans. The latter was a champion of free speech who was imprisoned for his beliefs and who died in the Tower. Three of Dilke's ancestors were said to have been among the judges of Charles I, while legend had it that Fisher Dilke, a Fifth Monarchy man, died of sheer grief at the Restoration in 1660, after digging his own grave.[9] More immediately, Dilke was strongly influenced by his grandfather's politics:

> My republicanism was...with me a matter of education. My grandfather was a conservative republican in old age; a radical republican in youth; but a republican through life; and...my young ideas were my grandfather's ideas.[10]

There was perhaps more than a grain of truth in the charge levied against Dilke, that he was reacting against the royal favour shown to his father.

In the early months of 1871 republican clubs sprang up across the country. Their progress was checked by news of the bloody events in Paris following the establishment of the Commune. The middle-class press and prominent radicals like Bradlaugh almost universally condemned the Commune. The English Positivists Beesly and Harrison, and a handful of middle-class radicals (including Dilke) who gave financial aid to the Communards, were notable exceptions, but even they were not prepared to go as far as Marx. His eulogising analysis of the Commune's significance alienated many working-class republicans and split the International Working Men's Association. Differences across the republican spectrum ranged from moderates on the right who favoured only political reform, to the extreme left who saw the establishment of the republic as the prelude to sweeping socio-economic changes.

The parliamentary middle-class radicals persisted with their campaign against the cost of the Crown. In July 1871 fifty-one MPs voted for a reduction in Prince Arthur's allowance. Soon afterwards an anonymous pamphlet entitled *What Does She Do With It?* appeared, which questioned the Queen's disposition of the civil list.[11] The pamphleteer had pointed to the savings made by Queen Victoria's withdrawal from public affairs and to the constitutional dangers inherent in a financially-strong monarchy.

Dilke drew upon the pamphlet's statistics to launch an attack on royal finances before a working-class audience at Newcastle on 6 November. In view of the uproar which the speech evoked, one might have expected to find in it a revolutionary declamation instead of, as was the case, a comparatively harmless survey of royal finances. The pith of Dilke's argument was that the cost of royalty was about one million pounds a year. A large proportion of this sum was squandered on sinecures, such as the employment of thirty-two doctors, and a 'host of confederates' whose jobs it was impossible even to surmise, such as 'the two "Green Office" men'.

He made no personal attack on the royal family or the character of the Queen, although he did aver, wrongly as it proved, that she paid no income tax. He emphasised that the responsibility for efficient administration of royal finances lay, not with the Queen, but with her ministers. The crux of the matter was that, without a periodic enquiry into the civil list, it was impossible to assess the size of the monarch's private wealth, a factor made even more pertinent by the Queen's withdrawal from social functions. The accumulation of large sums of money in the hands of the monarch was contrary to the principles embodied in the constitutional settlement of 1689.

Most of this was harmless enough and had already been argued in *What Does She Do With It?* In fact, the speech was not even reported in the

London newspapers until three days later, but when it was it unleashed a storm of protest. It had been delivered to a large gathering of working men (whose local leaders had shared the platform with Dilke) at a time of local industrial unrest amongst the miners and engineers,[12] and it was interpreted by some politicians as an incitement to violence and a call for the establishment, by revolution, of a republic. Dilke, unlike Bradlaugh, Odger and other republicans, was a Member of Parliament – a public figure and servant of monarchical government. Many of the republican clubs acclaimed the speech and made it appear more inflammatory than it was. Above all, newspaper criticism centred on his closing words, seeing in them a demand for revolutionary change:

> if you can show me a fair chance that a Republic here will be free from the political corruption that hangs about the Monarchy, I say, for my part – and I believe the middle classes in general, will say – let it come. [Cheers.][13]

He afterwards noted that in November and December 'English papers were filled with abuse of me, & the American papers with praise....'[14] Ashton reported from Cambridge on the general hostility shown there towards his brother. A Captain Maudsley remarked that Dilke had 'taken the oath of allegiance in the Rifle Corps [and] ... ought to be shot'.[15] That more was read into the speech than he ever intended is illustrated by his reaction to a congratulatory epistle from Chamberlain, who wrote: 'The republic must come, and at the rate at which we are moving it will come in our generation.' This was going, Dilke reflected, 'beyond my utterances or indeed my belief'. Although he never repented of his views, the outrage which his speech provoked afterwards led him to conclude that, though accurate, it was 'possibly unwise'.[16]

In the face of this hostile criticism, he continued with his series of speeches on 'Representation'. At Bristol on 20 November he announced: 'I make no concealment of the fact that I am a Republican myself.' The *Daily News* reported that 'from first to last his voice was drowned in the uproar, hisses, and other discordant noises made by a proportion of the audience'. The chairman of the Bristol Liberal Association refused to preside at the meeting because of Dilke's Newcastle speech. On one of the audience proposing three cheers for the Queen, the applause evoked was speedily overpowered by hisses and groans, whereas the mention of a republic was cheered with enthusiasm. Dilke's own admission that he was himself a republican caused applause which lasted a considerable time.[17] Two days later, a meeting of the Universal Republican League welcomed his declaration and decided to ask him to address them. One member reported that he had sent the programme of the league to Dilke some time ago and he had 'highly approved of it'.[18]

The Queen, alarmed by the course of events, urged her Prime Minister to take 'a bold line' against Dilke and the republicans.[19] However, Gladstone believed that they were becoming isolated by the loyalist reaction – a reaction fanned by the announcement, on 23 November, that the Prince of Wales was seriously ill with typhoid fever. That evening Dilke spoke at Leeds. Thousands could not get into the meeting. Yet, despite this enthusiasm, it passed off relatively peacefully, with only a few scuffles. Dilke was no demagogue: the monotony of his speeches accounted for the general lack of excitement with which the 'leader of republicanism' was greeted when he finished. As he disarmingly pointed out, 'there was something amusing to lovers of contrast ... between the stormy heartiness of my reception at most of these meetings and the ineffably dry orations which I delivered to them, between cheers of joy when I rose and cheers of relief when I sat down'.[20]

At Leeds he argued that the worst count against the monarchy was that it secured promotions according to birth not merit, denied having accused the royal family of malversation or of having used discourteous language, and again appealed for an investigation into the civil list.[21] Years later he reflected that, while the Newcastle speech had been on the cost of the Crown, the Leeds speech was a defence of the right to discuss that subject.

At Middlesbrough on 27 November, he spoke mainly of the need for a redistribution of parliamentary seats. The next day supporters and opponents among his constituents turned a meeting at Chelsea into a riot. It was surpassed in violence two days later when he spoke at Bolton. The following placard gives some sense of the excitement engendered by news of his impending visit:

To the loyal people of Bolton, Sir C. Dilke, the Republican, is coming to address you on Thursday night. Let it be seen that you are true-born Englishmen, and refuse a hearing to any man who preaches sedition and treason. As Englishmen you are accounted the most loyal people on the face of the earth, and your venerable monarchy of a thousand years is the admiration of the world. Prove your loyalty to it now when it is called for. Prove it nobly [*sic*] and worthily in defence of a woman – in defence of your own dear and lawful but much-injured Queen. Sir C. Dilke basely declares his wish to see our grand old monarchy overthrown. He has attacked his Sovereign in an unmanly and odious way, without the slightest consideration for her sex and august position. Men and women of Bolton, will you hear such a man? Forget for the moment your political differences, and rally in support of the throne ... God save the Queen.

The placard had the desired effect and a loyalist mob gathered outside the hall where Dilke was due to speak and smashed the windows with bricks and pieces of iron. He spoke for only a quarter of an hour. The crowd, bearing bludgeons, were eventually admitted. Rioting broke out in the hall and many people were badly hurt. One man died a week later from the injuries he had received. At the subsequent trial the defendants were acquitted by the jury on the grounds that they had merely been over-zealous in their loyalty to the Queen. Gwynn and Tuckwell repeated one eye-witness's account of the Bolton meeting – that Dilke coolly lit a cigar in the face of the howling mob. They failed to add that Dilke denied the story. He was, he said, well-protected by a large force of police. *The Times* and *Daily News*, in fact, reported that he and his friends left the hall unnoticed by the crowd. He later remarked that he was 'nearly subjected to physical martyrdom … and was actually and really subjected to moral martyrdom for a time'. Lord Chelsea, later to become his friend, regretted in a speech at Bath that the days of duelling were over.[22]

In the meantime, a Mr W. T. Manning had informed Dilke that his speech at Newcastle was inaccurate in as much as the Queen did pay income tax. Dilke had based his statement on an 1855 report by the Financial Reform Association, but apologised, in a speech at Chelsea, for having accepted what was in fact an error. Nevertheless, although he had been wrong, the exemption still existed and the monarch could cease to pay tax at any time without sanction from the Commons or any public acknowledgement of the fact.[23]

His next meeting, at Birmingham on 6 December, was interrupted by a few rowdies and some cayenne pepper was thrown, but the town hall was closely policed and the hecklers were ejected. He made a humdrum speech on the House of Lords. Chamberlain, who shared the platform and took up the same line of attack, was 'more lively'.[24]

Political meetings in Dilke's constituency were broken up by rival mobs. On one occasion 'no article or piece of furniture larger than a match was left in existence in the room', and the Dilkites had to wait until the gas had been put out and the place was in darkness before they could carry their vote of confidence. They contented themselves with marching on Sloane Street singing the Marseillaise. A meeting of anti-Dilkites at Knightsbridge on 12 January 1872, for which tickets were issued to prevent trouble, was raided by Dilke's supporters and the police had eventually to step in.[25] When he spoke at Chelsea on 19 February, he denied that he was conducting a republican campaign, and claimed that he had declined invitations from twenty-one large towns to speak on that platform. He again refuted allegations that he had maligned the character of the Queen, concluding with an observation that, mild and inoffensive as it was, marked the full extent of his republicanism:

For my part, I only say that I fail to see why men should be looked upon as dangerous revolutionists, who assert that a Republican form of government would tend to produce frugality and simplicity of life, and who regard as glorious the idea of a community in which there will be no claim to power but that which merit gives.[26]

The loyalist sentiment that greeted the Prince's illness,[27] the announcement of his recovery (on 14 December, the very anniversary of his father's death from the same disease), and the Thanksgiving Service in St Paul's on 27 February which was carefully staged in order to exploit this sentiment, were enough to kill off the 'respectable' parliamentary republican movement.

It was probably, therefore, only because he felt honour-bound to do so that Dilke went ahead, on 19 March, with the parliamentary motion for an inquiry into the civil list which he had put down prior to the Prince's illness. The House and galleries were full to overflowing. When he rose to speak he was interrupted by Viscount Bury, who questioned whether republicanism was compatible with the oath of allegiance to the Crown. Auberon Herbert leapt to Dilke's defence and the Speaker overruled Bury's objection. Dilke went on to criticise the civil list in a colourless speech occupying thirty-eight columns of Hansard. In brief, he opposed settlements at the beginning of a reign and pressed instead for periodic revisions by parliament and for the abolition of all sinecures. He repeated the point emphasised in his speeches in the country, that he regarded as most serious and contrary to the spirit of the constitution the threat inherent in the emergence of a wealthy monarchy independent of parliamentary grants.[28]

The speech was factual and monotonous. The House was not so packed when he sat down as it had been when he had risen an hour and a half earlier. He was conscious that his stand was 'studiously wooden, but the speech was solid and full of matter. It was, I think,' his account continued, 'unutterably dull, and however much tired of it the House of Commons may have been I certainly was more tired of it myself before I had "got through".' The banality of his delivery contrasted vividly with the scene and expectations in the House, but it was his intention to be 'mild and inoffensive' in order to secure a fair hearing for his opinions, and in this he was successful.[29]

The House filled again as the Prime Minister rose to reply. Spurred on by cheers from the Conservative benches, Gladstone attempted to discredit Dilke rather than his arguments. As *Punch* put it, he went 'smashing' into him as if he were Chelsea china.[30] The House did not, however, give full vent to its hostility until the courageous Herbert rose to second the resolution. By now the patience of MPs was exhausted and a most disgraceful scene ensued. Herbert's voice was drowned in a cacophony of hisses, shouts and cock-crows. In a belated attempt to preserve the House's dignity, Lord George Hamilton espied 'strangers', and the press and other witnesses were required to leave. When the division was taken, Dilke's arguments 'proved so far convincing', the *Manchester Guardian* sarcastically remarked, 'that he carried with him into the lobby only just so many followers as he could have carried away with him inside a cab'.[31] He was defeated by 276 votes to 2. He and Herbert were tellers, the minority comprising Sir Wilfrid Lawson, the temperance reformer, and George Anderson, one of the Glasgow MPs.

Dilke had been abandoned by erstwhile supporters and sympathisers, notably Fawcett, Fitzmaurice, Trevelyan, George Dixon and Joseph Cowen, the Newcastle radical. Dixon, a Birmingham member and an associate of Chamberlain's, had backed down at the last minute having earlier intimated that he would support Dilke in the debate; and Fawcett spoke against the motion on the grounds that he refused to link the lofty ideals of republicanism with a mere haggling over a few pounds.[32]

Although the parliamentary republican movement was now dead, the extra-parliamentary agitation continued for another two years; but it was riddled with divisions. The left republicans held a conference at Sheffield in December 1872; the moderates met five months later at Birmingham, whence Bradlaugh was sent forth with a message of support for the republicans of Spain. Thereafter, republicanism went into a steady decline, although activists from the metropolitan and provincial clubs re-emerged in the 1880s to play a part in the development of a socialist politics.[33]

The demise of republicanism is partly explicable in terms of a return of economic prosperity, but it has to be understood also in the context of shifting middle-class attitudes towards monarchy. There is evidence that the middle class, by mid century, was coming to recognise the institution's usefulness as a socially stabilising force. With the growth of the middle-class periodical press and of magazines targeted at women, the domestic virtues of the royal household were given increased publicity. The Queen was eulogised for her role as wife and mother (of nine children), the totemic symbol of bourgeois family life. Prince Albert, for his part, was praised not only for his exemplary personal character but for his evident interest in, and promotion of, industry. The proliferation of statues of Albert across the country, paid for out of the pockets of municipal men, is testament to his middle-class appeal. In effect, the monarchy underwent a process of 'bourgeoisification' in the 1850s, reflecting the confidence and optimism of an economically hegemonic class intent on restructuring the bases of social stability and harmony in the post-Chartist era. This was not an unproblematic process, as criticism of Albert during the Crimean War, and of Victoria's isolation (and the political inconvenience that this caused) and her relationship with her servant, John Brown, after Albert's death, illustrate. But criticism in the middle-class press was increasingly admonitory rather than adversarial, designed to keep or return the monarchy to the straight and narrow, not to do away with it.

After 1867 the economic progress and social stability of the fifties and sixties seemed under threat. The depression and rising unemployment, the disillusionment of many working men with the Reform Act and the rise of republican and revolutionary organisations served to elevate, in middle-class eyes, the need for a period of consolidation. The proliferation of republican clubs, whose history has never been written and whose impact therefore has never been fully comprehended, and the social programme that many of them embraced, underlined the importance of the monarchy as a socially stabilising force.

This is exemplified in the responses of two men to the post-1867 crisis: Walter Bagehot, editor of the *Economist* and perhaps the most perceptive political commentator of his day; and William Gladstone, the Liberal Prime Minister. It has frequently been pointed out that Bagehot's account of the role of the monarchy in his classic *The English Constitution* (1867) was as much prescriptive as descriptive. Bagehot, both here and in his many *Economist* articles, emphasised the importance to social order of a monarchy cognisant of its duties and prepared to play its proper, politically subordinate and *theatrical* role, within the constitution.

Gladstone's part in reconstructing the monarchy's social and ideological function is still more significant. It was largely owing to his efforts that the Thanksgiving Service of February 1872 became a major ceremonial occasion, orchestrated to exploit the loyalist sentiment attendant upon the Prince of Wales's illness and to counter republican criticism of the civil list.[34] Minute attention was paid by Gladstone to every last detail of the ceremony, and all of it was done very much in spite of, rather than with assistance from, the Queen herself. The irony of this should not pass without notice for, despite her frosty relations with Gladstone and her almost contemptuous regard for him, he more than any of her Prime Ministers (notwithstanding the imperial flatteries of Disraeli) helped to secure the place of the monarchy within the modern English constitution. Both Bagehot and Gladstone recognised that the Crown's loss of political power was being replaced by a social and ideological influence and they were determined to increase and exploit it. Gladstone perceived the monarchy's influence as primarily a moralising and religious one, not just upon the working class but upon the aristocracy as well, whereas for

Bagehot the monarchy was a show that served to entertain and distract the uneducated masses.

In the light of all this, the republican campaign of a handful of middle-class radicals appears aberrant – going against the grain of general bourgeois attitudes or, at best, opportunist in its attempts to exploit working-class unrest. These perspectives, however, miss the real significance of their involvement. In truth, they were faint-hearted republicans, with little more than a theoretical attachment to republicanism. Their prime concern was with the cost of monarchy not with its abolition, and in this they betrayed only a traditional middle-class interest in questions of economy and efficiency. By stopping short of outright abolition, they left themselves open to ridicule from the likes of Bagehot. Monarchy on the cheap, he told them, was a contradiction in terms.[35] Furthermore, their intervention in the republican campaign actually helped forward the process by which the social role of the monarchy was strengthened and thus, paradoxically, they made its future all the more secure. Once again it was Bagehot who grasped this point. Without the attack on the civil list, he wrote, 'the great outburst of popular sovereignty which we have seen would hardly have had the same significance'.[36] The press, whose influence was increasing along with its circulation, was able to treat the radicals as whipping-boys, exaggerating their republicanism and filling its pages with loyalist propaganda. Middle-class radicals like Dilke, therefore, did not occupy an alternative standpoint on a par with that of the left republicans. Their position was reformist and operated within the parameters of bourgeois liberal ideology and discourse. Like Bagehot and Gladstone, and the middle class generally, they were concerned with the duties of monarchy in relation to its costs.

This should not be mistaken for pusillanimity: evidence of the failure of the bourgeoisie to modernise a state apparatus dominated by the aristocratic and City segments of the ruling class.[37] The shift in attitudes towards the monarchy reflected the growing confidence of the middle class after 1850. By 1870 it had come to the view that it was not worth jeopardising economic and social progress for the sake of a theoretical attachment to republicanism. This was exactly the reason given by the old radical John Bright in refusing the invitation to preside at the Birmingham Republican Conference in 1873.[38] The middle-class radicals, therefore, were able quickly to back-pedal once the Liberal administration and the press had successfully orchestrated the pro-monarchy, anti-republican campaign in the winter of 1871–72.

In the course of that winter Dilke was frequently accused of showing disrespect for the royal person. He told an amusing anecdote of his first encounter with Her Majesty at the Great Exhibition of 1851: 'This was the occasion of which the Queen, twenty years afterwards, said that she remembered having stroked my head, and that she supposed she must have rubbed the hairs the wrong way.'[39] Because he had inherited the baronetcy awarded to his father, he was accused of biting the hand that fed him. This point was labelled in a flood of satirical verse which gained a brief popularity in the country in 1871–72. In one such poem, Dilke is reported as saying:

'But hold, – I got my title from the Prince Consort I ween,
Is it exactly gratitude to vilipend the Queen?
What matter – something whispers, 'tis the mission of my life
To spit my noxious venom on my benefactor's wife!'[40]

Dilke always denied that his father made as much as a farthing by his labours. Rather, he overspent his income on exhibition work and left his son less rich than he would otherwise have been.[41]

For a season, therefore, he was the butt of bad poets and a leper in high society. His close friends were reduced to only two – Trevelyan and Fitzmaurice – and it was rumoured that a moderate Liberal would run against him at the next election. Initially, Dilke was perturbed and looked for another seat. He was selected, with Odger's help, as candidate for Tower Hamlets. Indecision, however, rapidly hardened into a resolve that the best way to win Chelsea was not to run away. This temporary ostracism also had its brighter side in the renewal of an acquaintanceship with a Sloane Street neighbour, Miss Katherine Sheil.

Katherine Mary Eliza Sheil was an orphan whose father, an army captain, had died when she was a child. She had seen a great deal of Dilke in 1869, but they had quarrelled and she had entered into an affair with a much older man. They were reconciled in November 1871 when her sympathy was aroused by the attacks on Dilke because of his republicanism. On 30 January 1872, and in almost precipitate haste, they were married quietly at the local Trinity Church because her family objected to 'the republican'.[42] Dilke wrote exuberantly to Kate Field, the London correspondent of the *New York Times* and a close friend at this time:

You will be astonished to hear that I have married this morning Miss Sheil – to whom I have been long engaged. A real marriage, in a real church, with a real parson, and the whole thing! Is it not dreadful?[43]

The honeymoon was delayed by Dilke's attention to his parliamentary duties, but at Easter, with the civil list motion behind him, he and his new wife were at last able to get away to France. It was on this visit that he began his close friendship with Gambetta, whom he had arranged to interview in connection with a history of the nineteenth century, which he had begun researching and which he worked on spasmodically throughout the seventies, but which was never completed.

Dilke's description of his new wife was hardly a flattering one. She had, he wrote, 'a large mouth, small eyes, and a turned-up nose' and 'tiny ears'. He nonetheless made it clear that while these features would have ruined 'most reputations for beauty', she was in fact extremely attractive and spoken of by some as 'exquisitely lovely'. A 'perfect' voice enhanced her 'extraordinary powers of conversation'. Her fine taste in dress and beautiful singing voice made her a notable society lady, though her violent temper and ready sarcasm may have alienated many of the friends won by these attributes. 'She was extravagant', his pen-portrait concluded, 'and spent her capital as income – chiefly on horses and dress.'[44] Her faults were far outweighed by her capabilities as a hostess, and 76 Sloane Street was filled with distinguished dinner-guests during her short tenure. Dilke admitted on reflection that they were not in love at the time of their marriage. But they were both no doubt in love with an idea – he of adorning his drawing-room with a charming hostess, a useful asset for an aspiring politician, and she of making a match with the promising politician who dared to bait the Queen.

From Dilke's point of view, therefore, the marriage to Kate was partly a marriage of convenience aimed at the reconstruction of his badly-damaged reputation. Accustomed to high society, he detested the role of outcast. His republicanism had gained him notoriety but lost him respectability. He was regarded as wayward or dull. In this respect the marriage fulfilled its immediate purpose. The Dilkes were invited to many of the London houses that had recently closed their doors to 'the republican'. Their own dinner-guests included Mark Twain, Robert Browning and Garibaldi's son Ricciotti, as well as Dilke's political friends. Occasionally they engaged a French comedy actor to provide entertainment. During the first year of their marriage, 262 different guests dined at Sloane Street. Moreover, the marriage of convenience developed into a close relationship. Dilke and his wife shared many interests. They were both, for example, match croquet players and competed together at the All England Club. Dilke went so far as to buy land at Broadstairs for a house and three full-size croquet lawns, but building had made little progress and was abandoned following Kate's death.

Dilke also began to shift his politics from an outright republican stance to the rather less extreme strategy of attempting to form some sort of national pressure-group to push for greater democratisation. He was the moving spirit behind a conference on parliamentary reform held in London in November 1872. An organising committee was set up with himself as chairman. John Morley gave the committee financial support, and thirty-nine radical societies and fifty-two trade unions agreed to send delegates to the conference, which met in St James's Hall. Chamberlain presided in the morning and Dilke in the evening.[45] Resolutions in favour of a wider franchise and a redistribution of seats were carried. These proved to be more extreme, on account of working-class pressure, than the middle-class organisers had expected. Odger, for example, wanted universal manhood suffrage. There was some impatience with Dilke's emphasis upon the centrality of redistribution, a subject which many working men found too technical and a distraction from the franchise issue. It was only after the election of a Conservative government by a minority of the national vote in 1874 that his proposal began to receive more serious consideration. Even then working-class interest remained limited and he had to carry the campaign forward almost single-handedly.[46]

He kept the organising committee together by turning it into a small Electoral Reform Association. It issued circulars and whips in support of George Trevelyan's franchise and his own redistribution resolutions.[47] They were introduced separately at first and jointly from 1876. Dilke described redistribution as 'the hardest reform of all to *carry* – because the interest of the vast majority of members is the other way'.[48] His speech of May 1873 contained arguments that were to become familiar to the House over the next few years. Half the members represented fewer than half-a-million voters, the other half over two million. Manufacturing areas in the north were particularly under-represented. He was critical of the retention of the university seats, encouraged no doubt by the fact that his most vigorous opponent on the Liberal side, Robert Lowe, sat for one. Although the resolution was overwhelmingly defeated on this first occasion and in a Liberal House, it was to be a measure of Dilke's achievement that by 1877 only two Liberals (Goschen and Lowe) were opposed to it.[49]

At the same time as attempting to reconstruct a democratic alliance with the working class, he sought to produce a popular programme that would identify Liberalism with radicalism and thereby marginalise the persistent Whig influence within the party. At Derby in January 1873, at the height of the agricultural unrest, he spoke for the first time in favour of free land. A week later, at Chelsea, he focused upon free trade. On both occasions he used the phrase 'Free land, free church, free schools, free trade, free law'.[50] Historians have usually credited Chamberlain with the development of this so-called 'free programme'. But it was not, in fact, until nine months later that he published his famous article in Morley's *Fortnightly Review* promoting the 'Four Fs' (substituting 'Free Law' and 'Free Trade' with 'Free Labour') as the basis upon which to radicalise the Liberal Party. By choosing a prominent middle-class periodical with a national circulation as his platform, Chamberlain attracted greater attention and caused more of a political stir.[51] This should not disguise the fact, however, that Dilke's radicalism had been ahead of his Birmingham colleague's, not for the first or last time during their association.

Dilke continued the recuperation of his reputation in 1874 with the publication of a delightful novelette entitled *The Fall of Prince Florestan of Monaco*. It was written in Monaco in December 1873 where he had taken Kate, who was ill following the birth of a still-born son, and appeared the following March. It tells the story of a Cambridge undergraduate who, succeeding to the throne of Monaco, attempts to put progressive ideas into practice, alienates the church and is deposed. An extract will suffice to illustrate the light-hearted and self-deprecating vein which runs through the book. Prince Florestan, recalling his Cambridge days, observes:

> I had, by the way, almost forgotten the most amusing of all the Union episodes of my time, which was the rising of Mr Dilke of Trinity Hall, Sir Charles Dilke's brother – but a man of more real talent than his brother, although, if possible, a still more lugubrious speaker – to move that his brother's portrait, together with that of Lord Edmond Fitzmaurice, the communist brother of a Marquis and a congenial spirit, should be suspended in the committee room to watch over the deliberations of that body, because, forsooth, they had happened to be president and vice-president of the Society at a moment when the new buildings were begun out of the subscriptions of such very different politicians as the Prince of Wales, the Duke of Devonshire, and Lord Powis. Mr Dilke and his radicals were sometimes in a majority and sometimes in a minority at the Union, and the portraits of the republican lord and baronet went up on the wall or down under the table accordingly, Mr Willimott, the valued custodian of the rooms, carrying out the orders of both sides with absolute impartiality.[52]

The novel proved a more satisfactory vehicle for conveying republican sympathies than had platform oratory and was an immediate success in fashionable circles. The social set who had closed their doors to Citizen Dilke no doubt smiled at Florestan's description of English constitutional monarchy as 'a democratic republic tempered by snobbism and corruption'.[53] It is significant, however, that Florestan's republic is not acceptable to the people, a conclusion provided by Dilke to show his critics that, as he once privately wrote, 'to think and even to say that monarchy in Western Europe is a somewhat cumbersome fiction is not to declare oneself ready to fight against it on a barricade'.[54] Florestan's reflections upon his experiences, with which the novel concludes, mirror Dilke's own feelings:

As for my failure at Monaco, I went too fast. I agree with Mr Freeman, your English historian, that a sudden breach in the continuity of national institutions is an evil, and that 'the witness of history teaches us that, in changing a long established form of executive government, the more gently and warily the work is done the more likely it is to be lasting' ... If they take me back, which I really think for their own sakes they had better do, I will go much slower.[55]

In order to preserve his incognito, Dilke had made elaborate arrangements to publish the book, even to the point of keeping Macmillan in the dark as to its authorship. When the latter objected to the satire directed against the author of *Greater Britain*, Dilke had first to modify the disagreeable things he had said about himself and, when this failed to satisfy the over-scrupulous publisher, finally to let him in on the secret. The book was hailed by the press, and its authorship was variously attributed to Matthew Arnold, Benjamin Jowett and all manner of writers but Dilke. The *Pall Mall Gazette* used it as a base from which to attack him while the *Standard*, hitherto one of the most vitriolic critics of his republicanism, was overflowing with praise for the anonymous work.[56]

It was remarkable that the secret was so well kept. There were some clues in the novel as to its authorship – admiration for Disraeli in contrast to the dour Gladstone, praise of Gambetta, the Cambridge background, a knowledge of Monaco demonstrated in the text and its accompanying maps, and perhaps even, to those who knew Dilke well, the rather abundant satire directed against himself. Nevertheless, the social world was kept for two months on tenterhooks, during which time only Harrison tumbled to the secret. He wrote to Dilke on 5 May:

Prince,

You see how well I have respected your incognito, though I early saw the *republican* made your lace uniform, & the *secularist* in your softness for the poor Abbé. Your journey to Monaco, & your tale of its end is indeed a most palpable pit; but do you not think the time has come to let the world into the secret & fling off the royal mufti? For my part I think the best of all the good jokes of the book, is the name of the author, & since the dénoument of Tom Jones there was never yet a secret so well kept by an author. You have taken us all in, but most of all the dismal critics ... So now before the season ends ... out with it, or the fun will be spoilt.

To write a good book which pokes fun at your enemies is not amiss; but to write a book which dunces think is to poke fun at *yourself*, is a jest too good to be lost. Pull off the mask, Prince, before the town has finished its laugh, show us the brown beard & moustache underneath, & let the duffers see you have been laughing at *them*. It will hit the real Princes more than all the 'lugubrious' speeches of the entire family.

Ever Yours
Frederic Harrison.[57]

Dilke decided to break the secret by having his wife announced, on arrival at a party, as 'Princess Florestan'.

Overnight he had resurrected his reputation and reinvigorated his flagging political career. From being the most widely-shunned politician in London he became a central social attraction. His visits to Lady Waldegrave's house at Strawberry Hill, once frequented by Horace Walpole and his circle, date from 1874. She was the wife of Chichester Fortescue who later, as Lord Carlingford, served in the same cabinet as Dilke. She was perhaps the last of the great society hostesses – and to be invited to her Sunday gatherings was a mark of one's political progress, a sign that a politician was perceived as having an important future in the Liberal Party.[58] Here, ironically, Dilke came into contact with a fair number of European royals. Like Disraeli before him, therefore, he found that the *littérateur* possessed keys to the all-important doors of the socially and politically influential. The republican iconoclast had suddenly become fashionable.

By 1877 the parliamentary correspondent Henry Lucy was reporting that Dilke had 'travelled with seven-leagued boots away from the position' he had assumed in the early 1870s. He was now 'the most courtly-mannered Radical that ever shocked a duke, or fluttered an earl'.[59] However, while Dilke was less impractical and more wordly-wise after his experiences of 1872, there was no significant shift in his basic principles or in the content of his arguments. It was only in the atmosphere of the social unrest of the early seventies that his proposals had seemed so inflammatory.

He had never, at any stage, believed that an English republic was a practical proposition, nor had he subscribed to any attempts to bring it about. His preference was theoretical, his practice was radical but not revolutionary. Hence he remained adamant in his opposition to royal grants of any description. In July 1873 he opposed the Crown Private Estates Bill and produced, according to himself, 'an overwhelming weight of authority in favour of the view that it is unwise to allow the Crown to hold private property in land'. As a result, the Solicitor-General promised that the monarch's personal wealth would be taken into account in determining the next civil list. This practice was adopted in 1901 and endorsed by the civil list select committee of 1910, of which Dilke was a member, but was abandoned thereafter.[60]

Dilke was later to explain why he was against revolutionary change. 'I have always been ... favourable to a republican system of government,' he wrote, 'but I have never advocated ... sudden change, because any attempt to hasten things would be to cause an increase of the forces of obstruction to political and social reform by their gathering round the monarchic principle.'[61] He did not join a republican club, and was regarded with contempt by some left republicans. Karl Marx, for example, described him as 'a miserable creature, this swaggerer who has nominated himself as the future "President of the British Republic"....'[62] Other of the intellectual republicans were little different to Dilke. Charles Bradlaugh believed in establishing a republic by moral suasion and 'deprecated even ostentatious demonstrations, or the display of flags and banners'. As for Fawcett and his Cambridge followers, 'A little audacious talk over a glass of wine would be the outside of the offending.'[63]

It is essential to view Dilke's republicanism in terms of his whole political creed. It was the republican *virtues* which he espoused – reduction of waste, abolition of privilege, equal opportunity: in sum a system of government and of society based on merit and not on birth. Even at the height of his so-called 'republican campaign' of 1871–72, his speeches concentrated on social improvements in the spheres of education and land reform, and on the capacity of the state to cope with these problems. At Newcastle he showed how the monarchy might be made more efficient and less corrupt and corrupting; at Middlesbrough, Manchester and numerous other towns how the House of Commons might be democratised; and at Birmingham how the dead-hand of the Lords might be lifted from the people's government. In England revolutionary change was impractical, but the republican virtues could be cultivated in a constitutional monarchy. Dilke was no revolutionary. An explanation for the outcry against him has, as we have seen, to be sought in the broader context of the time, and above all in the growing conservatism of the middle class.

By the 1870s the ruling class as a whole, faced with unrest in town and country and by a more organised and politically-engaged working class, perceived monarchy as a vital element of social order and set about reconstructing its role. Many historians have acknowledged the changed function of the monarchy in the last quarter of the nineteenth century, usually attributing this to its promotion as a symbol of imperial unity and grandeur. Disraeli has been credited for his part in this shift, and his Crystal Palace speeches of 1872 which began the process were themselves responses to the republican unrest. However, the linking of Crown and empire followed on from and augmented the construction of a monarchist ideology. The essential elements of monarchism – its 'magic' and capacity to 'disguise' (this is Bagehot again), and its theatricality generally, along with its representativeness in terms of middle-class values of family, domesticity, religion and morality – had been stitched together prior to the grafting on to it of 'imperialism'. In an age of democracy the monarch could act as a figurehead, the cornerstone of national unity and class harmony, standing above the political fray and favouring no one class or party.[64]

This is the context in which Dilke's comparatively mild pronunciations were made to appear so seditious. Their very moderation also explains why, within a matter of months, he was able to reclaim his tarnished reputation and to recommence the forward march of his political career.

Chapter 5

Recovery

In February 1874 the Liberal government was turned out of office. Gladstone believed that it had been borne down in a torrent of gin and beer unleashed by its unpopular licensing legislation. But he was wrong. The reasons for the defeat were more complex than this. Indeed, the Liberals polled a majority of the popular vote but lost because of the vagaries of the electoral system. Nor does it appear that there was any major defection of Nonconformists, still smarting at the Education Act, as was once thought. It seems that the Liberals lost moderate voters frightened away by what had been a great reforming administration,[1] albeit one insufficiently radical for Dilke. In addition, the Liberal failure to carry an Irish University Test Bill in 1873 had alienated the Irish MPs and was the prelude to their defection and return at the general election as an independent group of fifty-eight Home Rulers. Finally, the Tories owed their victory as much to their own reorganisation as to Liberal weakness.

Dilke's rabid independence made him fear for his seat at Chelsea, where it was rumoured that he would be opposed by a moderate Liberal. On the eve of the election, therefore, he put out a statement qualifying his republicanism and, exceptionally for the time, enlisted his wife's help in his campaign. In the event, no such spoiling candidate was forthcoming and his efficient electoral management ensured that he again finished at the head of the poll, though with a Tory now in second place.[2]

Lady Dilke had campaigned for her husband despite being in the early stages of pregnancy. She had never fully recovered her health after her miscarriage, and she became full of foreboding as this second pregnancy approached its term. On 20 September 1874, two days after giving birth to a son, she suffered a sudden and fatal convulsion caused by a toxichaemic condition of the blood.[3] Dilke was traumatised by her death. In a dazed state, but still calm, he went to his grandmother, Mrs Chatfield, told her what had happened and lay quietly at her side for a few hours clutching her hand. Then, having given her charge of the house and the baby,[4] he shaved off his beard to avoid being recognised and fled to Paris, where he buried himself in historical work for a month, refusing all contact with the outside world. Later, he could remember little about this time and concluded that 'For all practical purposes I was mad.' Ashton, who by now was managing his own newspaper, the *Weekly Dispatch*, was left to take care of the funeral arrangements, which were complicated by Kate's sister's wish to have her cremated in Dresden.[5] Mrs Chatfield arranged for the baby to be baptised, in the family tradition, Charles Wentworth.

It was almost the end of October before Dilke began to pick up the threads of everyday life, though his first work was the morbid production of a 'Sonnet to Death', which appeared anonymously in the *Spectator* while he was still abroad. When he began writing letters again they were either highly emotional or incongruously flippant. The extent of his nervous depression was reflected in his abandonment of drinking, which he did not resume again until 1886, and by his adoption of an extreme vegetarianism, which led to his moralising on the rights of human beings to kill animals for food. He also took to philosophical discussions of church doctrine, particularly with his old tutor Leslie Stephen. Ashton tried to bring him to his senses by hinting that there were threats of a new election in Chelsea raised by his absence, and by reminding him of his responsibilities to the 'living as well as the dead'.[6]

Sir William Harcourt was also a great help to him at this time. He too had lost his wife, when his son Lewis was born. As soon as he heard of Kate's death he wrote to console Dilke: 'If only the child lives you will have a real comforter... If I can do anything to help you to share this weary burden it will be to me a true pleasure.' It was some time before Dilke was able to reply:

> I have been wandering in the South of France ever since – and my letters were all kept from me till Monday night. Yours was one of the first I read – and I addressed an envelope to you intending to answer it – but I couldn't – and I don't know whether I shall be able to finish this now. You see – I can write to the people she didn't know and to those she didn't love – but it is hard to write to those she loved ... It is awful, and she loved Loulou [Lewis's nickname] too – but above all she loved you for the tenderness of your heart which we know & which so few can guess the extent of as we could. I am afraid I can't go on. Do write to me. I don't know what I shall do.[7]

Harcourt did write again, on 1 November, another letter of great kindness and sympathy to which Dilke responded: 'with your heart you could write no other. How little credit you get for yours. How few people know you have one!', which was presumably intended as a compliment.

At present, he continued, 'the child is no consolation to me – but the contrary. Of course I know that if it lives it will become one.' He had now resolved to throw himself 'into Parliamentary work as a mere drudge voting in every division & sitting there all the hours in quiet. That if I *can* do it would be the best for me – together with hard exercise – for a long time.'[8]

Dilke claimed that reading Balzac, Madame de Staël, and Chateaubriand helped to sober his mind, but that it was the companionship of Gambetta, with whom he stayed for a while in Paris, that contributed above all to his recovery. He spent December and early January in Algeria before returning to Paris and then, on 24 January 1875, to England. He was immediately invited by Harcourt to live a bachelor's existence with him at Stratford Place, his London home: 'We will live together here as if we were in College rooms ... You will have your latch key and come and go when you please.'[9] Dilke accepted the invitation gratefully, moving in after getting over a mild attack of smallpox. He occupied himself by preparing for publication *Papers of a Critic*, a two-volume collection of his grandfather's literary writings with an introductory biography, which appeared the following summer.

Although his doctor now pronounced him well, Dilke recorded that 'my hand still shook and I contracted a bad habit of counting the beats of my heart, and was so weak of mind that the slightest act of kindness made me cry'. Many years later he wrote cryptically in the margin of the Memoir account of his stay at Harcourt's: 'My son knows (October 1904) of the circumstances at 76, which, from my return made life there specially unhappy for me.'[10] It seems that he never became strongly attached to the boy, who was associated in his mind with his wife's death. There is only one letter in the Dilke Papers from Wentie, as the child was nicknamed, to his father, and the latter's references to him are few and cool. When he was five, he was sent to Birmingham for eighteen months, to stay with Chamberlain's children, and then to school at Summerfields, near Oxford. In 1883 Dilke was wondering whether Wentie ought not to join the navy rather than go to Eton: 'The navy is a good school for a bad boy I think.'[11] In the end he was sent first to Rugby, where he did not make much progress, and then, in September 1889, to a school in Germany. Later he went to Trinity Hall, his father's old college, but left without graduating. He travelled abroad a good deal but he was an epileptic who suffered from a form of mental illness and had, before Dilke's death, to be put in an asylum.

Dilke's recovery in the spring of 1875 was assisted further by the development of a new friendship which was to shape the rest of his life.

He had first met Emilia Francis Strong briefly in 1859, when she was nineteen, through a mutual interest in the South Kensington Trap-Bat Club. She had enrolled that year at the local art school to pursue one of the major loves of her life – painting and the arts. Dilke had thought her lively and fascinating, but bigoted in her religious opinions and some-what supercilious. They met again in February 1875 when Emilia was in London convalescing from a severe bout of rheumatism. They were both at this time in need of companionship, Dilke because of his recent loss, Emilia because of a strained relationship with her husband, Mark Pattison, the Rector of Lincoln College, Oxford, whom she had married in 1861. He was a cold and unattractive character, almost thirty years older than her. She found intimacy with him difficult and ultimately loathsome.

Emilia Pattison was a talented, attractive and immensely capable woman. She had been born in Ilfracombe in 1840, the daughter of an officer in the East India Company.[12] She had a powerful intellect which was manifested in her fluent grasp of four languages and in her sophisticated knowledge of seventeenth- and eighteenth-century French painting. At twenty-five she was contributing to the *Saturday Review* and the *Westminster Review*, and later wrote numerous essays on art history for several journals, most notably the *Academy*. For some years she wrote the review of foreign politics for the *Annual Register*. Despite the difficulties in her relationship with her husband, she found the intellectual environment of Oxford immensely stimulating. Her circle of friends came to include Robert Browning, John Ruskin, Richard Congreve and George Eliot. The latter is said to have based her characterisation of Dorothea Brooke and Mr Casaubon in *Middlemarch* upon the Pattisons. Emilia's appeal to Dilke was very different from that of Kate, the society hostess. He recalled that, after his wife's death, 'Mrs Pattison's higher standards in all things greatly affected my way of looking at many matters and brought me back to where I had been before recent inferior days'.[13] Religion was one of those 'higher standards'. She had by this time lost her earlier bigotry and had developed a personal and deep mysticism. Under her influence Dilke recovered his own faith, which he kept until she died.

Art, too, was a shared passion, and her early correspondence with Dilke was concerned with attempts to reform the Royal Academy. Dilke not only possessed a valuable art collection, but was acquainted with famous artists such as Holl, Watts and Legros, who painted, respectively, portraits of Chamberlain, Mill and Gambetta for him. 'No one', he remarked, 'can care more for the National Gallery than I do. I know the pictures very well for I go there almost every week.'[14]

Mrs Pattison was also extremely interested in political questions, and she introduced Dilke to many of her fellow-workers in the women's trade union movement. By the end of the decade they were writing to each other almost daily; Dilke had no qualms about sharing confidential information with her or seeking her advice. Their correspondence is quite considerably mutilated and extracts from it in the official *Life* are cited as having come from Dilke's diary – undoubtedly an attempt on the part of Miss Tuckwell to disguise the fact that her aunt and Sir Charles were on intimate terms for some years before Mark Pattison's death.

With his health and spirits restored, Dilke was able in the parliament of 1875 to set about repairing also his political career, damaged as it had been by the republican interlude. He was spurred on by Gladstone's retirement as Liberal leader, and by a growing disillusionment with Disraeli's government, which he had at first welcomed but which he was soon attacking as vehemently as he had its predecessor.

Dilke was still *hors de combat* in February 1875 when Gladstone stood down. He had not participated, therefore, in the Liberal Party's internecine struggle to elect a successor, during which Hartington had managed to hold off a fierce challenge from Forster. Dilke had little sympathy for either candidate but, conscious that he would achieve little if he remained forever a pariah, he now took the opportunity afforded by the change in leadership to establish himself in the front rank of the party.

With this renewed determination, he was able to make the 1875 session his most successful so far. He gave a well-informed and effective, but rather dull, speech on the weaknesses of the Ballot Act of 1872; sparred with Lord Randolph Churchill over unreformed municipal corporations; and gained the support of the Liberal Party for a redistribution of parliamentary seats and for a future Allotments Extension Bill.

Among the pernicious abuses identified in his ballot speech was the 'Tasmanian dodge', whereby a voter was bribed to smuggle his paper out of the polling-booth and give it to an agent to mark. Another voter would cast this ballot and bring out his own, and so on. Dilke warned the government that unless something was done, costly petitions would be a feature of the next elections. The Attorney-General promised an investigation, and a select committee was set up with Dilke as chairman, but nothing came of its recommendations.[15]

The ballot speech was detailed and knowledgeable but dry. By contrast, his speech on those municipal corporations that had been left untouched by the reform of 1835 was detailed, knowledgeable and witty, and was sprinkled with anecdotes of corrupt practices which 'kept the Commons in a roar'. He made mention of ninety-six unreformed corporations, but focused on the three he considered worst: Queenborough and New Romney in Kent; and Woodstock in Oxfordshire.

When he sat down, Lord Randolph Churchill, the redoubtable and flamboyant Tory MP for Woodstock, sprang to the defence of his constituency. Dilke had developed quite a close friendship with Churchill at this time. Indeed, Disraeli recognised the pale emulation of the one by the other when he described Churchill as 'Dilke and water'. The two had spent Easter in France together and frequently dined in each other's company. Churchill had been briefed by his friend as to the nature of the impending criticism, and he replied, Dilke tells us, in a speech that was 'funnier than I was, though... not equally regardful of the truth'. Dilke had told the story of how the mayor of Woodstock, after being fined for breaches of the Licensing Act, had said, 'I have always had a high respect for the police, but in future I shall have none.' Churchill adroitly replied that the mayor's words had been misheard. What he had in fact said was, 'I have always had a high respect for the police, but in the future I shall have *more*.' After the debate was over, Dilke recorded, 'Randolph came up to me outside, and said: "I was terrified lest you should have heard anything to-day, but I see you have not." I said: "What?" He said: "He was fined again yesterday."'[16]

Although the parliamentary session of 1875 had been a successful one for Dilke, it had also been an exacting one – the first in which pillows were introduced into the House for those members who wished to sleep. At the end of it he gained a respite from politics by making another trip around the world. On this occasion he visited the United States, Japan, China, Java and Singapore, and an account of his travels was appended to later editions of *Greater Britain*.[17] Japan, whose people captivated him, and Java, by virtue of its natural beauty, made the biggest impression on him. He arrived back in England in January 1876.

He returned in time for the wedding, in March, of his brother Ashton to Margaret Maye Smith. She was the daughter of Thomas Eustace Smith, a Liberal MP who had made his fortune building ships on Tyneside. The Dilke and Smith families were already very close, indeed too close. Mrs Eustace Smith had been Dilke's mistress in 1868 and again in 1874–75, when he was deranged by his wife's death. Maye had a younger sister, Virginia, who was then only fourteen but who, a decade later, was to determine Dilke's destiny.

The recuperation of Dilke's political fortunes continued in 1876. His annual speech to his constituents was issued in pamphlet form alongside that of 1874, a deliberate juxtaposition intended to show just what a good Liberal he had become.[18] In the House he reprised his performances on redistribution and on unreformed corporations. With regard to the first, there were some tactical advances. Dilke and Trevelyan moved a combined resolution for the first time. Dilke tried to get together 'a small knot of young peers' to support redistribution in the Lords. Rosebery, the Scottish Earl and future Prime Minister, then only twenty-nine, was approached but was found to be 'too "canny"'.[19] With regard to the unreformed corporations, he was able to draw upon the deluge of letters that had followed his first speech, from correspondents who believed their own borough to be the least efficient and most corrupt of all, and whose experiences provided him with the wherewithal to entertain the House once again. One case, that of Corfe Castle, he regarded as 'a gem', for its corporation consisted of only one member – the ubiquitous Mr John Johnson, grocer, draper and mayor – who must, Dilke supposed, 'elect himself [and] hold frequent meetings with himself, but I am not aware', he added, 'of whether he keeps minutes of what passes'.[20]

The session of 1876 saw the education controversy flare up once more when the Tories attempted to remedy some of the deficiencies of the 1870 act relating to school attendance. The National Education League urged Dilke to move a free schools amendment to the bill, but he was unenthusiastic and told Chamberlain that he could not see the point. 'We don't care twopence about the *division* on Free Schools', Chamberlain retorted, 'the important point is to get a fair statement of the question in the House.' Dilke again hedged, before finally telling Chamberlain that he had decided to vote against the second reading 'and to do nothing else', as free schools would never be a practical question until linked with disendowment.[21] His timidity can be explained but not perhaps excused. It was a consequence of the new position that he was trying to establish within the party after his early independence, and which was already being rewarded. He was appointed that summer as chairman of the Liberal Central Association, which gave him enormous influence over the choice of parliamentary candidates. Moreover, from this time on he began to be summoned to planning meetings of the party leadership.

With regard to the other educational issue of that session, university reform, he took in his own words, 'a highly Conservative tone', though without securing the support of Conservative opinion.[22] In response to the report of the Duke of Cleveland's commission on university finances, the government introduced two separate bills to appoint commissioners empowered to impose reforms on Oxford and Cambridge. The need for reform was indisputable, but Dilke's opposition was based on the fear that the clerical composition of the commissions would result in an extension of the already overstrong clerical influence in the colleges, and in the destruction of fellowships open to competition, which 'gave a chance in life to poor men'. He would have preferred instead to reform the governing bodies of the universities. Nothing was done in 1876, but the following year a combined Oxford and Cambridge Bill was brought forward. Dilke persuaded a meeting of leading Liberals at Devonshire House to support his amendments to the bill. The key one, for a change in the qualifications for membership of the outmoded governing bodies, was defeated by only twenty-eight votes.[23]

Dilke's passivity over elementary education was symptomatic of the generally weak position of radicalism in 1876. Towards the end of the last Liberal administration there had been moments when the radicals had dreamt of a new party, purged of Whigs and moderates by popular support for the 'free programme'. In 1873 Chamberlain had told Morley that Whiggism would soon be extinguished,[24] but this had proved to be little more than bravado. The Conservative victory in 1874, the loss to the Liberals of Gladstone's towering authority, and the consolidation of the government around an active social and imperial policy had left many radicals demoralised. The Reform Act had evidently not transformed the political firmament in quite the way they had once expected. In these circumstances, they had to reconsider their strategy, to look to organisational progress in and out of parliament and, at least for the time being, to reach a *modus vivendi* with the Whigs and the duumvirate of Hartington and Granville.

Parliamentary radicalism and Dilke's position were, in the long run at least, immeasurably strengthened in June 1876 by Chamberlain's unopposed return for Birmingham, the city where as councillor and mayor he had established his reputation as a reformer. Dilke immediately invited Chamberlain to treat 76 Sloane Street as his home during the session. The two radicals had kept in touch since 1870, without yet becoming close. When Dilke was attacked in the London Liberal papers in 1874 for his independent criticism of the government, Chamberlain used his influence with the Birmingham papers to support him. In March of that year, Dilke had welcomed Chamberlain's suggestion for broadening the National Education League into a new propaganda vehicle for the radicals: 'If it were done now – I cd. get all the trades unions in to a joint movement – with you for its head.' Chamberlain never had the same rapport with the labour movement as Dilke, and what he thought of the idea of heading an organisation involving the trade unions went unrecorded. In any case, he had quickly grown lukewarm about reconstituting the NEL: 'I don't think the League will do', he told Dilke. 'It must be a new organisation although our experience & acquired information may be useful.'[25] Here was the germ of the idea that led, three years later, to the establishment of the National Liberal Federation.

Although the two men were both extremely wealthy, they came from quite different backgrounds and brought complementary qualities to their political relationship. Chamberlain had the more impeccable radical credentials. He was the son of a boot and shoe manufacturer, while his own fortune was made in the screw-making side of the Birmingham-based family business. He was a Unitarian; he did not have the privilege of a university education; and he had served a lengthy apprenticeship in provincial politics, reaching parliament only on the eve of his fortieth birthday. Nevertheless, it was to be Dilke – rentier, Cambridge-educated, Anglican, metropolitan and cosmopolitan – who was to prove the more advanced radical. On a wide range of issues – parliamentary reform, education, Ireland, women's rights, local government and labour questions – he revealed the more progressive views. For the moment, however, their cooperation held out the promise of a formidable alliance. Chamberlain was the more powerful orator; Dilke had a penchant for the minutiae of administration. Chamberlain stood large in the country; Dilke was a Londoner, a man at the centre of the political process, a skilled parliamentarian with an unrivalled knowledge of procedure and a reputation for self-discipline and hard work. A House of Commons' joke circulating by 1880, that B. C. meant 'Before Chamberlain' and A. D. 'Anno Dilke', was indicative of the prestige they had won for themselves by that date and of an awareness that their partnership presaged a new era in politics.

This could not have been predicted from its inauspicious beginnings. The first major issue confronting them left the two radicals struggling to find a common approach. In the summer of 1876 rumours began to appear in the press of a terrible massacre of Bulgars by the Turks at Batak. The government at first discounted these reports, but a despatch published in the *Daily News* on 7 August appeared to confirm them. Turkish repression was not unusual. What was new was the force of the moral reaction in England to it. Dilke contributed to the developing furore by being one of the first politicians to give, outside parliament, some substance to the press rumours. At Notting Hill on 15 August, he read from a letter sent to him by a member of the American Legation at Constantinople which gave details of the atrocities.[26] Protest meetings were held throughout England in the late summer. Then, at the end of August, the gathering moral momentum drew Gladstone out of semi-retirement with an emotionally-charged pamphlet on the horrors which raised anti-Turkish feeling to fever pitch.

Dilke eschewed these histrionics, telling Harcourt on 9 September that, 'If Gladstone goes on much longer I shall openly turn Turk.'[27] He was opposed to basing foreign policy on emotion. His speech at Notting Hill had been a reasoned and dispassionate survey of the situation, so much so that it had caused indignation among the moral crusaders. He had reminded his audience of atrocities committed by Britain in India in 1857, by Russia in Poland in 1863, and by French troops in Paris in 1871. The Conservative policy of allowing Russia to intervene in Turkey to her own advantage was equally objectionable to him. He advocated, instead, resistance to Russian aspirations and the despatch of a British representative to Constantinople to protect the Christian subjects of Turkey in the name of the western powers.

The position of Russia was the key to Dilke's attitude. The so-called Eastern Question was posed by Russia's encroachment on the declining Ottoman Empire in search of a warm-water outlet through the Black Sea, thereby threatening Britain's Near East route to India. Dilke shared Cobden's knowledge of Russia and interest in her future, but without the latter's benign regard for her foreign policy. He was isolated in the sense that he disliked the manner in which Disraeli manipulated anti-Russian, and Gladstone anti-Turkish, feelings. The vast majority of parliamentary radicals went along with Gladstone; Dilke and Joseph Cowen were the only leading ones not to attend the national conference on the Eastern Question held on 8 December 1876. Dilke, and more especially Cowen, were the voices of a longstanding but still widely-held anti-Russian strand in English politics. In this respect, Dilke stood nearer to Hartington and Granville. He did not, therefore, on this occasion, alienate the Liberal leadership in the manner of his intervention on the Black Sea question five years earlier. 'I was anti-Russian,' he recalled, 'and in this with Hartington. On the other hand, I was for armed intervention in the East, and in this more extreme than Mr Gladstone....'[28] A historian of British foreign policy has recently observed that the positions struck by both parties were inadequate.[29] Dilke's attempt to reconcile opposition to Russian expansionism with concern for the repressed Turkish minorities was therefore an altogether more balanced approach to the Eastern Question.

Sensing that Gladstone's intervention marked his likely return to the leadership of the Liberal Party, Chamberlain suggested to Dilke that it would be in their best interest to support him. Dilke believed that the radicals would gain more from Hartington, but he also wanted the new radical partnership to succeed. For this reason, he did not reject Chamberlain's proposal outright. 'I am not at all Gladstonian but short of bowing the knee in that quarter I will do anything possible to act with you', he wrote from Toulon, where he was holidaying, on 6 October. Chamberlain was grateful:

> Thanks: I don't believe I am more Gladstonian than you, but at this time I can't help thinking he is our best card ... and if he were to come back for a few years (he can't continue in public life for very much longer) he would probably do much for us, & pave the way for more.[30]

Chamberlain had made a miscalculation about Gladstone's resilience as glaring as one in the opposite sense which came to Dilke in the same post. 'There is no fear of a return from Elba', Harcourt confidently predicted. 'He is *played* out.' But this was a case of the wish being father to the thought, for Harcourt disliked Gladstone and did not want him to return as leader. Despite his assurances to Chamberlain, Dilke for his part continued to believe that Hartington was 'the best man' for the radicals. He was at a loss to explain Chamberlain's 'profound dislike of Hartington', which was, he told Harcourt, 'founded on no reasons at all'. He regarded this as a serious matter, for Chamberlain was a strong man unlikely to change, whereas Cowen was 'as fickle as the wind'.[31]

Chamberlain's estimate was flawed not only because of Gladstone's longevity, but also because of the old man's experience in containing radical aspirations. In his excellent study of the Bulgarian agitation, Richard Shannon contends that Gladstone's re-emergence proved catastrophic for the long-term radicalisation of the Liberal Party, and therefore for its ultimate survival. For the crisis paved the way for his return as Prime Minister and for the eventual enervation of radicalism in the Irish crusade: 1876 rather than 1886 was therefore 'the crucial year for the Liberal Party'.[32] Shannon's argument exaggerates the strength of radicalism in the 1870s, but it does raise doubts about the wisdom of Chamberlain's strategy of courting Gladstone. Hartington had recognised from the early seventies that it was necessary to give the radicals their head. 'I think that there is hardly any important question on which the Whigs and Radicals will not vote against each other', he had remarked shortly before his selection as the new leader, adding that party harmony would be best served by having separate leaders for the two groupings.[33] Dilke was perhaps right in thinking that the Whig leader would have to appoint more radicals to government than Gladstone needed to.

This would certainly be the case if the radicals could increase their parliamentary presence. Following Chamberlain's election, therefore, Dilke urged him to join the Radical Club 'in spite of having snorted at it ... for it is a useful means of getting at the press on special questions'. But

Chamberlain was scornful. 'If you say I must,' he retorted, 'I am ready to join what you call the *Radical* Club: but you ought to write a letter à la Reform to some of its present members.'[34] Chamberlain was right. The Radical Club was largely ineffective. He agreed, however, to cooperate with Dilke in forming a small parliamentary radical group designed to co-ordinate arrangements between its members 'for a proper representation of their views' in the House.[35] Together with Chamberlain and Dilke, the 'new party' consisted of Llewellyn Dillwyn, MP for Swansea, Joseph Cowen and Thomas Burt, representatives of north-east mining constitu-encies, and Edmund Gray, an Irish Nationalist. They evidently took their role seriously for they met at 76 Sloane Street on 6 February 1877 for a 'Queen's Speech dinner', but the government, taking them less seriously, did not venture to grace their gathering with a copy of the Address. Cowen was soon to leave, partly because he could never agree with Chamberlain, and partly because his strong antipathy to Tsarist autocracy led him to support the government over the Eastern Question. Burt's lack of originality made him ornamental rather than useful. Gray upset Chamberlain by getting drunk at Sloane Street and walking off with his hat. So the party dwindled to the ludicrous status of 'two leaders and a follower' – the hapless Dillwyn. However, its rank and file was doubled at a stroke when Morley joined as its link with the press.[36] The latter toyed for a while with the idea of a new weekly review to propagandise radicalism, with himself as editor and Dilke and Chamberlain as his advisory board, but the idea was as evanescent as the party whose views it was to represent.[37] Besides, the *Fortnightly Review* under his editorship was achieving much the same purpose.

Chamberlain believed that the radicals would not prosper until they harnessed their power in the constituencies to their claim for influence within the leadership of the party. To this end he set about creating the National Liberal Federation, drawing upon the organisational experience of the NEL. The NLF was launched in 1877 to reorganise constituency associations, with the aim of using local control as the basis for achieving power at the centre. The constituency associations would insinuate a greater degree of democratic organisation and practice into Liberalism, and agitate for a radical programme, which was essentially the 'free programme' of 1873, and which was elaborated in the *Fortnightly*.[38] For a time after the election defeat, Chamberlain had reduced the Fs to just one – Free Church – as a rallying cry to the Nonconformists, but by 1876 he realised that disestablishment was insufficient in itself for it had little appeal to the working class.[39]

The Bulgarian horrors, hitched to Gladstone's star, might mobilise

Nonconformist and popular support for radicalism in a way disestablishment had conspicuously failed to do. In 1877, therefore,
Chamberlain made a calculated attempt to capture Gladstone for the
radical cause by inviting him to address the inaugural conference of the
NLF.

Dilke and Chamberlain were pursuing two distinct strategies. Dilke
wished to see a well-organised body of radical MPs capable of extracting
concessions from a Hartington-led party; Chamberlain wanted to radicalise the party through the grass-roots and to harness Gladstone's
populist appeal. In the event, neither succeeded: the radical party
remained intractable and Hartington gave way to Gladstone; while the
NLF never managed under Chamberlain to impose its will on the party
leadership and Gladstone proved less pliable than Chamberlain expected.

Gladstone's emergence from retirement to harangue the Turk split the
Liberal Party, and it was to remain divided over the Eastern Question for
the next two years. Although Gladstone carried the north of England with
him, he was, according to Dilke, execrated by the London populace who
amused themselves by gathering to howl at 'bag-and-baggage Billy', a
pastime which soon became 'the ordinary Sunday diversion of the London
rough'. Dilke exaggerated the extent of the opposition to Gladstone in the
capital, but it was perhaps sufficient to make him, as a London MP, more
circumspect about taking sides. He was clearsighted enough to realise that,
while he might not agree with Gladstone, the former Prime Minister at
least had 'moral conviction', whereas Hartington was merely 'infected
with moral indifferentism'.[40]

Public fervour also drew from him a more impassioned assessment of the
Eastern Question. In his annual speech to his constituents at the start of
1877, he condemned Russian autocracy in language which, he recorded,
'moved the meeting ... more than I ever noticed to be the case with any
speech of mine'. He proposed the break-up of the Ottoman Empire and its
replacement by an enlarged Greece and a smaller Turkey.[41]

By March 1877, following a conference at Constantinople, the powers
had prepared a draft protocol outlining the steps to be taken to press
reforms upon Turkey. The Foreign Secretary, Lord Derby, would only
sign on the condition that Russia disarmed – a proviso which Dilke
believed took all meaning out of the protocol, as it would encourage
Turkey to resist reform and this in turn would encourage Russia not to
disarm. Dilke was right. Turkey refused to accept the reform programme
and war now seemed inevitable. On 6 April Hartington asked Dilke to
draft a resolution censuring Derby's terms, and Dilke agreed even though
he thought it would be easily defeated. In the event, the Opposition moved

only for papers. The debate took place on 13 April. Dilke ridiculed Derby's policy, which he characterised as a 'gospel of selfishness', in a speech interrupted throughout by 'ringing cheers & counter-cheers'.[42] Eleven days later, war between Russia and Turkey finally erupted.

Dilke next intended to censure the government for vacillation and non-cooperation with the other great powers, but his plan was derailed by Gladstone's determination to confront the official leadership of Hartington and the anti-Russian policy. The former Prime Minister indicated his intention to introduce five resolutions demanding the coercion of Turkey. Hartington and Granville regarded the manoeuvre as a direct challenge to their leadership. The party was on the verge of breaking up, as Dilke told Mrs Pattison on 3 May:

> The Liberal Party will next week cease to exist. I have got already 88 names of men who will vote with Gladstone – & the front bench having very foolishly decided to support the previous question, the party will be about equally divided, & Hartington will resign.[43]

At the last moment a compromise was reached when Gladstone agreed not to press two of his resolutions, but not without, Dilke believed, his position having been made to appear foolish. Dilke thought both sides at fault – Gladstone for instigating a hostile tactic that he was not prepared to carry through, and Hartington for 'not providing a better way out'. The day after Gladstone's partial climbdown in the House, Dilke wrote that the 'noble delivery of his peroration ... saved the evening from being a complete fiasco – but only just saved it'.[44] Chamberlain thought Gladstone had gone too far, but nevertheless sought to mobilise support for the resolutions in the constituencies as part of his strategy of undermining Hartington's authority. Gladstone, for his part, offended by the official rebuff, was prepared to accept Chamberlain's invitation to the inaugural conference of the NLF at Birmingham at the end of May, thereby falling in with Chamberlain's strategy – though for his own purposes, not Chamberlain's.[45]

The next six months witnessed a steady Russian advance towards Constantinople and intensified Russophobia, especially in London where the music halls gave a new meaning to the word 'jingo'. When Dilke addressed his constituents in January 1878, he dwelt for two hours upon the Eastern Question. His speech was a masterly critique of Conservative policy since 1875, which he summed up as 'isolated, undignified, inconsistent, and unsafe'. In it he sympathised with the nationalist movements in the Turkish provinces. He averred that Egypt would and should be acquired by Britain as an alternative to independence under the

Khedive. He warned that Europe was probably 'mined beneath our feet with secret treaties'. Finally, he repeated his views on the plausibility of creating a greater Greek state as an alternative to Turkish misrule.[46] At about this time he set up a committee of parliamentarians sympathetic to the Greek cause, which came to include Fitzmaurice, Lefevre, Landsdowne and Rosebery. According to Dilke, it did 'much good in the course of the next three years'.[47]

Russian successes in Turkey had jolted the government into recalling parliament early in order to ask for money for war preparations. The Liberals were once again divided over what action to take, as many were as anti-Russian as the government. As with Gladstone's resolutions the year before, the party very nearly split over the leadership's decision to oppose the vote of credit. Forster made a poor speech opening the debate. On the fourth day, Dilke backhandedly complimented the government for keeping the country out of war, adding that he would oppose the vote of credit to ensure that this success was continued.[48] The motion was withdrawn when it was rumoured, falsely as it turned out, that Russia had entered Constantinople. The Liberal Party's part in the debate had once again been a fiasco, and it seemed destined for many more years in opposition.

Dilke's independence on the Eastern Question led to an approach from Churchill, who suggested to him a joint anti-Turkish amendment that would tie the hands of the government at any future peace conference. Churchill then travelled to Dublin to canvass the Irish party. Dilke conveyed the gist of the proposal to Granville, who correctly perceived that the Tory rebel would be unable to deliver support for the motion – a reply which indicated, Dilke thought, that Churchill 'already suffered under that reproach of want of truthfulness which he has always borne'.[49]

The Russo-Turkish war was ended on 3 March 1878 by the Treaty of San Stefano, which created an enlarged Bulgaria and granted independence to Montenegro, Rumania and Persia. Its terms were not acceptable to Britain. The government decided to call up the reserves and secretly bring troops from India to the Mediterranean. Derby, who was opposed to this, resigned and was replaced as Foreign Secretary by Lord Salisbury. Dilke had never had a high regard for Derby's ability, though he found him agreeable enough in private. On one occasion, when he and his companions lost their way during a country walk, Fitzmaurice, sighting the approach of some dishevelled person, remarked, 'Here comes a clod. We will ask him.' The clod turned out to be Lord Derby.[50] Dilke regarded Derby as something of a yokel also in foreign affairs and at first welcomed Salisbury's promotion. However, his support for the government ceased after only a few weeks when he learnt of the reasons for Derby's resignation.

On 20 May Hartington introduced a motion of censure, seconded by Dilke, on the government's decision to employ Indian troops in Europe without having first sought the consent of parliament. By focusing upon the constitutional aspects of the government's action, Hartington succeeded in uniting the Opposition over the Eastern Question for the first time in many months. But the Liberals were once again outflanked. A disclosure in the *Globe* newspaper on 1 June revealed that the government had been in negotiation with Russia throughout the 'crisis'; that a secret agreement had been reached; and that a congress would meet in Berlin to consider revisions to the Treaty of San Stefano and, no doubt, to rubber stamp the deals already made in private.

The treaty which rose out of the meetings at Berlin in June was debated by parliament at the end of July. It aimed to achieve a balance in southeastern Europe by recognising the independence of several former Turkish territories in line with San Stefano, but with restrictions on some of Russia's ambitions in the east which Britain had found objectionable in that treaty. Britain, for her part, was given the right to occupy Cyprus. Dilke, once again speaking after Hartington for the Opposition, criticised the disregard shown by the government at the congress to the aspirations of Greece and argued that the occupation of Cyprus had been bought at too high a price. The speech was a good one, but it was overshadowed by an oratorical *tour de force* on the part of Gladstone.[51]

For the remainder of the Beaconsfield administration, Dilke's stand on the Eastern Question was one of straightforward opposition to certain aspects of the Berlin Treaty: the occupation of Cyprus; the treatment of Greece; and the non-execution of the articles pressing reforms upon Turkey. His criticism of the administration of Cyprus – the brutality of the ordinances concerning land, justice and the employment of forced labour – occupied much of his time during 1879 and brought down upon him such an enormous correspondence in modern Greek that he had to engage a translator. He debated Cyprus in the House to the point of boredom, and beyond. On one occasion he began a speech before a party of MPs left for a dinner at the Crystal Palace and was still on his feet when they got back. Greece was treated in no less detail, and the Greek Committee, which had remained clandestine for a year, was now given a formal and open existence. Part of its work was to put pressure on the government to enforce the treaty provisions rectifying the Greek frontier with Turkey and imposing reforms on Turkey. He believed that the failure to press these reforms provided Russia with a *casus belli* whensoever she needed one.[52]

The Opposition had suffered a series of rebuffs at each stage of the crisis over the Eastern Question. Had the Conservative Party gone to the country in the summer of 1878, there seems little doubt that the Liberals would have been routed. Yet all this was to change over the next eighteen months. Both the Whigs and the radicals had come to realise that they would have to work together if they were to have a chance of dislodging the Tories. Dilke was at the centre of this healing process. Since 1875 he had tacked his flag to Hartington's mast: the latter's willingness, by 1878, to entrust major questions of foreign policy to him demonstrates the extent to which he laid claim to a front-ranking position in the party by this date.

Ever the realist, Chamberlain too was swinging round to Dilke's view of Whig-radical relations. In the course of 1878, he told several correspondents that the best chance of success for the radicals lay 'rather in a hearty alliance and attempt to influence our present leaders, than in the formation of a new party'.[53]

Hartington likewise recognised the need to reach a *rapprochement* with the radicals. Liberal divisions over the Eastern Question led to a more determined effort on his part to use domestic isssues to unify the party. He found he could get on with the urbane Dilke far more easily than with the brusque Brummagen. He therefore made a concession to a plank in the radical platform that was very much Dilke's own. In June 1877, shortly after the débâcle over Gladstone's five resolutions, he pledged the Liberal Party to redistribution.

This official commitment freed Dilke to focus on other electoral reforms. In 1878 he was largely responsible for a Registration Bill, which was based on one he had helped draft in 1871, and which was now adopted in preference to two other schemes by a select committee upon which he served. It passed quickly through parliament as a non-party measure. Its effect was to make information on the electorate more readily available to overseers and thus to secure more accurate registers and restrict the number of purely frivolous and partisan objections. An authority on electoral reform, Charles Seymour, remarked that its effect 'was in certain boroughs very striking and resulted in a greater extension of voting rights than had followed the act of 1867 itself'. Dilke, typically, was disappointed that the 'best' parts of his 1871 bill were not adopted at all.[54]

There were, indeed, serious flaws in the act. It applied only to the boroughs. Many voters, especially lodgers, were disqualified by residence requirements. Others were struck off the registers for receiving medical relief, sometimes as a result of nefarious practices by party agents who arranged for 'presents' of boxes of pills to be distributed unsolicited to certain voters. These and other abuses were exposed by Dilke in a pamphlet on *Parliamentary Reform*. In February 1879 he and William Rathbone, MP for Liverpool, carried a bill designed to do away with some of these anomalies, but they dropped it after it was mangled by the Lords.[55]

On another electoral issue, Dilke met with rather more success. He had for some time been agitating for an extension of polling hours. In 1877 he secured the appointment of a select committee on the question, on which he served, and which reported in favour of his proposal for an experimental extension of the closing time of the polls in London from 4 p.m. to 8 p.m. His bill to that effect was passed unopposed the following session. A year later Chamberlain proposed, with Dilke's support, to extend the principle to the large provincial boroughs, but the House was not yet ready to go further.[56]

Dilke's mastery of the arcane intricacies of electoral law and parliamentary procedure was widely acknowledged. He considered the Commons to be a place for transacting business and was critical of the structuring of parliamentary sessions around aristocratic pastimes like the shooting season and Derby Day. His suggestion that certain bills might be disposed of on their first reading gained him a place on Stafford Northcote's Select Committee on Public Business. He regarded it as 'somewhat a distinction, as I was to be the sole representative of the English independent members'. Although little came of the committee, his participation converted him to the method of restricting the length of debates known as the closure.[57]

The reconstruction of Dilke's political career in the second half of the 1870s was further assisted by his readmission to the ranks of high society. His route back focused increasingly upon Lady Waldegrave's circle. By 1876 he was such a regular visitor to the grand mansion at Strawberry Hill that he was provided with a room of his own, which he used until his hostess's death in July 1879. He never much liked her, but her excellent *soirées* were useful to him, especially as mixed parties had not proved successful at Sloane Street after his wife's death.[58] His engagement books were always full in the late seventies. The only respite he allowed himself was escape from time to time to a house, La Sainte Campagne, at Cap Brun near Toulon, which he first rented in 1876, but which so captivated him that he bought it the following year.

Dilke's Memoir is full of anecdotes about the people he met at this time. Parnell, the Irish leader elected to parliament in 1875, advised him on a cure for baldness. The poet Swinburne came frequently to dine and usually left behind a collection of broken glassware. Henry Manning, the Cardinal Archbishop of Westminster with whom Dilke became particularly friendly from 1878, had a taste for gossip 'and even scandal'. He told Dilke that had he not been cardinal he would have stood for Westminster in the radical interest. 'But', Dilke mused, 'Radical though he be on social questions, he is a ferocious Jingo.' Gladstone impressed him with his conversation, though not by his 'habit of play-acting', by which Dilke meant that he was over-demonstrative at social gatherings. On one occasion, when the Duke of Cambridge offered him his left hand because his right was painful through gout, Gladstone threw his arms in the air 'as though he had just heard of the reception of Lord Beaconsfield in heaven, or of some other terrible news'. All the same, Dilke was not blind to the former Prime Minister's abilities and 'but for his Scotch toadyism to the aristocracy,' he wrote , 'I could admire him with little reserve'.[59]

The foreign policy of the government which had hitherto been its strength was now proving its undoing. Reverses in South Africa and Afghanistan sapped its popularity. In eastern Europe the glitter of 'peace with honour', as Beaconsfield had dubbed the Berlin Treaty, was already beginning to look like fool's gold. During the course of 1879, therefore, the Liberals found themselves increasingly united in their condemnation of Conservative foreign policy. Dilke's knowledge of foreign affairs was earning him a respectful and appreciative hearing from an assembly that had shortly before hissed him. He was now coming to be regarded as the Opposition's chief spokesman on overseas issues, a position that was confirmed by the decision to give him responsibility for opening the debate on South Africa, an opportunity which he used to devastating effect.

Accordingly, on 27 March 1879, he introduced a censure motion criticising the conduct of the British High Commissioner in South Africa, Sir Bartle Frere, for his part in precipitating the Zulu War and the massacre of British soldiers at Isandhlwana. The annexation of the Transvaal two years earlier had led first to territorial disputes with the neighbouring Zulus and now, with Frere's high-handed management of the crisis, to war. Dilke spoke for two-and-a-half hours, delivering a skilful and caustic indictment of the High Commissioner based on the evidence in the blue books.[60] During the whole time he was on his feet he never doubted his complete success, being 'greatly cheered by my own side, without being once questioned or interrupted by the other'. It was not his best speech, but it was opportune. He jubilantly informed Mrs Pattison of the compliments showered upon him. Granville for one wrote, on reading the speech in the newspapers the next morning, 'It struck me as excellent, and I have since heard that it is the opinion of all those who heard it.' What the speech meant for the Liberal Party was summed up by Lord Reay when he called it its 'Cape of "Good Hope"'.[61] Although the resolution was defeated by 306 votes to 246 after three nights' debate, it was the first seriously damaging attack on Conservative overseas policy. By forcing the government to defend Frere's conduct, a virtually impossible task, Dilke had exposed weaknesses on what had hitherto appeared to be an invulnerable flank, and had rallied the Liberal Party in a way that had not been seen for many years. An electoral victory no longer appeared an impossibility.[62]

In all, 1879 was a disastrous year for the government. The war in South Africa was followed in September with the massacre of the British Legation in Kabul and the renewal of the Afghan War. Dilke's polished contributions to the debates on imperial policy, which displayed an unsurpassed knowledge of their subject, had completed his political recovery. His republican *faux pas* was now largely forgotten and he was increasingly talked of as a likely member of the next Liberal government. Later events have obscured the fact that, in 1879, it was he and not Chamberlain who was perceived as the 'coming man' among the parliamentary radicals.[63] He had established good relations with Hartington and could expect to be well-rewarded in a Whig-led administration. Events did not, however, transpire quite as anticipated.

Chapter 6

At the Foreign Office

At the start of the 1880 session, the Beaconsfield administration was facing serious problems. The politically embarrassing overseas setbacks compounded an already very difficult economic situation. The economy was in recession. The harvest of 1879 was poor. A budget surpus of £6,000,000 inherited from the Liberals in 1874 had been turned into a deficit of almost the same amount. The country now found itself paying for an adventurous imperial policy through increased income tax.

In the face of these strains upon the government's popularity, it is curious that its downfall was triggered by a comparatively minor policy reversal, and one involving Dilke. At the beginning of March Richard Cross, the Home Secretary, introduced a bill to purchase the private London water companies. Dilke and Fawcett had been urging such a policy for several months. However, the government's compensation to the companies was overgenerous, leading to criticism of its handling of the buy out.[1] In the House, Dilke pressed a harassed Home Secretary for more information. He claimed that his question contained such a mass of searching statistics that it frightened Cross, created dissension in the cabinet, and was 'the immediate cause of the dissolution'.[2] In fact, it was a surprise by-election victory at Southwark that encouraged Beaconsfield to go to the country, but there is no doubt that the row over the Water Bill was a contributory factor.

In the April general election Dilke was returned by a comfortable margin at the head of the poll. A fellow Liberal, J. F. B. Firth, was in second place. Dilke had feared defeat and had briefly contemplated moving to a safe seat at Manchester. The Liberals finished with an unexpectedly large majority – 112 seats more than the Conservatives, with the Irish Nationalists holding 62. Among the new members was Dilke's brother, Ashton, victorious at Newcastle-upon-Tyne alongside Joseph Cowen.

It was not yet clear who would be the next Prime Minister. Hartington was still the leader of the party and had the backing of Harcourt. He was also the choice of the Queen, who wanted to avoid Gladstone at all cost. Chamberlain, ambitious for office after only four years in the House and confident that the caucus system had been responsible for the Liberal victory, was determined to press his own claim for a cabinet post. On 4 April he wrote to Dilke:

> I find the same fault with your letters that the Scottish laird found with the Dictionary – 'the stories are varra pretty but they are unco short!'
>
> The time has come when we must have a full frank explanation. What I should like – what I hope for with you – is a thorough offensive and defensive alliance and in this case our position will be immensely strong. I am prepared to refuse all offices until and unless *both of us are satisfied*.
>
> Can you accept this position with perfect satisfaction? If you think I am asking more than I can give I rely on your saying so – & in this case you may depend on my loyalty & friendship. I shall support your claims cordially & just as warmly as if I were personally interested. But my own feeling is that if you are stronger than I am in the House, my influence is greater than yours out of it – &, therefore, that, together, we are much more powerful than separated; and that, in a short time – if not now – we may make our own terms.
>
> To join a Government as subordinate members – to be silenced and to have no real influence on the policy – would be fatal to both of us. If we both remain outside, any Government will have to reckon with us and on the whole this would be the position which on many grounds I should prefer. I am ready to make all allowances for the difficulty of giving to both of us the only kind of place which it would be worth our while to accept. If these are insuperable, I will give a hearty support to any Gov. which is thoroughly liberal in its measures; but I am not going to play the part of a radical minnow among Whig Tritons.
>
> The victory which has just been won is the victory of the Radicals – Gladstone and the Caucus have triumphed all along the line, and it is the strong, definite, decided policy which has commended itself and not the halting half-hearted arm-chair business ....
>
> You will see that my proposed condition is – both of us to be satisfied.
>
> As to what *ought* to satisfy us, if you agree to the principle, we will consult when the time comes, but my present impression is – all or nothing. *Tout arrive à qui sait attendre.* Write me fully your views & tell me whether and when you will pay me a visit.[3]

Despite their developing friendship, there had as yet been insufficient political cooperation for Dilke to find Chamberlain's proposal anything other than presumptuous. They had attempted to organise a radical group in parliament and had discussed with Parnell the possibilities of radical-Irish cooperation. However, they had differed over the Eastern Question and over the party leadership. Chamberlain had shown signs of recognising the need for a *modus vivendi* with the Whigs, but he was by nature more belligerent than Dilke and had in recent months crossed swords with

Hartington in a particularly unpleasant way. The occasion was a debate in July 1879 on flogging in the army, when the Whig leader, on returning from a long break for dinner, had inadvertently lent his voice in support of the government. Chamberlain was stung by this and had responded with a bitter attack on 'the noble Lord, lately the leader of the Opposition'. Dilke later claimed that the incident had badly damaged Hartington and paved the way for Gladstone's return to the leadership. This was an inaccurate judgement based upon hindsight. The party in fact rallied to Hartington, Chamberlain being condemned for his divisive and offensive manner.[4] Dilke's continued support for Hartington suggests that at the time he did not appear to regard him as having been damaged. An explanation for Gladstone's re-emergence should be sought rather in the effectiveness of his barnstorming 'Midlothian Campaign' in the run-up to the dissolution.

At the time of the election victory Dilke was still of the opinion that the radicals could extract from Hartington terms that they could never hope to get from Gladstone. He was not blind to the fact that an alliance with Chamberlain would undoubtedly be of more advantage to his colleague than to himself. He foresaw that a position might arise whereby neither of them was in the cabinet: in that case they should both refuse minor office unless one of them was included and the other given a place of influence.[5] With these considerations running through his mind, he told Chamberlain that nothing had as yet happened to lead him to alter his plans for spending Easter in Toulon, adding:

> I quite agree generally to the position that we shd. continue to work together & that each shd. see that the other is satisfied. My first enquiry when I hear anything will be – what about you? I also think that we are far more powerful together than separated, & that we are in a position to make our own terms... If H[artington] is Premier – I don't see why they shd. not offer the cabinet to *both* of us.[6]

Chamberlain, knowing that Dilke's chances of promotion were better than his own, felt slighted by this response and by Dilke's preference at this critical juncture for holidaying in the south of France to conspiring at Highbury. It was therefore a fortnight before he replied. When he did, it was in a tone which, despite his avowal of support for Dilke and indifference to high office, could not disguise the fact that his true feelings were ones of jealousy and blighted ambition. Moreover, he signed himself coldly 'Yours sincerely' instead of the customary 'Your ever', a reliable indicator of his frame of mind at the time of writing:

> I am glad to see that all the Papers speak of you as a certainty for the Cabinet. These reports are unauthentic, but they have a tendency to secure their own fulfilment. I feel

that you may have a rather difficult question to decide, viz., whether you can safely take the *sole* representation of the radical element in the Government.[7]

On 22 April Dilke received a telegram from Harcourt summoning him to London. He arrived back from France the following evening to the news that, despite being sent for and pressured by the Queen, Hartington could not form an administration without Gladstone, and that consequently the latter was to be Prime Minister. Working on what he called 'Peel's Rule' of not allowing anyone to hold cabinet office who had not previously held a minor post, Gladstone offered Dilke the choice of Financial Secretary or Under-Secretary of State for the Colonies. Dilke declined both and immediately invited Chamberlain to come to London to consult.[8] This was not a narrowly selfish move. Chamberlain had received nothing and by joint action Dilke hoped they might both benefit. But Chamberlain was still sulking and refused to come. Stirred by the urgency of the situation, Dilke wrote once more:

> I have your telegram refusing to come to-morrow. If I were not so tired with my journey I'd come down. You see you talk of consultation, but I can't consult you by telegraph, & in Gladstone's stand & deliver kind of business there is no time for exchange of letters with Birmingham. My telegram of this evening was intended to mean that it was certain that Gladstone wd. not offer either of us the cabinet, & to ask you to come up to talk over whether it was clear that we ought to refuse all else ... .[9]

Chamberlain responded to this second appeal, arriving in London on the following afternoon, and spent the evening closeted with Dilke. He now accepted Dilke's proposal that neither should accept office unless one of them was in the cabinet. He was still inclined to feel that it would be better if both of them were in or out of the cabinet, for it still seemed likely that it would be Dilke rather than himself who would win preferment.

The next day the wheels turned quickly. Gladstone offered Dilke the Under-Secretaryship of State for Foreign Affairs, which he refused when he learnt that Chamberlain was not in the government. Gladstone, perhaps irritated by Dilke's recalcitrance, decided to offer the Presidency of the Board of Trade with a seat in the cabinet to Chamberlain, thereby going back on his earlier zealous adherence to 'Peel's Rule'. Dilke now agreed to accept the Under-Secretaryship.[10]

Chamberlain knew that Dilke's subordination to himself would excite 'a good deal of discontent and ill-feeling', and that many would 'resent the quick promotion' which he had 'unwillingly' secured.[11] As soon as the announcement was made public, Dilke's mail was, indeed, replete with complaints on his behalf. One correspondent spoke of his 'needless self-sacrifice', and another reflected that he 'ought to have had the seat in the

Cabinet 20 millions of miles in front of Chamberlain'.[12] These opinions were echoed in the press. Dilke derived a certain amount of masochistic satisfaction from his martyrdom, but his comment in his Memoir was somewhat disingenuous, for he had undoubtedly expected to be in the cabinet himself. 'As to my being annoyed by Chamberlain being put in over my head,' he wrote, 'so far was that from being true that I actually wished that to happen wh. did happen, seeing that we could not both be in.'[13]

When finalised, Gladstone's second administration, like his first, was dominated by the Whigs. He took the Exchequer himself. Harcourt was Home Secretary, Granville Foreign Secretary, Kimberley Colonial Secretary, Selborne Lord Chancellor, Hartington Indian Secretary, Childers War Secretary, Earl Spencer was Lord President, the Duke of Argyll Lord Privy Seal, Northbrook was at the Admiralty and Dodson at the Local Government Board. In addition, the old radical John Bright was Chancellor of the Duchy of Lancaster and W. E. Forster the Irish Secretary. However, with Chamberlain at the Board of Trade there was no longer any doubt that the radical viewpoint would receive more than just a token representation in the cabinet. Granville summed up this concoction as 'like bread sauce made of two substantial elements. The few peppercorns are obvious, and perhaps give a little flavour, but do not affect the food.'[14] But Granville underestimated the ability of the peppercorns in the coming months to leave a nasty taste in the mouths of the Whigs.

Queen Victoria was not at all happy with the appointment of a professed republican to her government. In September 1879, when Dilke's name was being floated as a likely member of a future Liberal cabinet, she had been emphatic that she 'never *could* take Sir C. Dilke as a *Minister*'. When the Prime Minister formally submitted his name to her on 27 April, she insisted that he make a formal retraction of 'his very offensive speeches on the Civil List & Royal Family'.[15]

Granville tried to mediate in the delicate exchanges with the Queen. He forwarded to her a letter addressed to himself from Dilke which said that while republicanism might be suited to those countries making 'a fresh start in life after a great convulsion', it was 'folly' to attempt to introduce it in England, where constitutional monarchy was well-established. The Queen, however, wanted reassurance that Dilke no longer intended to pursue his opposition to the civil list. He was forced to declare that he would not 'take any further part of any kind in the matter' before she was satisfied.[16]

Appointment to a junior position did not match either Dilke's talents or his aspirations: he was determined that he would be more than just a mouthpiece for the Foreign Office in the Commons. He wished to bolster the foreign policy of the Liberals by showing that they could be at least as assiduous as the Conservatives in promoting Britain's overseas interests. His preference for a more forward policy seemed likely therefore to bring him into conflict with Granville and with backbench radicals who remained wedded to the internationalism of Cobden and Gladstone.

At first, as Dilke tried to assert himself, his relationship with the Foreign Secretary was decidedly cool. Granville was an extremely experienced diplomat and he did not yet suffer from the senility that marred his last years in office. True, he had the malapropic habit of mixing up words and names, but Dilke found this an amusing and disarming trait. Granville was shrewd enough to give Dilke almost exclusive control of the commercial department, which meant that a great deal of his time was expended upon negotiating a new trade treaty with France and away from broader questions of foreign policy to which he would have preferred to devote himself. Relations between them therefore quickly improved. When Granville fell ill, in August 1881, Dilke noted with some alarm in his diary that 'It wd. be a great misfortune if he were to die or become incapacitated. We should have to choose between Derby who is undecided & weak, Hartington, – who knows no French & nothing about F[oreig]n affairs, Kimberley, who is a chattering idiot, & Northbrook who is weaker than Derby.'[17] His preference for Granville was not simply occasioned by contemplation of the alternatives to him. He had come to respect the Foreign Secretary, and mutual respect rather than friendship, characterised their relationship.

There were occasional moments of friction. For example, after one particularly carping note from Dilke in February 1882, Granville remarked sardonically that it should have come a little later as 'it would have been so wholesome in Lent. The tone of it is hardly that of two members of the same Govt., more particularly when they are excellent friends.' Dilke apologised.[18] More serious was a basic disagreement over the granting of a charter to the North Borneo Company, to which Dilke was opposed. As opinion in the cabinet was evenly divided, he pressed Gladstone for his casting vote which was given for the charter. 'So the job is to be jobbed,' he told Mrs Pattison, '& the Charter granted.'[19] The Prime Minister later forgot his decision, insisting that he had never heard of the matter, and would have stopped the grant had it not been too late. When the charter was published in December 1881 Dilke, who thought it did not go far enough in compelling the company to put down slavery and the opium traffic, refused to defend it in the Commons and outlined his objections in a memorandum. His opposition angered Granville. He had threatened resignation and had won begrudging support from Chamberlain who did not regard this as 'exactly the sort of question on which, if we had the choice, we would have elected to split'. Dilke was confident that there would be no split and that the charter would be amended to meet his objections. This proved to be the case and he was therefore able to defend it in the House.[20] It helped to keep North Borneo from Spain and served as a model for later charters apportioning Africa's wealth among various predatory companies.

Dilke's criticism had not derived from any principled opposition to English expansionism. Indeed, the radicals were now proving to be more clamorous imperialists than their Whig brethren, whom they condemned for failing to stand up to Germany in various parts of the world – Angra Pequena, Samoa, New Guinea and Zanzibar. With regard to the last, Dilke wrote to Northbrook in November 1882, 'Are you going to let Zanzibar die without a kick?'[21] The Sultan had proposed a British protectorate: Gladstone was against, and Dilke strongly for it. The outcome was an increase in German influence, which later, in 1890, was used as a bargaining-counter in negotiations with Britain – Germany giving back, in Dilke's opinion, what should never have been allowed to slip away in the first place. Likewise, when two native chiefs in the Cameroons asked Gladstone to take their country under British protection, Dilke urged acceptance on the grounds that it was the best and most healthy spot on the west coast of Africa. He convinced Granville,[22] but Kimberley, the Colonial Secretary, obstinately refused the request and no answer was given immediately, with the result that Germany seized the Cameroons in 1884. Dilke, who was by this time in the cabinet, told Grant Duff: 'Chamberlain & I are both angry at the loss of the Cameroons, both of us in turn having thought we had annexed them – only now to find that through F. O. & C. O. dawdling they have gone to Germany.'[23]

This support for a more forward overseas policy marks a significant moment in the history of middle-class radicalism and of intra-capitalist relations in Britain. Faced with international competition, sectors of British industry began to favour more interventionist imperial policies in order to secure markets and access to raw materials. As capital export increased, financiers too were anxious to safeguard their overseas investments. Empire was therefore beginning to have a centripetal effect on British capitalism, drawing together its various sectors. The appointment of a radical to the Foreign Office, a traditional fief of the aristocracy, was itself symptomatic of this process. At the same time the anti-colonial and pacifist elements of the Cobdenite tradition, represented in cabinet by the venerable John Bright, began to falter. Bright himself was very soon to leave over an imperialist issue, Egypt, that more than any other demonstrated this turning-point in radical imperialism. The persistence of Cobdenism among backbench MPs and in the country at large remained a serious obstacle to the creation of a separate Radical Party. Dilke recognised this and it perhaps explains why, in the short term at least, he was prepared to seek a *modus vivendi* with the Whigs. A future realignment of the Liberal power bloc did not therefore necessarily entail a Whig exodus, although there were other obstacles, such as the land question and Ireland, that would have to be overcome if any such new balance of forces was to be achieved without breaking up the party.

The Liberals had won the election largely as a result of a moral disillusionment with Beaconsfieldism. Now they had to come to terms with the legacy of the Tories' Eastern Policy. Dilke soon found himself defending strategems that he had shortly before condemned, including support for Turkey while it carried through internal reforms and, above all, the occupation of Cyprus. He was now in a much better position to champion the Greek cause and, a month after taking office, he floated the idea of a union between Albania and Greece. At the beginning of 1881, when war between Greece and Turkey seemed imminent, he suggested a naval occupation of the port of Smyrna to compel the Turks to vacate territory ceded to Greece by the Treaty of Berlin. He found himself without a single supporter in the government and momentarily considered resigning. When a settlement was finally reached, Greece had to be content with only a limited cession of territory.[24]

The two and a half years spent in a subordinate position at the Foreign Office were not, therefore, without their frustrations for Dilke. On the day prior to his contemplated resignation over Greece, he had noted in his diary that he could not 'always depend on Chamberlain to oppose foolish things in Cabinet'. The reference was to Chamberlain's support for the prosecution of *Freiheit*, a German anarchist paper published in London.[25] For the most part, however, he enjoyed his work. He was kept fully informed by Chamberlain of cabinet meetings. The extent of his inside information can be seen from his letters to Lord Ripon. The latter had been appointed Viceroy of India and Dilke wrote to him after each weekly meeting of the cabinet with a summary of its business. Their correspondence further illustrates Dilke's ability to cultivate his Whig colleagues, a fact which explains why many of them looked to him rather than Chamberlain as a future leader of the Liberal Party.

As for the two radicals themselves, they were now the closest of friends. In reply to Chamberlain's warm comment that 'in all my political life the pleasantest & the most satisfactory incident is your friendship', Dilke was no less complimentary. 'As for your good words about our friendship', he replied, 'it is curious that in spite of what people believe about the jealousies of politicians you should be one of the two or three people in the world about whose life or death I should care enough for that care to be worth the name of affection.'[26]

A large part of Dilke's time at the Foreign Office was taken up with negotiating a commercial treaty with France. The Cobden Treaty of 1860 had been renewed in 1872 but was once again about to lapse. As a Francophile, Dilke was naturally interested in any arrangements that would improve Anglo-French relations. Yet the negotiations were beset with difficulties from the outset. The economic depression had given rise to the fair trade movement and to a less than favourable climate for tariff concessions. It was from this time that the hitherto sacrosanct system of free trade began to be seriously questioned. A more immediate difficulty, as far as Dilke was concerned, was Gladstone's fiscal orthodoxy and his determination to balance the budget. Faced with the deficit bequeathed by the Tories, he was emphatic that '*At present we have not a sixpence to give away.*'[27] In May 1880 he flatly told Dilke that he could not contemplate any loss to the Exchequer in the coming financial year, adding that while he did not wish 'to shut the door to "negotiation"', he had little faith in it. However, when Léon Say, the French ambassador, attacked Gladstone fiercely in the French press for not offering to lower the wine duties, the Prime Minister, fearing the hostility of British merchants, backed down and instructed Dilke to proceed.

Dilke agreed several bases for negotiation with Say, the most important of which were the creation of a new class of duties for light French wines, and 'amelioration' in the level of French tariffs upon British goods. The failure of the French to satisfy the British upon the latter point was to lead eventually to stalemate and to the final abandonment of the Cobden Treaty.[28]

In June Say returned to France to become President of the Senate. The Queen objected to De Noailles, his proposed replacement, on the basis of a rumour that his wife had had four lovers prior to her marriage, one for each season of the year. The credentials of Challemel-Lacour, the alternative to De Noailles, appeared hardly more flattering. He was accused of living with a washerwoman who posed as his grandmother, and of shooting a number of monks at Lyons where he was prefect during the Commune. The Prince of Wales pressed Dilke as to the truth of these rumours. They had met at a dinner-party in March 1880 and had afterwards become quite friendly. Excluded from any real power by his mother's longevity, the Prince found in Dilke a useful and willing source of information on foreign affairs. Dilke, for his part, enjoyed the social set to which his acquaintance with the Prince admitted him and, though he had little sympathy for his politics which he thought both strongly conservative and extremely jingoistic, he did not underestimate the value of cultivating relations with the future King.[29] The Prince appeared to believe, Dilke told Ripon, that Challemel was 'all daubed with petroleum, & that some will come off on to his clothes'.[30] Dilke tried to reassure him by telling him that Challemel's only really objectionable characteristic was his violent temper, 'the worst ... with which perhaps any human being was ever cursed'. The farce had its sequel in the House when an Irish MP by the name of O'Donnell put down a question which revived all the allegations against Challemel. Dilke repudiated them, but a protracted scene ensued in which O'Donnell's attempts to press for an adjournment were met by equally futile attempts on Gladstone's part to prevent him from being heard. Dilke afterwards received from Gambetta a note which thanked him 'from the bottom of my heart for the lofty manner in which you picked up the glove thrown down by that mad Irish clerical'.[31]

The change of ambassador gave the French an excuse for postponing the treaty negotiations. Dilke's exertions to keep them afloat had taken their toll on his health and in August he was quite ill from an internal abscess that had to be lanced.[32] 1880 was an unfortunate year all round for the health of the residents of 76 Sloane Street. Two of them died – Dilke's grandmother and her niece – while a third, H. G. Kennedy, Dilke's private secretary, had to retire through illness. He was replaced in the new year by J. E. C. Bodley, afterwards a distinguished writer on France.

Dilke turned next, with no encouragement from Gladstone, to negotiating a tariff agreement with Spain. He hoped that the threat of a separate treaty favouring Spanish wines would bring France back to the negotiating-table. 'I have always', he wrote in his Memoir a decade before the tariff reform controversy, 'been a reciprocitarian to this extent, and was always backed in using such arguments by Chamberlain who held the same views in still stronger form.'[33]

The tactic seemed to work. In May the French agreed to resume the talks, though Dilke was not sanguine about the chances of success. He noted in his diary that he had been appointed to a commission 'to conclude the impossible Treaty with France'. Nevertheless, he felt that several months of negotiations might induce France to concede a most-favoured-nation agreement.[34] The preliminary meetings held in London succeeded only in wrangling over the meaning of the word 'amelioration' and in convincing Dilke even more firmly than ever that no treaty was possible – 'a sad pity' he told Ripon.[35] The commission therefore broke up in June, but it agreed to reconvene in Paris in the autumn.

Dilke was under some pressure from the Foreign Office to conclude a less than satisfactory treaty at this stage in order to ease relations with France in the wake of the latter's occupation of Tunis. He preferred to delay until after the French presidential elections, when it was likely that he would be able to deal with Gambetta. He was supported by Chamberlain, who ensured this view prevailed in the cabinet.[36] Accordingly, an informal cabinet on 2 August, attended by Dilke, decided not to go to Paris unless the French prolonged the existing treaty for three months.[37] They at first refused to accede to this arrangement but, following some politicking by Dilke on a visit to France in which he exploited the machinations that were taking place between the rival presidential contenders, they suddenly backed down and negotiations were able to resume in Paris on 19 September.[38]

Dilke invited representatives of the chambers of commerce to give evidence before the commission and much progress was made in the English direction. However, by the end of the month, an *impasse* had once again been reached on the question of British cotton goods and French wines. It was decided by the British delegation to adjourn the meetings until 24 October on the pretext of awaiting fresh instructions, the ulterior motive being to delay in anticipation of Gambetta's victory. This tactic angered Tirard, the Minister of Commerce, who attempted to make the conclusion of any treaty impossible for Gambetta by suddenly demanding, at the resumption of negotiations, a vast reduction in the English wine duties. Dilke surmised that his rudeness was calculated to produce 'an immediate rupture'.[39]

During the course of the talks in France, Dilke had kept Gladstone and Granville informed of progress and, on 27 October, he summed up for the Prime Minister the absurdity of the situation in which the English commission found itself: 'we are in the singular position of trying to arrange the terms of a Treaty with a minister who if the Treaty is made is likely to become the private member who will move its rejection'.[40] Granville, bemused by Dilke's intricate explanations of the minutiae of the negotiations – as to whether, for example, ivory buttons emerged at a higher or lower rate of duty – thanked him for the information which was 'as interesting as the lists of the betting in the newspapers, just before the Derby. I hope you will win the race, it will greatly redound to your credit'.[41] Dilke had so impressed his seniors that they were by this stage willing to allow him a free hand.

He returned to London for a fortnight at the beginning of November

until the French elections were over. Before leaving Paris, he had dined
with Rouvier, Gambetta's Minister of Commerce to be, but had found him
'far stupider than Tirard'. When he returned to Paris on 19 November,
Gambetta's new ministry was not yet ready to resume the negotiations, so
he travelled on to Toulon for a holiday.

Gambetta's government had settled its conditions for treating by
Christmas, but these showed no advance upon those of the previous
administration and, upon the thirty-seventh sitting of the joint commission
on the last day of the year, negotiations were once more broken off. Before
leaving France, Dilke had a final meeting with Gambetta from whom he
gathered that France might concede a most-favoured-nation treaty of one
year's duration. He also met Clemenceau, 'an inferior Randolph
Churchill' he told Ripon.[42]

Gambetta shortly afterwards fell, but the new French government did
agree to a most-favoured-nation arrangement. In the end, a treaty had not
been possible, primarily because protectionist interests in France resisted
any meaningful reduction in textile duties. The granting of most-favoured-
nation status meant, for all that, quite large concessions, especially on
certain yarns, without any corresponding reduction by Britain of her wine
duties. There was not, therefore, that loss of revenue which Gladstone had
feared. On the contrary, within a year exports of cotton and woollen
manufactures to France increased, though there was a falling off in
worsteds. The largest increase in trade came in cloths, casimirs and other
milled tissues of wool, which more than trebled by value. Dilke had reason
to regard the outcome of negotiations about which he had always been
pessimistic, as something of a 'triumph', if only on a small scale.[43]

His reputation had suffered no harm by the failure to conclude a treaty.
The Prime Minister did not allow his dislike for tariff treaties to diminish
his admiration for a man with an interest in the technicalities of finance
that matched his own. At one stage during their correspondence on the
negotiations he was signing himself 'Ever Yours'. Granville, too, flattered
Dilke on his 'commercial triumphs'.[44]

With the French negotiations over, Dilke tried to speed forward those
with Spain. He was prepared to use Spanish grievances about smuggling
across the Gibraltar border as a bargaining-counter to get a most-
favoured-nation agreement. Gladstone again proved a stumbling-block,
being 'averse on general grounds to purchasing m.f.n. treatment at any
price great or small'. The Prime Minister backed down a little, but the
discussions nevertheless dragged on and were not completed until 1885.[45]

The commercial negotiations had not been helped by the deterioration
in Anglo-French relations over North Africa. Trouble over Tunis flared up

in January 1881, when a dispute over an estate culminated in the expulsion of a British subject by the French consulate and the appearance off the Tunis coast of a French ironclad. Dilke, taking on the mantle of Palmerston, recommended sending a British warship if the French would not withdraw. Granville concurred, and on 5 February the *Thunderer* was despatched. When France offered to refer the matter to arbitration, the Foreign Office, again at Dilke's insistence, refused. A 'safe and easy way' to stop the French in Tunis, Dilke observed, would be to let him 'go to Berlin for one day and see Bismarck & talk about the weather, and then to Rome for one hour & see no one, merely to let the fact get into the newspapers'.[46]

Realistically, however, the British government did not wish to alienate France for the sake of Tunis. French enterprise had, in Dilke's phrase, 'knocked another bit out of the Ottoman Empire', demonstrating only too clearly the fragility of this traditional barrier against Russia and the vulnerability of Constantinople as the linch-pin of Britain's eastern route to India. The opening of the Suez Canal had reduced still further in value the overland route and had turned the eyes of English ministers away from Constantinople to Cairo. With France's predominance in Tunis a *fait accompli*, Hartington, Granville and Dilke discussed what compensation in Egypt could be extracted from her.[47] Egypt was beginning to overwhelm all other questions of foreign policy which the government had to face.

Dilke had welcomed Disraeli's acquisition of the Suez Canal and favoured annexing Egypt to the British Empire. 'Africa', he noted in his diary in June 1877, 'has still I believe a future before it of which we should, starting from Egypt, obtain the control, to the advantage of ourselves, the Africans and the world at large, for I take it we are the least unfit among the powers for the task'.[48] His support for annexation was later replaced by the more limited goal of maintaining British influence in Egypt. For the time being, he was a leading proponent of intervention and set about devising ways by which it could be secured.

Britain and France had attempted to rule Egypt through the imposition of the puppet Khedival system, but a costly programme of reforms had left the Egyptian government in considerable debt and led to the joint supervision of Egyptian finances under the dual control of France and Britain. Attempts to institute financial reform had succeeded only in alienating the landlords and the military and in uniting their discontents to those of an already depressed peasantry.

Events in Egypt now followed what soon became a familiar pattern in the history of imperialism. Faced with threats to its economic interests, the metropolitan government searched around for reasons to justify armed intervention and secure public support for a forward policy. British intervention was to be cloaked behind claims that had no solid basis in fact – that Egypt was sliding into anarchy at the hands of a tyrant; that Christian lives were at risk; that the Canal was threatened; and that the French would use the instability to steal a march on Britain. In fact, it was the intervention itself which caused many of the very problems that it was supposedly initiated to prevent.[49]

In September 1881 the military revolution led by Arabi Pasha, a colonel in the Egyptian army, reached crisis point when the Khedive's palace was surrounded and his chief minister overthrown. Although the Khedive, Tewfik, continued to rule in name, the military regime now held sway. Fearing that intervention by the one would be a loss of influence to the other, France and Britain resolved on a joint intervention – a policy facilitated in November by the presidential victory of Gambetta, who had all along favoured cooperation. The outcome was the despatch, at the start of 1882, of a joint note warning the nationalists that steps would be taken to uphold the Khedivate and preserve the dual financial control. Dilke, who was in France that winter to negotiate the commercial treaty and who discussed foreign policy with Gambetta at Granville's request, was accused of hatching and supporting the idea of the joint note in return for Gambetta's promise to back a most-favoured-nation agreement. He always denied this, claiming that the note was almost the only issue of foreign affairs upon which he was not consulted during his period as Under-Secretary.[50] These denials were made at a time when he had become a proponent of withdrawal from Egypt and are not consonant with his behaviour at the time. He and Hartington were the leading hawks pressing for the assertion of British supremacy in Egypt. To this end he intrigued with Gambetta and, as we shall see, manoeuvred for unilateral intervention when Gambetta was replaced by the more circumspect Freycinet, stiffened Granville's resolve at critical moments, and was the foremost spirit behind the show of British force at Alexandria.[51]

The joint note had the predictable effect of alarming the nationalists and encouraging their resistance. This, in turn, provided Gambetta with the grounds for implementing the note. Dilke urged the government to support Gambetta's demand for joint intervention, but the cabinet was divided. The question was temporarily put to one side by the fall of Gambetta on 26 January. [52] After several weeks of temporising, the two governments finally agreed in May to a joint naval demonstration supported by the Turkish army. Dilke told Grant Duff:

The French have completely 'caved in' to us about Egypt, discovering that a Turkish intervention at the request of England & France is not 'Turkish intervention'. Ld. G. is 10 years younger than he was when I closed my last letter to you.[53]

France had agreed that Turkey should intervene only as a last resort and when, on 24 May, Britain proposed to act at once by calling in the Turks, the French Prime Minister Freycinet, according to Dilke, 'went to bed to avoid answering'. The French, he grumbled, had 'completely sold us, and we once more realised the fact that they are not pleasant people to go tiger hunting with'. The naval demonstration, without backing from Turkey on land, was ineffective and served only to inspire the nationalists to further extremism, culminating in the massacre of fifty Europeans at Alexandria on 11 and 12 June.

Behind the pressure for intervention in Egypt was the combined weight of middle-class bondholders, bankers, merchants and manufacturers, in common cause with the aristocratic officer class. This alignment of the various sectors of capital found its political correspondence in the firm support given by Dilke and Chamberlain to Hartington's demand for immediate action. Indeed, Dilke decided on 17 June to resign if nothing was done. When he was called into the cabinet on 19 June, he could only say 'like the servants when they fall out, either Arabi must go or I will'. Two days later he withdrew a little. He would resign if Hartington was prepared to go too but, failing that, must insist upon intervention to safeguard the Canal, and a 'startling reparation for the murders & insult to our council at Alexandria'.[54]

Granville allowed Dilke to telegraph to Egypt to insist on the execution of the leaders of the massacre, on compensation to the injured and relatives of those killed, on damages for the destruction of property, and on a salute to the British flag at Cairo and Alexandria. Throughout the crisis he was only getting his way by threatening to resign. Granville rebuked him for this on 24 June. The next day Gladstone and Granville, without consulting their colleagues, rejected an offer from the Sultan to hand over the administration of Egypt to Britain.[55]

Dilke was determined to prevent the Prime Minister and Foreign Secretary from agreeing to any diplomatic compromise. On 3 July he peremptorily sent off a despatch drafted by Granville but without his prior consent, which rejected French proposals for opening negotiations with Arabi.[56] The next day he prepared a memorandum in favour of British intervention, arguing that it could be justified on the grounds 'either of the need for settled government at Cairo, in order to make the Canal safe and our route to India free, or else on that of the probable complicity of the revolutionary party in the Alexandria massacres, or on both'.[57] The army would be withdrawn once these objectives had been achieved.

Meanwhile, the nationalists had begun to fortify Alexandria. Admiral Seymour telegraphed for permission to present the Egyptians with an ultimatum to dismantle the shore batteries or have them destroyed. The cabinet agreed, despite opposition from Granville, Bright and Gladstone, who, in an 'homeric rage', threatened resignation. On this occasion, the radicals were prepared to go out with Gladstone despite their disagreement with him. Chamberlain was anxious to associate himself with the Prime Minister's moral authority, and persuaded a very reluctant Dilke to fall in with him.[58]

When the ultimatum expired on 11 July the bombardment of Alexandria took place. The Arabists responded by proclaiming a 'holy war' against the British. On the night of 20–21 July, Dilke informed Gladstone and Childers that Arabi had turned the salt water from the lake into the freshwater Canal: 'Their replies were full of character. Mr G. said "What a wicked wretch". Childers said "How clever".'[59] Despite his earlier incandescence, however, the Prime Minister did not join Bright in resigning over the bombardment. This old-fashioned piece of gunboat diplomacy had succeeded in generating support for the government at a time of its serious difficulties over Irish coercion. As Dilke told Ripon, 'The bombardment of Alexandria, like all butchery, is popular.'[60] This was in no small part due to his own successful manipulation of information designed for public consumption. He anticipated objections that they were engaged in fighting 'a bondholders' war' by insisting on amendments to a 'Historical Despatch', designed to justify British action, so as to blacken Arabi's reputation and play down the government's concern at the financial implications of his proposed reforms.[61]

The escalation of the Egyptian crisis had made intervention unavoidable, and it was now decided to despatch troops to safeguard the Canal. Dilke suggested inviting Italy to join England and France in this enterprise. The offer was made but declined.[62] On 24 July parliament overwhelmingly backed the government's request for credit for the expedition. In his speech to the House, Dilke described Arabi as a military adventurer rather than a national leader, and he dwelt upon the commercial and political importance of Suez. However, Freycinet failed to secure the backing of the French Chamber and fell from office. As a result, Britain was committed to unilateral intervention. The hapless Turks, having agreed to send troops, were now surprised to learn that Britain did not wish them to do so. Dilke remarked that 'it was so much too late that we had to tell them that we should sink them if they went – so doubtless the Turks were a little confused in their minds as to what we really wanted'.[63]

On 13 September the British army under Lord Wolseley routed Arabi's force at Tel-el-Kebir. The British government was now the *de facto* ruler of Egypt. While the invasion had been in progress, Dilke, Childers, Northbrook and Hartington had met regularly at the War Office to consider what to do once Egypt was conquered. On 19 September they decided upon free navigation of the Canal, greater influence for Britain on its directorate, and the demolition of Egyptian fortifications. Dilke remained committed to ultimate withdrawal, but with the retention of control over the Canal. Occasionally, his frustration at being unable properly to influence events from outside the cabinet surfaced. 'I wish they wd.n't first agree upon some ridiculous course,' he noted in his diary on 6 November, '& then call me in afterwards – when that has been taken beyond recall.'[64]

The radical preference for liberal institutions clashed with Whig support for a strong Khedivate. 'What do four peers [Hartington, Granville, Kimberley, and Northbrook] know about popular feeling?' grumbled Dilke.[65] More seriously, the twin aims of restoring and maintaining political authority and protecting the Suez route to India were impossible to sustain without a permanent presence. By bridling at formal annexation, the government effectively turned Egypt into a running sore. The ever-unfulfilled promise to withdraw became a source of irritation in Anglo-French relations, one that Bismarck was only too willing to exploit.

Dilke found himself for a time preoccupied with legal technicalities concerning the trial of Arabi, about which he was being questioned in the House. Trouble came from Liberal backbenchers rather than from the Conservative Opposition who had been silenced by the government's decisive intervention. Dilke's view that Arabi was simply a renegade and a troublemaker left him unsympathetic to demands for a fair trial:

> Here I find irritation among my Radl. friends, who seem to me silly. (I suppose Radicals out of office always seem silly to Radicals in office.) I cannot see the connexion between extreme Radicalism & weak government, wh. exists in their minds. It's a great pity Arabi was not shot a month ago & the others pardoned.[66]

Dilke's assessment of Arabi was shared by Gladstone who thought he should be tried as a criminal and hanged. When it became evident in court that Arabi was not the tyrant of their propaganda, the trial was exposed as farcical. He was found guilty of the lesser charge of rebellion and exiled to Ceylon.[67]

In a circular note to the powers of 3 January 1883, the British government announced that it would withdraw from Egypt as soon as the country was settled. Events in the form of the Mahdist revolt in the Sudan were already conspiring to make just such a withdrawal impossible. They came increasingly to preoccupy the later years of the Gladstone administration, and to dominate meetings of the cabinet – a cabinet which Dilke was now about to join.

Chapter 7

Into the Cabinet

By 1882 it was widely recognised that Dilke's entry into the cabinet could not be long delayed. His political talents were acknowledged by the leaders of both parties. In November of that year, Gladstone had intimated to Granville that he saw in Dilke 'a probable future leader'.[1] Beaconsfield had described Dilke as '*the* rising man on the other side',[2] and had modelled the hero of his last complete novel, *Endymion* (1881), on him. Endymion enjoys a meteoric rise from the office of Under-Secretary of State for Foreign Affairs to the premiership. Beaconsfield's biographer remarked that Dilke took this as a compliment; but he must have been politely flattering the dying statesman, for in his diary he privately mused upon the 'fitting termination of Dizzy's life, to get £12,000 from t[he] British public for such rubbish as *Endymion*'.[3]

The first government reshuffle which concerned Dilke arose out of developments in Ireland. He had devoted little time to the Irish question, and was to do so only in 1885 when it forced its way to the top of the political agenda and when he believed that a solution was possible. 'I was never given to saying much,' he admitted, 'because ... I never thoroughly saw my own way.' He believed that a timely programme of reform would quell Irish discontent and preserve the union. He was, in short, prepared to give Ireland control over its own internal affairs.[4]

During the first two years of the Liberal administration, with the land question still unsolved, events in Ireland assumed a particularly violent shape. Forster planned to introduce a land bill in 1880 which would grant compensation to evicted tenants, but inevitably met with Whig resistance in cabinet.[5] The radicals supported him by placing their resignations in his hands, though Dilke was rather diffident about doing so:

> I do not care in the least about the Bill, but I must either go out with these men or climb
> into the Cabinet over their bodies to either become a Whig – or to eventually suffer the
> same fate – so I prefer to make common cause. I suppose there'll be a compromise once
> more.

And so there was, but it did not last long. The Lords rejected the bill in
August and a bad harvest was sufficient to intensify the violence and
boycotting in Ireland. At the beginning of September, Dilke persuaded
Forster to consider a scheme of public works, and at the end of the month
he used the *Daily News* to squash a proposal to prosecute Parnell. He was
prepared to resign with Chamberlain if coercion was introduced without
a land bill, telling his friend that 'to try & stop the Land League agitation
by suspending Habeas Corpus was to fire a rifle at a swarm of flies – or –
let us say – gnats'.[6]

Forster, for his part, threatened to resign if the cabinet would not agree
to coercion. He was supported by Hartington, Spencer, Argyll and
Selborne. Ranged against them were Gladstone, Bright, Chamberlain,
Granville, Harcourt, Kimberley, Childers, Dodson and Northbrook. Dilke
thought this a not unreasonable divide from the radical point of view:

> As I suppose the split with Whiggery has got to come I had sooner it come now, but I
> shd. like the split to be *this* split – & to have the great names of Gladstone & Bright on
> our side. I fear that Gladstone may yield & Bright follow him – even at the risk of going
> out of politics altogether. If Chn. & I shd. be driven to resign alone we shall have a great
> deal of disagreeable unpopularity & of still more disagreeable popularity to go through!
> … I had sooner the great split came now – but it wd. *perhaps* mean semi-revolution in
> Engld. & Civil War in Ireland – wh. makes every one trouble – however right he may
> feel, & however necessary his course. On the whole I still think that Forster will yield
> again.[7]

The day after Dilke had penned this line to Mrs Pattison, Forster
reluctantly agreed to stay in the government. On 10 December Chamberlain, Dilke's 'stormy petrel', came to stay at Sloane Street, where the two
decided that unless there was a tangible move in their direction they would
resign, 'even tho' blackguarded in every paper & by all our friends, &
danced upon for years'. Hartington's secretary, Reginald Brett, called on
Dilke three days later to find out if the offer of Chamberlain's post would
tempt him to sell his ally. 'We won after all', Dilke noted with barely-
concealed delight.[8] Coercion was to be delayed until a land bill could be
prepared.

When published in the new year, the bill included the 'three Fs' – Free
Sale, Fair Rents, Fixity of Tenure – though Dilke believed they were 'so
wrapped up that nobody will find them'.[9] The Coercion Bill, which

accompanied it, met with two days of filibustering by the Irish MPs before they were forcibly ejected from the chamber. It was this fracas that led to the introduction shortly afterwards of the system of terminating debates known as the closure.

During February Dilke became involved in two incidents connected with coercion. The first concerned the use of secret-service money to buy information about Fenian plots, to which he was opposed, much to Harcourt's ire, because he thought it did little more than line the pocket of 'a sharp Yankee'.[10] The second, and more serious, was a complaint by Parnell that the British Embassy had employed men to spy on him during a visit to Paris. Lord Lyons, the ambassador, denied this and asked Dilke to contradict the allegation. It transpired that Harcourt had employed the detectives without the knowledge of the embassy, and he would not therefore allow Dilke to make the contradiction. One consequence of this spying was that Parnell's adultery with Mrs O'Shea was known by ministers who afterwards expressed surprise when it was made public. The two incidents illustrate well Harcourt's paranoia at this time with plots and conspiracies. When the Home Secretary went further and insisted upon the opening of the mail of the Irish leaders, Ashton Dilke quipped, 'What is the use of having a blind Postmaster General [Fawcett] if he reads our letters?'[11]

In the same month, news reached England of the massacre of British troops by the Boers at Majuba. Dilke and Chamberlain decided to use the crisis as an excuse to resign. Coercion, the weak Land Bill, and the preponderance of Whigs in the cabinet were the reasons which chiefly weighed with the radicals, but by choosing the Transvaal as the issue, they calculated that Bright, Courtney and possibly Lefevre would join them. In this way they were able to present a more united front than opposition to Irish policy alone would have allowed. Gladstone therefore had to take their ultimatum seriously, and he persuaded the Colonial Secretary Kimberley to capitulate to their demand for a negotiated settlement with the Boers.[12] The outcome was the Pretoria Convention the following October which granted a large degree of independence to the Transvaal.

Meanwhile, the ungainly trio of Land Bill, closure and coercion made their faltering progress onto the statute book. The last continued to cause the most trouble. On 12 October 1881, following a bitter exchange between Gladstone and Parnell in which each had publicly denounced the other, the latter was arrested under the terms of the new act and imprisoned in Kilmainham Jail. The Land League responded by orchestrating a rent strike, with the result that Parnell was very soon joined in prison by many of his compatriots. The winter months witnessed mounting violence in Ireland and the emergence of new terrorist organisations. When Dilke addressed his constituents in January 1882, the anger of the Irish at the acquiescence of the radicals in the coercion policy was vented by one over-zealous Irishman who attempted to storm the platform wielding a chair and shouting Bright's maxim, 'Force is No Remedy'.[13]

In April the cabinet decided to release Parnell on parole, ostensibly to attend the funeral of a nephew but in fact to visit Mrs O'Shea and their three-month-old child who was dying. The government, with the notable exception of Forster, recognised that the Coercion Act had not succeeded, and was anxious to find some other way of quieting Irish unrest. Chamberlain was therefore authorised to negotiate with Parnell through Captain O'Shea, the husband of Parnell's mistress. The captain, who was more interested in his own political advancement than in his wife's infidelity, proved an able intermediary. The outcome was the Kilmainham Treaty, by which the government undertook to release the Irish leaders and to extend the terms of the Land Act to tenants in arrears with their rents. In return, Parnell would call for an end to the outrages and the withholding of rents, a promise which Forster urged should be made public. Dilke thought that such a disclosure would be in effect to recognise Parnell as the government of Ireland, and his view prevailed.[14] Consequently, first Cowper, the Lord Lieutenant of Ireland, and then Forster resigned.

Cowper was replaced by Earl Spencer. The radicals, who had expected that the Chief Secretaryship would be offered to one of them, were surprised and rather relieved when that post was given to Lord Frederick Cavendish, Hartington's brother. However, their relief at being by-passed was shortlived. On 6 May Cavendish and his Under-Secretary were brutally murdered in Phoenix Park, Dublin. Early the next morning, Parnell, 'white and apparently terror-stricken', and accompanied by a fellow Nationalist, Justin McCarthy, called at Sloane Street. Parnell believed that the murders had been perpetrated by extremists angered by his conciliatory policy, and that he himself would be the next victim of the secret societies. He had come to Dilke in the expectation that he would be the new Chief Secretary, and found him unshaken by the recent tragedy though of the view that Chamberlain would be a more suitable candidate.[15]

The decision as to a replacement was taken, unusually, not by the Prime Minister alone but collectively by the cabinet on 8 May. It sent Chamberlain to offer the post to Dilke, who promptly refused it. Chamberlain knew from their discussions and from their most recent correspondence that Dilke would not take the post without a seat in the cabinet. For this reason, Dilke was incensed at Chamberlain's part in the business. He regarded it as the only occasion upon which he ever had a personal difference of opinion with him, one for which he never forgave him.[16] His refusal was widely regarded as having seriously damaged his chances of future promotion.[17] He explained his objections to Grant Duff:

> I should have had to defend any policy that Spencer chose to adopt, without having a voice in it. Acceptance wd. not have been only a personal mistake: – it would have been a political blunder. Outside the Cabinet I should not have had the public confidence, & rightly so, because I could not have had a strong hand. I should have inherited accumulated blunders, & I was under no kind of obligation to do so, for I have never touched the Irish question. Nor have I spoken on it from first to last. Many of the measures rendered necessary by the situation are condemned by my whole past attitude, but they have really been made inevitable by blunders for which I had no responsibility, & which I should not have been allowed to condemn.[18]

The murders inevitably tipped the scales towards the coercionists. The radicals, however, were now more than ever convinced that repression would very soon have to give way to a more constructive and lasting solution to the Irish problem. At the beginning of June, Chamberlain and Dilke placed their resignations in the hands of the new Chief Secretary, George Trevelyan, in case he wished to make a stand against coercion. 'I feel sure he won't', Dilke told Ripon.[19] Gladstone, too, teetered on the verge of resignation and ministerial crisis followed ministerial crisis during the months of June and July, with Egypt at that moment adding to the government's difficulties. The radicals were united with Hartington and the interventionists on Egypt but at loggerheads with them over Ireland, so the government was torn in all directions.

Dilke's fear that his refusal to go to Ireland had irrevocably damaged his chances of advancement for as long as Gladstone remained party leader proved to be exaggerated. The Prime Minister had probably offered him the job as a step towards overcoming royal objections to his eventual promotion. Two months earlier, when Dilke had abstained on the vote of an annuity to Prince Leopold, both Gladstone and Granville had done their best to mollify the objections of the Queen. Dilke had reminded them of his pledge of 1880 to take no further part in royal votes and, on the very day that the Irish Secretaryship was offered to him, Gladstone had sent a long memorandum to the Queen expressing his satisfaction with Dilke's position.[20] Against a suggestion that he could not take a diametrically opposite course *on the first occasion*, Dilke noted, 'This would assume that I should vote the other way next time. I said I would take no part and I shall take none.' In a tone that suggested he was heartily sick of the whole business, he told Chamberlain that he thought the Queen's object was to keep him 'out of the Cabinet for her life, and in this I think she can succeed'.[21]

Following Bright's resignation over the bombardment of Alexandria in July, Gladstone pressed Dilke once more to make some public statement regarding his republican views. After consulting with Chamberlain, Dilke replied that to do so would be interpreted as 'buying my way into the cabinet by a sham recantation', and would 'create a storm to no purpose'. He was prepared, though, to affirm in public his acceptance of the principle of collective cabinet responsibility and his willingness to vote for future royal grants in return for a promise that provision for the Queen's grandchildren would be referred to a select committee. Gladstone was agreeable, and Dilke therefore pressed him for an appropriate form of words that he could use when he next addressed his constituents.[22]

The cabinet reshuffle eventually took place in December. Gladstone relinquished the Exchequer to a younger man, Childers; Hartington took Childers' place at the War Office; and Kimberley was moved to the India Office. Derby, who had switched parties, entered the cabinet as Colonial Secretary. This left still vacant Bright's old office at the Duchy of Lancaster. The Prince of Wales had invited Dilke and Chamberlain to Sandringham in November to discuss how the promotion of the former might best be effected without offending the Queen, and had suggested then that he should go to the Duchy.[23] But the Duchy was effectively a royal sinecure and the Queen vetoed the Prince's proposal. She also demanded a public recantation by Dilke of his republicanism. Contrarily, she conceded in the same breath that she would rather have him in the cabinet than Lord Derby, whose ignoble tenure of the India Office in 1858 remained firmly implanted in the royal memory. The fact of the matter was that Dilke 'has *right* views on *foreign* politics, and knows what the honour of this country requires'.[24]

Gladstone asked Dilke if he could persuade Chamberlain to take the Duchy. In view of Dilke's sacrifice in 1880, Chamberlain had little option but to acquiesce, though he did so begrudgingly:

> Your letter has spoilt my breakfast. The change will be loathsome to me for more than one reason and will give rise to all sorts of disagreeable commentaries. But if it is the only way out of the difficulty, I will do – what I am sure you would have done in my place – accept the transfer ... .

Roy Jenkins regarded Dilke's satisfaction with Chamberlain's churlish reply as surprising.[25] But Dilke knew his friend well. He knew that Chamberlain was ambitious, that the Duchy was a degrading alternative to face and that, in these circumstances, he had acted with the greatest degree of magnanimity that could be expected from a power-hungry politician. Chamberlain was not the man to disguise his feelings on a matter as important to his career as this, and his letter to Dilke had concluded: 'I would gladly avoid the sacrifice but if your inclusion in the Cabinet depends on it, I will make it truly & *with pleasure* for your sake.'[26] He enclosed in the same envelope another letter, addressed to Dilke but intended for Gladstone's eyes, which threatened resignation if Dilke was excluded from the cabinet for holding opinions which he shared.[27] Gladstone decided to delay a week before taking up Chamberlain's offer in order to see whether Fawcett, who was very ill, would be fit to continue.[28] In the event, Chamberlain was spared the sacrifice, for the Queen found him just as unsuitable for the Duchy as Dilke.

The Prince tried to break the *impasse* by suggesting that Dilke should go the Admiralty, an office that he would dearly have loved, but one which, he believed, would not be offered because of his earlier refusal to go to Ireland.[29] Indeed, the proposal was ignored, but the Prince did come up with the eventual solution – namely, that Dodson should go to the Duchy and be replaced at the Local Government Board by Dilke.[30] It was not immediately taken up as Gladstone, protesting that he was 'between the devil and the deep sea', was anxious not to offend Dodson.[31] Dilke wanted the matter resolved quickly and was prepared to take Lefevre's place, though with a place in the cabinet, if the latter could be moved to the Duchy. Dilke's description of his suggestion as '"amateur Cabinet-making" with a vengeance',[32] was not far off the mark, for Lefevre held the minor post of First Commissioner of Works, but it does illustrate his anxiety to settle the matter and to accept any post that took him into the cabinet.

The whole business was resolved two days before Christmas, after Hartington had persuaded Dodson to accept the Duchy.[33] The Queen was insufficiently touched by the Christmas spirit to abandon her demand that Dilke should take 'an early public opportunity of making recantation or explanation of his former crude opinions'. A rather more emollient version of this communication was conveyed by the Prime Minister to Dilke. The Queen was looking, he wrote on 28 December, 'with some interest or even keenness to the words of explanation' that he proposed to use. 'Notwithstanding the rubs of the past,' he added, 'I am sanguine as to your future relations with the Queen.' He did not, however, have the same confidence about his own relations with her. 'I am convinced', he told Dilke, 'from an hundred tokens, that she looks forward to the day of my retirement as a day, if not of jubilee, yet of relief.'[34]

When Dilke addressed his constituents on 29 December, he adopted the line on collective cabinet responsibility agreed with Gladstone in August. The only personal allusions he made were to the 'scatterbrained' opinions of political infancy which, 'as one grew older, one might regard as unwise, or might prefer not to have uttered'.[35] There was no mention of republicanism, but the press, as intended, construed his statements as referring to that.

The Queen was not so charitable. 'This gentleman [Dilke] has not yet fulfilled the *condition* on which ... the *Queen alone* consented to admit him into the Cabinet', she wrote darkly to Gladstone on New Year's Eve. 'It will be *very* serious if he does not do this.' Given the limitations of her constitutional position, this was little more than bluster. Gladstone believed that Dilke had gone far enough. Nevertheless, the Queen's obstinacy was causing him to lose sleep, so, before departing for a long holiday in the south of France, he made one last appeal to Dilke to publicly renounce his 'crude ideas'.[36]

Dilke complied by inserting just such a form of words into a speech at Chelsea on January 5:

> In the autumn of 1873 ... I had to ask the constituency to accept a renunciation of certain crude and visionary ideas which were supposed to be ascribed to or which were supposed to be held by me, on the strength of rather Academic statements which had been made by me on a certain occasion.[37]

These opaque remarks by no means amounted to a recantation of republicanism. Dilke was referring to ideas about the imminence of an English republic which had been attributed to him but which he had never in fact held. His words were enough, however, to satisfy the Queen.[38] He afterwards left for Paris, where he paid his last respects to Gambetta, who had died suddenly in December from wounds incurred in an accident with a revolver. He went on to Toulon and several times visited Gladstone, who was convalescing in Cannes.

Dilke had joined the government on the tacit understanding that royal grants to the Queen's grandchildren would be preceded by an inquiry, and he carried his point in April 1884 when the cabinet was discussing arrangements for the posthumous child of the Duke of Albany. In his diary he noted laconically, 'Qn. angry at Cabt. backing me on this.' The principle was formally enshrined by Gladstone in a memorandum drawn up at the end of 1884 at the time of the settlement on the marriage of Princess Beatrice, the youngest of Queen Victoria's daughters, and conceded only after Dilke had threatened to resign.[39] He had achieved a small but notable victory. The first inquiry was held in 1889, and thereafter at each accession of a new monarch.

At the time of his promotion, Dilke was still not forty. He was the youngest man in the cabinet, yet already had fourteen years of parliamentary experience behind him. Many contemporaries singled him out as a future leader of the Liberal Party. No one doubted his ability, though there were different estimates of it.

One of his greatest advantages was his excellent memory. He was a voracious and quick reader with a reputation for meticulous preparation. These qualities influenced his style of speaking. His ability to draw upon an unrivalled storehouse of knowledge had the effect of stunning his audience, sometimes with admiration but more often with boredom. Austen Chamberlain regarded him as 'an appallingly dull speaker', Asquith as 'a dull and ineffective speaker who acquired fluency, and an adequate equipment of debating capacity, by long practice and experience'. Perhaps Asquith came nearest the mark when he added that Dilke assumed that his audience had the same intimate knowledge as himself, which therefore 'often gave an air of pedantry to really good stuff'.[40]

Dilke was aware of his deficiencies as an orator, but worked hard at improving his delivery, which was marred at first by a nervous pivotal movement. This soon left him, and he gained the reputation for being a calm and assured speaker. He replaced the habit of twisting his body with that of revolving his hat in his hand, perpetually rubbing it as if 'endeavouring to dislodge imaginary creases'.[41] That self-same hat was also the repository for his notes during long speeches, and it was often quite full before he sat down. Dilke mused in his diary in February 1884 that his increase in prestige as a debater was 'a curious position for a man who has no natural gift of speech. I can remember when I was the worst speaker that ever spoke at all.'[42] When, in April of that year, Edward Hamilton dined with a group of Conservatives and conversation turned to a consideration of the oratorical talent in the Commons, he found that, Gladstone apart, they were for awarding the accolade to Joseph Cowen, but that the 'speaking power they most coveted was ... Dilke's'.[43]

References to Dilke's encyclopaedic knowledge were commonplace. One journalist described him as 'a walking *Whitaker*', another as 'a parliamentary pantechnicon', while a third believed that he 'more nearly approached omniscience than most men'.[44] O'Connor, in analysing his ascendancy over the Commons, summed it up as follows:

> It is an ascendancy not due in the least to oratorical power. Sir Charles never made a fine sentence or a sonorous peroration in his whole life. It is that power of acquiring all the facts of the case – of being thoroughly up in all its merits – in short, of knowing his business – which impresses the House of Commons ... It is derived from a perfect House

of Commons mind ... There is no man in the House of Commons so thoroughly political.[45]

Dilke had a deep-seated hatred of inefficiency and waste and a corresponding regard for the organisation and management of his time. He had the reputation of making appointments weeks or months in advance and keeping them to the minute. He was intolerant of inaccurate statements and slovenly argument. He was a model House of Commons man, regular in attendance, knowledgeable of its procedures and well-versed in its immediate business. His commitment to parliamentary matters led him, from the early eighties onwards, to refuse invitations to speak outside London during the session. For a radical parliamentary reformer he was curiously protective of its traditions, always attending in the conventional frock coat and tall hat. He was well-known for the speed at which he moved along the corridors of the House, and cartoonists portrayed him with his coat-tails flapping behind him; and he was first into the division lobbies, or busy in the library snipping his papers, letters and engagement books down to the minimum of important detail.

This idiosyncratic obsession with reducing material to its essentials was manifested also in his concise letters and in his precise answers to questions in public and in private. A correspondent of the *Manchester Guardian* related that he 'was an excellent man to interview for those who knew the way to take him. He always asked at the beginning: "Now, do you want me to talk or do you want to ask questions?" If you chose the latter you were wrong. He would answer your questions in a dozen compact words and shake hands. If you chose the former you would get all you wanted and much besides that you had not hoped for.'[46] The combination of an excellent memory with an unrivalled knowledge of people, places and culture made him an excellent and fascinating conversationalist. His knowledge leavened his conversation at the same time as it overloaded and deadened his speeches.

Similarly, at question time, he was admired for the way in which he disposed of probing interrogations, particularly during his spell at the Foreign Office where discretion was imperative. Frederic Harrison, in writing a criticism of parliamentary practice, was obliged, he told Dilke, to take his name in vain 'as the greatest master of the art of answering questions in modern times'. The Prime Minister, by contrast, was renowned for turning his answers into lengthy expositions. Dilke commented airily to Chamberlain that 'Mr G. will fight a whole day in Cabinet to avoid telling Parlmt. something, and then after all will tell them twice as much in reply to Ashmead [Bartlett] or Hicks [Beach]'. Henry

Lucy, the 'Toby' of *Punch*, thought Dilke's answers so perfect that one should be 'framed and glazed, and hung in the bed-room of every Minister', as an example for them to follow.[47]

Dilke justified the brevity of his private letters to one correspondent as follows:

> I always hold that it is absurd to write a real letter to any one who sees a daily paper. Daily papers killed letters – and very properly. Go and live with the Modocs in the lava-beds; and then I'll write you long letters.[48]

The habit sometimes produced mild rebukes from his friends. Sir Mountstuart Grant Duff, the Governor of Madras from 1881–86 and a regular correspondent of Dilke's during that time, thanked him for his 'short pithy letters'. John Morley, the disciple first of Mill, then of Chamberlain, and later of Gladstone, wrote on one occasion: ' ... I can't for the soul of me make head or tail of the little blue scrap of paper you sent me. Use twice as many words and I shall understand.'[49] In general, however, in an age when correspondence took up a considerable part of a politician's day, his ability to get straight to the point was welcomed.

He continued as well the practice learnt at Cambridge of keeping his body as active as his mind. He would invariably row at the weekends, and enjoyed riding and the occasional game of lawn tennis. This sporting regime was supplemented from 1879 with a daily bout of fencing, which he had tried before but only spasmodically. He was instructed by a French master, and would fence for an hour or so each morning during the session on the terrace at the back of 76 Sloane Street. His obsession with his physical condition is reflected in the fact that he kept a daily record of his weight, which had been eleven and a half stones while a student, but which fluctuated between thirteen and fourteen stones in later life. From 1880 the pressures of office compelled him to give up the practice of spending Sundays out of town with friends. Instead, he would go to bed on Saturday evening at around 8 p.m., then rise early to work on his red boxes before attending morning service at Westminster Abbey. The afternoon would be spent on the river and he would retire once again at around 8 p.m.

Dilke's elevation to the cabinet in 1882 marked a turnaround in the political influence of the middle-class radicals. Down to 1882 Whig ascendancy within the Liberal Party had not been seriously threatened. Hamilton believed that Chamberlain's tenure of the Board of Trade had in fact led to a diminution in radical authority and that he had become 'the best-hated man in the country'. It would therefore be some time, he added, 'before we see the radical party reigning alone & supreme'.[50] In truth, the unseemly and protracted parliamentary wrangling over

Bradlaugh's refusal to swear the oath of allegiance,[51] and the distraction created by Irish problems and the Egyptian crisis, had temporarily elbowed radicalism to the political margins.

Dilke's promotion revived expectations, especially among radicals in the country, who were becoming increasingly exasperated by the diversion of Liberal energies into foreign and imperial issues. He sat next to Chamberlain in cabinet and, according to Derby, they 'backed one another up'. They were also among its most vociferous members.[52] They wanted, and they believed that recent setbacks in by-elections showed that the people demanded, a more constructive programme. Chamberlain's antennae had alerted him to this groundswell and he at once urged Dilke to mark his entry into the cabinet with a speech on the pauperism of the agricultural labourers and the need for a solution to the land question, thereby issuing a challenge to the Whigs.[53] Three weeks later, on 20 January 1883, he told Dilke that he believed that 'the country – (*our* country that is – the great majority of Liberal opinion) is ripe for a new departure in constructive Radicalism & only wants leaders. So if we are driven to a fight, we shall easily recruit an army.'[54] At the end of March he made a populist speech at Birmingham in which he attacked Lord Salisbury as the 'spokesman of a class ... who toil not neither do they spin'. It was now, as well, that he began to flesh out the details of what later became known as the 'unauthorised' radical programme, and which was presented to the country in a series of articles in the *Fortnightly Review* by different contributors. The tone was set by its editor, T. H. S. Escott, with a piece on 'The Future of the Radical Party', in which he emphasised the importance for the progress of Liberalism of the constructive radicalism of Dilke and Chamberlain, based as it was on a practical and realisable programme unlike the 'crotcheteering' radicalism of men like Lawson, Cowen and Labouchere.[55]

Three years later the Liberal Party was to split apart. Some historians have concluded from this that a compromise between the Whigs and radicals was never possible, and that the break derived in large measure from the fundamental irreconcilability of the two groups and the determination of the radicals to force a rupture. Great stress has been placed upon the quarrels within the cabinet, the resignations and the threats of resignation, and the uncompromising anti-Whig diatribes that Chamberlain in particular was prone to make from time to time. It is important, however, to avoid judging Whig-radical relations teleologically, from the perspective of the terminal crisis in the Liberal Party. Apart from the inconvenient fact that the great divide found the Chamberlainite radicals in the same camp as the Hartingtonian Whigs, there are other reasons for caution. The constant threats of resignation were part of a strategy that stemmed from the radicals' minority position within the cabinet, through which they sought to bolster themselves and their policies – not least of all by attempting to identify their cause with that of the 'people' in the country against the 'peers' in the cabinet. The press was used for much the same end – the radicals leaking sensitive information when it served their purpose.[56] Chamberlain in particular was a master of bluff and bluster and used these arts to perfection to nudge the Whigs forward.

Imperialism, as we have seen, was beginning to produce strange bedfellows, with the leading radicals not infrequently aligning themselves with the Whigs. Indeed, they found themselves closer to the Whigs on these questions than to many back-bench radicals. Dilke was concerned at the paucity of radical talent and acknowledged the value of Whig experience. Conflict was therefore spasmodic and interspersed with moments of peace and constructive government.[57] The balance of power in the cabinet still favoured the Whigs, and the old wealth appeared confident that it could tame the new. The Fifteenth Earl of Derby, an immensely rich member of an old landed family who joined Gladstone's cabinet at the same time as Dilke, was not at all perturbed at the prospect of sharing power with men who were *nouveau riche*, even if they were radical. He noted in his diary that Dilke and Chamberlain 'belong to a distinctly different class, & probably represent a different class of ideas'. But, although they were 'Of the middle or trading class ... one is a baronet, & the other they say not far from a millionaire.' Besides, the cabinet, he was reassured to find, was 'as little democratic as any we have had in the present century'.[58]

In the face of rapid industrialisation, the progress towards monopoly capitalism and the rise of an organised working class in the latter half of the nineteenth century, it was unlikely that industrial and financial interests would be prepared to leave politics indefinitely to what Marx had earlier called their 'aristocratic representatives'. Some political realignment was therefore inevitable. That it would be the Conservative Party which would survive to represent the interests of capital, or that a new party would emerge to represent those of labour, was by no means predestined. The debate surrounding the demise of the Liberal Party really hinges upon whether it was capable of adapting to fulfil either of these two roles – that is, of becoming the party of a consolidated capitalism; or a social democratic organisation in the Labour mould. Imperialism had provided one basis for a Whig-radical compromise. Yet imperial could not be separated from domestic questions, even if classical political economy taught ministers to treat them as discrete areas of policy. For they arose out of the same macroeconomic context. The depressed state of the British economy contributed to increased unemployment and political and social unrest, but also, through capital export and the search for and safeguarding of raw materials and markets, to the various overseas crises. The middle-class radicals wanted action on *both* fronts. They were understandably frustrated when the Whigs did not repay their support on foreign and imperial questions with some movement on domestic issues.

What mattered to the radicals at the start of 1883, therefore, was the degree to which they could persuade the Whigs to swallow their domestic programme. If still a minority in the cabinet, they were nonetheless confident that the balance of power was on the point of shifting to them. They asserted themselves by whatever means were at their disposal to advance the radical programme – speeches in the country, leaks to the press, destabilising threats of resignation, and so forth. The ultimate prize was the leadership of the party in succession to the aged Gladstone, who frequently intimated that he was on the point of retiring. This encouraged but also, at the same time, frustrated the plans of the radicals, for they were never quite able to fathom his intentions. In terms of political astuteness he was more than a match for them.

After two years of ploughing the sands, Dilke and Chamberlain believed that the moment had arrived for the realisation of a middle-class radical programme that would determine the future of Liberalism. The emphasis within it upon land reform may appear with hindsight to have constituted an insurmountable obstacle to any permanent arrangement with the Whigs. Still, the latter had succeeded in preserving their political influence by timely concessions to middle-class pressure, and there appeared as yet no reason to believe that they would not continue to do so. Indeed, the latter half of Gladstone's administration saw further evidence of this *sauve qui peut* pattern of behaviour – beginning with Whig acquiescence in the fundamental demand of the radicals for the democratisation of the local and the central state.

Chapter 8

Local Government

Dilke had become President of the Local Government Board simply because John George Dodson was a political lightweight and therefore dispensable. Dodson was a worthy man but one not, unfortunately, held in much esteem by the radicals. Dilke remarked of his arrival late at one cabinet that no one had noticed his absence. The radicals were supercilious as well about Dodson's less than sartorial appearance. Chamberlain, who was always immaculately dressed, sarcastically observed that his boots would be more appropriate for a Minister of Agriculture and, on another occasion, Dilke was amused to find that Dodson had 'added to his other crimes that of hair dye'.[1]

There is no doubt that Dilke preferred the glamour of the Foreign Office and the broad sweep of international policy to the mundane and minute affairs of local government, where the mills of administration ground exceedingly small.[2] However, the LGB was by no means a political backwater. Quite the contrary: local government was of major importance to the progress of the nineteenth-century middle class, whose political power had been established in the first instance here rather than in central government. Town councils dealt with issues that directly impinged upon its economic interests – rate-fixing, land purchase, pollution, transportation, municipal improvements and so on. An urban power base also conferred status upon the new wealth. Reform of the local state, therefore, was at least as important to the middle class and its political hegemony as reform of the central state.

In fact, the two went hand-in-hand. The Reform Act of 1832 had been followed by the great municipal reform of 1835, while the 1867 Act had led to the establishment of the LGB in 1871 and to a series of abortive county government bills. Now, as Gladstone's administration contemplated a further instalment of parliamentary reform, adjustments to the local state apparatus were once again perceived as integral to the whole reforming process.

Other factors as well were pushing local government to the top of the political agenda in the 1880s. Population growth and the increased costs of urban management had placed the financial system under great strain, and the Liberals were anxious to shift the emphasis from the central grants-in-aid to a reformed local rating system. To this end, a more efficient and accountable local machinery was needed. Above all, a new dimension was added to local government reform in the course of the 1880s. Many middle-class radicals came to see it as an answer to the social problems, such as housing, that were now demanding attention. Democratised local authorities with a strong sense of community politics might counter the rise of socialism and preserve working-class attachment to liberalism and the Liberal Party.

Dilke's appointment to the LGB was therefore timely and pertinent to middle-class concerns. Having said that, Victorian ministers were less constrained than their twentieth-century counterparts by their departmental portfolios, and Dilke was able to involve himself in most of the major questions of the day. After his very first cabinet on 6 February 1883, from which Gladstone, who was convalescing in Cannes, was absent, he noted in his diary, with typical arrogance, 'I wrote most of the Queen's Speech'.[3] The issues that figured prominently in it – London government and local government – were, indeed, ones that directly affected his department. His two-and-a-half years at the LGB, his only experience of cabinet office in a long career, were extremely busy ones. They saw the production on his part of two Local Government Bills, the Redistribution Bill, and his chairmanship of the Royal Commission on the Housing of the Working Classes. His industry and talents were exploited by several of his colleagues. Harcourt thrust a great deal of Home Office business on to the LGB. Granville insisted that he should be kept in touch with Foreign Office communiqués, which meant that he was often doing his old job as well as his new, which was perhaps no bad thing in view of Granville's declining faculties. Gladstone and Hartington did not help him in the laborious preparation of the redistribution scheme as much as they might have done. Dilke excused himself the brevity of his Memoir account of his work at the Board 'because, though heavy, it was of an uninteresting nature'. Nevertheless, it was his own appetite for work that created the burden, and he would not have been happy had he not been kept busy. All in all, his final judgement was that he 'liked the L.G.B.'.[4]

He began by reorganising the Local Government Board itself. Clerical positions were thrown open to competition, which led to a beneficial

" SEEING'S BELIEVING."

Mr. P. " QUITE RIGHT, SIR CHARLES! *THAT* MEANS BUSINESS!!"

["The President of the Local Government Board yesterday visited the most overcrowded neighbourhood of St. John's-street Road and Goswell Road ; he also made a renewed inspection of the worst parts of St. Luke's, which he had already visited this week."— *Times*, Nov. 24.]

Punch, 1 December 1883

infusion of new blood. He also resisted making 'political' appointments, preferring instead to promote able men from within the service. He instructed his private secretary, Bodley, to carry out these arrangements.[5] A paradox of the amount of work which he took upon himself was that his purpose in doing so was to divest the Board of many of its functions. The key themes of his time there were simplification and decentralisation. These reforming principles were applied in four broad areas: county government; London government; housing; and public health.

Dilke was undoubtedly familiar with Mill's classic exposition in *Representative Government* (1861) of the importance to liberal democracy of achieving a balance between central and local power. His tour of Greater Britain had convinced him that local government was 'the greatest of the inventions of our inventive race, the chief security for continued freedom possessed by a people already free'. It had enabled him also to bring to his new office an unrivalled knowledge of comparative systems.[6]

The organisation of local government in the third quarter of the nineteenth century was chaotic, costly and inefficient, the product of a century of piecemeal legislation. Every important aspect of local government had its own separate boards, officials and areas of jurisdiction. There were highway boards, sanitation boards, poor law boards and, after 1870, school boards. Some, but by no means all, towns had their own corporations. The counties were governed by justices of the peace whose powers were increasing at the same time as those of the parish vestries were declining.

Dilke's first achievement was to complete the process of reforming the municipal corporations. A commission of inquiry had been set up following his satirical speech of 1876. He prepared a bill based on its report which, after some delay, reached the statute book in June 1883, though it did not come into force until 1886.[7] Thereafter, the only important corporation left unreformed was the City of London. Middle-class progress towards making municipal government uniform, democratic and free from corruption therefore stood in stark contrast to practice in the Tory-governed counties. It was unlikely that the aristocracy would be able to resist reform of their county bases for much longer.

In fact, the process of reform had been set in train immediately after the election. Dodson had drafted a bill providing for the election of county councils every five years by the ratepayers by ballot, with the JPs comprising not more than one-third of their membership. The councils would take over from the quarter-sessions the responsibility for highways, river-pollution and licensing. Some form of local taxation, such as a house tax, would be levied to supplement the rates. However, the bill had to be shelved in the face of the Egyptian and Irish difficulties, and Dilke was not prepared to revive it. It was, he said, 'a poor thing which I should not like to father'.[8]

Sir John Lambert, who had recently retired as Permanent Secretary at the LGB, had advised holding back upon local government until after parliamentary reform, on the grounds that the latter would provide a new electoral register and polling districts suitable for local elections. Dilke concurred with this view and circulated Lambert's memorandum, but only Chamberlain supported it.[9] The peers objected that parliamentary reform would necessitate a general election before the government had introduced any practical legislation. The radicals, restive at the lack of progress on the domestic front and determined not to be outmanoeuvred by the Whigs, now therefore settled upon the strategy of playing off local against central government reform. Dilke met Whig objections by proposing that they concentrate on London government in 1883 and make a Local Government Bill the big measure of the following session. If it was met with resistance, they should produce the Franchise Bill and be prepared to go to the country on both issues. He set about drafting a more advanced measure than that bequeathed by Dodson. 'I desire', he wrote to Chamberlain in February, 'to burn down this office & give all its powers to the County Bds.'[10] He was assisted by Sir Henry Thring, the parliamentary counsel and principal draftsmen of government legislation. The bill was 'the most important work', he told Mrs Pattison, 'on which I have yet been engaged in my political life'.[11] The understanding that it would not be introduced until the following session was ratified by the cabinet on 7 April.[12]

The bill was ready by the end of July. It proposed to create county councils and urban and rural district councils elected quinquennially by the ratepayers by secret ballot. Dilke provided the councils with extensive powers. The district councils would take over the functions of the poor law guardians and of the numerous ad hoc authorities (improvement boards, highway boards, and so on). However, opposition to entrusting education to the councils compelled him to drop the school boards from this clause in his bill. The county councils were to take over the powers of the justices in quarter-sessions with regard to county rates and other financial business, licensing, county police, major roads and water supply. They were also given many of the coordinating and supervisory powers of the Local Government Board. The bill provided for a consolidated rate paid equally by owners and occupiers, but supplemented through loans and central government grants. 142 towns and cities of over 20,000 population were to become county boroughs, exercising all the powers of county and district councils.[13]

Thring wrote to Dilke, 'Your plan when carried into effect will disturb most things no doubt but will at the same time settle everything.' Dilke was well pleased with the bill. He described it in a letter to Grant Duff as 'revolutionary:– a sort of 1789'. He continued to regard it as a useful device for forcing the county franchise, and this tactic was now beginning to have its desired effect.[14]

Alarmed by the far-reaching nature of Dilke's bill, the Whigs underwent a volte-face. Gladstone had gradually come round to the radicals' preference for giving priority to the Franchise Bill. When he proposed this to the cabinet on 25 October, all the Whigs, except Hartington, agreed. Dilke found himself in the unenviable position of having to negate his summer's work. 'I locked up my now useless Local Governt. Bill ... ', he recorded, having been instrumental in changing Gladstone's mind at the very time he was completing the bill's details, and thus contributing to its demise.[15] It would be misleading, however, to assume that he considered his work wasted effort. The pessimistic 'now useless' was written with hindsight in the 1890s. At the time, the radicals adhered to their original plan – county franchise first to be followed by local government reform.

Moreover, the bill was not locked away, but kept alive as a standby in case the Tories threw out the Franchise Bill. The cabinet committee therefore continued to meet. On 19 November Dilke informed Gladstone that the bill's prospects did 'not look rosy'. Of the committee, only Childers and Chamberlain supported it. Derby, Kimberley, Carlingford, Fitzmaurice and Dodson favoured a more moderate scheme of Fitzmaurice's, which Dilke thought 'good, but very timid'. He was forced to swallow alterations which he disliked, but which made the measure more acceptable to the Whigs.[16]

The membership of the county councils was changed to include certain *ex officio* elements such as the lords lieutenant and the MPs for each county and the boroughs within it. Dilke was favourable to the inclusion of MPs, for they at least were subject to popular election and would provide an important link between central and local government. He also recognised the wisdom of raising the population limit for the county boroughs to 100,000, thereby reducing their number to a more practicable eighteen. Other changes he found less palatable. In particular, he objected to the retention of certain supervisory powers by central government. He would have preferred, he said, to abolish his own office entirely and replace it with an elected board.[17]

On 15 January 1884 he informed the Prime Minister that the final draft of the bill was ready and that the committee had held their 'funeral meeting over it... I wish to tell you with what spirit & skill Edmond Fitzmaurice has gone into the matter. He is the only man I know who is fit to be President of this board.'[18] Praise, indeed, for the man who had helped to water down his original scheme. In the event, progress with county franchise meant that it was never necessary to lay the bill before parliament. The constitutional changes of 1884–85 made new elections imperative in advance of any further legislation. Local government reform would have to wait.

The Liberals also failed to deliver on the other big local government issue they faced. London, as we have seen, remained the one major municipality untouched by reform. Moreover, the self-interest and privilege of the City was obstructing metropolitan reform in general. The City corporation, composed as it was of rich and privileged men elected through the livery companies, met the demand of the reformers for the creation of a single democratic corporation for the whole of London with the alternative and reactionary scheme of creating corporations modelled on its august self. In this way, it cleverly posed as a defender of decentralisation against the centralising reformers. Had the City's proposal been implemented it would, of course, have perpetuated its own vested interests and at the same time created others.

Two of Dilke's Chelsea neighbours, J. F. B. Firth and James Beal, were leading lights in the metropolitan reform movement. Firth, the second member for Chelsea, was the author of a mammoth reform tract entitled *Municipal London* (1876). Beal, the honorary secretary of the Metropolitan Municipal Association, had been pressing for London reform since the 1850s. Dilke shared their commitment to creating a single democratic corporation for the whole of the metropolis and, following the Liberal victory, the three Chelsea men had begun to lobby for reform. The agitation was orchestrated by the London Municipal Reform League: Dilke's brother Ashton was a member of its executive committee. Harcourt, who as Home Secretary was nominally responsible for London government, had agreed at the beginning of 1882, while Dilke was still at the Foreign Office, to take charge of a bill which they had drafted. In his diary Dilke recorded that Harcourt had 'adopted all my scheme for his Govt. of London Bill'.[19]

A cabinet committee was appointed to flesh out the bill's details, 'but it met only once', Dilke recalled, 'for the informal committee of Harcourt, Beal, Firth & myself did the whole work'. The one occasion of its meeting, on 11 January, was spent in discussing the Borneo Charter![20] Progress was slow, and the bill was not finalised until Christmas, by which time Dilke had moved to the Local Government Board.

The government's intention to make the bill the centre-piece of the 1883 session was thwarted by a serious disagreement over control of the Metropolitan Police. Harcourt, alarmed by the renewal of Fenian activity in the capital, which a few months earlier had seen an attempt on the Queen's life, wished to retain Home Office control over the police, whereas Dilke was for handing it over to a watch committee of the new corporation. Dilke pointed out that a watch committee worked tolerably well in Liverpool, 'the most Fenian town in Engl[an]d' and, supported by Gladstone and Chamberlain, refused to yield to Harcourt.[21]

This was the first measure in which Dilke had been closely involved to come before the cabinet since his promotion, and he was dejected at the prospect of his energies being dissipated by one man's obstinacy. 'It is heartbreaking work is drawing great bills', he wrote to Mrs Pattison on 14 March. 'I believe that all our labour on the London bill is wasted. That is one reason why the F.O. is pleasanter, – as nothing is wasted there.' Ironically, a dynamite explosion at the Local Government Board the next day helped to stiffen Harcourt's resolve. Dilke dismissed the incident as trivial. 'The dynamite people only chose a quiet corner,' he told Mrs Pattison, 'the quietest anywhere about the offices, & they chose a time when nobody is about, which shows that the object is to get money from America – not to hurt anybody.' All the same, the explosion caused quite considerable damage. There was now little hope of shaking the Home Secretary. At a cabinet on 17 March, Dilke rather sourly observed to Chamberlain that 'Harcourt thinks himself a Fouché & wants to have *all* the police but nothing but the police'.[22]

Dilke's commitment to the London bill led him to search anxiously for a compromise. On 11 April he told the Prime Minister that he would yield on the police question if Gladstone would make a declaration to the effect that in due course the police powers would be handed over to the new corporation. 'I fear that my judgment may be disturbed by my extreme anxiety to save the Bill', he wrote. 'I feel it all but a point of honour with myself after the declaration which I made at my election in 1880 & re-election of this year.' Gladstone agreed that the withdrawal of the bill would be 'a serious mischief, and a blow to the Government', but he had reservations about giving in to Harcourt.[23] However, Dilke's concern was acknowledged; at a cabinet three days later it was agreed that he, rather than Harcourt, should conduct the bill through committee.

Nine members of the cabinet met at the Home Office on 24 May to finalise arrangements. Dilke was jubilant. 'Victory!' he wrote to

Chamberlain, 'Hartington alone dissenting, everybody was for going on with everything, and sitting in the autumn.' His optimism was premature. Gladstone had no enthusiasm for the compromise and, just one week later, the measure was abandoned.

Dilke persisted, however, in the role of mediator and managed to resuscitate it. On 8 November he persuaded Gladstone to allow a decision on the police question to be deferred for the time being. London government was again to figure in the Queen's Speech for the coming session and was to be given precedence over his own local government bill.

Dilke finalised the details with Harcourt early in the new year. The bill provided for a unified London, with a vastly expanded city corporation elected triennially by the ratepayers as its main authority, and with popularly-elected district councils exercising only such powers as the corporation chose to delegate to them. Its jurisdiction was to be limited to the area covered by the Metropolitan Board of Works, but it was generally understood that it would be extended to the whole of London in due course. The Home Office, in line with Harcourt's wishes, was to keep control of the Metropolitan Police.[24]

The measure failed to make progress because of obstruction and time-wasting by the Tories, and because of the determination in the Liberal Party at large to secure the Reform Bill. Dilke's commitment to it and his feelings of isolation were conveyed in a confidential letter to his Chelsea agent:

> One unfortunate fact for the London Bill is that no one *in the House* cares about it except Dilke, Firth, & the Prime Minister, – & no one outside the House except the Lib[era]l Electors of Chelsea ... I am personally so strong for the Bill that I have not at any time admitted this to Harcourt, & I have only hinted it to Firth, but I fear it is the case. At the same time even unanimity & violence on the part of London if they existed or cd. be created would not I fancy overcome the determination of the party generally throughout the country to have 'the Franchise Bill only' in sight in view of the great row with the Lords.[25]

Tory obstruction in the Commons was only one part of a programme of full-scale opposition launched by the City. In 1882 it had set up a committee to organise against the bill and devoted nearly £20,000 to that task, much of it expended on bribery, corruption and the hiring of bullies to break up metropolitan reform meetings. By contrast, the reformers had relied almost exclusively on the parliamentary process for achieving their objective and made no attempts at mobilising popular support – a tactical error that goes some way towards explaining their failure.[26] Dilke tried a flanking manoeuvre aimed at weakening the City's power to resist reform when he used the report of a Royal Commission on the City Guilds in 1884 to attack them, but he got no support from Selborne, the Lord Chancellor, a member of the richest guild, the Mercers' Company and, according to Dilke, with all the personality of a 'a cross between a mummy and an icicle'. He therefore made no headway. A small bill which he introduced to limit the power of the companies was overtaken by the dissolution in 1885.[27]

Looking back on the futile attempts to reform London government, Professor W. A. Robson wrote in 1939 that 'The Harcourt Bill had a number of defects; but it cannot be doubted that it would have removed once and for all the worst evils which had afflicted London since the early years of the nineteenth century... London would today be a far finer and better-governed city if [it] had been passed into law.'[28]

The pressing need for the reform of the capital's administration was driven home by its housing crisis, and by doubts about the capacity of the vestries to alleviate it. Dilke had been at the LGB for just ten months when an anonymous pamphlet appeared which caused a national outcry and which for a short period pushed the housing question to the front of the political stage. *The Bitter Cry of Outcast London*, subsequently attributed to the Congregationalist minister, the Rev. Andrew Mearns, was a searing indictment of society's toleration of the slum conditions of London's East End. Its thesis, that poverty and bad housing caused irreligion and immorality, was not new. But it touched middle-class consciences in a way that no social writing had since Mayhew. The explanation for this lay partly in Mearn's choice of a dramatic title for his pamphlet, partly in its opportune timing. For it appeared just at the moment when politicians, from a mixture of guilt about overcrowding and fear about its possible implications for social stability, were tentatively turning their attention to the housing issue.

Lord Salisbury, the Conservative leader, had spoken and written on the subject in the spring of 1883. His intervention had attracted widespread publicity. In October, the same month that *The Bitter Cry* appeared, Morley's *Fortnightly Review* published an article on 'The Housing of the Poor in the Towns' by Frank Harris (later to achieve notoriety for a particularly salacious autobiography). This was the third in the series of contributions to Chamberlain's new radical programme. Dilke, for his part, had made the acquaintance of Mearns and had supplied him with evidence of church-going habits for inclusion in his pamphlet.[29] He realised that the housing crisis could be used to reinforce the case for municipal reform in general and at once set about accumulating information that he hoped would demonstrate the failings of the vestries in this matter.

The Bitter Cry moved the Queen to write to Gladstone on 30 October expressing her distress at what she had read, and asking him what he proposed to do. Less important questions were presently under discussion, she averred, and these 'might wait till one involving the very existence of thousands – nay millions – had been fully considered by the Government'.[30] Gladstone forwarded the letter to Dilke.

Cross's Housing Acts of 1875 and 1879 had empowered local authorities to condemn, demolish and rebuild deficient areas. The legislation was discretionary and made no provision for rebuilding to keep pace with demolition. Consequently, the acts were, in Dilke's view, little more than street improvement schemes which drove people away from their places of work and, 'in many cases to starvation'. He was in favour instead of investing large sums of money in construction programmes, to be carried out by reformed local authorities.[31]

He discussed the Queen's letter with Harcourt, who was nominally responsible for working-class housing in London but who, because of his preoccupation with Fenianism, had once again handed the matter over to the LGB. He also wrote to Chamberlain for details of housing conditions in Birmingham. In November he decided to use a scheduled visit to the East End workhouses to look into the housing situation there.

These preliminary inquiries escalated during November and December into a full-scale survey of housing conditions throughout London. Dilke had written to several prominent social reformers for a list of the worst areas, which he visited in the company of the district surveyors and the local medical officers. Houses in central London had been pulled down to make way for warehouses, businesses and other such developments, thus driving some of the population to the periphery and intensifying overcrowding in the remaining tenements. The worst areas were those which had refused to adopt by-laws to enforce existing provisions, usually because of propertied interests on the vestries. However, only Clerkenwell provided him with the sort of ammunition against the vestries that he had hoped to find. Here 'the two great dictators or potentates of the parish who had the control of the Vestry and its leading committees ... were the largest owners in the whole district ... of bad or doubtful property'.[32]

Dilke intended to compel the districts on his 'black list' to implement existing by-laws and to enact and enforce new ones. Shortly before Christmas, he published two circulars reminding vestries of their responsibilities under existing legislation and of their powers to inspect and regulate certain properties. Ministers were presented with copies of his conclusions.[33] On 8 February 1884 the government decided to appoint a royal commission to inquire into the housing of the working classes. Dilke was given charge of selecting and chairing it. He secured the services of several distinguished figures, most notably, the Prince of Wales, Cardinal Manning and Lord Salisbury. Richard Cross, the former Home Secretary and housing legislator, Jesse Collings, an acolyte of Chamberlain's and a spokesman for the agricultural labourers, and Henry Broadhurst, an active trade unionist, were also included.

Such an impressive commission was not assembled without difficulties, the principal of which concerned the rank of Manning. Harcourt, in theory responsible for the commission, did not like the Queen's suggestion that Manning, in his capacity as cardinal and therefore as a foreign prince, should be given precedence over Salisbury. Fortunately, his lordship had no objection to the lower ranking. A further source of conflict arose over Dilke's desire to co-opt a woman, Octavia Hill, onto the commission. The cabinet refused to establish such a precedent, even though the Prime Minister supported Dilke. He had to be content with Lyulph Stanley as the representative of, and poor substitute for, his more knowledgeable sister, Maud. Finally, the veteran social reformer Lord Shaftesbury complained at being overlooked. Dilke managed to pacify him by calling him as the first witness and making much use of his evidence.[34]

With the difficulties smoothed over, the Queen complimented Dilke on his 'excellent selection'.[35] He remarked, with typical candour, that the royal commission had 'fewer fools on it than is usual'. Much of the hard work was left to him. The commission began its inquiries in March, often sitting twice a week, for which meetings he had, as examiner-in-chief, to prepare in advance by drawing up the appropriate questions and corresponding with all the witnesses. He continued to visit areas which were reported as being particularly bad. Of the commission's leading members, the Prince of Wales proved little more than a figurehead, although he took part whenever other distractions were not too great; Manning was the 'greatest revolutionist'; and Salisbury provided the most practical assistance.

Manning owed his place to a correspondence with Dilke in October 1883 and to his concern at the moral consequences of overcrowding emphasised in *The Bitter Cry*. They agreed that reform was urgent and that, as Manning put it, 'construction must keep pace with destruction', but they were not of one mind on the type of action that was required. Manning favoured strong central control. He wanted to give the Local Government Board greater powers to compel the valuation and de-struction of condemned houses. 'Without a high-handed executive', he wrote, 'nothing will be done till another generation has been morally destroyed.' His ideas were in advance of his time. He advocated a scheme of town-planning which would have involved the removal out of London of prisons, infirmaries, breweries, ironworks and all factories not needed for daily or home work, in order to give more room for housing. Dilke regarded Manning's proposals as 'wild' and 'ill-considered', and so impracticable as not to warrant discussion. They went, he believed, beyond the remit of the commission and the expectations of the country. Moreover, he disliked suggestions that would increase the power of the executive at the expense of a system of reformed local authorities. All the same, Manning was a valuable contributor to the commission, and Dilke was not slow to acknowledge this.[36]

Salisbury, who had been among the first to press for a royal commission, worked out with Dilke the procedure which it should follow. Together they drew up, in April 1884, a questionnaire for circulation to the local authorities. Its aim was to elicit information about overcrowding and room-usage, which became the central concerns of the whole inquiry. When Salisbury further suggested that they inquire about sanitary and structural defects, Dilke objected that this would produce too much evidence to handle satisfactorily. At the end of April Dilke asked: 'Are we after finishing our enquiry as to the Evil in London, to go next to the Remedy in London, or to the Evil in the great provincial towns?' Salisbury plumped for the latter on the grounds that they might from their inquiries get 'hints' as to remedies, though there was 'a good deal to be said for either course'.[37] The close cooperation of Dilke and Salisbury on the housing question developed into a friendship which was to become important during the intricate negotiations on the Redistribution Bill a year later. Salisbury secured the election of Dilke to membership of Grillion's, an exclusive dining club of major politicians, which he at first rather ungraciously declined until reprimanded by Carlingford.

Salisbury was a big London property-owner himself and his suggestions for housing reform, in Dilke's opinion, 'throw much light on his temporary Radicalism which unfortunately soon wore off'. Among his proposals were schemes for making loans available on easier terms; fairer arrangements for leaseholders; rate-relief from taxation; more effective implementation of existing legislation enabling districts to build lodging-houses; the lowering of the qualification for membership of vestries; empowerment of the police to inspect tenements; better railway facilities for linking job and home; and a yearly census of housing conditions in selected localities.

Despite its glittering composition, Dilke found the commission not only hard work but also inordinately dull. When Chamberlain was due to give evidence, the anticipated clash with Salisbury (whom he had been haranguing in the country over his opposition to parliamentary reform) proved a damp squib, and the interview passed off uneventfully. Almost the only amusing incident that Dilke could recall was an occasion when, following 'a rather wild suggestion' from Salisbury, 'Broadhurst put down his pen and ... said with an astonished air "Why that is Socialism"; at which there was a loud laugh all round'.[38] The work of the commission continued into 1885, when it extended its scope to include Scotland and Ireland. Burdened though he was by this time with the Redistribution Bill, Dilke still found time to visit Edinburgh in April and Dublin in May.

The publication of its report met with a mixed response. *Reynolds's Newspaper* was cynical. It was, it said, 'as disappointing an official deliverance as ever we remember to have read ... [It] carries us no further than we were at New Year's Day, 1884. If we needed the lesson, the report tells us not to put our faith in Royal Commissions.' The newspaper's central contention was that the commission merely exposed conditions that were already well-known, without offering any adequate remedies.[39]

The criticism was justified. The report did not say much that had not already been said by social reformers, journalists and philanthropists. It drew attention to the well-known evils of overcrowding, poor water supply, disease, structural defects and the moral effects of slum conditions on their inhabitants, and attributed them to numerous causes: low wages and high rents, job proximity, demolition without reconstruction, 'landlordism', and the failure of local authorities to use their legitimate powers. The significance of the report has to be sought rather in the fact that it was the product of an *official* inquiry, not only promoted by parliament, but conducted by some of the most important people in the land – the heir to the throne, the emissary of the Catholic church in England, a man who, even before the commission had dissolved itself, was Prime Minister of a Conservative government, and a man who seemed destined to become Prime Minister in a future Liberal government. National, non-sectarian and non-party, the royal commission was all these things, and it created a sense of optimism that something might at last be done to tackle a serious social evil. In many respects, therefore, the commission was more important for the new awareness that it signified than for providing any concrete solutions to the housing problem. It had demonstrated that the housing crisis affected the 'respectable' as well as the 'dissolute' poor and thus challenged orthodox assumptions about the causes of urban poverty. Thereafter it was no longer possible to separate the symptoms of slum life from the deep-seated economic problems that caused them.[40] The report formed an element in that revaluation of classical liberalism that was being forced forward by the socio-economic crisis and the impact of socialism. It was in this sense that the *Manchester Guardian* could with some justice describe it as 'one of the most important and most instructive documents ever laid before Parliament'.[41]

Its recommendations bore the stamp of Dilke's influence: on the one hand, in the emphasis placed upon the consolidation and implementation of existing statutes, particularly with regard to sanitation and public health; on the other in the need to reform London government in order to make the local authorities more responsive. He would have liked to have gone further and given municipal bodies extensive powers to clear slums, purchase land and build new houses, but the collective opinion of the commission was that there had been a 'failure in administration rather than in legislation'. Among its other recommendations were the appointment of sanitary inspectors; the planning of buildings in terms of space and height; the granting of powers to requisition prison-land in London for house-building; and improvements in the facilitation of loans.[42]

The commission had failed to come up with any major new initiatives, so it is hardly surprising that the Housing Bill which arose out of its findings was a timid measure. None of the commissioners was consulted in its drafting, though Salisbury was amenable to taking charge of it in the Lords. The bill's emphasis, like the commission's, was on the consolidation and enforcement of existing legislation. Its most important clauses concerned the easing of loans for building purposes, the assignment to local authorities in England and Scotland of compulsory powers to take land for cottage gardens (though this was dropped by the House) and, potentially the most progressive in the whole bill, a clause which made the letting of an unfurnished house imply a guarantee that it was reasonably fit for human habitation, thus rendering the landlord liable to damages for loss by injury to health in consequence of defects.[43]

The royal commission of 1885, and the housing bills that followed it, formulated no dynamic state housing policy, and the very poor continued to subsist in squalid conditions. At the turn of the century, social investigators and novelists like Jack London were still able, like Mayhew, Mearns and others before them, to shock their readers with descriptions of the ghetto conditions, slums and doss-houses that persisted in London's East End. Manning's 'next generation' was, as he had feared, tainted by the depravity of such living conditions. In England and Wales in the decade 1891–1901 demand continued to outstrip construction, with the population rising by 12.17 per cent and the total number of tenements by only 11.51 per cent.[44]

Improvements did not come until local authorities embarked on more interventionist housing policies, and in a sense Dilke had been right in advocating local government reform as a necessary priority. Too much faith was placed in the efficacy of existing legislation. Many interventions that were thought to be progressive, such as sanitary improvements and the clearance of slums, merely forced up rents and threw more of the poor onto the streets, thus exacerbating an already acute problem. Reformers tended to work on the assumption that vested interests were exploiting, rather than fulfilling, a very real need for cheap housing. The poor were still regarded as demoralised and their housing plight capable of amelioration by way of orthodox liberal remedies such as self-help, religion and temperance. Without state-supported schemes for rehousing, industrial planning and cheaper transport, areas of London were condemned to remain overcrowded. Local bodies were dependent on guidance and aid from the centre, but in this Dilke and his fellow Liberals were not yet prepared to give a lead.

One important spin-off from his work on the housing commission did assist Dilke's intellectual progress from individualism to collectivism. Towards the end of 1884 he had been invited by Frederic Harrison to preside at an Industrial Remuneration Conference, to be held in the Prince's Hall, Piccadilly, from 28 to 30 January 1885. 'The conference has no party character, & no distinct economic doctrine. Its business', Harrison wrote, 'is discussion & suggestion ... We think that your work on the Royal Commission will have turned your attention directly on the general industrial question.'[45]

The conference was, indeed, a politically eclectic gathering. It included three delegates from the Marxist-inspired Social Democratic Federation at one extreme, and the future Tory Prime Minister, A. J. Balfour, at the other. Among the speakers were leading economists such as Professor Alfred Marshall, Liberal politicians such as Morley and Shaw Lefevre, labour leaders like Thomas Burt and John Burns, the republican and social theorist Professor E. S. Beesly, the women's trade unionist Emma Paterson, the employer Thomas Brassey and the Fabian playwright Bernard Shaw. The timing of the conference reflected the unease of the middle class at the growing social unrest during the recession. Its central purpose was to consider ways in which labour might gain a more equal share in the products of industry. Among the topics debated were the benefits to the working classes of industrial progress, remedial legislation and the state management of capital and land. The conference was firmly within the tradition of attempts at maintaining class cooperation and class harmony which had been a key characteristic of nineteenth-century middle-class radicalism.

In his opening remarks from the chair, Dilke revealed the extent to which his capacity to break with classical political economy was still inhibited by a moral perspective:

> By laying ... greater burdens on the wealthy, society may make the rich poorer, but it cannot make the toilers really richer unless the relief obtained is applied in such a way as to tend to the mental and moral development of the people. This is, to my mind, one of the greatest problems of our modern social change, and I shall look most anxiously for any light which your discussions will throw upon it.[46]

The discussions did, however, make one important impression upon him. They converted him on the question of the eight-hour day 'from a position of absolute impartiality to one strongly favourable to legislative limitation'.[47] Legislative interference with hours of work was contrary to classical theory on the free play of economic forces and, in this one area at least, the conference had moved him towards accepting the need for greater state intervention on certain social questions. In other respects he was still a bondslave of *laissez-faire*. When a demonstration of the unemployed led by Burns gathered outside the offices of the LGB a fortnight after the conference, Dilke was unmoved by their demand for a programme of public works to alleviate the distress.[48] It was to be some time yet before he took a more active political part on social issues.

Control over the spread of disease was another issue under Dilke's jurisdiction at the LGB which stretched *laissez-faire* to its limits. It had been one question upon which the state had been compelled, long before the housing crisis and at least since the time of Edwin Chadwick, to play a more interventionist role. For while it was possible (at least until the mid 1880s) for the middle class to believe that the poor themselves could be kept quarantined in their overcrowded ghettos, this was decidedly not the case with their nasty infections and contagions. At the LGB Dilke was faced with two recurrent and interrelated public health problems. The first was a panic caused by news of the sudden outbreak of a cholera epidemic in Egypt in 1883; the second, concern over the effectiveness of vaccination in controlling and preventing such epidemics.

Dilke used the cholera panic to introduce legislation to provide more rigorous quarantine arrangements in London. He considered cholera a less serious threat than smallpox, and drew up a bill which provided for the compulsory acquisition of wharves for floating-hospital ships on the Thames to which smallpox cases could be moved from the London hospitals. Gladstone thought this contentious and likely to waste government time when more important matters were pending. Dilke, however, had used scare tactics to secure Harcourt's backing and he noted in his diary with ill-concealed glee that the Home Secretary was 'as frightened now about cholera as he used to be about dynamite'. The combination of Dilke and Harcourt was sufficient to overcome Gladstone's resistance, and the Prime Minister gave way, though not without first protesting 'in a very strong letter'.[49]

Dilke's Diseases Prevention (Metropolis) Bill permitted not only the impounding of the smallpox wharves but also the establishment in an emergency of one sanitary body for the whole of London. It quickly became law. Thereafter, Dilke frequently visited the hospital ships and the smallpox camp at Darenth to which convalescents from the ships were moved. He spent a weekend at Darenth in the summer of 1885. In preparation for one such visit in September 1884 he was revaccinated, and his arm was, for a while, in 'a frightful condition'. Vaccination gave him more than just a sore limb. It placed him at the centre of a perennial and arid controversy about its effectiveness and about the intrusion of compulsory programmes upon the rights of the individual. He defended the practice, and was theoretically in favour of compulsion, but shied away from using the power of his office to prosecute objectors.[50]

At the LGB, Dilke had demonstrated a determination to simplify the structure and administration of local government, and to rid central government of duties more appropriate to reformed local bodies, in order to achieve an improvement in administration at the centre and at the periphery. Decentralisation and democratisation were his twin ambitions and were key motifs in radical liberal theory. He perceived efficient administration as the means to all sorts of beneficial ends. Above all, one end-product would be the active participation of the citizen in government, which would act as an antidote to social disturbance. Local government reform was seen as the answer to many social and political problems: housing, land, licensing and even the question of what to do about Ireland. For this reason, it had by 1885 become the most important single element within the radical programme. Strategy, however, dictated that parliamentary reform should take precedence over local government. The radicals were nevertheless confident that they would be able to reform the local state from a position of dominance in the next Liberal government – a government which would, in fulfilment of their strategy, be elected under a democratised constitution.

Chapter 9

Towards Democracy

Although the Reform Acts of 1832 and 1867 had achieved a quite substantial numerical increase in the franchise,[1] and had disfranchised some of the more corrupt boroughs, they had brought about little in the way of a corresponding shift in the disposition of political power. London and the expanding industrial society of the north of England were grossly underrepresented compared with the stagnant and declining agricultural communities of the south. The reformers of 1832 and 1867 had deliberately strengthened the disparity between town and country – through the Chandos Amendment in 1832, and by the deliberate exclusion of agricultural workers and the increase in county seats in 1867. When combined with plural voting,[2] the disfranchisement of working men through registration anomalies, restricted polling hours, the persistence of bribery and corruption, the exclusion of women and the aristocracy's maintenance of a second line of political privilege in the shape of the House of Lords, it will be appreciated just how far removed from democracy the British constitution remained.

Whatever concessions had been extracted from the landed oligarchy in the form of the vote had been limited therefore by a gamut of restrictions on its effectiveness. As a result, the landed gentry remained the largest single economic interest within the House of Commons and by far the preponderant interest within the cabinet. The disjunction between the economic hegemony of the middle class and its subordinate position within the political structures of the state was one which the radicals were now determined to correct. It is in this context that the democratic importance of the Redistribution Act of 1885 has to be understood. For the creation of equal electoral districts entailed an equalisation in the value of each vote and the destruction of most of the remaining corrupt boroughs. Redistribution therefore gave meaning to the Reform Act and the Corrupt

Practices Act so that, taken together, the constitutional changes of 1883–85 prepared the way for the decisive transfer of political hegemony from the landed aristocracy to the middle class, and the end of Whig ascendancy within the Liberal Party. For this reason, it was, Dilke told a Glaswegian audience in 1883, 'the keynote of the whole future of our politics'.[3] At the same time, the democratic reforms encouraged longer-term trends that the Liberals for the most part had not intended or anticipated and which they would find difficult to offset: namely, the migration of the middle class to the Conservatives and the emergence of a separate party of the working class.

An end to corrupt practices was dictated by the cost of the 1880 general election, which had reached a startling £2,000,000.[4] On the eve of the dissolution, Dilke had called for the government to act to put a brake on expenses. Instead, it had proceeded by somewhat devious means to produce what one historian has called 'the only piece of reactionary [electoral] legislation of the century'.[5] A large part of electoral expenditure went on paying for the conveyance of voters to the polls, a practice permitted in the counties but not in the boroughs. On the day the dissolution was announced, Stafford Northcote, the Conservative leader in the Commons, had assured Dilke that this discrepancy would be dealt with before the elections were held.[6] The Tories then carried post-haste a bill placing the boroughs on the same footing as the counties, rather than the other way round as the Liberals had expected. At the general election this retrograde measure benefited the richer candidates in the boroughs and the cabbies who reaped the profits.

In November 1880 Dilke was placed on a cabinet committee to consider the question, though it was not, he noted, 'a harmonious body'.[7] It nevertheless agreed the terms of a Corrupt Practices Bill which was introduced in 1881, and again in 1882, but which made insufficient progress owing to Irish obstruction. It was eventually carried with little opposition in 1883, skilfully steered through the House by Dilke, during the period when he was taking charge of measures that were more properly the responsibility of the Home Secretary. It did not completely end corruption but it did signal a change in political morality. The following year he succeeded in extending his Metropolitan Hours of Polling Act of 1878 to the counties and the larger boroughs, which now joined London in closing at 8 p.m. instead of 4 p.m.

These were minor achievements when set alongside the big con-stitutional issues of the day. The radicals were determined that, if the government did nothing else while in office (which in the early years of Irish obstruction and Bradlaugh did not seem at all improbable), it would carry a Reform Bill that would extend the franchise to the agricultural workers. It was always likely that such a major constitutional change would be left until towards the end of the life of the administration. Dilke for one was strategically consistent in regarding county franchise as a useful and popular measure to have in reserve on which to go to the country if defeated in the early days on less stirring issues, such as Ireland and the closure.[8] By the autumn of 1883, however, he believed that the Reform Bill should now take precedence over all else, including his own Local Government Bill. Pressure for reform was beginning to build at the grassroots. In October 1883 delegates from 500 Liberal associations met at Leeds and demanded prompt action. A few days later another reform demonstration was held in Glasgow with Dilke as the principal speaker. In the face of all this, the cabinet agreed to give county franchise priority in the next session, Hartington alone dissenting on the grounds that it should be dealt with alongside redistribution.

During December Chamberlain, angered by Hartington's obstructionism, harangued the landed oligarchy at a series of public meetings where he used language which, in its invocation of class war, alarmed the Whigs and moderates. Even if reform was not possible now, the radicals calculated that by provoking a Whig secession they would secure its future success.[9] The Prime Minister, however, was able to use Chamberlain's demagogy to persuade Hartington of the advisability of compromise. He gave the Whig leader 'a strong dose of Chamberlain', warning him that his secession 'would leave Chamberlain and Co. masters of the situation and accordingly obliterate the moderate section of the party....' A chastened Hartington-intimated that he would fall in line, provided Gladstone made a statement of the government's policy on redistribution when the Franchise Bill was introduced.[10]

Dilke recognised that compromise with the Whig leader would mean a less radical measure, and so it proved. Hartington was appeased by the retention of the forty shilling freehold suffrage in the counties. Nor was Gladstone willing to support the simple 'one man, one vote' franchise demanded by the radicals. Dilke was 'grieved' by this.[11] At the root of radical difficulties was the Prime Minister's basic conservatism on reform. 'Our not getting one man one vote', Dilke opined, 'was entirely Mr Gladstone's fault, for the Cabinet expected & would have taken it; Hartington alone opposing, as he opposed everything all through.'[12] The failure to adopt a simple franchise to replace all the complex incremental legislation of the past meant the continuance of registration anomalies and the inevitable exclusion of many men from the vote.

The main decisions were made in cabinet during late January and early

February. The radicals were overruled in seeking to end plural voting and the university franchise. Dilke did manage to protect the voting rights of certain special groups (such as Scottish shepherds) who occupied dwellings not separately rated as part-payment for their services. In a speech at Chelsea, he tried to win the support of Irish MPs by reassuring them that Irish representation would be unaffected by any subsequent redistribution.[13]

The bill, introduced on 28 February 1885, extended the borough householder franchise of 1867 to the counties. In this regard, it embodied no new principle and fell far short of the democratic sentiments of the radicals. Nevertheless, it was the first to treat the whole of the United Kingdom in the one measure. Above all, it was designed to have a dramatic numerical impact. Its net effect would be to raise the number of voters, in round figures, from three to five million. In accordance with an agreement in cabinet, however, it included no clause to enfranchise women. Yet, their participation in municipal, school board and board of guardians elections had created a not unfavourable climate of opinion, and 1884 was perhaps the most propitious moment in the last quarter of the nineteenth century for some progress on this question. Accordingly, a limited measure of female enfranchisement was introduced in an amendment to the bill moved by William Woodall.

During the Easter recess Dilke wrote from Antibes, where he was holidaying, to sound the Prime Minister as to the consequences of his support for the amendment. He inferred from the reply that Gladstone would enforce the principle of collective responsibility. In these circumstances he decided, after much heart-searching, to abstain.[14] On 9 May Gladstone circulated a memorandum to the cabinet making it plain that if the women's suffrage amendment was carried, the bill would be dropped and the government would be forced to resign.[15]

When the debate was held on 12 June, Gladstone's opposition rallied the party against the amendment and it was defeated by 136 votes. Dilke maintained a discreet silence, but refused to follow his cabinet colleagues into the 'No' lobby. Hartington was furious and wanted him sacked. At a cabinet two days later he was reprieved, despite Hartington's anger, not least because Chamberlain, though opposed to women's suffrage, indicated that he would resign if Dilke went. Gladstone drafted a minute pointing out that in 'ordinary circumstances' Dilke would have had to go, but that in view of the grave situation in Egypt, such resignations would be 'unfortunate'. Faced with either agreeing or disintegrating, the cabinet chose the former and the crisis for Dilke passed.[16]

He had risked his career for what many contemporaries thought a minor issue. It has been estimated that 104 Liberals who normally supported women's suffrage had followed Gladstone's lead and voted against it.[17] Dilke, with more at stake, refused to compromise and, writing to Mrs Pattison a year later, made it clear that he would take the same stand again: 'When the day comes that all our people are raving for manhood suffrage & that I have to join the Tories in carrying adult suffrage as an amendment – I may if in office have for a time to go out by myself or nearly so.'[18]

With the publication of the Reform Bill, the Tories suddenly discovered the importance of redistribution. Salisbury later dismissed as a calumny the claim that this conversion was merely convenient.[19] Overwhelmingly defeated in 1880 on a very large turnout, the Conservatives had little to lose and perhaps much to gain from a redrawing of constituency boundaries. Nevertheless, it is difficult to avoid the conclusion that their initial opposition was little more than an obstructionist tactic. To oppose the Reform Bill on the grounds that it was a *reactionary* measure, duplicating anomalies that could only be removed by redistribution, was a shrewd move. They could pose as the more popular party, embarrass the Liberals and buy valuable time. The Liberals were walking into deep water over Egypt, and delay and assault on this flank might result in the fall of the government and no reform.[20] In this way, reform and Egypt became imbricated. For the Conservatives, Egypt was an opportunity to derail reform; while for the Liberals, reform was a distraction from Egypt. The government only narrowly survived two votes of censure on its Egyptian policy in the early months of 1884. When this strategy failed, Salisbury, fearing the consequences for the Conservative Party of an election held on the enlarged county franchise, took the battle into the Upper House.

On 8 July the Lords rejected the bill. The cabinet, in anticipation of this outcome, had already decided to call a special autumn session to reintroduce it. On 9 July Dilke launched an all-out attack on Salisbury in a speech to the Middlesex Liberal Association, in which he warned the House of Lords of the danger of not using its authority prudently. It was the duty of the elected representatives of the people, he concluded, to reintroduce the measure until the Lords were forced to swallow it. The Queen protested to Gladstone about the tone of this speech, and Churchill complained in the House about references which Dilke had made to his quarrels with the Tory leadership.[21]

The rumbling threat of a constitutional crisis disturbed the summer of 1884. Demonstrations and meetings were held throughout Britain. On 21 July, referred to as '*Intimidation Monday*' by some Tories,[22] a franchise procession in London took three hours to pass by the Houses of Parliament.

There were demands for universal suffrage and for the immediate abolition of the Lords, while some socialists called for the abolition of the Commons as well. The middle-class radicals sought to harness this advanced radicalism of the working class to their own more limited objectives, a strategy which had been deployed successfully at various times in the past, though there was always a danger that the latter would push reform further than the former were prepared to go. This consideration explains the dichotomy between the words and the actions of the radicals. Their rhetoric was often fierce, but they stopped short of any attempt to force a terminal confrontation with the Lords. Chamberlain, for example, vehemently condemned the Conservatives and the Lords as he stumped the country addressing mass meetings in language that once again whiffed of class war. It was he who coined the slogan 'the Peers against the People'. Likewise, John Morley spoke of 'mending or ending' the Lords. Morley had given up the editorship of the *Fortnightly Review* in order to enter parliament for Newcastle in 1883, taking the seat vacated by Dilke's brother, Ashton, who had died of tuberculosis in Algiers in March of that year.

Dilke himself was no demagogue and left the rabble-rousing to his colleagues. He preferred instead to begin preparing the ground for a compromise with the Tories. Had it not been for this initiative, Gladstone's second administration might very well have been remembered only for an ignominious foreign policy. Dilke took up the redistribution gauntlet thrown down by the Conservatives: he was the linch-pin of the negotiations between the parties in the autumn of 1884 and steered the resultant bill quickly and skilfully through the House of Commons.

He had begun preparing a scheme without prior instruction while the Lords were still debating the Franchise Bill. On the evening of 14 July he discussed it with Gladstone and they 'practically hatched the Bill'. Dilke now called in Sir John Lambert to assist him. Lambert had taken part in drafting the Reform Bill of 1867 and had become the LGB's first Permanent Secretary in 1871, a post which he held until his retirement in 1882. By 9 August their proposals were ready for circulation. A redistribution committee of the cabinet was set up which included Hartington, Kimberley, Childers, Chamberlain and Lefevre, but was by-passed by Dilke who preferred, in the interest of time and efficiency, to work with Lambert alone.[23]

The prorogation of parliament on 14 August helped to dissipate some of the tension that had arisen in relations between the two Houses during the summer. A week later Dilke went to Hardwick Hall, at Hartington's request, to discuss the possibility of introducing redistribution alongside the Franchise Bill. Hartington informed Gladstone that he did not think Dilke was opposed to this himself but that many Liberals would be angry about making such a concession to the Opposition.[24] Salisbury and Balfour were by this time making it clear in their speeches in the country that they did not fear a fair redistribution scheme. The Tory leader had been so won over to the idea of a far-reaching plan that, Kimberley wrote, 'it will become a sort of open competition, which party can go furthest. I should not be surprised if he [Salisbury] were to trump us by proposing to abolish the H. of Lords.'[25] Several proposals for a bipartisan agreement were therefore being floated during the late summer and autumn. Chamberlain, however, remained hostile, telling Dilke that he hoped all thoughts of compromise had been 'extinguished'.[26] In these circumstances, Dilke had to keep his own more conciliatory views private, even from his closest ally. He continued to work behind the scenes, putting the finishing touches to a plan that he hoped would be acceptable to all parties, and which would facilitate the passage of the Reform Bill.

Dilke and Lambert had at first contemplated grouping small constituencies together but had abandoned the idea because of its impracticality. Their scheme was completed on 18 September. It divided the English counties into two-member constituencies, apart from Lancashire and Yorkshire which were classed as 'urban counties' and divided into single-member districts. Fifty-three borough constituencies with a population of less than 10,000 were merged into the counties. Boroughs with populations between 10,000 and 40,000 lost one member, releasing thirty-three more seats for redistribution. A further twelve came from the merger into counties of six district boroughs,[27] and these went to Scotland. Glamorganshire gained four while the total number of Irish seats was left untouched. Wales and Ireland were therefore to be somewhat over-represented compared with England and Scotland.[28]

This fairly modest set of proposals undoubtedly favoured the Liberal Party. While disfranchising completely those boroughs where the Tories predominated, it took only one seat from the medium-sized boroughs where the Liberals were strong. It left the Liberal Celtic fringe overrepresented. Certain features were kept in order to appease the Whigs. For example, sufficient two-member seats were retained to allow for the continuation of the practice of running Whigs and radicals in harness. Likewise, university representation was left untouched. 10,000 for the lower limit meant the retention of many ancient and corrupt boroughs and the underrepresentation of large industrial towns.

Dilke disliked the scheme but, motivated primarily by the desire to make it uncontroversial and acceptable, purity of conviction had perforce to be strained through the sieve of realism. However, as the negotiations unfolded, he used all his guile to radicalise it. In so doing, he demonstrated that disinterestedness in party which he had always professed. His subsequent success in increasing the population limit for the loss of both members and in greatly extending the single-member system was detrimental to Liberal interests, and he consciously pursued these changes when the highest office was within his grasp. His motives were not entirely altruistic. He gambled on the Liberal caucuses in the single-member constituencies selecting radical rather than Whig candidates so that, while in the short term the party as a whole might suffer, in the long run the radicals would gain by the purging of Whig influence.

On 20 September he sent Gladstone a secret memorandum, not generally circulated until October, in which he apprised the Prime Minister of his doubts about the plan. Basically, he wanted the population levels for disfranchisement to be carried above 10,000 and 40,000 respectively and the universal adoption of single-member districts. 'Summing up on our English borough scheme', he wrote, 'I am struck by its timidity. I do not see how it is to stand the revolutionary criticism of Lord Salisbury.'[29]

The 'revolutionary criticism' of the Tory leader was to be an important card up Dilke's sleeve with which to trump the conservative criticism of Gladstone, who disliked the destruction of ancient borough seats. When, years later, Dilke sent Morley notes for his biography of Gladstone, he said of the redistribution negotiations: 'I treated Mr G. as the Tory on this question, which he was.'[30] Nine days elapsed before Gladstone offered any comments upon Dilke's memorandum. He agreed to an increase in the number of single-member constituencies but was opposed to altering the 10,000 and 40,000 limits. Indeed, he wanted to create new borough seats of less than 40,000 population. He inclined towards the retention of the status quo in Ireland and Wales, and favoured increasing the House's membership to 670 rather than disfranchise some of the smaller English boroughs. Finally, he approved of Dilke's decision to appoint inspectors to make a private inquiry into boundaries.[31]

Dilke strongly objected to the Prime Minister's predilection for creating new boroughs of less than average size. He told him that, while he was prepared to put up with 'existing & ancient anomalies', he could see no point in 'creating fresh ones'.[32] He spent the last day of September with Lambert redrafting the plan to accommodate some of Gladstone's suggestions. The size of the House was increased by twelve, these new seats going to Scotland, with a further ten released for England, five for the counties and five for the largest boroughs.[33]

At the beginning of October Tory pressure for compromise began to produce friction in the cabinet. Chamberlain wrote to Dilke on 3 October advocating resignation if Gladstone surrendered to Tory demands for redistribution without any guarantee that the Franchise Bill would be passed.[34] Tension was heightened the following day when Hartington made a speech in which he suggested that the Lords should first be allowed to see the Redistribution Bill and satisfy themselves as to its fairness before they passed the Franchise Bill. His remarks provoked a great row in cabinet, where Dilke and Chamberlain attacked any such truckling to the Tories.

There is no doubt that Dilke himself wanted to reach a *modus vivendi* and, while publicly aligning himself with Chamberlain, he was privately contriving to engineer a settlement. To this end, he tried to avoid any discussion of his plan in cabinet. 'They drive me wild', he told Chamberlain, 'with piddling points.' He may also have been responsible for leaking the scheme to the press. On 9 October the *Standard* 'sprang a mine' by publishing the gist of it. Dilke claimed that it had been leaked by the Queen's Printer, but there is no doubt that its publication seemed calculated to serve his private purpose. It might compel the Tories to respond with their own proposals and thus provide a basis for negotiation and, at the same time, counter the distracting manoeuvres of some of his Liberal colleagues, such as the attacks on the Lords (Chamberlain) or the making of indiscreet offers (Hartington).[35]

If this was Dilke's plan, it backfired. The Tory chiefs were at that moment meeting, at the Queen's behest, at Gordon Castle, the Scottish seat of the Duke of Richmond, to see if they could find grounds for compromise. Salisbury had, until its official repudiation, believed that progress might be made on the basis of Hartington's proposal. He was now convinced that compromise was impossible, and told the Queen's private secretary as much. The talks in the castle broke up, and a truculent Salisbury left for Kelso where, on 11 October, he denounced the leaked Liberal scheme.

He proceeded to engage in a public exchange of insults with Chamberlain. In reply to Salisbury's wish that he would lead a planned procession from Birmingham to London and get his head broken for his pains, Chamberlain expressed a hope that his lordship would meet the procession so that his head might be broken in very good company. Threatening language of this sort was infectious. A banner at a reform demonstration in Bristol bore the clever legend: 'The Lords will be done ... .'[36] Dilke, too, now jumped on to the demagogic bandwagon, attacking the Tories in a series of speeches in the textile centres of north-west England – Oldham,

Manchester and Stockport – on the 14, 15 and 16 October respectively. He spoke out against 'reform' of the Lords, because he understood by this the correction of abuses. Reform would therefore entail the rehabilitation of a moribund and unrepresentative institution. This was not just semantic pedantry on Dilke's part, for there were many of his contemporaries who proposed reform precisely in order to revive the Lords' role within the constitution. Gladstone, for example, wanted 'to make the two Houses sit in congress and vote together!!!'[37] Dilke preferred to leave the Upper House unreformed but to neutralise it by enhancing the powers of the Commons, though he recognised that certain restrictions upon its rights (such as that of legislative veto) might have to be introduced in the future.

On 21 October, in response to a complaint from the Queen, Gladstone asked Dilke to persuade Chamberlain to tone down his speeches. In conveying these sentiments to his friend, Dilke suggested that he declare in a letter that he was 'shocked to hear that such an interpretation as that of incitement to violence should be placed on words which were only a fair and obvious reply to Salisbury's monstrous violence'. As a postscript, he added: 'Of *course*, in any case, I make common cause.'[38] At a cabinet the next day, Chamberlain agreed to Dilke's suggestion but doubted if it would do much good. He duly despatched a public letter to a Birmingham constituent, Thorold Rogers, couched in Dilke's terms.

By late October no progress appeared to have been made towards averting a constitutional crisis. At the opening of the autumn session on 23 October, the government made clear its intention to push through the Franchise Bill, and confrontation with the Lords seemed unavoidable. The situation was further inflamed on 28 October when Randolph Churchill accused Chamberlain of provoking the Aston riots, which had broken out when Churchill had tried to address a Birmingham meeting. Later on the same day, Gladstone informed Dilke that Chamberlain's letter to Rogers had not 'come up to the mark', and asked him if anything more could be done. The Queen, he lamented, not only attacked Chamberlain 'but me through him, and says I pay a great deal too much attention to him'. Dilke forwarded the Prime Minister's letter to his friend with the note: 'It is clear that the Queen has written to him [Gladstone] a *serious* letter. Shall I say that *I* thought your letter to Rogers met the case, or what?' Chamberlain replied, 'Yes, I cannot & *will not* do more.'[39] A direct approach by the Prime Minister also failed. Following their interview, an implacable Chamberlain rushed into Dilke's office 'much worried & excited & broke out v. Mr G. "I *don't* like him, really. I *hate* him"'. The intermediary concluded his account of this episode with the classic understatement:

'Next day I warned Mr Gladstone that it would not take much to make a serious row.'[40]

The crisis was defused by conciliatory talks between the two parties. Several unofficial meetings had already taken place between the re-distribution committee and a group of Conservatives led by Sir Michael Hicks Beach, a former Irish Chief Secretary and later Chancellor of the Exchequer. Lord Carnarvon, on behalf of the Conservatives, now approached Gladstone with a view to making the Hicks Beach talks official. Gladstone demurred and suggested instead that they appoint a committee of their own to draw up a scheme. On 30 October Hicks Beach, acting in a purely personal capacity, proposed taking both seats from constituencies below 25,000 and one seat from those below 80,000. 'We've got a revolutionary scheme from Hicks Beach,' Dilke wrote to Grant Duff in Madras, 'wh. we wd. take if S[alisbur]y wd. support it!'[41] This went beyond the levels agreed by Dilke's cabinet committee, which he had persuaded only five days earlier to move from 10,000 to 15,000 for complete disfranchisement, still way below Hicks Beach's proposal. Nevertheless, Hartington was directed to begin talks with the Tories on the basis of Hicks Beach's unofficial scheme.

The lack of any coherent Tory plan for redistribution had bemused Dilke in his attempts to find a compromise. In early November he told Hamilton that he was willing to draw up a bill based on 'suggestions from the other side' but, unfortunately, there appeared to be no 'agreement among the Tories as to the general lines on which they wish us to proceed'.[42] The Tories were in fact slowly moving towards the view that the best way to neutralise the extension of the franchise and the challenge that this posed to their traditional county bases, was to go for single-member constituencies and the strict separation of urban and rural populations. This would mean a much more thoroughgoing reform than the Liberals had so far proposed, and one to which the Whigs, whose interests would be squeezed by such a scheme, would probably not be sympathetic.

A request by the Queen for a meeting of the two parties to discuss the situation, mooted on 31 October, was accepted by Salisbury four days later. On 7 November the cabinet appointed Hartington and Dilke as official plenipotentiaries in the negotiations. The conciliatory spirit was reflected in Dilke's speech on the Franchise Bill that same day. Any Redistribution Bill, he said, must satisfy both sides of the House.[43]

Progress was interrupted when a group of leading Tories, encouraged by an overwhelming by-election victory at South Warwickshire on 9 November, pressed once more for the Franchise Bill to be thrown out.

Dilke's role as mediator became especially critical at this time. He demonstrated consummate political skill in playing diverse interests off against each other. His objective was to come up with a scheme that would be radical enough for the Tory leaders and the left-wing Liberals, and at the same time acceptable to a cabinet dominated by Whigs and a conservative Prime Minister. His pragmatism is well-illustrated by his assertion in cabinet that the Redistribution Bill was not being constructed on 'tenable principles' but would be 'the best we can carry'.[44] Gladstone's letters to him were full of suggestions for keeping the scheme moderate. The only way to force his hand was to throw the Tories into the scale against him. Hence Dilke's seemingly ambiguous statement that he was inclined 'to compromise far more than I need, for the sake of getting a revolutionary Bill. I think', he added, 'there will be a *mutiny*'.[45] This strategy inevitably plunged him into deep water with those radicals opposed to any concession to Tory obstruction. Chamberlain was to remain bellicose throughout the negotiations, threatening resignation in the early stages. He did not like single-member seats or share Dilke's view that they would strengthen radicalism within the Liberal Party, but Dilke handled him with great tact and carried him along by his own commitment. His hold over the important radicals therefore enabled him to forestall any 'mutiny' and to confine objections to sections of the Liberal press. His role in these machinations was immeasurably strengthened by the fact that he was one of very few who fully understood the complexities of redistribution. The only politicians to match his grasp were Salisbury and Gladstone: the eventual settlement was to be a product of the 'politicking' of these three men.

For the time being, Dilke had to ensure that the Conservatives stuck to their radical guns. He saw Salisbury frequently in the summer and autumn of 1884 in connection with their work on the housing commission, and took the opportunity to show him his papers on redistribution. These included figures for the division of London and Lancashire where the Tories stood to gain by the carving out of residential single-member constituencies. Salisbury was at first lukewarm, and Dilke concluded that the division, harmful to the Liberal Party, could probably have been avoided: 'But, as I liked them myself, I fought the other way, against Mr Gladstone.'[46]

On 13 November Gladstone instructed Dilke to approach the negoti-ations with the Conservatives armed with the original, moderate re-distribution plan. Dilke agreed, though he privately believed that it would not be acceptable. At the same time he tried to ensure that it was not by encouraging the Conservatives to press for a more radical scheme. 'If they won't,' he told Hartington, 'Lefevre has an ingenious plan for putting fire under the bellies of the Lords, which I have told him to send to Mr Gladstone.'[47]

Lefevre's 'ingenious plan' was to make public the steps so far taken in the direction of compromise and thereby put the onus of responsibility for the continuing stalemate on the Tories and the Lords. Gladstone, who had been negotiating with Northcote in secret,[48] informed the cabinet on 15 November that the Lords would not part with the Franchise Bill, which was sent up to them on that day, until the Redistribution Bill was in their House, and so it was decided to issue a statement in both Houses on the lines of Lefevre's plan. At the same time Gladstone privately satisfied Salisbury as to the conditions upon which negotiations would proceed and this was sufficient to break the deadlock. The Tories met at the Carlton Club on 18 November and, according to Hamilton, '*Pax* was the *mot d'ordre*, much to the discomfiture of the hot-headed ones'.[49] The Lords agreed on the same day to pass the second reading of the Franchise Bill.

The next day Salisbury and Northcote, for the Conservatives, and Gladstone and Granville, for the Liberals, met to fix a date for negotiations. On 21 November Dilke continued his 'private conference' with the Tory leader at a meeting of the royal commission, where they agreed the composition of the boundary commission. A motion by Labouchere to reform the Lords was easily defeated that same day in the Commons. Dilke and Chamberlain had absented themselves before the vote was taken.[50] The following afternoon the historic meeting of the parties took place at 10 Downing Street, Salisbury, Northcote, Hartington and Dilke attending. According to the last, 'there never was so friendly & pleasant a meeting!'[51] Northcote and Hartington were largely bystanders. Salisbury had dropped many of his preconditions for a settlement and, Dilke informed Chamberlain, seemed really anxious that a bill should be passed. At the same time, Dilke had to pacify radical opinion in the country, reassuring Frank Hill of the *Daily News* that the compromise was not a 'surrender', and that they were likely now to get a larger redistribution scheme than Gladstone would have agreed to in any other way.[52]

No written agreement resulted from the Downing Street negotiations, but the foundations for a Redistribution Bill had been laid.[53] Certain important details were settled in the next few days. Salisbury was in favour of creating a number of urban constituencies by grouping small boroughs with small manufacturing towns. Dilke had at one time advocated a similar proposal but was now 'aghast' at the idea.[54] The possibility of a settlement was momentarily jeopardised. However, Salisbury was simply engaging here in the old political game of pressing for one thing in order to get something else,[55] and Dilke was willing to let him. The radical and the Tory had their own reasons for wanting to manoeuvre Gladstone into conceding an extensive scheme and they were quite prepared therefore to let each other gain negotiating victories which served this mutual purpose.

At a further meeting of the party leaders, on 26 November, it was decided that the population limit for the loss of one member should be raised to 50,000 and for both members to 20,000, and that the number of single-member constituencies in the counties should be vastly increased. Salisbury abandoned grouping in return for an agreement that the boundary commissioners would be instructed to separate, as far as possible and without creating constituencies of utterly eccentric shape, urban from rural areas. This procedure commended itself to the Tories in that it would create Conservative pockets in the boroughs and at the same time preserve landed interests in the counties. Sir Francis Sandford, a Tory, was to balance Sir John Lambert on this commission. The Conservatives suggested reducing Irish representation to 100 but backed down when they realised that the three seats to go would be Tory. Agreement on the single-member principle for boroughs would have to await cabinet approval.[56] After the meeting, Dilke told Chamberlain that he was somewhat pessimistic about the chances of immediate success: 'I think it very likely the Bill will be wrecked by the House at large, for the real Tories hate single member seats, & the County Tories hate single member seats in Counties. But we shall have Franchise, & get our own way in the next bill.' Dilke may, however, have been feigning pessimism in the knowledge that Chamberlain was not enamoured of the scheme. Certainly, and in the same letter, he attempted to sugar the pill with the bribe of an extra seat for Birmingham.[57]

There was dissatisfaction in cabinet with the provisional arrangements when it met to discuss them on 27 November. Childers, who disliked the 20,000 base for complete disfranchisement, threatened to resign, and Grosvenor (the Chief Whip who had been called in to the meeting) was 'most hostile'. Dilke argued that the extra seats that would be released would go to the large towns to '"sweeten" the division into wards wh. will be unpopular' and compensate the Tories for abandoning grouping. His manoeuvrings to secure the single-member system did not fool Hartington, who recognised that it would 'ruin the Whigs'. Chamberlain, despite his misgivings, had been won over by the offer of the extra seat and as he, Dilke and Gladstone were the only ones who really understood the complexities of the proposal, they carried the day. 'I was sent off from the Cabinet', Dilke afterwards related, 'to Lord Salisbury to tell him that we could agree. At three o'clock we had a further conference with the Conservative leaders, and came to an agreement on my base, Chamberlain, who was somewhat hostile, yielding to me; I going in and out to him, for he was at Downing Street in another room.' Gladstone, Dilke and Hartington were, according to Gladstone's daughter, 'like 3 boys out of school with a sort of devilish twinkle in their eyes'; and at tea, the Prime Minister was 'splitting and chuckling'.[58]

The agreement was drawn up and Dilke, acting as go-between, traversed the ground from Downing Street to Salisbury's house on Arlington Street four times on 28 November before the Tory leader's consent was finally given to the document, afterwards known as the 'Arlington Street Compact'. The adoption of single-member constituencies satisfied both Tories and radicals but not the Whigs, who feared, with good cause, that their power would be diminished by radical domination of the caucuses. One sop was offered to them at Gladstone's insistence in the form of the retention of a handful of two-member constituencies. The 15,000 level was also restored, largely because Dilke was unable in this instance to get the Tories to stick out for 20,000. On 1 December, the day that the Redistribution Bill was introduced into the Commons, Salisbury pronounced the arrangements 'quite satisfactory'.[59]

During the next few days a number of minor difficulties were smoothed over. Gladstone made a personal pledge to Salisbury that he would endeavour to safeguard the nine university seats. Sir Henry James pointed out that no provision had been made to prevent voters in large boroughs from voting in more than one division. This was put right on 2 December. A more serious matter was a complaint by Spencer about the appointment of the Irish boundary commissioners. Dilke had originally decided not to have a separate Irish commission, but had been persuaded to do so by Spencer. He had gone ahead without consulting Salisbury, who protested angrily to Spencer. The latter in turn upbraided Dilke for his lack of consultation. 'I had undoubtedly been wrong,' observed Dilke, 'and can only say that Spencer let me off cheaply.'[60]

This incident did little to soften Tory suspicions. The redistribution agreement had been born out of mistrust and political self-interest and these, rather than any spirit of bipartisan cooperation, were what now carried it forward. Northcote, in particular, distrusted Dilke. On 4 December he complained to Gladstone that Dilke had leaked details of the Arlington Street negotiations to Churchill. Dilke strenuously denied the allegation. Northcote, however, continued to regard Dilke as 'a slippery fellow', and grumbled next about the appointment of Donald Crawford to the Scottish Commission, partly because he was a distant relative of Dilke's, but more particularly because he believed that he would be overfavourable to Liberal interests.[61] All this did not augur well for the smooth passage of the bill, for it was likely that the two men would have to work closely together to steer it through a potentially hostile House.

By the end of the first week in December, the Franchise Bill had passed through the Lords and the Redistribution Bill through its preliminary stages in the Commons, following which parliament was adjourned until February. On 10 December Dilke defended single-member constituencies in a speech at Aylesbury. One of their advantages, he believed, was that they would enable working men to stand for parliament because they would be cheaper to contest.[62]

A week later he departed for a well-earned rest in the south of France, but he found relaxation difficult as his mind was preoccupied with the arrangements for conducting the bill through its committee stage. The compact with the Tories meant that there would be little scope for amendments. He was concerned that the effete Northcote would not be able to manage his own back-benchers, and he therefore wrote to Gladstone suggesting that he should be asked to nominate a stand in, otherwise they would be left to negotiate with Hicks Beach, 'who makes no secret of his hostility to the Bill & desire to wreck it'.[63] On 23 December he wrote to Hartington from Antibes:

> Mr G. sends me everything on Redistn. & expresses no opinions of his own. Salisbury & Northcote write to me only, and the whole thing is more & more in my hands. If I let things drift it is clear that I shall practically have sole charge of the Bill, for no one else will know anything about it. I don't shrink from this at all. It is work I like. But, as you will probably be called on to form an administration after the passing of the Bill, don't you think it wd. look well, & that our people, & the press, & the country wd. like it, if you were to take charge of the Bill?

Hartington was less than enthusiastic, but suggested that they discuss the matter on Dilke's return.[64] The latter stayed at Hardwick Hall from 10–12 January 1885, but little was accomplished because Hartington still fought shy of mastering the bill's details. Elsewhere, Dilke had remarked of the Whig leader that, 'with his stables and his wealth it was useless to expect him to do serious work'.[65]

Dilke was left to steer the bill through the Commons almost single-handed. The task was not an enviable one. He had always recognised that redistribution would be difficult to carry because it lay contrary to the interests of many MPs. The support of the rank-and-file Conservatives was by no means guaranteed. In reply to Dilke's letter from France, Gladstone had advised him to by-pass Northcote, who had 'little weight or influence', and deal directly with Salisbury whenever possible.[66] Moreover, the unity of the government was threatened at the start of the year by Chamberlain's 'Unauthorised Programme', and its very existence by the news of the fall of Khartoum. In February a vote of censure on its foreign policy failed by only fourteen votes. Both Gladstone and Dilke were determined to stay in office in order that the Liberals and not the Conservatives earned the kudos for carrying redistribution.[67]

The House went into committee on the bill on 19 February. The boundary commission had completed its work to the satisfaction of both parties, which helped to expedite business. Nonetheless, because the bill involved the interests of every MP, its passage was to be a lengthy and, for Dilke, an extremely heavy and tiring task. Despite his sympathy for amendments tabled by the radical wing of the Liberal Party – for example, for the abolition of the university seats – he had to ask the House to reject them as they contravened the Arlington Street Compact. He also had to admonish Northcote for failing to keep the Tory rank-and-file in line. Between 11 and 13 March they gave him a great deal of trouble. The question of grouping was resurrected, as was that of the anomalous retention of two-member boroughs. With regard to this last, Dilke had again to abjure his own natural sympathies and refuse the amendment. He and Northcote had anticipated difficulties regarding the increase in the size of the House to 670, and he skilfully defended the decision. Courtney resigned over the failure to incorporate into the bill the principle of proportional representation, but failed to muster backbench support for his stand, which was seen as threatening the whole franchise-redistribution package. The Conservatives caused some further trouble at the end of April by asking for Westminster to be divided into three and not four. Dilke gave way on this point. The Irish wanted better representation for Dublin, despite the fact, crucial a generation later, that the settlement left Ireland grossly overrepresented. But the greatest single opponent of the bill, according to Dilke, was Mr Wiggin, the blind MP for East Staffordshire, who 'addressed the House so often upon the question that they at last learnt to roar with laughter each time he rose'.[68]

At the end of the day, no substantive amendments were made to the bill. It had been little changed despite, or perhaps because of, the many individual interests involved, for Dilke was able to play them off against each other. Alternatively, he could plead *non possumus* and invoke the sanctity of the 'compact' whenever problems arose. *The Times* was fulsome in its praise of his handling of the measure, commending his 'tact, patience and courtesy' as well as his knowledge of its 'bewildering multiplicity of details'. Perhaps more important for Dilke's future prospects was the Prime Minister's estimation. Nothing, he told his private secretary, 'can be more masterful than Dilke's conduct of the Bill'.[69]

On 11 May it was sent up to the Lords. Dilke, meanwhile, was engaged in securing three Registration Bills for England and Wales, Ireland and Scotland. Although dependent upon the prior enactment of redistribution, their early preparation would expedite the compilation of up-to-date registers in readiness for an early general election.[70] The strain to which Dilke had been subjected in the past twelve months was now beginning to tell on him, and he contemplated escaping from office for a while. 'All *creative* energy has been driven out of me by the overwork,' he told Mrs Pattison, '& *that* I think will not come back.'[71] In declining an invitation to address the TUC, he told Broadhurst that he was looking forward to 'a complete rest after the end of the session'.[72]

By 15 June the bill was back in the Commons. In the previous week, the government had been defeated on the budget. The group of Tory malcontents known as the Fourth Party, whose members (Churchill, Gorst, Balfour and Drummond Wolff) were no longer on amicable terms, was temporarily reunited by the smell of blood and, supported against his own front bench by the irascible Hicks Beach, attempted to upset matters by moving the adjournment of the debate on the Lords' amendments until a new government had been formed. Dilke replied that the leaders of both parties were agreed in their response to the amendments and Northcote corroborated this.[73] The threat to the bill evaporated and, by the end of July, it was ready for the Queen's signature.

Despite declarations that he would have liked to have gone much further, Dilke had good reason to be satisfied with what he had achieved. In all, 142 seats had been redistributed. The great reduction in the disparity between the largest and smallest constituencies, the disappearance of many hitherto corrupt boroughs, and the increased representation for the large industrial towns and the metropolis (from twenty-two to fifty-nine seats), were important democratic advances. For the first time in English electoral history, the counties and boroughs were placed on an equal footing. The counties, under the new scheme, had a population of 12,506,000 with one MP to every 53,400, while the boroughs, with a population of 12,106,000, had one MP to every 53,600.[74] The disproportion between the largest and smallest constituencies prior to 1885 stood at 252 to 1. It was now reduced to 8 to 1.[75]

The change to single-member constituencies marked a dramatic new departure in British parliamentary history and introduced an electoral structure that has remained in place with little fundamental change ever since. There were only three exceptions to this – the six universities with nine seats; the twenty-four two-member boroughs, kept largely in deference to Gladstone; and the twenty-two boroughs created by grouping rural towns in Scotland and Wales. These were all removed in later legislation. The institution of the single-member system changed the pattern of politics. Electoral influence shifted for the first time ever from the agricultural south to the industrial north. Dilke had correctly calculated that single-member constituencies would put an end to Whig and radical electoral cooperation and would lead to the demise of the latter and the radicalisation of the Liberal Party. However, he and other Liberals do not appear to have anticipated just how advantageous the change would be for the Tories – or if they did, they were prepared to put party interest to one side.[76] While the number of landowners returned for county seats declined quite rapidly after 1885, there was a corresponding increase in the influence of the Conservatives in urban seats. The result was the emergence of 'Villa Toryism', the progress of the Conservative Party in the suburbs of the towns and in the county towns, and the increase in Liberal influence in the countryside – a process that coincided with the shift of middle-class voters to the Conservatives but which was magnified by the single-member system. Redistribution, albeit not alone, contributed to the ending of forty years of Liberal parliamentary hegemony and the beginning of twenty years of Conservative and Unionist dominance. At the same time, as a result of the instruction to the Boundary Commissioners to have regard to local interests, it created the compact mining constituencies from which the first working-class parliamentarians came, and prepared the way, therefore, for independent labour representation. The fate of the Liberal Party would be dependent to a large degree upon its capacity to adapt to this new political firmament.

Dilke found two reasons for particular satisfaction with the new arrangements. In the first place, the settlement had been achieved by agreement between the two parties: for someone who disliked 'party warfare' this coming together on a major constitutional issue was an important precedent. Secondly, redistribution laid the basis for further reforms and for the implementation, in a reformed parliament, of the radical programme. This lay in the future. While the Seats Bill had been making its way through the House, the Liberal administration had been beset by increasing difficulties and divisions which had paved the way for its disintegration.

Chapter 10

Things Fall Apart

At the start of 1885 the government was deeply divided. A developing crisis in Egypt and the Sudan threatened to overturn it. It managed to remain in office for a further six months partly because of the ineffectiveness of the Opposition and partly because both the Whigs and the radicals had their own reasons for wishing to retain and support Gladstone's leadership even as they were engaged in manoeuvres to secure the succession to him. In this power struggle, the radicals as a minority in the cabinet sought, as we have seen, to get their way by bluster, threats of resignation, calculated press-leaks and inflammatory speeches in the country. Their short-term aim was to push through franchise and redistribution as a prelude to achieving ascendancy in the Commons and the longer-term realisation of the other planks in the radical programme.

Despite the many threats of resignation, and not a little irritation on the part of the Whigs at the radical tactics, the administration as a whole had suffered remarkably few casualties. Lansdowne, a junior minister, Argyll and Forster had resigned over Irish issues; Bright over foreign policy; and Rosebery, Under-Secretary at the Home Office, out of petulance and ill-humour at not receiving a cabinet post. Dilke himself, in a brief moment of weariness, had contemplated taking the Speakership when it became vacant in 1883. Gladstone had been able to exploit the demonstrations of loyalty towards him that arose from the rivalries of the various pretenders by periodically hinting that his retirement was imminent. When, at the start of 1885, the Prime Minister's poor health made his retirement seem once again a very real possibility, it provided the context for several more weeks of political intrigue, the only result of which was to reaffirm his 'indispensability' for a little longer yet. Finally, a disastrous climax to the unfolding events in North Africa quite improbably gave the administration a new, if brief, lease of life, when one might reasonably have expected entirely the opposite outcome.

After Arabi's arrest in September 1882 there had been a temporary lull in the Egyptian crisis and preparations went ahead for the withdrawal of British troops. The process was interrupted by disturbances in the Sudan. Proto-nationalist rebels led by a religious reformer, Mohammed Ahmad, the self-styled Mahdi, were seeking to exploit the troubles in Egypt to gain Sudanese independence. The Egyptian government, despite discouragement from Britain, sent in an army under the command of a British officer, Colonel Hicks, to suppress the uprising. On 5 November 1883 Hick's Egyptian army was massacred by the Mahdists. The Sudan was not perceived as essential to the defence of Egypt and the Canal and it was decided, therefore, to evacuate the country. General Charles Gordon was appointed to supervise the operation.

Why Gordon was selected remains something of a puzzle. His fame rested upon a series of brilliant campaigns in China and Africa. But he disagreed with the government's policy of evacuation, possessed a reputation for unreliability and rivalled the Mahdi in his religious fanaticism. He seems to have been chosen by Granville,[1] who perhaps hoped that his popularity would rub off on a lack-lustre government. Dilke was initially opposed to sending anyone, but on 18 January 1884 he was summoned suddenly to a meeting at the War Office with Hartington, Granville, Northbrook and Gordon, who were already there when he arrived. According to Dilke, they instructed Gordon to go to Suakim to collect information and report on the situation in the Sudan. That night he set out on his fatal mission. The next day Dilke wrote to Granville expressing alarm at Gordon's parting hints to the newspapers that he was going to Khartoum. It seems that such licence may have been given to him by the other ministers prior to Dilke's arrival at the War Office.[2]

En route to Brindisi, Gordon telegraphed the government with a series of decrees which he intended to get the Khedive to issue, which would proclaim him Governor-General of the Sudan and authorise him to go to Khartoum. His independent action split the cabinet and led, over the next few months, to a series of confrontations on a range of issues: first over whether to send an expedition at all to relieve him; next, when that issue had been resolved affirmatively, over the size of the force to be sent; and, concurrently, over which route it should take.

Gladstone, from the moment that Gordon broke his orders, was for disavowing him, whereas Hartington, supported by Dilke and Chamberlain, favoured sending an expedition to bring the garrison out. Dilke believed that the government had been placed in an impossible situation by Gordon, and that no one, except Gordon himself, was responsible for what subsequently happened:

> I thought and still think that Gordon had lost his senses, as he had done on former critical occasions in his life; but the romantic element in his nature appealed to me, and, while I could not but admit that he had defied every instruction which had been given to him, I should have sent an expedition. to bring him out, altho' thinking it probable that when Wolseley reached him he would have refused to come.[3]

On 8 February, following the defeat of the Egyptian army at El Teb, the cabinet considered sending British troops to Suakim. Gladstone and Granville were opposed, and 'broke up the meeting sooner than agree'. Three days later, Granville changed sides and the deployment was agreed upon, the whole of the cabinet being against the Prime Minister. During February and March the government wavered as to whether to accede to Gordon's request for the appointment of Zebehr Pasha, a notorious slave-owner, as Governor of Khartoum. This time Gladstone was in favour, but again in a minority of one. When Gordon heard of the refusal, he telegraphed that he now intended to smash the Mahdi and requested British troops for the purpose. 'We were evidently dealing', Dilke observed, 'with a wild man under the influence of that climate of Central Africa which acts even upon the sanest men like strong drink.'[4]

On 14 February Dilke defended the government's Egyptian policy against a vote of censure. His speech strove to inspire a confidence which he himself lacked. It contained one interesting admission. Because Gordon was in the best position to judge the situation for himself, Dilke said, he had been asked by the government 'to draft his own instructions'.[5] The government had clearly been guilty of giving Gordon the impression that he had a free hand. At the same time, they were naturally angry when he refused to obey orders. It was from this mutual misunderstanding and conflict of authority that the tragedy of Khartoum was to ensue.

At a cabinet on 5 March, Chamberlain proposed that Dilke should be sent to Egypt to supervise operations; Hartington wished to go himself; but Granville, through jealousy according to Dilke, would have neither.[6] At the same cabinet it was decided to instruct the army under General Graham to attack the force of the rebel leader, Osman Digna. When Dilke heard twelve days later that a reward had been offered for the capture of Osman dead or alive, he wrote to Granville, Hartington and Northbrook to protest and to say that 'if a proclamation calculated to lead to Osman's murder in cold blood' had been issued, and was not publicly disavowed and withdrawn, he would resign.[7] The proclamation was withdrawn.

The deep despondency within the cabinet at this time was well summed up in a letter written by Dilke to Grant Duff on 26 March: 'Egypt looks black. Finance impossible; – Gordon shut up in a place where he can't be got at. No ray of light.'[8] Finance was impossible because Egypt had been presented with a bill of £4,500,000 for damages to the property of Europeans arising out of the Alexandria riots, which she could only settle by borrowing under terms agreed by the five European powers who constituted the Commission of Liquidation, and who had reasons of their own for obstructing a settlement.

Despite the disagreement over the need for an expedition to relieve Khartoum, Dilke and Hartington were already considering possible routes. Wolseley had advised them on the viability of the overland route from Suakim to Berber,[9] but Dilke favoured a naval expedition up the Nile on the grounds that 'the Admiralty were likely to do the thing better than the War Office'. For the time being, in the face of resolute opposition from Gladstone and Granville, the cabinet decided against any expedition, but Dilke noted in his diary that, 'It will *have* to be sent next autumn I believe',[10] that is, when the river was at its most navigable. Gordon had recently asserted that Khartoum had six months' provisions and Dilke believed, therefore, that an expedition sent at high Nile would be in time. During April he privately sounded ministers about an autumn expedition and, of those whose views he could ascertain, six were for (Hartington, Northbrook, Selborne, Derby, Chamberlain and himself) and five against (Gladstone, Granville, Harcourt, Kimberley and Dodson).[11]

On 13 May the Conservatives again sought to censure the government's Egytian policy. Dilke rose after midnight to wind up the debate. In an hour-long speech, he ridiculed proposals for early intervention. He afterwards observed that the debate was the best he had ever heard, not because of his own contribution but because of the general high quality of all the speeches. At its conclusion, the government's majority had shrunk to only twenty-eight. Many radical backbenchers were at odds with their more jingoistic cabinet brethren and, following another narrow vote a month later, Gladstone remarked sarcastically to Dilke, "'How splendid is the discipline of our party. Not a man but voted against us!'"[12]

During May Dilke circulated a memorandum proposing the neutralisation of Egypt which gained the support of ten ministers. Hartington dissented so fiercely that Gladstone declined to press the matter, and therefore the ten were overruled by the one. The question was to be taken up again later. On 24 May the cabinet discussed the desirability of making a statement in the Commons on the number of years British troops would remain in Egypt. Hartington and Northbrook suggested five or three years from January 1885, and Carlingford, supported by Dilke and Gladstone,

one year. Three years prevailed. In this way the cabinet, divided one way over the expedition, was sliced in yet another way over withdrawal.

Meanwhile, the Prime Minister was slowly coming round to the view that a small expedition, which could move quickly and with the least fuss, might be the best solution. This was in line with the opinion of Dilke, who canvassed the support of Northbrook and Hartington, but with little joy. The fact of the matter was, he told Gladstone on 4 June, that Hartington was determined 'on giving Wolseley his big job'. Little progress was made until 25 July when, for the first time, a large majority of the cabinet pressed for an expedition. Despite momentary resistance from Gladstone, Harcourt and Kimberley, it was finally agreed on 1 August to seek the necessary credit of £300,000.[13]

With the money in hand for an expedition, there remained the problem of the Egyptian debt. When the matter had first been raised in April, it had been decided to call a conference to change the arrangements by which Egypt could only borrow with the consent of the powers on the Commission of Liquidation. 'Is there anything else?' Chamberlain had asked as the meeting was on the point of breaking up. 'No', replied Gladstone. 'We have done our *Egyptian* business, & we are an *Egyptian* government.'[14]

France, in safeguarding the interests of her bondholders by refusing to acknowledge the debt, was largely responsible for the breakdown of the conference on Egyptian finances when it met in July. Faced with French obstruction, the cabinet decided on 2 August to send Northbrook, 'just a nice idiotic banker's clerk' according to Dilke,[15] to Egypt to try and find a solution. At this meeting, notes exchanged between Dilke and Chamberlain illustrated their exasperation at the way in which the cabinet conducted its business:

Dilke	We _always_ have 2 subjects
	A. Conference
	B. Gordon.
Chamberlain	Yes – subjects of equal importance. The first always taking up 2 or 3 hours & the 2nd 5 minutes at the fag end of the business.[16]

Hartington wanted to guarantee the whole Egyptian debt; Dilke and Chamberlain wished to declare Egypt bankrupt; Northbrook himself favoured redeeming the debt by loans at guaranteed minimum rates of interest. The wrangling continued for several days and was such that, at one meeting, Dilke noted that Northbrook, 'instead of sleeping (his usual practice at a Cabinet) on this occasion fainted'.[17]

When Northbrook reported in November, he proposed that Britain should take sole financial control and assist the bondholders with a guaranteed loan of £9,000,000. Dilke, however, argued in a memorandum of 19 November, that parliament would never agree to a scheme which imposed sacrifices upon the taxpayer for the sake of the bondholders. The cabinet divided eight for and six against: 'All the Lords on one side, curiously enough,' Dilke observed, 'and all the Sirs and Mr's on the other ....' Gladstone's propensity for winning on behalf of the minority this time worked for the commoners. At a cabinet on 2 December, when Northbrook's proposals were on the point of being adopted, he declared that 'he did not much care for himself, as he now intended to retire, but that had he been 25 years younger nothing would have induced him to consent. A loan he would not tolerate. Then there was a general veer round ....'[18]

The disagreement in the cabinet as to the future of Egypt, which lay at the root of the debate on Northbrook's proposals, continued into the new year. Chamberlain summed it up in a letter to Dilke on 3 January 1885 as '"Scuttle & Bankruptcy" against "Protectorate & Guarantee".' At that moment, the two radicals were contemplating resignation. Dilke had been deliberating whether to go out over the Princess Beatrice dowry question and Chamberlain, though reluctant to resign on this particular issue, was nonetheless prepared to go with him. The situation was suddenly changed by news that Gladstone was ill and the speculation, once more, that he would soon retire. A period of political manoeuvring ensued in anticipation of a possible Hartington administration. On 4 January Hartington and Harcourt discussed its likely composition. They agreed on Dilke as the putative Foreign Secretary, but could find no place for Chamberlain.[19] It has been suggested that Dilke may have been party to this intrigue to remove Gladstone, and that Chamberlain responded by launching his Unauthorised Campaign because no office had been identified for him in the proposed reconstruction: he was determined to assert himself and make it clear that any such reconstruction could only take place on his terms.[20] There is no evidence, however, that Dilke was plotting behind Chamberlain's back. Indeed, he told Grant Duff that he did not want the Foreign Office, despite pressure on him to take it if offered. He wrote immediately to Chamberlain proposing, if Gladstone went, that they should force their own terms upon Hartington, or at any rate strike some distinctively radical note.[21]

Chamberlain, once again wary of appearing anxious to usurp Gladstone's crown, and understandably alarmed at the prospect of being marginalised in a Hartington-led administration, told Dilke that they

1 Sir Charles Wentworth Dilke (1810-69). Sketch of Dilke's father as member of the International Exhibition Commission of 1862
Illustrated London News, 1 March 1862

2 Dilke as a child. Miniature by Fanny Corbaux

3 Charles Dilke in 1860 (*British Library*)

4 Dilke the frontiersman, San Francisco, 1866. Apart from a brief period in 1874, Dilke kept the beard acquired on his transcontinental journey for the rest of his life
(*British Library*)

5 Dilke at the time of his entry into the cabinet. Intriguingly, Virginia Crawford kept a
copy of this photograph until her death in 1948. It was dated in her hand 'Apr. 83'
(*British Library*)

6 Joseph Chamberlain (1836–1914). Portrait by Francis Holl. Commissioned by Dilke at a cost of 350 guineas, this portrait of his radical friend was completed, ironically, at Christmas 1885, just when their alliance was to be severely tested (*National Portrait Gallery*)

7 A meeting of the cabinet, 7 July 1883. Sketch by Chartran for *Vanity Fair*, 27 Nov. 1883. Gladstone is standing. Seated clockwise round the table from him are Carlingford, Childers, Northbrook, Spencer, Chamberlain, Dilke, Selborne, Harcourt, Hartington, Dodson, Kimberley, Derby and Granville (*Birmingham Library Services*)

8 W. E. Gladstone (1809–98). Portrait by John Everett Millais. (*National Portrait Gallery*)

9 Henry Labouchere (1831–1912). Portrait by Walery (*National Portrait Gallery*)

10 Katherine Sheil (first Lady Dilke) on the eve of her wedding (*British Library*)

11 Emilia Frances Pattison, *née* Strong (second Lady Dilke), September 1904. This was the last photograph of her, taken a month before she died

12 Dilke with his second wife in the 1890s (*British Library*)

13 Ashton Dilke (1850–83)
(*Churchill College, Cambridge*)

14 Mrs Robert Harrison (Helen Smith)
(*British Library*)

15 Mrs Ashton Dilke (Margaret
Maye Smith) (*British Library*)

16 Mrs Victor Stock (Fanny Grey)
(*British Library*)

17 Virginia Crawford (*née* Smith) at about the time of her marriage to Duncan Crawford and her affair with Captain Forster
(*British Library*)

18 Virginia Crawford in later life, when she was trying to put the scandal behind her
(*Churchill College, Cambridge*)

19 Mrs Eustace Smith. The mother of Virginia Crawford. She had been Dilke's mistress in 1868 and again in 1874–75.
(*Churchill College, Cambridge*)

20 Dilke at home in the country

21 Dilke and his son Wentie rowing on the Thames. From *Cosmopolitan*, June 1904 (*Manchester Central Library*)

AN ATHLETIC STATESMAN

Sir Charles Dilke, who is very generally considered to be the foremost authority on British colonial and foreign problems today, is, at sixty years of age, a famous athlete. He is an expert fencer and boxer, a noted horseman, pulls a strong oar and plays cricket. He is present at the House of Commons, notwithstanding, when Parliament is in session, from three o'clock in the afternoon until midnight.

The secret of Sir Charles's ability to crowd so much work into a day is that he does everything according to a system. Each hour is marked off in this system almost with the same exactness that the day is divided on the face of a clock. At 7:45 he rises. By 9:30 he has breakfasted, read the papers, and dictated his correspondence. At 10:15 he fences, and at 10:30 he rides. Luncheon and work keep him busy until 3, when he goes to the House of Commons and stays there until midnight. Saturday and Sunday afford departures from this routine, for on Saturday he makes it a rule to retire early, and he always goes out of town for Sunday.

must not arouse any possible suspicion that they had joined in an intrigue against Gladstone, or were party to 'dividing the Lion's skin'. He suggested that, if they resigned over Egypt, their terms for joining a Hartington administration should be, in addition to immediate withdrawal and bankruptcy, insistence on a conference to settle details for the neutralisation of Egypt. Dilke doubted whether Hartington would give way on bankruptcy and, in any case, thought that Egypt should not be at the centre of their dealings with the Whig leader. In the event, Hartington, Northbrook, Carlingford and Childers were overruled by the rest of the cabinet, which decided on 20 January, after a heated discussion that nearly broke up the government, to accept a French proposal for neutralisation and an international loan to Egypt guaranteed by all the powers.[22] This position was ratified by the London Convention in March, which in effect gave the European powers complete control of Egyptian finances and made any further attempts at Egyptian reform dependent on European cooperation.

In the meantime, Chamberlain had responded instantly to Dilke's promptings to him to strike a distinctively radical note by launching an acerbic and populist attack on the Whigs. The opening salvo in what came to be called the campaign for the Unauthorised Programme was delivered at Birmingham on 5 January. 'What ransom will property pay', demanded Chamberlain, 'for the security it enjoys?' This was followed by provocative speeches at Ipswich on 14 January and at Birmingham again on 29 January. It was not their content that caused alarm, most of the proposals having already appeared in the pages of the *Fortnightly Review*, so much as the language of class conflict in which they were cast. Gladstone warned Chamberlain that he was going too far in raising topics which had not yet been considered by the cabinet, and on 2 February the latter told Dilke that the alternative seemed to lie between resignation and a censure of his conduct. His preference was for the former but, he added, '(until I see you) I have no right to assume that you will accept a joint responsibility'.[23] Dilke immediately informed the Prime Minister that he made common cause with his Birmingham ally, privately believing that Gladstone would not accept Chamberlain's resignation.[24] At the same time, he tried to persuade Chamberlain to draw in his horns:

> The object of the Whigs is to force us to war with Mr G. who is strong, & not with Harty whom we shd. break. We therefore play into their hands by going *now* ....
> Mr G. does not I think *wish* yr. resignation. (He knows I shd. go too).

Later that same day, in a second letter, Dilke suggested that they should clarify their demands.[25] Both radicals recognised that the time had now arrived to lay down the terms upon which they consented to serve. To that end, a letter expressing their 'joint view of the situation' was drafted by Chamberlain and annotated by Dilke, and sent to the Prime Minister on 7 February. There were no 'rules' binding members in the 'liberty of personal opinions', they argued, especially in view of recent reforms and political developments 'which make the customs of the past no absolute guide for present practice'. The platform had become 'one of the most powerful & indispensable instruments of Government & any Ministry which neglected the opportunities afforded by it would speedily lose the confidence of the People'. The radicals regarded themselves as representing the majority of the people, and they had a 'public duty' to perform which exempted them from 'the narrow limits of a purely official programme':

> The legislative work of a Liberal Administration is always decided by the maximum which the Moderate section is ready to concede, and the minimum which the Advanced party will consent to accept. It is recommended to the constituents of the former as the least which it is imperative to grant; while it must be defended by the responsibilities of the latter as an instalment of the full measure of justice which may some day be hoped for.[26]

The letter was designed to encourage Gladstone to remain as Prime Minister by emphasising the constraints that a Whig-led administration would face. At the same time, by spelling out the terms upon which they consented to remain, it provided the radicals with principled grounds upon which to resign if they were compelled to do so. In the event, this particular domestic difficulty had already been overtaken by events in the Sudan. Nevertheless, it provided one more instance of the radicals' growing dissatisfaction and impatience with Whiggism and their determination to ensure that they were given the voice in government to which they believed their support in the country entitled them.

On 5 February news had reached London of the massacre at Khartoum, which had taken place ten days earlier. The crisis postponed for the time being the political manoeuvring. Since the late summer Dilke's diary had made only occasional references to the Sudan. On 17 September 1884 he had written, 'A telegram from Gordon which shews he's quite mad', but the next day he had noted almost apologetically that 'Some of the other telegrams sent from him at the same time are sane enough.'[27] The diary had made no reference to Wolseley's expedition, as it had slowly made its way up the Nile. Gordon's mission had been reported in the newspapers, often using telegrams from the general himself, which had built up the drama during the winter months and helped to heighten the reaction against Gladstone and the government when it culminated in tragedy. The disaster, however, had been totally unexpected. When the news arrived that Wolseley had entered the beleaguered city on 28 January 1885, two days too late to save its inhabitants, the only ministers in London were Dilke and Chamberlain. The rest had to hurry to town to a hastily summoned cabinet on 6 February.

Despite the popular outcry at Gordon's death, Dilke did not believe that the crisis would overturn the government though, he told Grant Duff, 'I rather wish it would, myself.'[28] In fact, the cabinet was now as much galvanised into action by the crisis as it had hitherto been paralysed by the run-up to it. Wolseley was instructed to crush the Mahdist revolt and steps were immediately initiated to restore order throughout the Sudan. Firm action came too late to rescue the government's reputation in the country, where its ability to conduct an effective imperial policy was henceforward seriously questioned.

In the longer term this apparent shortcoming was to be exploited by a Conservative Party that strove to wrap itself in the Union Flag. For the present, the Opposition, weakly led in the Commons by Stafford Northcote, was unable to capitalise on the government's unpopularity. On 28 February a vote of censure failed by fourteen votes. In the debate Dilke repeated his opinion that the expedition could not have left any earlier than it did.[29] The cabinet decided only on the casting-vote of the Prime Minister to continue in government. The radicals' first inclination had been to resign and Chamberlain had voted accordingly. Dilke, however, had swung round when he saw that Gladstone was determined to stay on. He had invested a great deal in the success of redistribution and wanted to see the bill safely through committee before going out.

Gladstone, meanwhile, had resorted to the usual face-saving act of a Prime Minister in difficulties, namely that of changing the faces. Shaw Lefevre had been brought in as Postmaster-General in November and was joined by Rosebery, appointed First Commissioner of Works, in February. What, Granville asked the latter, had he thought of his first cabinet? 'More numerous than the House of Lords', came the reply, 'and not quite so united.'[30]

Wolseley's success in repressing the Mahdist revolt was such that by April the cabinet was considering pulling him out. A war scare over Afghanistan, where an Afghan force was defeated by Russian troops at Penjdeh, revived the old bogey of the threat to India and provided the government with a justification to redeploy Wolseley's men. Dilke had been a member of the Central Asian Committee and had unsuccessfully urged the demarcation of the Afghan frontier. Following a Russian climbdown in the face of the British military preparations, it was now decided to press ahead with demarcation. In this way the limits of Russian expansion were fixed at a point where it did not threaten India. Dilke's attitude to the whole affair was summed up in a letter to Fitzmaurice: 'I'm as great a jingo in Central Asia as I am "scuttler" in South Africa...."[31]

The Gordon and Penjdeh crises broke at the same time and the government had to find some way to pay for them. A vote of credit of £11,000,000 to deal with both was raised in April. Childers proposed to recoup some of the costs in his budget. This was to be the first to break the psychological barrier of £100,000,000, though in terms of percentage of GNP it was in fact no greater than the budgets of twenty years earlier. Childers wanted to increase income tax from 5d. to 8d., and to raise indirect taxes on drink.

When these preliminary budget proposals were discussed in cabinet in April, Dilke, who was strongly opposed to an increase in the duty on beer, threatened to resign. He had always disliked the regressive nature of indirect taxes and had opposed the match tax in 1871 and the match and tobacco duties in 1882.[32] He thought it particularly unwise to introduce a tax that would bear heavily on the agricultural labourers in the run up to a general election in which many of them would be voting for the first time. With redistribution now virtually secure he was looking for an opportunity to go. The prospect of a radical government elected under the new arrangements was increasingly proving to be more appealing to him than persisting in the present one. He therefore produced a memorandum on the condition of the poorer classes in which he spelt out his objections.[33] He was persuaded to back down for the time being, partly by an appeal from Gladstone, who told him that 'any secession at this moment would be a blow to the Govt.', and partly by Chamberlain's reluctance to go out just when he was proposing a major new *démarche* on Irish policy.[34]

Precisely at the point when Egypt had momentarily gone quiet, Ireland had returned to centre stage and, like Egypt, split the cabinet in two. The Crimes Act of 1882 was due to expire in September and so placed the question of coercion and reform once more upon the political agenda. The radicals had consented to an interim land purchase measure of one year's duration and the land question remained, therefore, an unresolved issue. It had been agreed to only in the context of the need for local government reform which, in the grandiose plans for wholesale local democratisation that the radicals were now devising for the next parliament, would be shaped to encompass most of the pressing Irish issues. An alliance with Parnell's Irish Party on the basis of an agreed programme of self-government would strengthen the hands of the radicals in their struggle for control of the Liberal Party, and pave the way for the implementation of this and other parts of the radical programme after the next election. It was this context and these calculations that prompted Chamberlain to put forward a comprehensive measure of local self-government for Ireland, and one which he believed would be radical enough to quieten demands for outright independence. A Central Board for Ireland made up of representatives from elected county councils would be set up and given powers to deal with the non-imperial aspects of Irish government.

On 23 April Dilke saw Manning at the latter's request. He was told that the Irish bishops and Roman Catholic clergy would exert their influence to pacify Ireland and would denounce talk of total separation and an Irish parliament if the government would pass Chamberlain's central board scheme. A cabinet committee was set up to consider the plan. On 30 April Manning had an interview with Parnell, following which he recommended its prompt introduction. At the same time, Dilke learnt from Captain O'Shea that the Irish leader had agreed to support it. According to Dilke, O'Shea showed him 'a paper unsigned, which purported to be, & which, knowing the hand, I believe was Parnell's writing, somewhat to this effect'.[35] O'Shea was prepared to act as go-between in negotiations between the government and his wife's paramour, Parnell, but for reasons of his own, made it appear that Parnell was more favourable towards the central board than in fact he was. What O'Shea did not make clear to the radicals was Parnell's unshakeable commitment to Home Rule, towards which the central board could be no more than an interim arrangement. The negotiations were therefore destined to collapse, once Parnell's true position emerged.

At the same time, Manning was complaining to Dilke about the interference of George Errington, a Liberal MP, in the election of the archbishop of Dublin. Errington had proved a thorn in Dilke's flesh on a previous occasion. In 1881 the government had employed him in unofficial negotiations with the Vatican. When questioned in the House about this, Dilke, who had not been informed about the mission, had irritated Granville by refusing to give an answer. Now Spencer was seeking to use Errington to swing the Dublin election against Manning's candidate, Dr Walsh, and the cardinal expressed his 'great vexation' at this. Dilke and Chamberlain protested to Spencer, who replied simply that 'H.E. the Cardinal is wrong in his estimate of Dr Walsh'.[36]

When Chamberlain's scheme was put before the full cabinet on 9 May it was rejected, all the members of the Commons, except Hartington, supporting it and, with the solitary exception of Granville, all the peers once again on the other side. As the ministers were leaving, Gladstone turned to Dilke and said: 'Within six years, if it please God to spare their lives, they will be repenting in ashes.'[37] The day before, Dilke had prophesied in a letter to Grant Duff that the scheme would 'either pacify Ireland or break up the Govt.'.[38] With Gladstone threatening to resign, and the radicals truculent over renewing the Crimes Act, the latter now seemed the more likely.

The cabinet met the following week to discuss coercion and land purchase. Dilke, Chamberlain and Lefevre declared that both were out of the question without the central board.[39] Afterwards Harcourt told his son that he now dreaded 'each successive Cabinet which is sure to be ... more painful than the last ...'. Hartington was determined to disagee with his colleagues on every question, while Dilke and Chamberlain were 'preparing deliberately to break up the Govt ... and finally separate from the Whigs'.[40] Dilke wrote a very frank and despairing letter to Harcourt explaining why he was ready to resign. 'There is nothing in politics about which I care so much as the peace of Ireland', he began. With the rejection of the one-year limit on coercion and of Chamberlain's scheme:

> The last chance of the pacification of Ireland has been jeopardised, & my interest in being in office has been destroyed. Neither do I desire to return to office in the next Parliament, inasmuch as I now see ... no chance whatever that a Hartington–Chamberlain govt. can be formed, when Mr Gladstone retires as he says he will do. Chamberlain's scheme for Ireland would be to me essential, & the absence of it I fancy is equally essential with Hartington & perhaps yourself. I now feel, therefore, that I am working for nothing for which I care ... I who have lost all interest in the future of the govt., & all interest for some years to come in the future of the party, am asked to consent to a tax which I abhor when the need for it has gone. I most unwillingly yielded before when I thought that I was saving Chamberlain's great scheme from wreck. Now, I am saving nothing.[41]

Dilke's judgement was affected by overtiredness, partly brought on by his labours on the Seats Bill but also by the fact that he was receiving anonymous letters questioning the probity of his private life and hinting that a conspiracy was brewing against him. At moments of great stress the 'nervousness' that had been present in his childhood resurfaced. He was then capable of reacting emotionally or rashly to situations which in normal circumstances he would respond to in a more considered way. Ireland had never been as central to Dilke's politics as his letter to Harcourt suggested, but it provided one more rationalisation of his evident determination to break up the government in anticipation of a future radical administration.

On 20 May Gladstone announced in the House, without any further cabinet discussions, the government's intention to bring forward a land purchase bill. He had consulted Chamberlain and had gathered from him that he would not be opposed to another short-term measure. Dilke immediately resigned. He must undoubtedly have been irritated by Chamberlain's failure to pass on the details of his private dealings with Gladstone and may even have suspected that his friend was trying to steal a political march on him. More likely in explaining his precipitate behaviour was his sense that Chamberlain was far too willing to compromise, especially as an agreement on land purchase entailed an acceptance also of coercion with which it was linked. He had learnt only three days earlier, from a dinner conversation with Churchill, that the Conservatives would oppose coercion in a bid for the Irish vote: this knowledge would have increased the importance in his eyes of radical rectitude on the question. He saw opposition to coercion and support for the central board as something that radicals could unite behind, and therefore his action was not quite as 'extraordinarily inept' as Roy Jenkins maintained.[42] However, there is no doubt that his behaviour was less circumspect than usual and that the stress and mental tiredness he was suffering were responsible for the abrupt tone of his resignation and the manner in which he challenged the Prime Minister's authority in specifying the terms for its retraction.

Chamberlain was startled by his colleague's action but decided, along with an equally reluctant Lefevre, to go out with him. Gladstone was also taken aback. He complained to Chamberlain that he understood that the radicals had agreed to an interim measure which would provide funds for one year only, and that any renewal would be considered alongside Irish local government. Chamberlain was prepared to suspend his resignation, at least until the bill had been introduced. Dilke would only withdraw on condition that Gladstone circulated a memorandum explaining the radicals' position and pointing out that they had not consented to the reversal of the cabinet's decision. 'We differ so completely on the questions which will occupy the time of Parliament for the remainder of the session', he observed, 'that I feel that the Cabinet cannot hold together with advantage to the country.' Gladstone accepted Dilke's terms in what can only be described as a humiliating climbdown.[43]

Despite his doubts about making land purchase the issue, Chamberlain too recognised that the battle with the Whigs for control of the Liberal Party was approaching its climax. On 21 May Hamilton reported in his diary a conversation with him in which he had emphasised the pointlessness of continually postponing the 'evil day':

We must part company sooner or later with the Whigs. We are tired of conceding this & conceding that. We have a duty towards the radicals whom we represent. Moreover, is it fair to the electors that we should go on any longer concealing our differences? Have they not a right to know the truth? so that they may choose their leaders ... .[44]

Chamberlain had told Mrs Pattison much the same thing four days earlier. The 'struggle between us & the Whigs' could not be long postponed. The radicals would only join another administration on their own terms. If these were not accepted, they would remain out of office until they could lead 'a purely Radical administration'. 'We must win in the end', Chamberlain prophesied, 'but the contest will be a bitter one & may lead us farther than we contemplate at present.' Still, it would all be 'settled in the next few months ... The ultimate victory is to the strong & Providence *est toujours du côté des gros bataillons.*'[45] The radicals were therefore making no secret of the fact that they wanted to break up the government, were looking to success at the general election, and were cultivating Irish support with that end in view.

Dilke now urged that, as a *quid pro quo* for radical support for the Land Purchase Bill, the party should commit itself to introducing the central board scheme in 1886. Gladstone was amenable and suggested that Dilke raise the matter with Spencer during his visit to Ireland, where he was going on housing commission business on 22 May.[46] His discussions with Spencer only served to convince him that the Lord Lieutenant's position in Dublin was no longer tenable and that he should be allowed to resign. The 'Red Earl', as Spencer was nicknamed (on account of the colour of his hair not his politics), was persistently taunted for his failure to reprieve Myles Joyce, who had been hanged for the Maamtrasna murders despite testimonies to his innocence by the other conspirators. On 27 May Hartington arrived in Dublin to add his weight to the negotiations, but illness compelled him to take to his bed and he therefore contributed little of importance. Spencer was prepared to accept four separate elective boards for Ireland but not one, so the talks came to nothing. When, six months later, he went to the opposite extreme and supported Home Rule, Dilke was at a loss to account for his earlier stubbornness. He believed that if Spencer had yielded there would have been a fair chance of settling the Irish question in 1885.[47] Shortly before leaving Ireland Dilke light-heartedly summed up his sentiments in a letter to his friend Grant Duff: 'A pretty pass you Whigs have brought this country to. I really think we Radicals ought to be allowed to try. We certainly cd. not do it *worse.*'[48]

On 29 May Dilke crossed on the mail steamer to England. In a further and this time very candid letter to Grant Duff, he tried to explain his conduct during the past two months. Threats of resignation, he argued, were the only way that radicals could get their own way as long as they remained a minority in a Liberal government. Furthermore:

> Mr G. keeps on saying he is going at once. Therefore we have to count with Hartington. Now we doubt if we can form part of a Hartington govt., & we *certainly* can't do if we do not threaten, & impose our terms by threats. If we were to join a Hartington govt. without making our own terms we shd. be lost & the party paralysed. This is why *I* have been forcing the pace of late, with much help from Lefevre. Chamberlain is a little timid just now, in view of the elections & the fury of the Pall Mall. I cd. not drive Chamberlain out without his free consent, so I am rather tied.[49]

On 5 June Dilke reported his discussions with Spencer to the cabinet. He had suspended his resignation upon receiving a promise from Gladstone that the latter would support a compromise proposal of Lefevre's for introducing coercion by proclamation – that is, to make it dependent upon executive discretion. A letter from Spencer was read out protesting against this, as it would allow the radicals to veto any attempt at coercion. The meeting broke up without agreement being reached. A further cabinet on 8 June failed to break the deadlock. So ripe was the ministry for disintegration that, in spite of some last minute concessions by Spencer, it seized upon defeat on the budget that night as an excuse to be out.

Childers had tried to meet radical objections to his budget by limiting the beer increase to one year and thereafter replacing it with raised wine duties. The Chancellor was not the most astute of politicians, and the radicals had little time for him. On one occasion, in 1884, when he had put his sinking-fund proposals to the cabinet, Dilke had sneeringly remarked to Chamberlain that he had gone away 'quacking like an old duck that's been frightened by a dog'. 'I'd frighten him to some purpose if it weren't for Mr G.', Chamberlain had scoffed, '- & blow his whole d-d scheme out of the water.'[50] Now, in June 1885, far from appeasing his colleagues, Childers found the whole cabinet ranged against him. Three days before the Finance Bill was due to be debated in the House he tendered his resignation. But ministerial resignations had latterly become so commonplace – there had been no less than nine since the middle of April – that, unless they were persisted with, Gladstone appears to have felt it safe to ignore them.[51]

On 8 June Dilke criticised an Opposition amendment to tax tea instead of beer. He then proceeded to build the question into one of confidence in the government:

> This question cannot be considered as a mere question of change of Budget. It is a question of life and death; and if the right hon. Gentleman defeats us on this occasion he must try to form a Government on the policy he has placed before the country to-night.[52]

When the vote was taken in the early hours of 9 June, the government were in a minority of twelve. Later that day the cabinet decided to resign.

Dilke's part in the *débâcle* did not pass without comment. Henry Cowper, MP for Hertfordshire, told his sister-in-law, Lady Florence Herbert, wife of Dilke's old comrade Auberon Herbert, that:

> The Government are all delighted to be out, and most people, myself included, believe it to be a half trick... Some say it was Dilke when in his speech he nailed colors [*sic*] to the mast and said it was a matter of life and death who saw the opportunity of getting out of the prospective difficulty of his and Chamberlain [*sic*] leaving the Cabinet on Irish policy, and that simple old Gladstone fell into the trap and repeated the same thing more emphatically in his speech. The members of the Government are *indecently* delighted at being out of it, and don't seem to be aware of how inglorious a thing it is to step out of all the difficulties they have themselves created in this way.[53]

Following the rumpus in the cabinet over the budget on 5 June, Dilke had sent an apologetic but resigned note to Gladstone: 'I'm very sorry. I fear this looks like a break up.'[54] There is no doubt that he wanted to go. It is also the case that the rest of the cabinet and many backbenchers were unenthusiastic about continuing in office, although the Prime Minister himself does not appear to have anticipated defeat. The Finance Bill provided a convenient raft on which to escape. Seventy Liberals were unpaired and absent from the division lobby on 9 June. The government had simply given up.

An immediate dissolution was not possible because the new parliamentary registers had not yet been prepared. Salisbury was therefore asked to form a minority government which, after some delay, finally took office a fortnight later on 24 June. In the meantime, the radicals turned to plotting strategy for the coming elections. On the night following the adverse vote in parliament, Dilke spoke at the City Liberal Club where, in the political game of poker with the Whigs, he began by playing the Gladstonian card. His fulsome eulogy of Gladstone must have brought a wry smile to the old man's lips when he read it in the next day's newspapers. For it was essentially a challenge couched in sweet language. Dilke's sugared message was that the radicals would be content, indeed pleased, to follow Gladstone to victory at the general election, but that it would be a radical victory, and Gladstone must lead on radical principles.[55]

That same day Dilke told Chamberlain that it was essential that they should be consulted in the choice of the next Chief Whip, for it meant that 'a fair share of the party fund & of such patronage & honour as we may require shall go to our people, in place of going to Whigs who stay away'.[56] It was important also at this point to resolve any political disagreements that existed between them. They had differed over London government reform but that was a comparatively minor issue. On Egypt, Dilke had found Chamberlain to be 'rather in the clouds for a practical politician'.[57] More serious was the question of women's suffrage and, after broaching the subject with Chamberlain on 16 June, Dilke concluded that this was 'the only question of importance on which we differ, and the only question which seems likely ever to divide us'. They agreed to postpone the inevitable difference for as long as possible.[58] Curiously, Irish nationalism did not figure on Dilke's agenda of potential radical disagreements. It was certainly in his mind that day, for he wrote telling Grant Duff that he believed Home Rule would be 'tried too late, as all our remedies have been'.[59] However, their joint support for the central board scheme, which was still regarded by them both at this time as a sufficient measure of Home Rule, was enough to disguise the fundamental differences that were shortly to emerge.[60] Perhaps they chose not to look beyond it out of a sixth sense that to do so would reveal what neither of them was yet willing to acknowledge.

On 22 June Dilke announced that he and Chamberlain intended to visit Ireland with a view to assessing the viability of their wide-ranging plan of devolved local government. However, Manning, who was now confident of gaining concessions from the incoming Conservative government, told Dilke that he could not give him the letters of introduction to the Irish bishops which he had requested. He feared that they might conduct a 'Midlothian in Ireland'. 'How can I', he asked, 'be godfather to Hengist and Horsa?' Dilke assured him that their visit would be for the purpose of acquiring information and would be strictly private.[61] The planned visit was also attacked by *United Ireland*, while Parnell too appears not to have wanted it. It was evident that the Irish hoped to hold the political balance after the election and to extract thereby more than the radicals had been offering them. Any possibility of an alliance between the radicals and the Nationalists had disappeared. Chamberlain felt bitterly betrayed by Parnell and his alignment with the Tories, and hardened against further concessions to Irish nationalism.[62]

Just how lightly Dilke held to his eulogy of Gladstone became clear at the end of June when he had one last brush with him. The occasion was the conferment of a baronetcy upon Errington for his part in the Vatican negotiations. He had thought the whole affair improper from start to finish, and protested to Gladstone, but failed to gain the backing of his colleagues. 'Chn. & Lefevre think I went too fast & too far,' he told Mrs Pattison, 'so I must draw in my horns.' He was obliged to despatch a demeaning apology to Gladstone and to fall in with Chamberlain's pro-Gladstonianism:

I had understood from you that you did not wish Mr G. to lead at the next election, but from your letters & still more from Harcourt's I find that you have changed your mind as to this? As long, however, as he consults only Ld. G[ranville] & Grosvenor we must be slaves on many points to the Whigs & this ex-cave. If he wd. be himself Mr G. wd. be great indeed, but he seems almost as much in slavery as we are, & we are enslaved thro' him.[63]

Gladstone had decided to stand again at the election, and Chamberlain, always keener than Dilke to inherit Elijah's mantle for the radicals, had turned to courting the Grand Old Man once more.

By the end of June radical plans were taking shape. Gladstone would lead, with Dilke and Chamberlain as the crucial supports upon which he would depend. They would occupy major posts in the next Liberal government whose balance, they believed, would be tilted for the first time towards them and not the Whigs. They were convinced that, at seventy-five, Gladstone could not long remain at the helm. On 30 June Chamberlain wrote confidently to Dilke that the radicals had never held so strong a position in the country and that 'the whole atmosphere of the H. of C. will be changed after November ... A little patience & we shall secure all we have fought for.'[64]

That last day of June was a day for reflection and Dilke too, as he looked towards a promising future, was in contemplative mood:

It is in old age that power comes [he wrote to Mrs Pattison]. It is possible for an old man in English politics to exert enormous power without effort & with but little call upon his time, & no drain at all upon his health & vital force. The work of thirty or more years of political life goes in England to the building up of political reputation & position. During that period no power is exercised except by irregular means such as the use of threats of opposition. It is in old age only that power comes that can be used legitimately and peacefully by the once strong man.[65]

At that moment Dilke was being canvassed in the press as the likely next Liberal Foreign Secretary. It was widely recognised that no one else came near to possessing his knowledge of foreign affairs, and few had as many international contacts. He tried to reassure Granville, who was by this time increasingly senile and rather deaf, that he had no designs upon his office. '... Heaven forbid', he wrote, 'that I shd. ever occupy your room, in wh. I shd. feel as tho' unworthily trying to drive the horses of the sun!'[66] This was not simply a tactful attempt on Dilke's part to assuage Granville's jealousy. He had, on more than one occasion, repeated his belief that the Foreign Secretary should be a peer for as long as there was a House of Lords. There is no doubt, however, that he was in line for one of the major ministerial portfolios, and it is unlikely that he would have turned down the Foreign Office had it been pressed upon him.

His experience in office had done nothing to diminish his reputation for painstaking ability, while his handling of redistribution had greatly enhanced his stature. Chamberlain told Mrs Pattison that Dilke had 'deservedly gained universal praise for his management of the Seats Bill':

> Nothing could be better & his knowledge, courtesy & tact are in everyone's mouth. I have long since known that he would always do any work that fell to him in the best possible way but he has undoubtedly added to his expectations with others by the masterly manner in which he has carried through this difficult business.[67]

Tact was not a quality that Chamberlain could easily claim for himself. Heading the fight against Salisbury, the Aston riots, and the Unauthorised Programme may have made him popular in the country, but they did little for his standing in the hierarchy of the Liberal Party and damaged his chances of ever leading it. Hamilton was quick to point the contrast between the speeches of the two radicals. 'They are both pitched in the same key;' he observed, 'but while Chamberlain always manages to rub people up the wrong way, Dilke hardly ever treads upon people's corns.' Hamilton summed up Dilke's comparative advantages when he wrote in his diary of his 'greater personal popularity, his higher social position, his being more of a man of the world, his superior faculties of leading or influencing others'. Hence, he concluded, while there was 'more in Chamberlain's little finger than in the whole of Dilke', the latter would win 'the political race'.[68] Salisbury is reputed to have said that 'No one ever loved Joe', and the Marquess of Bath described him as 'thoroughly unprincipled and without scruples'.[69] When the two radicals were threatening to resign in November 1884, Derby observed that while Chamberlain 'is not much liked: Dilke on the contrary is popular'.[70] Following Dilke's fall, Chamberlain was said to have asked Labouchere what was being said about Dilke, to which Labouchere replied, 'Oh, they all say that they are sorry it was not you.'[71] Yet Dilke has been relegated by many historians to the role of Chamberlain's lieutenant. This is partly explicable in terms of his subsequent fall from grace. Some politicians conveniently 'forgot' him when they came to write their memoirs, or were churlish in view of the scandal. Chamberlain, with his demagoguery and flair for publicity, was much more difficult either to ignore or forget. His public *persona* made him therefore the more memorable of the two radicals and certainly the more feared. Moreover, it has to be said in mitigation of some of the harsher judgements of his character, that there was an element of snobbishness in them. The *nouveau riche* businessman, in spite of his fine dressing and the orchid in his button-hole, lacked a pedigree and was not regarded as a gentleman.[72]

If we are to believe Dilke's own testimony, Chamberlain recognised that his friend possessed the more respectable and presentable qualifications for party leadership, for he agreed in that fateful summer of 1885 that Dilke should be the leader when the radicals were finally victorious.[73] This is quite plausible. Dilke had been in parliament seven years longer than his friend and his reputation there stood higher. He had chaired meetings of the radical cabal when it met at Highbury in the early summer. He had, largely through his views on foreign policy, become less objectionable in the eyes of the Queen,[74] whereas Chamberlain, by his 'unauthorised speeches', had become more so. Above all, he had Gladstone's tacit blessing for the succession, his devout Anglicanism at this time giving him something of an advantage in this regard over the Unitarian Chamberlain.[75]

Looking back upon the members of Gladstone's ministry, T. P. O'Connor 'pronounced Dilke as the most successful'.[76] He had emerged from the government with a record of solid achievement in both foreign and domestic affairs, and he appeared to be on the threshold of the highest public office. On the eve of this fateful year, he had written an intimate letter to Mrs Pattison which the passage of time was about to render pungent with irony:

> Many Happy New Years to Hoya & [erased] besides this one, please, Mr God, but *this* one blessed above all other years, I mean *this coming* one of 1886 [*sic*]. Zz plays but Hoya knows how the tears of joy are rolling down his cheeks as he says and writes this solemn prayer.[77]

1885 was to be a year of destiny for Dilke, but not in the way he had prayed for or expected. His promising career was about to be shattered.

Chapter 11

A Personal Tragedy, 1885–86

With a lengthy apprenticeship and a solid reputation for administration behind him, and with speculation about Gladstone's imminent retirement circulating, Dilke's future had seemed set fair when he left office in June 1885. But within six weeks all that had changed. On Saturday 18 July he attended a Reform Club banquet held in his honour in recognition of his role in bringing redistribution to pass. On returning home, a note was awaiting him from Mrs Rogerson, an old friend and near neighbour, asking him to call on her on serious business. The next morning he learnt from her that Mrs Donald Crawford had confessed to her husband that she had committed adultery with him, and that consequently the husband was to file a petition for divorce naming him as the co-respondent.[1]

Dilke's immediate thought was to abandon political life forever and slip into the shadows. On the Monday he presided at the last meeting of the housing commission, when the Prince of Wales, no stranger to scandal himself, moved a warm vote of thanks on his behalf. Next, he called on the former Lord Advocate, J. B. Balfour, to see if he could persuade Crawford, who had been a secretary in his office prior to the fall of the government, to agree to a private investigation of the charges. That same day he wrote to Mrs Pattison: 'The only thing I can do in future is to devote myself to *you* and helping in your work. To that the remainder of my life must be dedicated.'[2] On Tuesday, boiling with rage, he confronted Mrs Crawford at the home of Mrs Ashton Dilke, her sister and his sister-in-law, where she was now staying, and tried to extract a written retraction from her. When this failed, and with the news that Crawford had refused a private investigation, he became resigned to his fate. On Thursday 23 July he wrote in his diary:

Left for the last time the House of Commons, in wh. I have attained some distinction. It is curious that only a week ago Chn. & I had agreed at his wish that I shd. be the future leader, & that only three days ago Mr G. had expressed the same wish. A sudden fall, indeed! Such a charge – even if disproved – which is not easy against perjured evidence picked up with care, is fatal to supreme usefulness in politics. In the case of a public man a charge is always believed by many, even tho' disproved, & I shd. be weighted by it throughout life. I prefer therefore to at once contemplate leaving public life for ever.

Scribbled in the margin alongside this passage are the words, 'Chn. overpersuaded Hoya [Mrs Pattison], & through her me, but he was wrong' – a comment which indicates that, with hindsight, Dilke believed his spontaneous decision to go was the right one.[3]

Encouraged by his closest friends he became more resolute and determined to fight. Mrs Crawford's purpose seemed momentarily shaken by this.[4] He put himself in the hands of Balfour, Henry James (the former Attorney-General) and Chamberlain, with whom he went to stay on 30 July. He remained at Highbury for much of that summer but returned to London for a few days at the beginning of August, when he visited the Commons. He also saw Cardinal Manning and told him 'everything'. In early September he attended the funeral of his great uncle in Chichester. The companionship of friends and the channelling of his abundant energy into physical activity helped to save him from mental breakdown. Chamberlain's son, Austen, who was only half Dilke's age, found during that summer that their guest was 'very tiring to entertain because he required two hours riding, two hours lawn tennis and some fencing daily'.[5] According to Austen, Dilke showed remarkable composure and revealed nothing of the turmoil that he must undoubtedly have been experiencing, but some evidence of morbidity could be seen in his decision at that moment to make his will.[6]

He was also distressed in case the news should prove to be a serious blow to Mrs Pattison, to whom he had become secretly engaged in the previous autumn and who was at that moment ill with typhoid in India. Mark Pattison had died in July 1884. Emilia had decided to spend the year's withdrawal from society, expected by Victorian convention, in Madras with her friends the Grant Duffs. She quickly dispelled Dilke's fears by immediately telegraphing the announcement of their forthcoming marriage to *The Times*, where it appeared on 18 August. In mid September Dilke travelled to Paris to meet her on her way home, and their wedding took place in St Luke's parish church, Chelsea, on 3 October, with Chamberlain as best man.[7] She brought to the marriage no mean dowry, having been left £50,000 by her late husband.[8]

Thereafter, Dilke began to pick up the broken threads of his political career. Three days after his wedding, he spoke at Chelsea in favour of local government and elective self-government for Ireland consistent with the integrity of the empire. A few days later he made a major speech on local government at Halifax. He held Chelsea, now a redrawn single-member constituency, by a narrow margin in the November general election, despite Tory successes throughout the metropolis. His political activities had so far revived that he was to be instrumental in goading Gladstone into declaring his conversion to Home Rule for Ireland. However, his direct part in the turmoil of events that followed this declaration was negligible, for Gladstone courteously but firmly refused to contemplate him for office when forming his third ministry in January 1886, in view of the impending trial.[9]

The case was heard on 12 February. It was a brief affair consisting mainly of Crawford's evidence of his wife's confession. Donald Crawford had married Virginia Smith on 27 July 1881. He was a former Fellow of Lincoln College, Oxford, and a lawyer with political aspirations. His job in the Lord Advocate's office had brought him into contact with many politicians, and he had, coincidentally, been working closely with Dilke during the winter of 1884–85 on the Redistribution Bill. Dilke, for his part, was doing what he could to secure Crawford a safe seat at the next general election.

Crawford told the court that he had received an anonymous note early in his marriage claiming that his wife was flirting with medical students at St George's Hospital, but with a postscript warning him to 'Beware of the member for Chelsea'. He had not taken it seriously and the letter had been thrown on the fire. In March 1885 he had received a second letter naming Dilke as the man who had ruined his wife. Once again he refused to believe the allegation and did nothing about it. He understood that Dilke had learnt about the letter from Mrs Rogerson, who had been told about it by his wife. A third letter in June informed Crawford that Virginia had been seen at the Hotel Métropole with a Captain Forster. When, on 17 July, he received a fourth anonymous note, he instantly confronted her with it. 'Fool', the note read, 'looking for the cuckoo when he has flown, having defiled your nest. You have been vilely deceived, but you dare not touch the real traitor.' Crawford, who had been having his wife watched by detectives (though he did not divulge this to the court), believed her paramour to be Henry Forster, the army captain referred to in the third note. When challenged with this suspicion, she categorically denied it. Her lover, she said, had been Sir Charles Dilke.

The affair had begun, according to Crawford's account of his wife's confession, shortly after their marriage, when Virginia was still only eighteen. Dilke had kissed her at a hotel where they were staying after their honeymoon. Adultery had not taken place until the following year and had continued intermittently, at various houses of assignation as well as at 76 Sloane Street, until the summer of 1884, when Dilke had finally tired of her. He had also made love to two of his servants, the sisters Sarah and Fanny Grey and, in what was the most sensational part of the confession, had introduced Fanny, who was much the same age as Virginia, into their bed. 'He taught me every French vice', she had told her husband. 'He used to say that I knew more than most women of thirty.'

The confession was nothing more than hearsay, but it was all that was needed under English law to secure Crawford his divorce. There was no requirement of 'proof' and, accordingly, no corroborating evidence whatsoever was produced to incriminate Dilke. Indeed, only two other witnesses were called, primarily to show that Mrs Crawford had spent two nights away from home in February 1883 during her husband's absence, and that they were not spent with one of her sisters as she had claimed at the time. Neither Dilke, on the counsel of his legal advisers, nor Mrs Crawford, who was not even present in court, went into the witness-box. In his summing up, Mr Justice Butt stressed that there was not 'the shadow of a case' against Dilke, and he awarded the latter his legal costs. At the same time, however, he granted Crawford his divorce.[10]

Legally sound but illogical, the decision was not allowed to rest there by the newspapers. Virginia Crawford had committed adultery with Dilke but he had not committed adultery with her. The contradiction was absurd. Dilke's failure to deny the charge under oath proved a monumental blunder. He had been advised not to go into the witness-box by Chamberlain, who was in court to lend moral support, and by his legal counsellors, Sir Henry James and Sir Charles Russell. James, who would have been Lord Chancellor but for his disapproval of Gladstone's Irish policy, was a close friend of Dilke's and acted as an unpaid adviser. By contrast, Russell, the newly-appointed Attorney-General, had been hired at considerable expense. They had arrived at their recommendation after discussing the matter during the lunch-time adjournment. Dilke had not been party to their deliberations and he accepted their advice unquestioningly. What appears to have weighed with them was partly the thinness of the evidence adduced in support of Mrs Crawford's allegations,[11] and partly the fear that Dilke's past would be raked over.

During the preparation of their brief, Dilke had told his lawyers of his past relations with the Smith family, including details of his two short adulterous affairs with Virginia Crawford's mother, Mrs Eustace Smith, during 1868 and 1874–75. Roy Jenkins regarded the decision to keep him out of the box to avoid possible disclosure of these affairs as an extraordinary indictment of his advisers' legal competence. For such evidence would have been inadmissable under the existing rules and any line of questioning leading in that direction would, on objection, have been ruled out of order.[12] However, they may have decided that, on balance, having Dilke face questions about his past behaviour that were overruled would be more damaging to his reputation than not having him face them at all. Far more serious was the gross misjudgement made by Russell when, in explaining their reasons to the court, he referred to the past 'indiscretions' that a man might be forced to reveal if put in the box. Dilke recorded in his diary that Russell had done this 'clumsily' and without his permission, which raises questions not just about Russell's judgement but about his part in the whole affair.

The newspapers soon latched on to Dilke's failure to testify under oath. He was made to appear to have sheltered behind government influence. Two of his advisers were ministers of the Crown. The whole business smelt of a cover up. He was therefore hounded by the press to prove his innocence before resuming public life.

The lead in this was taken by W. T. Stead, editor of the *Pall Mall Gazette*, who had only recently been released from prison following his famous 'Maiden Tribute' exposures of child prostitution. Morley, his predecessor at the *Gazette*, described Stead, with some justification, as 'for a season the most powerful journalist in the island'.[13] Rather aptly nicknamed 'Bed-Stead' by one of his colleagues, he was among the first to realise that a vicarious obsession with sex and scandal sold newspapers. He seized upon the Dilke case as the sensation of the day that would revive the flagging fortunes of the *Gazette*. Indeed, he became so obsessed with it (his notes occupy hundreds of pages of his letter-books) that he alienated many of his own friends. At first he posed as a sympathetic supporter of Dilke, anxious to afford him the opportunity definitively to clear his name before returning to active public life and thereby to honour a pledge which he had made to his constituents in August 1885.[14] Later, he became more virulently and persistently hostile. He disliked Dilke, but his motives in hounding him were more subterranean than this. For he was possessed by an intense hatred of Chamberlain. He told a friend that his morning exercises included six kicks forward with each foot 'and, to put vigour into them, I say with each kick, "That's for Joe!"'[15] The Crawford case gave Stead an excellent opportunity to get at Chamberlain through Dilke, and it was he who began the story that Chamberlain, in anticipation of the consequences, had advised Dilke against going into the witness-box. On one occasion he offered to whitewash Dilke if he would throw over Chamberlain. But the two friends remained unshaken, Chamberlain avowing that he was glad to share Dilke's burdens and 'act as a lightning conductor'.[16]

The newspaper campaign was the background to Dilke's decision to invoke the Queen's Proctor to reopen the case. The idea was floated by Chamberlain in a letter of 22 February and Dilke later noted that this was the first occasion it was suggested to him. However, as Jenkins points out, Stead had mooted the idea in the *Pall Mall Gazette* that same day and Dilke would undoubtedly have seen it there. Stead himself later claimed that Dilke had visited him after the first trial, and had asked him 'with tears in his eyes' how he could prove his innocence, and that he had advised him there and then to apply to the Queen's Proctor for a new trial.[17] Stead is not a reliable source but it does seem in this instance that the idea originated with him. Moreover, James believed that Dilke felt 'goaded' into a second trial by the need to prove his innocence to Lady Dilke.[18]

The Queen's Proctor, Sir Augustus Stephenson, was a legal representative of the Crown in the Probate and Divorce Division of the High Court. He could intervene on the Crown's behalf to prevent a decree *nisi* being made absolute if he could prove that facts had subsequently emerged to alter the original decision. In this particular case, the Queen's Proctor would have the extremely difficult task of proving a negative – that Mrs Crawford had *not* committed adultery with Dilke.

Nonetheless, Dilke was optimistic that such a course would be to his advantage. His solicitor had found Fanny, the former servant named in Mrs Crawford's confession, and had taken a favourable statement from her. Also, he had known for some time before the first trial of Mrs Crawford's affair with Forster, and he was now amassing evidence to prove it. Some of this appears to have come from Virginia's elder sister Helen, who was married to Robert Harrison, a stockbroker and brother of Dilke's former friend, the positivist philosopher Frederic Harrison. She had quarrelled with both Virginia and Maye and in September 1885 had made a secret approach to Dilke offering him information that would be to his advantage. The Dilke Papers refer to the approach in an oblique way, but it appears that she may have told him of the use made by Forster and Mrs Crawford of a brothel at 9 Hill Street (now Trevor Street).[19]

This accumulation of new evidence prompted Dilke to write confidently to Chamberlain on 1 June 1886 that: 'Things are now changing so fast that I do not believe that at this moment Crawford himself believes me guilty. It will still be a *hard* and a *long* fight, but I am not now hopeless of coming out right even within a few years.'[20] His confidence was misplaced.

Against the advice of many of his friends, including Manning who told him to let the bad publicity die a natural death, he grasped with almost blind desperation at the opportunity to clear his name afforded by the intervention of the Queen's Proctor. It is amazing, once again, that not one of the legal *glitterati* advising him alerted him to the potential pitfalls involved in this particular course of action. For, having been dismissed from the suit at the first trial, he was now no longer a party to it and could not therefore offer a defence. Belatedly, on 11 June, when the implications had dawned upon him, he applied to be reinstated, but was turned down and also failed on appeal. Nor could he take comfort from the decision of the Queen's Proctor to try the case before a special City of London jury of propertied men who, politically at the least, would be out of sympathy with an advanced radical. His earlier optimism understandably evaporated and he became filled with a deep sense of foreboding – that 'untruth would triumph' and that he would be prosecuted for perjury and imprisoned.[21]

The trial began on 16 July before Sir James Hannen, President of the Probate, Divorce and Admiralty Division of the High Court. Dilke's apprehensions were soon shown to have been well-founded. The president rejected an application from the counsel for the Queen's Proctor to call Mrs Crawford immediately. Consequently, Dilke gave evidence before her, and she was able to weave her story around his, altering details of her original confession where he had found plausible alibis. She proved a calm, collected and apparently truthful witness, while Dilke, uncharacteristically verbose and relying on his lacerated diaries and engagement books for verification of dates, appeared transparently guilty.

Nor was Dilke fortunate in the Queen's Proctor's choice of counsel. Sir Walter Phillimore was an able lawyer but not experienced in divorce-court practice. He was assisted by H. Bargrave Deane, and by Edward Marshall Hall, who went on to become one of the most celebrated advocates of the late Victorian age, but who had then only recently been called to the bar and played no part in the proceedings.[22] By contrast, Crawford's advocate, Henry Matthews, a Tory soon to enter politics, was a skilful exponent of the gruelling art of cross-examination.

Dilke was in the witness-box for the whole of the first day and for a brief period at the start of the second. Phillimore's examination of him was concerned with establishing details of his acquaintanceship with Virginia Crawford, his daily routine and particularly his whereabouts at the times of the alleged assignations. Mrs Crawford had named places and dates in her confession. She claimed that Dilke had seduced her at 65 Warren Street on 23 February 1882 and that she had slept at Sloane Street on the nights of 13 and 14 February 1883. With the aid of his engagement books, Dilke was able to give fairly precise details of his movements on those days and was particularly able to provide an alibi for the first of them. He firmly denied both the adultery with Mrs Crawford and the alleged affairs with his servants, Fanny and her sister Sarah Grey.

Matthews' cross-examination opened on a subtle note. What, he asked, did Dilke think Mrs Crawford's motives were in bringing accusations against him? Dilke suspected a conspiracy got up by the author of the anonymous letters in league with Mrs Crawford and Captain Forster. Why then, he asked, had he not gone into the witness-box at the first trial to confound the conspirators? Matthews attempted to establish that Dilke's moral character would not stand up to close examination. He got Dilke to admit his 'indiscretions' with Mrs Eustace Smith, evidence which should have been inadmissable but which was allowed to pass. A few moments earlier Hannen had interrupted the cross-examination to tell Dilke that he would be protected from any improper questions by his counsel. But, of course, Dilke was now only a private party to the case and was not represented in court. Hannen's remarkable ignorance on this point not only explains why *he* did not intervene to stop Matthews' questions, but is also symptomatic, by treating Dilke as if he were on trial, of his generally hostile manner towards him. Matthews emphasised Dilke's habit of snipping out parts of his diaries.[23] He intimated that Dilke had tried to bribe Mrs Crawford to arrange a quiet separation from her husband during his visit to her at Mrs Ashton Dilke's house in the week after her confession. And he endeavoured to blow holes in Dilke's alibis. Above all, he introduced new dates into the evidence, of assignations with Mrs Crawford on 5 and 6 May and 7 December 1882, for which Dilke was not prepared, and he tried to show that Dilke was far friendlier with Mrs Crawford than his replies to Phillimore had suggested. He concluded with an innuendo about Dilke's familiarity with French ways which was deliberately intended to hark back to Mrs Crawford's confession that he had taught her every French vice. When his cross-examination had finished things already looked black for Dilke.

Phillimore briefly re-examined after which Dilke finally left the witness-box. His ordeal had lasted in all five hours. The next two and a half days of the trial were spent in hearing twenty-three other witnesses called by Phillimore – servants, secretaries, family associates, lodgers at the alleged houses of assignation, and so on.

Phillimore was particularly anxious to provide an explanation for the absence from court at both hearings of Fanny Grey, whose implication in the scandal by Mrs Crawford made her a vital witness and whose absence was therefore remarkably convenient for one of the parties. Dilke's solicitor had obtained a signed affidavit from her in which she had expressed her reluctance to appear in court at the time of the first trial and in which she denied any impropriety with Dilke. Apart, however, from the speculative mileage that could be made from Fanny's disappearance once again, there was nothing whatsoever in the evidence of Dilke's employees to corroborate Mrs Crawford's allegations. This was not because of any misplaced loyalty, for some of them had been in his service for only a short time. Next a handwriting expert testified that the last anonymous letter received by Crawford, on 17 July 1885, had probably been written by Mrs Crawford herself in a disguised hand.

By far the most interesting of Phillimore's twenty-three witnesses was Mrs Rogerson, the family friend who had broken the news to Dilke of Mrs Crawford's confession. Christina Rogerson was the daughter of Duncan Stewart, a Liverpool merchant. She had become Dilke's neighbour in 1869 when the family had moved to 101 Sloane Street following her father's death. Her brother, Charles Stewart, was a solicitor who acted in the case for Donald Crawford. Her husband was an alcoholic. She was probably the mistress of Dilke's great uncle, and possibly of Dilke as well. She certainly told the novelist Henry James that she had been. When her husband died in 1884 it seems likely that she hoped to marry the man who then stood on the verge of the highest political office. There is no doubt that she played a pivotal role in the scandal, which it will be necessary to unravel later.

She told the court of how, in the summer of 1884, Mrs Crawford had come to her with the story of her adulterous affair with Dilke and, later, with details of her love-affairs with other men, including Forster. Following Mrs Crawford's confession to her husband in July 1885, Mrs Rogerson had tried to persuade Donald to agree to a quiet separation. Shortly, afterwards, however, she had lost her sanity and her mental instability had persisted for nine months. This disclosure conveniently protected her from further questioning, but it was not strictly true. There is interesting information about her behaviour in this period that the court never heard.

She had, indeed, suffered from mental illness in September 1885. She had recovered, however, during the autumn and early winter and had contrived to ingratiate herself with the new Lady Dilke. She had gone out of her way to befriend the latter. The Dilkes were invited to dine at her house on 17 November, on which occasion she had taken Lady Dilke to one side and reassured her that her husband had led a blameless life for the past five or six years. She was insistent, in the manner of one who doth protest too much, that she had had nothing to do with the accusations levelled against him.

Dilke had, in fact, suspected her of conspiring with Virginia Crawford following his engagement, but he had no proof. As Mrs Rogerson was friendly with the Crawfords, he perhaps hoped that she might provide some evidence that would exonerate him, or possibly intercede with Virginia to persuade her to retract. But Christina Rogerson was wholly unreliable. She was an unpredictable, neurotic and wickedly clever woman who took delight in stringing Dilke and his new wife along. She called on them several times in December, on one occasion claiming that she had broken with Mrs Crawford, on another bearing the draft of a letter which withdrew the charges against Dilke, which she believed she could get Virginia to sign in return for providing full evidence of her adultery with another man as a basis for her divorce. As she had lent her home as a place for Forster and Mrs Crawford to conduct their liaison, and as the latter had obviously confided in her, this might have seemed a plausible scheme to her deteriorating mind. Virginia, was most unlikely to have agreed to such a proposal; but it was perhaps enough to keep the Dilkes' hopes alive. Mrs Rogerson spent Christmas Day with them and they dined with her two days later. In January her mental health completely collapsed and she was unable to appear at the first trial.[24] By the time of the second trial, she had recovered sufficiently to give the partial evidence which, in confirming the details of Mrs Crawford's confession through her account of its prior disclosure to herself, lent some credence to it.

Further witnesses called by Phillimore verified the intensity of Virginia's relationship with Forster. Lady Dilke and her niece, Gertrude Tuckwell, confirmed Dilke's alibi for 6 May 1882. The former had met him at the London home of the Earles in the early afternoon, while the latter, who was staying with Mark Pattison, testified that the Crawfords had arrived in Oxford in the late afternoon in order to spend the weekend there – a coincidence worthy of a penny dreadful.[25]

When the counsel for the Queen's Proctor had finished presenting his side of the case, the outlook for Dilke looked bleak but not hopeless. He had not performed well but there had been no concrete evidence as yet to confirm Mrs Crawford's allegation. Moreover, the latter had now been exposed as a liar. She had lied to her husband about her relationship with Forster. Under skilful cross-examination, this young woman, still just twenty-three years old, might well break down. The outcome of the case would therefore rest upon how she handled herself in the witness-box.

Virginia Crawford was the daughter of a wealthy Tyneside ship-builder, Eustace Smith, who lived in a fine eighteenth-century mansion,

Gosforth House, near Newcastle. Its park later became the site of Newcastle race-course. Smith was elected MP for Tynemouth in 1868 and bought a house in Princes Gate, Kensington, for use during the parliamentary session. Virginia was born on 20 November 1862, the sixth of ten children.[26] Her mother, Martha, was ambitious, overbearing and possessed of a violent temper. Her daughters appear to have been educated at home by a strict Calvinist governess.[27] 'Nia', as she was known within the family, grew up to be pretty but not exactly beautiful, with blue eyes, brown hair and a *retroussé* nose. She had a very fine complexion but was slightly plump. 'Milk-maid looks' was the phrase she herself chose to sum up her appearance. It was in large part to escape from her mother that she had agreed, at the age of eighteen, to marry a man more than twice her age. One of her nieces recalled that she had already refused two proposals of marriage – one of them from the young Baden-Powell – and that when at first she rejected a third suitor, Donald Crawford, 'her mother shut her up in her bedroom on bread and water'.[28] The marriage was an unhappy one from the start.

A cursory knowledge of the scandal and its shocking revelations might give the impression that Virginia Crawford was a shallow, two-dimensional character. It is important to review her life in order to demonstrate that this was emphatically not the case. She was an intelligent and shrewd woman, a talented linguist, with a keen interest in art and art history. She was also possessed of a strong social conscience, and she had worked in the poor settlements of London's East End prior to the scandal. But it was only afterwards that her obvious talents blossomed. She was employed for a while by Stead on the *Pall Mall Gazette*, where she displayed an undoubted literary ability. In 1888 she began to correspond with Canon H. P. Liddon, the Dean of St Paul's, on questions of faith and morality.[29] At the same time, she was developing a close affinity with Cardinal Manning and his blend of 'religious socialism'. In consequence, she was received into the Roman Catholic Church on 4 February 1889 by Father Robert Butler of St Charles' College, Bayswater.

The rest of her long life was devoted to social, political and literary work. For a time she ran a home for unmarried women. In 1903 she entered a convent at Mill Hill with a view to becoming a nun, but left after only a few months.[30] She afterwards became extremely active politically. She joined the Labour Party, and served for fourteen years after the First World War as Labour councillor for Marylebone.

From 1895 until his death in 1933 she was employed in literary research by George Moore. She also produced a fair number of publications of her own. In addition to *Studies in Foreign Literature*, which displayed an informed familiarity with contemporary European literature, and many journal articles, she wrote political and religious pamphlets, several of which revealed her passionate opposition to the rise of fascism, and which led to her being placed on a black-list by Mussolini's government.[31] She was a member of St Joan's Alliance and its delegate to the International Woman Suffrage Alliance in Berlin in 1929. She helped found the Catholic Social Guild and, in her seventies, chaired the People and Freedom Group, an organisation which promoted peace in Spain during the Civil War and which included such luminaries as Wickham Steed, G. P. Gooch and Harold Nicolson. She wrote papers which advanced a Catholic Democratic form of corporatism as an alternative to fascism and socialism.[32] Her last book, on Frederic Ozanam, was written when she was eighty. She died in a nursing home on 19 October 1948, one month short of her eighty-sixth birthday, by which date the affairs of her youth had become a distant memory.[33] The details of her life make it difficult to believe that this was the same woman who, in July 1886, stood at the centre of one of the most notorious scandals of the Victorian age.

In his questions to Mrs Crawford, Matthews prompted her to elaborate upon her relationship with Dilke. This she did with calm and assured ease, embellishing her evidence with convincing details, weaving into it points derived from Dilke's testimony that lent verisimilitude to her own, and introducing further meetings, at 3 Sydney Place, the Crawfords' London lodgings in 1882, at 27 Young Street, their house for the 1883 season, and at Sloane Street. She confidently described the interior of Dilke's bedroom and regaled the packed court with details of the occasion in the spring of 1884 when Fanny had joined them in bed. She had resisted this arrangement for some time but it had ultimately been forced upon her by Dilke's insistence. In this way she presented herself to the twelve upright jurymen as the submissive, if not entirely innocent, partner, forced against her will into unholy activities by a sexual monster. They had no way of knowing that she was, as we shall see, no stranger to the practice of sharing her lover in this way. The affair had ended, she said, in the autumn of 1884.

Her evidence differed materially from that given in her original confession to her husband. In view of Dilke's explanation of his movements on 23 February 1882, she changed the time of their liaison from afternoon to morning. The two nights spent at Sloane Street were 7 December 1882 and 13 February 1883, not the two consecutive nights in February 1883 alluded to by her husband who, she claimed, had made a mistake in his recollection of her confession. She also now testified that it was she who had ended the affair after discussing it with Mrs Rogerson and acting upon her advice, whereas earlier she had told her husband that Dilke had grown tired of her.

Phillimore, surprisingly, failed to capitalise upon these changes. When he pointed out in his cross-examination that her maid had sworn at the first trial that her mistress had been away on two consecutive nights in February, she replied that she supposed that this was what she had been told to say. Incredibly, Phillimore did not follow up this admission. He did succeed, however, in getting her to admit her adultery with Forster from 1884. He also questioned her about initials pencilled in her diary, but failed to press her upon her explanation that whereas 'F. W.' and 'R. C. P.' (Frederick Warner and Robert Priestley, the aforementioned students at St George's Hospital) probably indicated that they had come to tea, the entry 'C. W. D.' for 23 February 1882 had, according to her replies to Matthews, indicated an assignation. She further claimed that Dilke had told her he had four other mistresses: Mrs Rogerson, Martha Smith (her mother), and the two servants Fanny and Sarah Grey. She believed that Dilke had asked Mrs Rogerson to marry him in the spring of 1885, but that she had refused. (That Dilke should have done such a thing when engaged to Mrs Pattison is highly improbable, though it is not at all unlikely that the unstable Mrs Rogerson should have said as much to Mrs Crawford as, indeed, she did to Henry James.) Mrs Crawford was also of the opinion that the anonymous letters had been written by her mother. Finally, Phillimore tried to suggest reasons why she should have invented the plot – that it was to cover up her affair with Forster, and that Dilke was chosen because she thought Crawford would not dare to proceed against such a prominent figure.

Matthews then briefly re-examined his witness. He got her to tell the court that her first meeting with Forster had been at a ball in February 1884 – an attempt to demonstrate that the new relationship was only emerging as the old one with Dilke began to fade. At this stage the jury asked her to draw a plan of the bedroom in Warren Street, which she did with apparent ease.

Among the remaining witnesses called by Matthews were Crawford, who contributed little of importance, and Forster, who introduced into the story for the first time the brothel at 9 Hill Street where, he admitted, he had met with Mrs Crawford. Above all, there was the evidence of Mrs Ashton Dilke, who was in the unenviable position of being both Mrs Crawford's sister and the widow of Dilke's brother. Maye Dilke was an enigmatic character and her role in the scandal, like that of Mrs Rogerson's, merits special attention. Dilke had grown to like Maye very much after her marriage to his brother in 1876. He had made a gift to her of a brougham identical to his own, and had become joint guardian of her three children after Ashton's death in 1883. Like Mrs Rogerson, she remained on friendly terms with Dilke after her sister's confession, and congratulated him on his marriage. According to Lady Dilke, Maye called on her on 9 December 1885. When asked whether her sister was prepared to back down, Maye had replied that it was important that Virginia obtain her divorce for, if the proceedings failed now, two other suits would immediately be commenced against her. (Presumably because, as it later transpired, Donald Crawford was extremely anxious to obtain a divorce in order to remarry and perhaps also to distance himself, as a prospective MP, from this unsavoury business. Hence, the employment of detectives to watch his wife.) When Lady Dilke then asked if she was prepared to screen her sister at the expense of an innocent man, she had replied with cynical laughter, 'Oh! Innocent people can take care of themselves.' Thereafter, Lady Dilke cut Maye, who now took the side of her sister against that of her brother-in-law and the guardian of her children. 'I cannot', she wrote, 'sacrifice the truth even to their interests.'[34]

In her evidence to the court, she confirmed Matthews' earlier intimation that Dilke had tried to bribe Virginia to retract her confession. However, she also testified that servants had been interchanged between Dilke's household and her own, thus providing a possible source of information for Mrs Crawford. She admitted that she had remained on friendly terms with Dilke after her sister's confession but claimed that other information had later come to light that made her still more convinced of its truth. Historians have usually placed great stress upon the absence of Fanny and the general plausibility of the young Virginia Crawford as the telling factors damaging to Dilke's case. But there is no doubt that Maye Dilke's testimony weighed heavily with the jury in convincing them of his guilt. For here was a woman prepared to sacrifice the undoubted advantages that her relationship to Dilke brought her for no obvious gain beyond satisfying sisterly solidarity.[35]

Equally damaging at this particular stage in the proceedings was the evidence provided by Mr and Mrs Hillier and their daughter, lodgers from 1882 to 1884 at 65 Warren Street, a house kept by a pensioned servant of Dilke's, Mrs Anna Dessouslavy. They claimed that a man and woman had visited the house frequently, and that man they now identified as Sir Charles Dilke. However, the lady they had seen accompanying him was not Virginia Crawford but a fair-haired woman aged about twenty-eight. What the jury made of this is not known. They may, of course, have regarded it as further evidence of Dilke's sexual promiscuity.

Finally, Matthews attempted to contradict the claim made by

Phillimore's witness that the last anonymous letter had been written by Mrs Crawford herself. According to his handwriting expert, the last two letters had, in fact, been written by Mrs Rogerson. Mrs Rogerson's brother and son-in-law both contributed their belief that she had been the author of at least one of the letters.

The trial had clearly gone disastrously for Dilke. Matthews, in his closing address, reminded the jury that the Queen's Proctor had to prove a negative – namely, that Dilke had not committed adultery. In his opinion he had not done so. Phillimore, for his part, reviewed the evidence in an attempt to demonstrate that nothing had been proved against Dilke. But Hannen's unfavourable summing-up reflected the way the trial had gone against him. It took the jury only fifteen minutes to decide, on 23 July 1886, that the Queen's Proctor had not proved his case. The decision in the first trial was left to stand: Dilke had *not* been found guilty of adultery, indeed he had not been on trial – but his career was ruined.

On returning home from the court, he immediately drafted a farewell address to the electors of Chelsea in which he proclaimed his innocence while recognising that he must perforce accept the verdict. It appeared in the newspapers the following morning. If any doubt still lingered as to Dilke's political future, it was quickly dispelled by the hostile press comment on the outcome of the trial. The Queen, who was delighted that the republican had at last got his come-uppance, tried to get him removed from the Privy Council. The outgoing Gladstone administration was happy to leave this delicate matter to Salisbury's new government, and in the event nothing was done.[36] Dilke for a while became the object of popular ridicule, the butt of music hall songs and jokes,[37] and he was ostracised by many of his own social circle. More seriously, he faced the threat of a possible prosecution for perjury, and was advised by Chamberlain and others to flee the country, a course which he defiantly refused to take. In the event no charges were initiated.[38] Having satisfied himself on that score, he took his wife to Royat in France so that she could convalesce after a bout of rheumatism, and they stayed there from mid August to mid September. After a brief return to England, the Dilkes were once again in France, spending a month in Paris before Christmas.

A number of sympathisers subsequently collected around Dilke and formed the Chesson Committee for the purpose of unearthing new evidence to prove his innocence. It was named after F. W. Chesson, one of Dilke's former Chelsea constituents and a colleague in the Aborigines Protection Society; it also included an old Cambridge friend, D. F. Steavenson, and a minor official from his days at the Local Government Board, Howel Thomas. It was joined by three others – Clarence Smith, a former sheriff of the City of London, W. A. McArthur, a Liberal MP, and Malcolm MacColl, a canon of Ripon – who were not particularly close friends of Dilke's but who were interested in getting at the truth. The mass of new information they produced resides in several large volumes of papers in the British Library not generally made available until 1955, though the substance of their findings was published in a pamphlet of 1891 which helped to clear the way for Dilke's return to politics.

The committee turned up several interesting facts. They found that the affair between Mrs Crawford and Captain Forster had begun long before 1884, possibly as early as 1881, though the weight of the evidence points to its commencement in 1882, when the pair began regularly to frequent the brothel at 9 Hill Street. Moreover, salacious details of Helen Harrison's involvement in a triangular relationship with Virginia Crawford and Forster were assembled by the committee.[39] There was strong circumstantial, but not conclusive, evidence that the two sisters had several other paramours in common, including Frederick Warner and Robert Priestley, before the latter's engagement in 1884 to their younger sister, Ida. These dalliances *à trois* may have inspired Mrs Crawford's astonishing and damning three-in-a-bed story. The committee also found evidence to show that Mrs Crawford had spent the night of 13 February 1883, not with Dilke as she had alleged, but with Forster at his lodging-house at 32 Earls Court Gardens. Indeed, the committee believed that she contracted syphilis from Forster who, according to Dilke, eventually died of the illness, and it may have spurred her in her desire to get a divorce as quickly as possible. Doubt was also cast upon the use of 65 Warren Street as a place of assignation. Mrs Crawford's drawing of its interior was shown to be wrong in almost every detail (another remarkable fact overlooked by the court), while the Hilliers subsequently proved less certain about the identity of the man they had seen entering the house. Lastly, the committee collected signed deposits from many of Dilke's servants testifying to the virtual impossibility of his conducting a clandestine relationship at Sloane Street without their knowledge.

Of these statements that of Fanny, whose absence from both trials had been extremely damaging to Dilke, was the most intriguing. It was suggested at the time that Dilke had been responsible for her disappearance and had paid to keep her away. Prior to the first trial, Crawford's detectives had found her and had pressured her to give evidence. She had then gone to Dilke's solicitor, Mr Humbert, who had arranged for her to stay on a farm in the village of Stebbing in Essex. In November 1885 she had married Victor George Stock and they had left Stebbing and could not be found at the time of the first trial. They resurfaced in April 1886 when Humbert took the statement from Fanny denying any impropriety with Dilke, which had been forwarded to the Queen's Proctor. She then disappeared again. She had refused to reveal her whereabouts between March 1883 and July 1884 which, she said, had nothing to do with the case. She was tracked down again in early 1887 when she gave a false account of where she had been during these crucial months. It subsequently transpired that she had been in lodgings at the home of a Mrs Anne Thorpe at 14 Grafton Street, London. Mrs Thorpe stated that there had been nothing untoward in her behaviour during that period. When questioned by the investigators again in 1890, Fanny admitted that she had lied in 1887, and now made a sworn declaration that the room she had taken in Grafton Street had been rented on her behalf by an artist to whom she had then been engaged. She refused to divulge further details of this relationship, but repeated her denial of any involvement with either Dilke or Mrs Crawford.

The evidence assembled by the Chesson Committee leaves no doubt that the divorce court had been misled and had based its verdict upon false information. That Mrs Crawford wove a net of fabrications in which Dilke became inextricably enmeshed is beyond dispute. It is quite remarkable that she was unable to produce any evidence that could be clearly substantiated of an affair which reputedly lasted for two years. Yet this is not to exonerate Dilke. The baffling question still remains: was he guilty or was he the victim of a conspiracy?

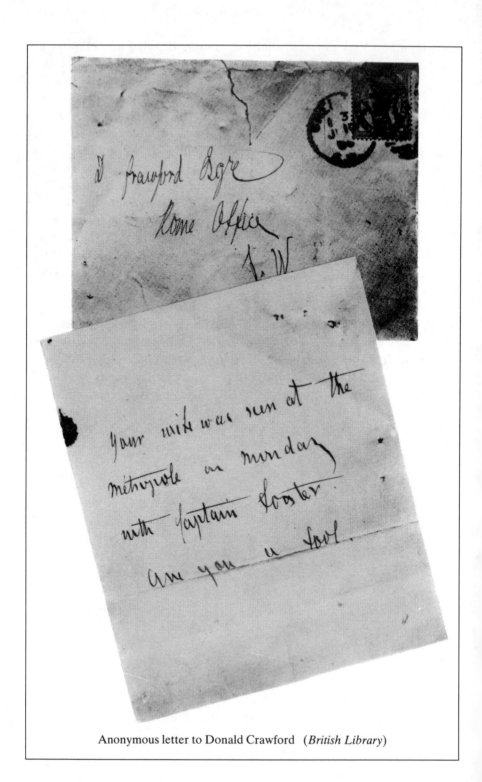

Anonymous letter to Donald Crawford (*British Library*)

Chapter 12

Of Conjectures and Conspiracies

Historians who have studied the divorce case in any depth have concluded that Dilke was in all probability innocent of any adulterous relationship with Mrs Crawford.[1] They have therefore been left wondering why she chose him as her victim. Their accounts at this point inevitably enter the realms of speculation.

In the most complete review of the whole affair, Roy Jenkins conjectured that Virginia Crawford may have been motivated as the result of a chance affair with Dilke *before* her marriage.[2] But this seems unlikely. She had returned from finishing school in Lausanne at the start of the 1880 season for her 'coming out', and would have been strictly chaperoned until her marriage the following summer. Moreover, if such an affair had taken place, why had Virginia not mentioned it, the one truthful event in the whole litany of imputations against Dilke's character?

The novelist and historian Betty Askwith believed that Fanny was the key to the mystery. Dilke had kept her unavailable for the trial because, though he had not had an affair with Mrs Crawford, the young servant girl was probably his mistress during that period from March 1883 to July 1884 about which she had been so tight-lipped. When the affair had ended, Dilke had found her a position with Mrs Dessouslavy at Warren Street.[3] The difficulty with this surmise is that Dilke allowed his supporters to track down Fanny and question her; and that Mrs Crawford, if she was not intimate with Dilke herself, must have been either incredibly lucky to have fixed upon Fanny or have been given information about Dilke's sexual relations by someone else (her mother or Mrs Rogerson?) who was. Above all, capable as Fanny was of lying, she never produced anything to incriminate Dilke.

Sir Shane Leslie, the biographer of Manning, was convinced of Dilke's innocence. On various occasions he promised to produce proof to that effect. He had interviewed Dilke's two private secretaries, J. E. C. Bodley (1881–86) and H. K. Hudson (who did not, however, join his staff until 1887), who were both of the opinion that household arrangements at Sloane Street made it impossible for their employer to conduct a clandestine relationship there. He never produced his proof, but he wrote a number of articles which took Dilke's side. According to Leslie, Dilke was the victim of a conspiracy engineered by Mrs Eustace Smith, a woman twice scorned by Dilke and therefore doubly determined to out-fury Hell itself in her determination to gain revenge upon him. She was behind the anonymous letters and, in the wake of Dilke's courtship of Mrs Pattison, prompted her daughter's confession.[4] However, there are sound reasons for doubting this particular hypothesis. Mrs Smith had never been on close terms with Nia and it is unlikely that her daughter would have initiated a scandal solely at her mother's bidding, though her desire to protect Forster and to obtain a divorce may of course have out-weighed this reluctance. More pertinently, it is questionable whether Mrs Smith would have welcomed a scandal. She was a minor society hostess who revelled in the role. She had been delighted by Maye's marriage into the Dilke family,[5] and she was sufficiently shrewd and ambitious to have recognised that there was more to be gained from maintaining good relations with a putative Prime Minister than from ruining him. Indeed, the publicity generated by the case proved immensely damaging to the Eustace Smiths who were forced to give up their house at 52 Princes Gate and move to Algiers.[6] An outcome of this sort was quite predictable and one which a society animal like Mrs Smith was unlikely to have wished upon herself.

The most damning of Mrs Crawford's critics has been John Juxon, the biographer of her solicitor, George Lewis. He regarded her as no more than a 'psychopath' and 'a liar of genius' whose whole life was a series of 'masks' – artistic young wife, common prostitute, Catholic social worker – and who was able to assume throughout her long life 'the mask of the moment'.[7]

It was because of the heavy weight of opinion against Mrs Crawford, in the wake of Jenkins's biography, that members of her family began to assemble evidence to portray her part in the case in a much more favourable light. They found it difficult to reconcile the woman that they knew, a social and religious activist, with the description of her in the history books as the perpetrator of a vile, unprovoked and premeditated calumny. The lead in assembling new evidence was taken by Stephen Roskill, the historian and the grandson of Ashton and Maye Dilke, a descendant therefore of both parties to the scandal.

The papers now reside in the Roskill Archive at Churchill College,

Cambridge, and comprise three main sections: papers of the Roskill family, some of which came from Stephen's mother, Mrs John Roskill, the only daughter of Ashton Dilke, and others which represent his own researches into the case; the papers of Ashton Dilke, largely unrelated to the scandal but of great historical interest; and the Enthoven collection of information about the case that came via the descendants of Rosalind, the youngest daughter of Eustace Smith. Some of this evidence, particularly in regard to the last-named section, has to be treated with great caution, for much of it is opinion rather than fact. Virginia Crawford's nieces and nephews, and great nieces and great nephews, were obviously as bemused and divided about the truth of the scandal as all other students of it have been. Partly because of his relationship to both parties, Stephen Roskill endeavoured to steer 'a middle course', but he did so as well partly in order not to offend those members of the family, principally the descendants of Rosalind Smith, who passionately believed in Dilke's guilt.[8] Marion Rawson, Rosalind's daughter, claimed that her mother never budged from the view that Dilke was wholly guilty. Her mother had told her that, as a small child, she had been 'played with in an unpleasant way' by Dilke. She believed that Dilke was possessed of an extreme sexuality and that he may have 'indulged in perversions'.[9] Stephen Roskill's brother Ashton quite rightly cautioned him as to the use made of this second-hand evidence from 'a possibly tainted source'.[10]

Beyond this prejudiced, uncorroborated and therefore unreliable information, there is new evidence in the archive which, while it does not resolve the truth about the case, nevertheless throws additional light upon it. Much the most valuable of this, which relates to the character of Virginia Crawford, her family background and her life after the trial, has been incorporated at the appropriate point in this narrative. In addition, there are some tantalising but incomplete bits of evidence.

The first of these is a photograph of Dilke dated in Virginia's hand 'April 83'.[11] Who gave it to her, why she kept it, and whether it was dated at the time are intriguing but unanswerable questions. Secondly, there is an undated love letter to Virginia from a woman with the initials F. A. D., but no evidence of reciprocation or of a lesbian relationship.[12] Finally, there are three letters to her from Forster, written after the scandal. Two of them, dated 9 and 10 October but with no year, refer to his marriage as having 'taken almost everything from me'. He urges Virginia to let him call on her: 'you know how we were friends once, in the best sense'. The third letter, of 9 March 1899, refers to a chance meeting in the street: 'Your face was so full of annoyance when I passed you five minutes ago ... .' Virginia had decreed that Forster should no longer see her but he had walked in the same direction as her 'with no idea of offending you or breaking your ruling in any way ... You have an unpleasant recollection of me indeed. Please try to believe that, although I did you so much harm, I was not altogether bad. It sounds like more of my stupidity to say so, but it is true that you are the best recollection I have. When I saw you I wanted to make life a laugh, as it used to be .... '[13] Why did Virginia keep these letters? The reference to his stupidity and the harm he caused her probably harks back to the way he abandoned her for Miss Barry at the very moment when she had sacrificed so much for him. Perhaps Virginia kept the letters as a reminder of the one man she had really loved and who belatedly came to recognise and acknowledge his love for her.

Despite the years of searching, Mrs Crawford's family were unable to produce anything to substantiate her allegations against Dilke. Nevertheless, their diligence is a reminder of the extent to which the historical record is slanted by the documentation left to us. Dilke was much more able, through the Chesson Committee and through the censorship exercised over his private papers, to influence historical judgement than was Mrs Crawford, who undertook at the time of her conversion never again to refer to the affair. It was obviously in Dilke's interest to blacken and vilify her character as much as possible, but there are aspects of his own character that do not bear too close scrutiny.

The news of the scandal did not come as a shock to many people. Hamilton noted it in his diary with the comment, 'It does not much surprise anyone who knows Dilke. He is extraordinarily free & easy with ladies.'[14] There is no denying his appeal to the opposite sex, which came from a natural charm and conversational ease, and a seductive voice of 'brown velvet',[15] rather than from good looks. By the 1880s his hair was well in retreat and his beard had become bushier, hiding most of his face and helping to focus attention on his eyes. These, according to one contemporary, would have had an hypnotic appearance but for the fact that from time to time they moved furtively from side to side – a characteristic which, combined with his easy fluency, led some people to believe that he 'was never quite candid'.[16] But his great wealth and political power together made him a most desirable match, so much so that the announcement of his engagement to Mrs Pattison lost him the sympathy and support of many influential society ladies.

From Dilke's adultery with Mrs Smith, which came out at the trial and was therefore not cut from his papers, it is not unreasonable to surmise that there were more such affairs, possibly with other ladies such as Mrs Rogerson, and possibly with servants in his own household, which might explain his initial reluctance to make a fight of the scandal. A lady by the name of Mrs Sands was alarmed when she heard that Crawford intended 'to go into all Dilke's amours ... and did not know whether she might be included'.[17] One wonders how many other London hostesses felt a similar apprehension. Labouchere, who knew Dilke quite well, is said to have remarked of his relations with the Smith family that 'I have no doubt that the wolf got into the fold, but I feel convinced he didn't get hold of this little lamb!'[18] The Hilliers were convinced at the time of the trial that they had seen Dilke entering 65 Warren Street with a tall, fair lady of about twenty-eight. Mrs Anna Dessouslavy, the one-time servant and pensioner of Dilke's who also lodged at 65 Warren Street and who had given evidence on his behalf at the trial, later made accusations about him which he put down to her going 'cracky'.[19]

The fact that Mrs Crawford did not, after her conversion to Catholicism, make restitution to Dilke in accordance with the sacrament of penance might appear to prove his guilt. However, Catholic doctrine does not point to such an unequivocal conclusion. The principle of restitution does, indeed, require reparation of the damage done to another person's reputation, but only has force where the circumstances are such that the injurer is able to make good the damage. Mrs Crawford may have believed that Dilke's reputation could not be restored, particularly in view of the revelations about his adultery with her mother. Dilke himself was certainly of the opinion that the damage once done could never be undone.[20] Manning, to whom Dilke had told 'everything', appears to have believed that no good could come from keeping the scandal alive. Beyond theological considerations, perhaps his knowledge of the circumstances and his friendship with both parties account for his discretion in leaving things as they stood, for what purpose would it serve to absolve Dilke of one charge by showing that it had been prompted by his guilt elsewhere? Shane Leslie, when working on his biography of Manning, wrote to Miss Tuckwell in 1916, 'There is no doubt the Cardinal thought your uncle innocent of the *extreme* charge ... .'[21]

There is also the question as to why Dilke never prosecuted Mrs Crawford for perjury, particularly once he had assembled the new evidence about the extent of her affair with Forster. Similarly, Stead invited Dilke, by repeating Mrs Crawford's allegations, to prosecute him for libel.[22] Dilke never took up these challenges. He was prepared to face a perjury charge himself and risk 'penal servitude', but not to initiate one. The only hint as to why he didn't proceed against Stead was that it would have been difficult to recover costs and would have served no purpose in view of the fact that Stead lacked sufficent support to obstruct his return to politics.[23] Moreover, it was unlikely after 1886 that he would ever be able to regain the pre-eminent position in politics that he had once held. By 1892 the best he could expect was to return to parliament, which was achieved regardless of Stead. In sum, his experience at the hands of the courts may have led him to conclude that the risks outweighed the perceived advantages.

Dilke's reputation as a ladies' man may help us to understand Bodley's cryptic statement that 'the truth lies between the narrative which was recited in the witness box and the illusion which poor Lady Dilke cherished'.[24] In his capacity as Dilke's secretary, Bodley perhaps had reason for not himself cherishing any illusions about Dilke, though he was adamant that Dilke had not had an affair with Mrs Crawford. It was possible for Dilke to allow the investigations into the case to continue long after the trial, because his committee were engaged in unearthing proof of the innocence of his relationship with Mrs Crawford, not in establishing his guilt with other women. But Dilke was not an innocent. He was guilty of at least one affair and possibly several more. Those of his contemporaries who knew the truth perhaps concluded that, by the moral standards of the day, he had not been unjustly punished.

Against all this, it has to be admitted that there has never been any firm evidence to link Dilke in an adulterous relationship other than with Mrs Smith. It was perhaps inevitable that, in the wake of the scandal, he would be the subject of rumour and gossip, and that there would be hints in memoirs that would cast doubts upon his moral character. Yet, despite the occasional innuendo, it is remarkable that no 'kiss-and-tell' story was ever published or, indeed, has turned up in private collections, to besmirch his reputation seriously. The purchase of a kiss from Margot Asquith's sister in return for a signed photograph of himself appears to have been the extent of his philandering.[25]

If he was innocent of the charge made by Mrs Crawford, were personal motives the only ones involved in choosing him? The murky world of the scandal, combined with the fact that Virginia Crawford had patently lied, has inevitably encouraged a number of writers to claim that she was simply the tool in a much larger conspiracy. The tightly-interwoven structure of Victorian upper middle-class society provided fertile conditions for the nurturing of dark plots. In the story of the case, the personal inter-relationships and the chance encounters are reminiscent of a Dickens novel. It is hardly surprising, therefore, that it has fed the imaginations of conspiracy theorists and dramatists.

Three *political* conspiracy theories have been advanced implicating, quite separately, Albert Venn Dicey, Lord Rosebery and Joseph Chamberlain. The Dicey theory can be summarily dealt with. It is the contention of Trowbridge H. Ford that Dilke's downfall was orchestrated by the famous constitutional theorist in order to prevent him from becoming Liberal leader and introducing Home Rule for Ireland.[26] Aside from the fact that at the time of Mrs Crawford's confession, Dilke was still strongly backing Chamberlain's central board scheme and was always lukewarm about Ireland, Ford's account is based upon unsubstantiated suppositions, factual inaccuracies and a circumstantial use of evidence. To take just one example – for his theory merits no more space than this – he argues that, for the conspiracy to succeed, Dilke had to be built up into 'a modern Oedipus'. The only support he gives for this is to cite Mrs Crawford's claim in the witness-box, that Dilke had compared his affair with her to his relationship with his mother. Upon this blatant inaccuracy – Mrs Crawford, of course, had alluded to Dilke's relationship with her own mother – Ford proceeds to hang his Oedipus theory. In short, it is impossible to give any credence to his extraordinary thesis.

Almost as implausible is the second of the political conspiracy theories, which points the accusing finger at Rosebery and his wife. The Crawfords often stayed with the Roseberys and Virginia and Lady Rosebery were friends. A rumour circulated shortly before the first trial that the latter had assisted Donald Crawford financially to pursue his case against Dilke in an attempt to clear out of the way a rival to her husband's career. Dilke reported the rumour to Rosebery, who vehemently denied that there was any vestige of truth in it. Dilke fully accepted this. Rosebery went on to follow the political path that had seemed Dilke's destiny – Foreign Secretary in Gladstone's third and fourth administrations, and his successor as Prime Minister. Convenient as Dilke's fall was to his own future, there has never been the slightest evidence linking Rosebery or his wife with the scandal, but Rosebery never forgave Dilke for implying that there might have been.[27]

It was Bodley who first started the theory that the plot against Dilke had been engineered by Chamberlain, a man whom he disliked intensely.[28] It will be recalled that Crawford had been having his wife followed in order to gain evidence of her infidelity. A detective employed by him had seen Virginia call on Chamberlain two days before her confession. Chamberlain was not at home but arrived a few minutes later. The detective did not see Mrs Crawford leave the house although he waited until dark, and he surmised that she must have left in a closed carriage during the evening. When the Chesson Committee got hold of the detective's notebooks in 1887, Dilke broached the matter with Chamberlain who admitted the visit, but added that the lady, finding no one at home, had not waited. Dilke thought this reply unsatisfactory (without saying why), but refused to believe that Chamberlain had betrayed him.

In recounting this incident, Jenkins posed questions about it which indicated why it was troubling. Why had Mrs Crawford called on a man with whom she was not familiar in the first place? Why had a trained detective not seen her leave immediately? And why had Chamberlain not mentioned the visit to Dilke? Chamberlain had the motive – he was a ruthless and ambitious politician who perhaps saw in Dilke a rival for the premiership. On breaking with Gladstone in 1886, almost his first act was to turn the Birmingham caucus to securing the election to parliament of Henry Matthews, Crawford's skilful advocate who had done so much to blow holes in Dilke's evidence at the second trial. Chamberlain had also been apprised by Dilke of the 'vile letters' that he had, since about 1882, been receiving, and which contained anonymous charges and hints at conspiracy.[29] Did he unearth its roots and use it to his own advantage? On 23 June 1885 Dilke had asked him to see Crawford about the latter's proposed candidature for Motherwell, and had given him his whereabouts for the following three weeks.[30] Did he meet with Crawford and promise him political advancement if he fell in with the conspirators? Crawford, anxious to sue for divorce, might well have been tempted by such an offer. Why else was he so calm and friendly towards Dilke, his wife's lover by her confession of the previous night, when they met at the Reform Club on the afternoon of 18 July, if not that he had no reason to bear Dilke any malice?

How credible is a conspiracy theory involving Chamberlain and one or both of the Crawfords? In the Roskill Archive there are two further vital pieces of evidence. Chamberlain wrote to Mrs Eustace Smith on 27 January 1881 returning an Academy catalogue and arranging to call on her for Sunday lunch.[31] There is also a copy of a letter dated 5 February 1886 from Chamberlain to Sir Charles Butt, the judge at the first hearing, thanking him for agreeing to a meeting at his chambers.[32] At first glance these two letters might appear to confirm Chamberlain's complicity in a conspiracy – the first indicating that he was on good terms with the Smith family in 1881 and therefore able to join the plot against Dilke from its very early days; the second suggesting, in the words of a note attached to it by Stephen Roskill, 'highly improper' conduct on Chamberlain's part designed 'to prejudice Butt against Dilke' as part of his broader strategy to destroy him.[33]

Although the evidence is ambiguous there is a far less sinister interpretation of it and one which entirely exonerates Chamberlain.[34] Jenkins had thought Mrs Crawford's visit to Chamberlain's house suspicious because she did not, he believed, know him. Jenkins was wrong. In 1880 Chamberlain had taken a house in Princes Gardens very near to the Smiths' in Princes Gate. He was a Liberal colleague of Eustace Smith's in the House of Commons, so his visit to the lunch parties given by Mrs Smith should be no cause for surprise. It is conceivable that Virginia called at Chamberlain's house on 15 July 1885 to visit his sister, who was keeping house for him, or one of his daughters. It is impossible to say, but the visit is perfectly comprehensible in view of their neighbourly acquaintanceship.

The visit to Butt was part of Chamberlain's unstinting attempt to save his radical friend from disaster. He knew that Crawford would secure his divorce solely upon the uncorroborated confession of his wife. It is probable, therefore, that he called at Butt's chambers in order to impress upon him the importance of stressing in his summing-up that there was not a shred of evidence against Dilke. This the judge proceeded to do, emphasising that not only was there absolutely no case against Dilke, but that Mrs Crawford's absence from the witness-box further weakened her allegations against him.[35]

Far from plotting against Dilke to remove him from his path to the premiership, Chamberlain was desperately trying to save him.[36] He was partly motivated by altruism but partly as well by the political circumstances of 1885. For Chamberlain was above all a political realist, and his instinct told him how crucial Dilke's survival was to the future success of the radical wing of the Liberal Party, with which his own fortunes were then bound up. During the summer of 1885, when Dilke had stayed at Highbury, Chamberlain had treated him with a sympathy and kindness which he could never forget. Along with Mrs Pattison, he had encouraged Dilke to put up a fight when the latter had been quite prepared to abandon political life. Why should he have bothered if his aim had been to ruin Dilke? He could, of course, have wanted to cover his tracks by continuing to pose as Dilke's dear friend, but it would have taken a consummate hypocrite to act in such a manner, and Dilke was probably right when he professed his belief that Chamberlain was not of that stamp. Moreover, by standing by Dilke throughout his ordeal he risked damage to his own career. The whole course of politics in 1885 suggests that Chamberlain would have been foolish to destroy Dilke at that moment, when they appeared to be on the verge of usurping power from the Whigs. He may have been prepared to postpone this if it meant an eventual clear run at the premiership – *reculer pour mieux sauter*. But this seems most improbable. For Chamberlain was a man of action who wanted power quickly, who preferred going up the ladders to sliding down the snakes.[37]

It is unlikely now that the full story of the Dilke-Crawford affair will ever be known. The two principals who knew the truth, together with the Roman Catholic priests, Manning and Butler, to whom it was presumably vouchsafed, are long dead and there appears to be no further evidence that will resolve the matter conclusively. For this reason, the scandal has been, and will no doubt continue to be, the subject of imaginative and dramatic reconstructions.

The first of these appeared soon after the trial. In 1887 a French author by the name of Hector Malot published a novel entitled *Vices Français*, deliberately echoing the phrase used by Mrs Crawford in her confession. The characters and the plot were undoubtedly based on the Dilke scandal and, most curious of all, there are passages in it that are virtual paraphrases of extremely personal letters that passed between Dilke and his wife.[38] These could only have come from the Dilkes and probably from Lady Dilke herself, who knew Malot. The extraordinary latitude of allowing a popular novelist to make use of such private correspondence can only be accounted for by his sympathy for the Dilkes and his determination to portray the character representing Sir Charles in a sympathetic light. Malot's plot suggested that Dilke was traduced because he rejected the advances of a lady (the character representing Virginia Crawford) who was in love with him. The novel appeared in English translation under the title *Josey*, produced by an obscure little firm that disappeared shortly after its publication. Dilke was said by Lady Dilke to have told Malot that he was 'most unwilling there shd. be any English translation of his novel about us'.[39] However, there are interesting parallels here with a previous occasion when Dilke, at the nadir of his fortunes, had turned to the imaginative genre of the novel as a means whereby to capture the sympathy of an audience deaf to more conventional appeals. *Prince Florestan* had also been published in French and English. Dilke may have hoped that *Josey* would have the same restorative impact on his career.

The publication of Jenkins's biography prompted further fictional interventions. Betty Askwith's novel *The Tangled Web* appeared in 1960 and, in the same year, *The Dilke Case* was presented in the form of a courtroom drama by Granada Television. In 1964–65 *The Right Honourable Gentleman*, a play by Michael Bradley-Dyne based on the affair, enjoyed a successful run in a West End theatre. Television returned to the scandal in 1981 with the broadcast of Ken Taylor's *The Member for Chelsea*.[40] Imaginative and ingenious as all these undoubtedly were, they contained no new hard evidence.

If a final solution to the mystery is therefore unlikely, what, at the distance of over a hundred years, seems the most likely explanation? Sufficient evidence is available to permit a reasonably credible reconstruction of the narrative of events. What will never be resolved are the more intangible questions to do with the psychology of motive.

Virginia Smith had returned from finishing school in Lausanne. She was almost immediately thrust into the adult world through her marriage, at the age of eighteen, to a man more than twice her age. She had acquiesced in this arrangement largely to escape from her hot-tempered mother. She soon found consolation elsewhere, falling in love with a handsome army captain named Henry Forster. Along with her elder sister, Helen, trapped in a similar unhappy relationship, she embarked on a series of amorous adventures. The one egged the other on. They hunted for lovers together among the medical students at St George's Hospital. By 1882 they were both involved in an adulterous relationship with Forster and frequently met him at the brothel in Hill Street.

Donald Crawford was alerted to his wife's behaviour by letters from one or more informants. At first, he dismissed them. Later his suspicions became intense, and he decided to have his wife watched. He was now strongly motivated by the desire to gain the necessary evidence to secure a divorce, for he wished to remarry and embark on a respectable parliamentary career. The situation was becoming critical for Virginia Crawford. The Métropole letter of June 1885 had, for the first time, named Forster. She was aware that she was being followed and had therefore made elaborate arrangements to communicate with Forster to avoid detection. Moreover, their affair had reached a delicate stage. In September 1884 Forster had become engaged to Miss Smith Barry, but had broken off the engagement the following January after only four months. Virginia was still very much in love with him. She perhaps hoped to marry him. The Crawfords, therefore, had strong reasons over and above their mutual dislike for wanting to terminate their marriage by the summer of 1885.

Two intriguing questions arise at this point: what was Mrs Rogerson's part in the sordid business; and why did Virginia choose Dilke? Virginia Crawford and Christina Rogerson had become very good friends. The latter knew of Virginia's affair with Forster and occasionally allowed them to conduct it under her own roof. In September 1884 the two friends suffered simultaneous blows. Forster became engaged to Miss Barry and Mrs Rogerson was stupefied by Dilke's engagement to Mrs Pattison. Recently freed by the death of her alcoholic husband, Mrs Rogerson had set her sights on the rising politician. She began to spread the story that she had been Dilke's mistress (which may have been true – we shall probably never know) and that she expected to marry him. She certainly fed the novelist Henry James with this story.[41] She perhaps wrote one or more of the anonymous letters sent to both Dilke and Crawford in the spring of 1885.

As a close friend of the Dilke family for many years, she was quite familiar with the interior of 76 Sloane Street and could have supplied Mrs Crawford with some of the details that embellished her story. Henry James knew her very well and is reputed to have said that 'had she been beautiful and sane, she would have been one of the world's great wicked women'. Perhaps she was anyway – her mental instability feeding her wickedness. Her behaviour towards the Dilkes in the autumn and winter of 1885, and her evidence at the second trial, smack of duplicity. Dilke was perhaps never nearer the mark than when, on first hearing of Virginia's confession, he wrote to Mrs Pattison: 'The blow long threatened in the wicked letters has fallen at last. The instrument chosen by the conspirators is Donald Crawford ... In my belief the conspiracy comes from a woman who wanted me to marry her – but this is guesswork. I only know that there is a conspiracy, from one or two women, perhaps from both.'[42] At the end of the long investigation by the Chesson Committee, one of its members, Judge Steavenson, a man who had studied the evidence closer than anyone and was familiar with most of the principal players in the drama, was likewise convinced that the whole conspiracy had been got up by Mrs Rogerson and Mrs Crawford in collusion – the first because she had wanted to marry Dilke, the second because she wanted to rid herself of her husband.[43] The present writer shares this opinion, while believing that Mrs Crawford's motives were more complex than Steavenson suggested.

While one can only speculate as to her reasons for choosing Dilke as her victim, his affair with her own mother must have had a considerable influence. Even if restitution was impossible, one might have expected some sign of remorse for the disgrace she had brought upon Dilke, but never once did she show him the slightest compassion. For she knew Dilke to be an adulterer. Instead, she chose to atone for her own sins by embarking on a life of good works, following Manning's advice to the letter and never, in the over fifty years that remained to her, divulging any clue as to the truth of her accusations, not even to her close family.

There may have been other reasons for choosing Dilke. Perhaps he had made advances towards her, soliciting a kiss in return for a photograph, as he had once done with Margot Asquith's sister. Perhaps this was how she came by the photograph that she kept among her possessions for the rest of her life, where it resided as a reminder that the man she had ruined was not guileless. Dilke had been mentioned in the anonymous letters to her husband from as early as 1882 and any confession of adultery with him would therefore have the ring of authenticity. While Dilke's engagement to Mrs Pattison can be adduced as a motive for Mrs Rogerson's animosity, it cannot be entirely discounted in regard to Mrs Crawford's behaviour. For Mrs Crawford had been a close friend of Meta Bradley, who was the mistress of Mark Pattison in the early 1880s at the very time that Dilke's relationship with Mrs Pattison was beginning to flourish. Perhaps somewhere in the labyrinthine reaches of her mind, she had convinced herself that *both* the Dilkes deserved retribution.

Forster and Nia also believed that Dilke was 'interfering' in their affair.[44] In June 1885 he had been summoned to Mrs Rogerson's home at Forster's instigation, where he was accused of attempting to damage the captain's career by writing a letter to the War Office mentioning his affair with Mrs Crawford. Forster was spoiling for a fight. Dilke assured him that he had not written such a letter and managed to calm the situation, but the incident can only have increased Mrs Crawford's resentment of Dilke.

Above all, she appears to have believed that naming Dilke would be enough to secure her a divorce and protect her real lover and other members of her family. She did not want Forster, who was perhaps pressuring her, to be dragged into the divorce court. Any case in which Forster was cited as co-respondent would cause unpleasant ripples throughout the Smith family, engaging not only her own interests but those of Helen and, more pertinently, Ida, who was now happily married to Robert Priestley and perhaps knew nothing of her husband's earlier dalliance with her two sisters. In these circumstances the diversion of attention towards another person appeared altogether a more attractive option. Virginia therefore precipitated the crisis and distracted Crawford from his pursuit of Forster by sending him an anonymous letter herself – written in her own disguised hand or by her friend Mrs Rogerson – which in turn prompted her 'confession' of adultery with Dilke. In confessing, she was extremely careful to stress that Forster had never been her lover.[45] Now and afterwards she covered up for him by an act of mental transference, exchanging his name for Dilke's in descriptions of her adultery. However, she was genuinely scared when Dilke revealed his determination to fight. In July 1885 she told Mrs Rogerson's brother, Charles Stewart, who was acting for Crawford and was anxious to get her to put her confession in writing, that 'I am horribly frightened at the prospect of Sir Charles Dilke fighting the case, as it complicates it so dreadfully'. Stewart then threatened that the divorce was unlikely to be settled quietly if she did not comply, and that his client, who was 'resolved at all costs to obtain a divorce', would be obliged to implicate others, including 'female relations of your own – and another co-respondent, Captain Forster. It will depend on you, therefore, which course is adopted'.[46] Only then, when her sisters and the man she had endeavoured all along to protect were threatened with exposure, did she determine to press on.

Forster repaid her fidelity by renewing his engagement that same month to Miss Barry, whom he married in September. But for Virginia there was now no going back – the die had been cast. The Smith sisters closed ranks, only Helen having a twinge of conscience about the consequences for Dilke. She quarrelled with Virgina and Maye over what they were doing, but their purpose was not to be shaken for, as Maye told Lady Dilke at their December meeting, if Virginia withdrew now, two other suits would immediately be commenced by her husband against her. The threat issued at the outset to other of her 'female relations' was therefore probably the strongest motivating force of all in compelling Virginia to see through what she had begun.

Despite the grand political conspiracies that have been advanced to explain Dilke's downfall, the genesis of the scandal appears to have been entirely domestic. Its progenitor was Mrs Crawford acting alone or, more likely, prompted and encouraged by the neurotic and vengeful Mrs Rogerson. Political factors exercised only a negative sway. It is undoubtedly the case that many politicians were not sorry to see Dilke ruined. The Liberal leadership had been under constant pressure from the radicals, and the trial came at the very moment when the Dilke-Chamberlain alliance seemed on the point of success. There were many members of the establishment who had been alarmed by Chamberlain's Unauthorised Campaigns and rabble-rousing speeches. They rubbed their hands when his co-adjutant landed in the divorce-court. Within the higher echelons of the state there was a fair degree of satisfaction at radical discomfiture. The Queen, of course, was pleased. Lady Salisbury, the wife of the new Prime Minister, was 'delighted because it will smash Chamberlain'.[47] Above all, the legal establishment had hardly done justice to Dilke's case, and he met with coolness and at times outright hostility from its members, not least from the president of the court at the second hearing. Most suspect was the advice tendered by Dilke's counsel at the first trial. Sir Charles Russell was reputedly one of the finest barristers of his day. Yet he was not only partly responsible for the decision that kept Dilke from the witness-box, he made the incredible reference to 'indiscretions' in explaining the reasons. It is not possible to say how deliberate that was. The damage may have been done in an unconscious way. Conscious or unconscious, it was perhaps symptomatic of an anti-radical conservatism that persisted for a long, long time. When, many years later, Lord Simon, a former Solicitor-General, was asked for his legal opinion as to whether, under the existing rules of evidence, Dilke would have been protected had he entered the witness-box, he replied in the affirmative: 'Of all the courses open to him Charles Russell took the one most damaging to his client.' But, he continued, 'Charles Dilke was an unscrupulous and ambitious populist – the Tony Benn of his day. That he was hounded out of public life postponed the degradation of our country for 90 years.'[48] This is a remarkable insight into the depth and longevity of the fears within the establishment of Dilke's brand of radicalism. The scandal may not have been political in origin, but its political ramifications were great indeed. To the delight of moderate and conservative opinion, it terminated or hampered most of the policies which Dilke was pursuing. Together with the split over Home Rule, the divorce case helped to destroy the momentum which had been gathering in the reforming wing of the Liberal Party, with incalculable consequences for its future.

It was not the only society scandal of the day nor was it the most famous. That dubious accolade goes to the Mordaunt trial of 1870 involving the Prince of Wales. By bringing discredit to the monarchy it had given impetus to the republican movement and, it will be recalled, to Dilke's demands for a reduction in royal grants. There were some interesting parallels between the Mordaunt and Crawford cases. Sir Charles Mordaunt, a Conservative MP, had filed for divorce after his twenty-one-year-old wife had confessed to him that she had committed adultery with Lord Cole, Sir Frederick Johnstone, the Prince of Wales 'and others'. Lady Mordaunt's counsel served the Prince with a subpoena to appear as a witness at the trial. Unlike Dilke, the Prince was advised to go into the witness-box to refute the allegations – which he did during an examination lasting just seven minutes. His denial of any impropriety with Lady Mordaunt was greeted by applause from the galleries of the court. Despite some embarrassing details relating to private meetings between the Prince and Lady Mordaunt, Sir Charles's petition was dismissed on the grounds of his wife's insanity and the Prince was effectively exonerated.

Another sensational trial began just four months after the end of the Dilke case when Lady Colin Campbell instigated divorce proceedings against her husband, the Liberal MP for Argyllshire and youngest son of the Duke of Argyll. She accused him of cruelty (he had infected her with venereal disease) and adultery. He responded with a cross-petition, charging her also with adultery. The case involved many of the legal players who had participated in the Dilke drama – George Lewis, Sir Charles Russell and Mr Justice Butt – and was replete with similar salacious details embracing all ranks of society from family servants to the Duke of Marlborough.

The Campbell trial did not, however, have the same political ramifications as the Crawford-Dilke case, which was paralleled in this regard only by the scandal involving the Irish Nationalist leader Charles Stewart Parnell. His affair with Katherine O'Shea, the wife of the Irish MP Captain William O'Shea, had begun in 1880. The latter had soon learnt of his wife's infidelity and, in a moment of impetuousity, had challenged Parnell to a duel. Kitty had calmed him and persuaded him to accept her new relationship – partly by threatening to make public his own adulterous affairs, and partly by bribing him with an allowance that she received from a rich aunt. The government also knew of the liaison and had paroled Parnell from Kilmainham prison in 1882 to allow him to attend the funeral of his child by Mrs O'Shea. She afterwards bore him two more children. Both of the O'Sheas were involved as political intermediaries between Parnell and the government in the negotiations which culminated in the Home Rule crisis.

At the end of 1889, O'Shea unexpectedly decided to sue for divorce. The case was heard in November 1890. The presiding judge was once again Mr Justice Butt. Neither Parnell nor Mrs O'Shea attended court, and therefore O'Shea effectively won his case by default. Parnell was shortly afterwards removed from the leadership of the Irish Nationalist Party. His health went into rapid decline and he died in October 1891, less than four months after marrying Katherine.

Just as Dilke was distrusted for his advanced radicalism by some members of the establishment, so too were there many who took pleasure in the discomfiture and ruin of the leader of Irish nationalism. Parnell's downfall may appear therefore to give some support to the conspiracy theorists. The fact that establishment politicians like Lord Hartington were able to conduct adulterous affairs with impunity compounds such suspicions. Hartington carried on a love affair with the Duchess of Manchester for thirty years before finally marrying her in 1892, shortly after her husband's death. The relationship was no secret: it earned Hartington the nickname 'Harty-tarty'. Dilke occasionally made reference in his diary to it – not to moralise but to grumble about the Duchess's influence over the Whig leader's politics. Dilke's attitude was not untypical of the prevailing morality within the ruling class. The sexual pastimes of politicians were rarely censured by their colleagues and only became a cause for concern when they entered the public domain. Dilke and Parnell were not the victims of political conspiracies. They were ruined when details of their private lives were paraded before the divorce courts in what were essentially domestic disputes. Hartington by contrast was lucky. His affair remained private simply because the Duke of Manchester, wishing to avoid a public scandal, preferred to keep it that way. He chose to turn a blind eye to his wife's infidelity, which never therefore entered the public arena to become the subject of an outraged Nonconformist conscience.

These various scandals throw an interesting sidelight on Victorian attitudes and standards. By prising open the lid of Victorian morality they provide an insight into contemporary sexual mores. They reveal a society where débutantes were married off to elderly gentlemen and where many of them turned to finding solace elsewhere, even to the extent of hunting in pairs for lovers. This was a society where houses of assignation flourished, with rooms let by the hour to gentlemen as places to conduct their illicit liaisons, and where both class and family barriers fell before the pleasures of seduction. Whenever evidence of these sexual pastimes surfaced, it was greeted by the fulminations of a section of the middle class whose puritanical consciousness managed to square an outraged morality with a prurient concern for exposing every immoral detail. The 'respectable' bourgeoisie could tut-tut at the scandals chronicled in the name of public morality by a burgeoning 'sexational' press, and hound from public life politicians, like Dilke and Parnell, who were 'found out'.

Yet, refreshingly, this hypocrisy does not appear to have penetrated very far in society (though the Dilke scandal did produce the expected crop of smutty jokes and the occasional obscenity chalked on the walls and doorstep of 76 Sloane Street). Despite being accused of adultery and, more heinous still, of bedding two young ladies at once, Dilke remained popular with the working-class voters of Chelsea. His eventual defeat there was the product of a political rather than a moral reaction against him.[49] The Chelsea Liberal Association repeatedly expressed its faith in him, local bodies elected him as their chairman, and numerous constituencies sought him as a candidate. Many leading politicians remained his friends, and within six years he was to be back among them in parliament.

Chapter 13

A Political Tragedy, 1885–86

During the twelve months in which the Crawford scandal was unwinding, political events were following an equally dramatic course. At the time of the fall of the government, in June 1885, the radicals had every reason to be optimistic. The redistribution maelstrom had been successfully circumnavigated, while the end of the year would see new elections, a purging of Whig influence, and the implementation of the radical programme. They looked forward to a Liberal administration in which radicalism would for the first time be in the ascendant, reflecting what they held to be the changed balance of power between the landed aristocracy and the middle class in the country at large.

Local government reform was now the keystone of the radical programme, 'the necessary first step', Dilke told a Chiswick audience on 21 July, 'to every reform which is pressing at the present time'.[1] That same day he received a letter from Gladstone pleading for agreement upon Irish policy:

> I cannot forbear writing to express the hope that you and Chamberlain may be able to say or do something to remove the appearance now presented to the world of a disposition on your parts to sever yourselves from the executive and especially the judicial administration of Ireland as it was carried on by Spencer under the late Government ... we have been for five years in the same boat, on most troubled waters, without having during the worst three years of the five a single man of the company thrown overboard. I have *never* in my life known the bonds of union so strained by the pure stress of circumstances: a good intent on all sides has enabled them to hold – is there any reason why at this moment they should part? A rupture may come on questions of future policy; I am not sure that it will. But if it is to arrive, let it come in the course of nature, as events develop themselves.

Gladstone went on to say that past decisions were the collective responsibility of the late government and therefore the singling out of

Spencer for criticism was not justified.[2] He was appealing here, as he had done so often in the past, for Dilke to act as a moderating influence – and, indeed, the latter immediately wrote to ask Chamberlain, who was due to speak at Hackney, if he could say something flattering about Spencer. Chamberlain thought not, though he could perhaps make 'a personal tribute'.[3] Gladstone had despatched the letter before news of Mrs Crawford's allegations had reached him. Henceforward, the Liberal leader switched to negotiating directly with Chamberlain. The removal of Dilke's mediating abilities thereby materially contributed to the political tragedy that was to unfold over the next twelve months.

Chamberlain, meanwhile, affronted by the Irish rebuff to his central board scheme, had begun campaigning on other of the planks in his Unauthorised Programme. The articles from the *Fortnightly Review* in which these reforms had been outlined were now gathered together and published in September as *The Radical Programme*.[4] Land, local government, housing, finance and taxation reform, together with free primary education, disestablishment and further electoral reform, were its main elements. To a degree, therefore, it echoed the 'free' programme of the early 1870s, but the centrality of local government as a panacea embracing many of the other reforms, especially the provision of allotments for the agricultural labourers, was the most significant new departure, being partly a response to the popular land schemes of Henry George and Alfred Wallace and the ferment of new social ideas. The programme was therefore a deliberate counter to the growing currency of socialist proposals and an affirmation of the reforming potential of radical Liberalism. The attacks on the landlords and the church were intended to serve, as they always had done in the middle-class radical tradition, as a rallying-call to middle- and working-class voters alike (the latter now augmented by the agricultural labourers) and as a distraction from the evils of industrial capitalism. In this respect, *The Radical Programme* was essentially conservative, aimed at forestalling rather than inaugurating a social revolution.[5] This does not mean that it was not at the same time progressive. On the contrary, local government was seen as a mechanism for extending individual liberty and democracy. Land reform was presented as an urban issue. It would resolve many of the problems created by economic depression and unemployment in both town and countryside – rural depopulation and the impact of this on the towns, allotments for urban as well as the famous 'three acres and a cow' for rural workers, housing shortages and high rents associated with 'landlordism' and 'rack-renting', and the taxation of the unearned increment on land to pay for reform.[6] On top of this, free education was also perceived as primarily an urban issue that would retain working-class support for radical Liberalism. In sum, the radical programme was a response in part to the economic recession and in part to the new social ideas of the 1880s, aimed not at driving the propertied classes out of the Liberal Party but at making them aware of their obligations to address the problems of poverty. It was in this sense a defence of a capitalist system faced by the challenge of socialism and by the need to win over the new democracy. At the same time it continued to seek solutions at the expense of the landed establishment and it nowhere probed the deficiencies in the industrial system. It was therefore Janus-like in looking backwards to the traditional forms of middle-class radicalism, and forwards to the social welfare radicalism of the new liberalism (in Chamberlain's language it sounded 'the death-knell of the *laissez-faire* system').

With Dilke disabled by the scandal and temporarily out of the running, Chamberlain now embarked on a bid for the leadership of a party that he believed would be radicalised at the elections and swept to victory on his programme. He was encouraged in his calculations by the fact that Gladstone had once again been ill and was recuperating that summer in Norway. But he reckoned without Gladstone's resilience and proceeded to make a series of strategic mistakes which would have been less likely had Dilke been able to play a full part.

At the beginning of September, James asked Dilke to mediate in a row which had flared up over the radical programme between Chamberlain and Hartington.[7] In a speech at Waterfoot, the latter had challenged the radicals' land reform scheme. As Dilke's confidence returned, so too did his optimism about the possibilities for radicalism. The democratic reforms, he told James, had made the Liberal Party vastly more radical and any future cabinet must reflect that fact. Chamberlain was therefore quite right to make clear to the electorate the differences that existed between the Whigs and the radicals, and to announce that he was not prepared to join an administration dominated by Hartington.[8] It may be that Hartington's speech had been deliberately calculated to outmanoeuvre Chamberlain by drawing from Gladstone a commitment to lead the party.[9] If so, then it succeeded. Hartington and Chamberlain had their own separate reasons for keeping Gladstone as leader. Chamberlain did not wish to risk antagonising the popular following of the 'People's William'; Hartington clung to him as a moderating influence. The irony of this should not go unremarked. For Gladstone returned to lead the party into a campaign for Home Rule that neither of them wanted.

On 10 September Chamberlain told Gladstone that he could not concur with Hartington's opinions and that Dilke, who was still at Highbury, 'agrees in my conclusion'. Despite the distraction caused by the need to prepare his case, Dilke had nevertheless found time that summer to take out the draft Local Government Bills of 1883 and 1884, dust them down, and incorporate Scotland and Ireland into a revised and enlarged scheme. In addition, he proposed to extend the principle of decentralisation by revivifying the parishes. The preoccupation of the radicals with land reform prompted this move. Dilke regarded the parish as the ideal body to provide allotments for agricultural labourers. Chamberlain now conveyed the substance of these new proposals to Gladstone, adding that it would be impossible for the radicals to join a government that would not concede them or free education. He reaffirmed their support for Gladstone's leadership but urged him to consider their demands.[10]

These entreaties failed to sway Gladstone, who proceeded to publish his own moderate manifesto on 18 September which, leaning as it did towards Hartington's view of land reform and making no concession on education, was regarded by Chamberlain as 'a slap in the face'. On returning from a speaking tour of Scotland, he informed Dilke, who had now left Highbury, that he was going to tell Gladstone of his dissatisfaction with the manifesto and of his intention not to join any government confined within its narrow lines: 'If we chose to go into direct opposition we might smash him but the game is not worth the candle I think. I miss you here – I wish you were still with me.'[11] The game was not worth the candle because, as Chamberlain told Collings, Gladstone was 'squeezable' and would probably give way to radical pressure.[12] He therefore warned Gladstone once more that the radicals would not join any government which did not give them a free hand on local government and education.[13] Four days later he delivered what came to be called his 'ultimatum speech', in which he made public his desire to stand aside rather than join a government on Gladstone's limited programme.

He was convinced that Gladstone would give way, if not immediately then certainly after a radical victory at the elections. On 28 September he advised Dilke when he next spoke 'to emphasise our determination not to be lay figures in a Cabinet of Goschens. I do not think they can or will try to do without us, but if they do we will make it lively for them!'[14]

Following his role as best man at Dilke's wedding, Chamberlain, much to his surprise, was suddenly summoned to Hawarden. From there he wrote to Dilke praising a speech the latter had made the previous evening, and pouring scorn on the attempts of the press to create differences between them: 'I verily believe that if I spoke your speech & you spoke mine, they would still find the distinguishing characteristics of each speaker unchanged.'[15] This was a happy sentiment but hardly a true one.

Two days later he informed Dilke of the outcome of his conversation with Gladstone. The old man, he believed, was 'more than ever impressed with the advantages of the Central Council scheme' for Ireland. But, when presented with Dilke's plan for a multi-purpose local government reform and their request for a free hand in education, he 'boggled a good deal... & said it was very weakening to a Government but I told him we could not honestly do less & that I expected a large majority of Liberals in favour of the proposal'. Gladstone remained non-committal and indicated once again his intention to give up the leadership in the near future. Chamberlain told him that the radicals would expect far greater concessions from Hartington than from him, and that they expected the next cabinet to reflect the growth in radical influence. 'He seemed impressed', Chamberlain concluded, 'but did not say anything – nor give any hint as to the composition of the next. The only suggestive remark was his warm praise of Lord Granville, which I thought suspicious & indicating an intention to have him again in the Government.'[16]

If Hartington wanted war, Chamberlain told Harcourt on 9 October, then 'Dilke and Morley and I will in that case formulate a still more definite and advanced policy and we will try to run a Radical in every constituency. We have no alternative. If we were now to give up the very moderate minimum to which we are committed, the very stones would cry out and we should simply be elbowed out of the way to make room for more advanced and less reasonable politicians.'[17] In other words, it was imperative to radicalise the Liberal Party and to introduce the reforms that would neutralise the socialist challenge.

On 13 October, Dilke unveiled his local government proposals in a lengthy, detailed and complex speech at Halifax. *The Times* praised him for his pluck in dealing with such a subject in a non-party manner on the eve of an election. There is no doubt that the speech was probably beyond the comprehension of a large section of his audience. He was not therefore thinking of their grasp of its details, but rather of its impact upon their everyday lives, when he described the plan as 'English constructive Radicalism['s] ... first grand chance of winning the affections of the people'.[18] The creation of popularly-elected county councils, county borough councils and district councils envisaged in the draft bill of 1883 was now to be rounded off by the establishment of democratic parish vestries and of elective boards for England, Ireland, Scotland and Wales. The vestries would be given powers to manage parochial charity lands, to control commons and recreation grounds and resist enclosures, and to take land compulsorily for allotments and housing. In the setting up of the national boards, Ireland would be given priority as it was now a matter of urgency that she should be given the widest form of elective self-government 'consistent with the integrity of the Empire', a phrase that was beginning to become almost ritualistic in the speeches of proponents of devolution.

By this stage Chamberlain had cooled completely on Irish reform. He had been angered by Manning's refusal on 'so small a matter' as the letters of introduction to the bishops and, in October, he refused to have further talks with the cardinal. 'The Irish business is not the first just now', he told Dilke, but a little over a week later was expressing uneasiness at hints from Gladstone that Irish matters might elbow out all others.[19] He was still at loggerheads with Hartington, and he informed Grosvenor, the Liberal Chief Whip, that, without certain concessions, the radicals would not join a Liberal administration and would form a separate party if Gladstone retired. This information was passed on to Gladstone, who regarded it as 'putting a pistol to the head of a man with whom he is in negotiation'. Chamberlain retracted the threat.[20] He was now inclined to be more conciliatory but, in emphasising other planks in the radical programme as alternatives to the Irish question, made a series of miscalculations that led many to question his political judgement.

His principal error was to introduce disestablishment into the campaign in an attempt to rally Nonconformist support. Instead, it united the Conservatives around the cry of 'The Church in Danger'.[21] Nor did free education – which was linked to disestablishment through disendowment as one means of meeting the cost – prove a popular campaigning issue. It posed a threat to Roman Catholic schools and provided an additional reason, along with Parnell's instruction to them to do so, for Irish Catholics to vote Tory.[22] There were also fears that free education would lead to higher taxes at a time of economic recession. Unemployment was at its highest level since 1879 and there had been a rise in industrial disputes. A fair trade campaign was effective in swinging votes to the Conservatives in many of the boroughs. Grosvenor placed the blame squarely on Chamberlain's shoulders for frightening away 'shoals' of voters from the Liberals.[23] As Chamberlain sought to extricate himself from these difficulties by amending his proposals for disestablishment and disendowment, he only succeeded in making matters worse, not least by alienating the Nonconformists whom he had set out to capture.

Chamberlain's choice of campaign issues made it even more difficult for Dilke to defend what was becoming an increasingly marginal seat. 'Even my Nonconformist friends come to me to implore me to pledge myself against disestablishment ...', he told Chamberlain on 19 November, 'and free education is unpopular. I'm now fighting the election entirely on City guilds, and against protective duties – these are the only two questions on which I find our views popular.'[24] Dilke was therefore having to back-pedal fairly smartly on the radical programme. In the event he scraped home on 25 November with a slender majority of 175 votes. His verdict was that disestablishment had allowed the church 'to beat the non-cons out of the field'.[25] His own inclination had been to focus on local government and it is difficult to believe that Chamberlain would have made such a serious tactical blunder in going for disestablishment had Dilke's influence not been diminished.

Despite Chamberlain's *faux pas*, the radicals had reason to be satisfied with the outcome of the November general election. The reformed constitution resulted in the return of 335 Liberals and 249 Conservatives. The Irish Nationalists, with eighty-six, exactly held the balance, a vindication of Parnell's strategy and a tense curtain-raiser to what was to follow. Single-member constituencies worked their magic for the Con-servatives in the boroughs where the 'Villa Tories' made significant gains, especially in London and the Lancashire towns. The Conservatives finished with a majority in the English boroughs for the first time since 1832. It is difficult to estimate how permanent this pattern would have been, as Home Rule was to transform the picture. The shift probably reflects the gradual consolidation of middle-class Conservatism, but it may partly be explained by the swing of the pendulum. More certain and permanent was the decline in the landowning Whig party; and the increase in the business and, more especially, professional composition of the parliamentary Liberal Party. Moreover, nearly half of the Liberal MPs were new – a very high turnover.[26] In these circumstances, the radicals could look forward with confidence to the formation of the next Liberal government and expect it to reflect these broader changes.

On 5 December the radical cabal of Chamberlain, Morley, Lefevre and Dilke met at Highbury to conduct an election post-mortem and to consider future strategy. What transpired in that weekend of talks is not certain but, in view of the probable balance that the Irish would hold in the next parliament, the radicals appear to have agreed that the Tories should be allowed to remain in office. Trevelyan, who had been unable to attend the meeting, wrote to Highbury in favour of this course, and Morley was inclined to support it. Chamberlain had suggested to Dilke in the previous week that they should keep the Tories in for a couple of years and then once again go for disestablishment of the church. Dilke, having apparently learnt more from the recent experience than his friend and conscious that disestablishment was more of a vote-loser in London than in Birmingham, poured cold water on this particular addendum to their strategy, and persuaded him to drop it from the radical agenda.[27] The cabal searched for an alternative. On 6 December Chamberlain admitted in a letter to Harcourt, that 'we are dreadfully in want of an "urban cow". The boroughs do not care for our present programme and I confess I do not know what substitute to offer them.'[28]

Dilke was more certain. He believed that local government was still an effective rallying-issue. On leaving Highbury, he pressed ahead with a series of speeches urging the priority of local government over any Irish settlement. At the Central Poor Law Conference on 9 December, he promised the Conservative government his support if they introduced a bill on the lines of his Halifax proposals.[29] Three days later, in a speech to the Eleusis Club, he firmly grasped the nettle by announcing that the radicals were in favour of keeping the Tories in. It has been suggested that Dilke wanted to delay the formation of a Liberal administration until the Crawford case was out of the way.[30] If this was indeed his motive then it badly backfired, for the government's resignation in January could not have come at a worse time. Nor does it explain Dilke's part in drafting, three weeks before the first trial, the amendment which precipitated the change in government, an action which if anything demonstrates either foolhardiness or a complete lack of self-interest on his part.

The full tragedy of Dilke's temporary withdrawal from politics was revealed by his Eleusis speech. He had lost contact with Gladstone and, as he afterwards admitted, did not know the direction his thoughts were tending at that moment. In fact, Gladstone's mind was undergoing one of its periodic seismic upheavals, the tremors on this occasion being brought on by the Irish problem. By late summer he had come to the realisation that the central board scheme would not be sufficient to satisfy nationalist sentiment. Chamberlain later claimed that Gladstone went for Home Rule in order to dish the radicals and their programme and to unite the party around a single issue under his leadership. This is unlikely. Gladstone's motives derived from a mixture of long political experience and deep-seated moral conviction. Crude pressure from Chamberlain characteristically made him more rather than less combative and he was able to draw upon a well-honed political cunning when Chamberlain tried to 'squeeze' him. Far more important, however, in determining his commitment to Home Rule was his strong sense that justice demanded it.

Dilke's speech set off a chain of events. Wemyss Reid, the editor of the *Leeds Mercury*, told Herbert Gladstone that he detected in it a 'clever trap' designed to keep the latter's father out of office.[31] Gladstone himself, however, refused to be bounced into any premature announcements. 'I agree most strongly that I must remain obstinately silent as to my plans', he told Rosebery. 'If P[arnell] and the Government cannot agree, that opens a new situation … I do not mean to be sat upon by D[ilke] or by D. & C[hamberlain], if other things call on me to act … I think it may be best to ignore Dilke.'[32] But Herbert was not prepared to sit back and let the radicals make the running and, on 14 December, he announced through the press his father's conversion to Home Rule. The launching of this, the so-called 'Hawarden Kite', was directly attributable to Dilke's speech, as Harcourt informed Chamberlain a fortnight later:

> … I have discovered today on the *most authentic information* that the *démarche* of Herbert [*sic*] was a deliberate countermove to Dilke's foolish speech which as you know gave great offence to the Party generally but especially at Hawarden. At the latter place it was regarded & was no doubt represented as the outward & visible sign of a plot believed to be hatched at Birmingham to keep the G.O.M. out of office. The chivalrous Herbert therefore thought it his duty to defeat this plan & took his measures accordingly. This you may depend upon it is the true history of this extraordinary & mischievous proceeding. It is a good illustration of how one folly begets another & one piece of mischief has the most unexpected results. If Dilke had only held his tongue 'the fire would not have burned the stick & the stick would not have beaten the dog & the dog would not have worried the cat etc. etc.' & we should not have been in the very infernal mess in which we find ourselves, all at loggerheads because one man chooses to play his own game off his own bat. The only thing now to do is to wipe up this nasty mess as soon and as well as we can.[33]

The mess was not so easy to wipe up, despite anxious attempts by Herbert to make it clear that no plan for Home Rule had been drawn up and that there had been no negotiations whatsoever between his father and Parnell.[34] Nonetheless, the antagonism between Gladstone and Chamberlain on the Irish question now came out into the open. The next six months witnessed the political machinations that culminated in the defeat of the Home Rule Bill and the secession of Chamberlain and his followers from the Liberal Party. The divorce case prevented Dilke from playing a major part in these events and they are of interest to this narrative only in so far as they marked the break-up of his longstanding friendship and alliance with Chamberlain, which delayed, with in-estimable consequences for the Liberal Party, the radicalisation of its leadership.

At the outset, Chamberlain was supportive of Dilke, despite the furore that his speech had caused. When Morley denounced it as 'a downright false move', Chamberlain dissented. He told Morley on 15 December that he thought Dilke was, in principle, right: 'If Mr G's manifesto is the be-all and end-all of the Liberal policy I am glad that the Tories are to carry it out. It is good enough for them – it is not nearly good enough for us.'[35]

Within twenty-four hours, Chamberlain had completely veered round. 'We must temporise', he told Dilke:

> It will be better to stick to Mr G. ... The Press, I suppose, is sure to try & find differences between you & me but it does not matter. They have done it before & we understand each other.
>
> Besides it will puzzle them – it is a good thing. They know that we are working together & they will perhaps think it is some astute Machiavellianism on our parts to differ slightly at times.[36]

The next night, in a speech at Birmingham, he shifted his position to one of 'cooperation' with Gladstone for the introduction of some form of Home Rule consistent with the integrity of the empire. Chamberlain was no mean practitioner of the art of 'astute Machiavellianism'. The 'Kite' had shifted the political agenda, away from the radical programme to Home Rule, and he had to respond to this changed circumstance. He now calculated that the only way to prevent the creation of a separate Irish parliament was from the inside. Surely Gladstone would compromise rather than split the party for Irish independence? Even if he did proceed with his intentions, the radicals would defeat him, and Gladstone would be forced to retire. Who would replace him? Dilke had suffered a setback from which he seemed unlikely to recover. The leadership of a radical Liberal Party would inevitably fall, therefore, to Chamberlain.[37] Such was the logic behind his sudden change of front. Dilke excused Chamberlain because he thought he was opposing Gladstone and Home Rule out of a commitment to the central board scheme. But Chamberlain had already made up his mind that the Irish would never accept such a moderate change, and that it was necessary therefore to prepare for an all-out battle against Home Rule and damn the consequences. The consequences were to be fearful – the loss of close friends such as Dilke and Morley; the division of the Liberal Party; and, above all, the defeat of Home Rule.

Dilke was initially stung by Chamberlain's sudden turnabout. 'I expected you to "temporise"', he wrote on 17 December, 'but not to go right round.' On giving the matter more thought, he recognised that there was some justification for Chamberlain's action, and sent a second letter to Highbury that day:

> I find no fault at all & think what you do inevitable. It is a little 'rough on' me to have to be converted to your view & then converted back again (I mean as regards *Ireland*) so rapidly, but I saw both sides before & I see both now. We last week sacrificed principle in my opinion to expediency (dissolution will smash us). I consider that we are returning to principle as regards Ireland, tho' I am hopeless about it.
>
> But for myself personally, the situation is grave. I shall appear to have taken a line for personal reasons of a not very creditable nature & then for the same reasons to have got

frightened & backed out of it. Also, I shall be beaten at Chelsea when we are driven to dissolution.[38]

Chamberlain's reply began somewhat tongue-in-cheek in view of the fact that it was he who had suggested keeping the Tories in power in the first place. 'Have I turned around?' he asked. 'Perhaps I have but it is unconsciously.' He 'honestly' believed that Dilke had gone beyond what they had agreed, but he assured him that he would not put him 'in a hole for a King's ransom'. His conclusion was uncompromising:

> Finally, my view is that Mr G.'s Irish scheme is death & damnation; that we must try & stop it – that we must not openly commit ourselves against it yet – that we must let the situation shape itself before we finally decide ... .[39]

Both men spoke in public that evening. 'The Papers seem to show that I have succeeded in avoiding any kind of conflict with you', Chamberlain wrote to Dilke the next morning, adding 'Your speech was most judicious.' Dilke replied: 'You have not turned round a bit in yr. speeches, it is in private I mean – as to the *possibility* of supporting Mr G.'s scheme. But yr. letters today are plainer, & are in *full* harmony with my view.'[40] The first crack in the radical alliance was thus rather clumsily papered over.

Chamberlain had not been quite frank with Dilke. He had not yet intimated that he no longer regarded the board scheme as viable. Therefore Dilke did not recognise the situation for what it was – a full-blooded battle with Gladstone for the leadership of the Liberal Party. When Dilke announced his intention to speak at Rugby on 31 December in favour of the scheme, Chamberlain at first urged him not to do so. Dilke's insistence, however, led Chamberlain to inform him at last of his decision to abandon the board scheme on the grounds that it was unacceptable to the Nationalists. Irish independence, on the other hand, would lead eventually to a war with England in which Ireland would have the support of some other power. The *via media* of Home Rule would grant Ireland separation and its attendant dangers without at the same time removing Irish obstructionists from Westminster and was, therefore, even less desirable than independence, to which it was but a step. An alternative would be a federal arrangement with national parliaments for England, Scotland, Wales, Ulster and the rest of Ireland; an imperial parliament in charge of defence, foreign affairs, post office and customs; and a supreme court. In such a settlement there would be no place for the House of Lords or, indeed, the monarchy. 'As a Radical, all these changes have no terrors for me', Chamberlain claimed, but was such 'a clean sweep of existing institutions' necessary, he asked, simply to satisfy the Irish demand for Home Rule?[41]

Chamberlain appeared to have no doubts that Dilke would fall in with him. The next day, in reviewing Gladstone's Home Rule proposals, he asked, 'What are *we* to do?' On 31 December he wrote, 'I have had a great row with Morley over his speech. I am afraid our Party will again be reduced to two.' But Dilke had not accepted Chamberlain's analysis. The fact of Irish opposition to the central board scheme was not, he replied, sufficient reason to abandon it, and he went ahead with his speech in its favour at Rugby.[42]

The next day, the first of the new year, Hartington, Harcourt, Chamberlain and Dilke met at Devonshire House to seek a solution, but the ethics of Herbert Gladstone's action in launching the Hawarden Kite seemed to take precedence in their discussions over any serious attempt at agreeing future policy. They gave notice that they would call a party meeting if Gladstone did not disavow Home Rule. As he had not yet made any public commitment, the threat was meaningless. Dilke was acutely conscious of his inability to carry much weight during these deliberations. Not only had he to face the distraction of the impending trial but, until it was out of the way, many of his former colleagues refused to deal seriously with him. When Gladstone came up to London on 11 January, and held a conclave of leading Liberals, Dilke was perplexed to hear him whisper to Harcourt, 'this is very awkward', in reference to his presence. Then he was kept in ignorance of the arrangements for the Queen's Speech dinner and, he opined to Chamberlain, 'I did not like to *ask*'.[43] The extent to which he was becoming out of touch with the party leadership became clear on 26 January, when he was sternly advised against moving a resolution condemning Salisbury's threat to send the Mediterranean fleet to dissuade Greece from naval operations against Turkey.[44]

Later that same day, Salisbury's interim minority government was defeated on a radical motion in favour of the provision of allotments for agricultural workers. This 'three acres and a cow' amendment was proposed by Jesse Collings, a Birmingham acolyte of Chamberlain's, but had, according to Dilke, been drafted by himself and Chamberlain over breakfast at 76 Sloane Street on 21 January.[45] Gladstone's third administration was assembled just a fortnight before the first trial and there was no place in it for Dilke. Gladstone was under pressure from the Queen to exclude him. He did, however, write a kind note on 2 February expressing his regret, which Dilke found touching.[46]

The radicals were therefore unable to dominate the new government in the manner they had anticipated. Although the radical balance in the cabinet was ostensibly strengthened by the inclusion of Morley, as Irish Secretary, and A. J. Mundella, at the Board of Trade, the former was increasingly gravitating towards Gladstone, to Chamberlain's great ire, while neither of them was an adequate replacement for Dilke. Henry Campbell-Bannerman entered for the first time at the War Office. Harcourt and Childers exchanged the posts which they had held in the previous Liberal administration, with the former now taking the Exchequer and the latter the Home Office. Old Whigs like Granville, Kimberley, Spencer and Ripon remained. Rosebery became Foreign Secretary. In a kind note to Dilke he wrote with some truth that, had the latter not been compelled to stand aside, the office would have been his by 'universal consent'. Dilke, who for a time regarded Rosebery as the most ambitious man he had ever met, replied with equal magnanimity that he hoped Rosebery would always hold the post while the Liberals were in power.[47]

Nor did Chamberlain get the high office he had once expected. Gladstone was able to treat him with something approaching disdain and to take little account of his views in planning Liberal strategy. This was possible partly because of Chamberlain's tactical errors during the election campaign, which had tarnished his star, and also because of Dilke's weakness. However, in view of the repeated radical emphasis on the immediate importance of local government reform, Chamberlain's appointment to Dilke's old office was probably not intended by Gladstone to be quite the severe snub which Chamberlain clearly felt it to be.

That Chamberlain interpreted it in this way is evidence of his preoccupation now with the grander struggle for control of the Liberal Party. In these circumstances, he was happy to let Dilke take charge of drafting a Local Government Bill. Dilke therefore found himself in the rather curious position of presiding over the committee which drew up the legislation, even though he was not a member of the government. His scheme of 1883–84 was expanded to include the parochial reforms outlined at Halifax, but the bill was never brought forward because of the Home Rule crisis.[48]

In that developing crisis, Dilke increasingly felt the seriousness of his inability to act as mediator in the stand off between Gladstone and Chamberlain. He tried to persuade John Morley to take his place: 'My *one* hope', he wrote to him on 2 February, 'is that you will work as completely with Chamberlain as I did. It is the only way to stand against the overwhelming numbers of the Whig peers.'[49] But Chamberlain had already dispensed with Morley. The showdown between the radicals and the Whigs had been displaced by the imminent showdown between Chamberlain and Gladstone. Sensing what lay ahead, Dilke wrote to Chamberlain on 31 January:

I feel that our friendship is going to be subjected to the heaviest strain it has ever borne, & I wish to minimise any risks to it, in which, however, I don't believe. I am determined that it shall not dwindle into a form or pretence of friendship of which the substance has departed. It will be a great change if I do not feel that I can go to your house or to your room as freely as ever. At the same time confidence from one in the inner circle of the cabinet to one wholly outside the Government is not easy, & reserve makes all conversation untrue. I think the awkwardness will be less if I abstain from taking part in home affairs: (unless, indeed, in supporting my Local Govt. Bill, shd. that come up). In Foreign Affairs we shall not be brought into conflict, & to Foreign & Colonial affairs I propose to return .... .[50]

During February he was preoccupied with the divorce trial, and it was not until 3 March that he reappeared in the House, attending it for the first time since the formation of the new government. The next day he called on Chamberlain and told him that if he resigned over the Home Rule Bill and led a radical secession, he would wreck the party. Chamberlain felt that he was obliged to go because of the opinions he had expressed since before Christmas. 'Certainly', Dilke responded. 'But do not go out and fight. Go out and lie low.'[51]

Later that month, he sent Chamberlain a copy of the resolution he proposed to move at a meeting of the Chelsea Liberal Association: 'That while this meeting is firmly resolved on the maintenance of the Union between Great Britain and Ireland, it is of opinion that the wishes of the Irish people in favour of self-government as expressed at the last election should receive satisfaction.' Chamberlain replied that the two things were inconsistent, that Irish wishes as voiced by Parnell were for separation, and suggested the substitution of 'satisfaction' with 'favourable consideration'. Dilke thought the change insignificant and carried the resolution in its amended form. In the course of his speech he attacked land purchase, but reserved judgement on the Home Rule Bill until its details were known. He believed, however, that he would be able to support it.[52] Even now, Chamberlain was convinced that Dilke was still on his side. Balfour dined with him on 22 March and attributed his truculence and inclination to resign to 'Dilke's position' and Gladstone's 'refusal to have anything to do with him'.[53] Four days later Chamberlain resigned. The next day he told Dilke: 'We have a devil of a time before us.'[54]

Dilke's main concern now was to save the Liberal Party for radicalism and radicalism for the Liberal Party. At the beginning of April Hartington asked him to arrange a meeting with Chamberlain on behalf of the Whigs. He did so, but warned Chamberlain against allying with them and 'being driven into coercion as a follower of a Goschen-Hartington-James-Brand-Albert Grey clique'.[55] Labouchere too was trying at this time to convince Chamberlain that the future of radicalism was more important than the

Irish question. He wanted Chamberlain to use Home Rule to drive the Whigs out as a prelude to becoming leader of a radicalised party.[56] Dilke still believed that a compromise might be arranged between Gladstone and Chamberlain, possibly on the basis of a scheme which kept Irish representation at Westminster, but Chamberlain, now thoroughly disillusioned with Gladstone and bent on seeing the battle through to the end, refused to make conciliatory overtures, while Gladstone simply ignored Dilke.

With Chamberlain unwilling to compromise and Dilke unwilling to vote against a measure which he had never opposed in principle, their political alliance was finished. The Home Rule Bill was brought before the House on 8 April and debated over the next few weeks with great passion. On 30 April Chamberlain read in the *Daily News* of Dilke's intention to vote for it. He immediately wrote to him to the effect that he hoped they would not be separated upon 'this vital question', adduced evidence to show that the bill was 'doomed' and invited him to Highbury to discuss the situation. The letter was signed 'Yours very truly' instead of the customary 'Yours ever', indicating Chamberlain's displeasure.[57] Dilke refused to go to Highbury but made one last attempt to persuade Chamberlain to change his mind. Although personally against it, he would be prepared for the sake of the party to accept Chamberlain's demand for the retention of Irish representation at Westminster and would not openly declare his support for Home Rule:

> The reason, as you know, why I am so anxious for *you* (which matters more than I matter at present or shall for a long time) to find yourself able if possible to take the offers made you & vote for the 2R [second reading] is that the dissolution will wreck the party, but yet leave *a* party, – democratic, because all the moderates will go over to the Tories, – poor, because all the subscribers will go over to the Tories, – more Radical than the party has ever been, – & yet – as things now stand, with you outside of it .... .[58]

Most rank-and-file radicals wanted to clear Ireland out of the way and move on to the pressing domestic reforms of the radical programme. Many of the Liberal intelligentsia of the Second Reform Bill era – such as Dicey and Goldwin Smith – deserted the party over Home Rule. They were soon replaced by new liberal intellectuals – such as Hobson and Hobhouse – who were prepared to address social reform issues. Grassroot support for Gladstone came through the backing of the NLF, once Chamberlain's own creature. Nonconformists and labour leaders also supported Gladstone. But this radicalised Liberal party – radicalised by the election and then by the Whig exodus – lacked a leader to take it towards the twentieth century. Chamberlain had the opportunity but spurned it, his conservatism on Irish nationalism evidence perhaps that he was never in any case suited to the task. Dilke would have fitted the role, and herein lay the tragedy of his political ruin. In these respects, it might be said that the plans of the two radicals for the future of the Liberal Party had been thwarted by a pretty young woman and an old man in a hurry. After Gladstone, it had only the leadership of Rosebery to fall back upon, a peer who lacked radical vision and the capacity to transform it into a vehicle of social democracy that would retain working-class support. Liberalism in the end had to undergo a period of sand-ploughing that was disastrous for its long-term prospects.

It was two days before Chamberlain could bring himself to reply to Dilke's appeal, perhaps aware for the first time of the enormity of the course upon which, without his erstwhile colleague, he was about to embark:

> Yr. letter has greatly troubled me. My pleasure in politics has gone & I hold very loosely to public life just now. The friends with whom I have worked so long are many of them separated from me. The party is going blindly to its ruin & everywhere there seems a want of courage & decision & principle which almost causes one to despair ... .
>
> During all our years of intimacy I have never had a suspicion, until the last few weeks, that we differed on the Irish question ... .

He would vote against the Home Rule Bill, while Dilke must do as his conscience directed him:

> But you must be prepared for unkind things said by those who know how closely we have been united hitherto.
>
> The present crisis is of course life and death to me. I shall win if I can and if I can't I will cultivate my garden. I do not care for the leadership of a party which should prove itself so fickle & so careless of National interests as to sacrifice the unity of the Empire to the precipitate impatience of an old man, careless of the future in which he can have no part – & to an uninstructed instinct which will not take the trouble to exercise judgment & criticism.[59]

Chamberlain did not pause to consider the extent to which his own lack of 'judgment & criticism' contributed to the *impasse*. He closed the letter once more with a 'Yours very truly', and on the following day used the still more formal 'Yours sincerely'.[60]

Dilke, who had always been the more emotionally involved in the friendship, was stung into writing what was for him an exceptionally long letter:

> I need not say to you who know what I am what it has been to receive from you a letter which ends with a form of words intended to be cold by the side of that which for so great

a number of years you have used to me. Your letter must have been written just at the moment when I was trying to express something of what I owe to your affection, which, it seems, that at that very time I had lost. It is a curious fact that we should without a difference have gone through the trials of the years in which we were rivals, & that the differences & the break should have come now that I have, – at least in my own belief, & that of most people, – ceased for ever to count at all in politics ...

I am so anxious for you personally, & for the Radical cause that anything shall be done by the Govt. that will allow you to vote for the 2R., & so succeed to the lead of the party become purged of the Whig element ... *I care (in great doubt as to the future of Ireland & as to that of the Empire) more about the future of Radicalism & about your return to the party & escape from the Whigs than about anything else as to which I am clear & free from doubt ...* As to inclination, – I feel as strongly as any man can as to the *way* in which Mr Gladstone has done this thing, & all my inclination is therefore to follow you, – where affection also leads. But – if this is to be, – what it will be – a fight not as to the way & the man, & the past, but as to the future, the 2R will be a choice between acceptance of a vast change which has in one form or the other become inevitable, & on the other side Hartington-Goschen opposition, with coercion behind it. I am only a camp follower now, but my place is not in the camp of the Goschens, Hartingtons, Brands, Heneages, Greys.[61]

Dilke concluded by saying that if he voted against the bill, he would be betraying his principles and the constituents who had elected him knowing his views. He believed that Chamberlain would win the battle, signed 'Yours ever', and added a postscript reaffirming his faith in their friendship – 'I don't believe in the difference, & I have merely scribbled all I think in the old way.' No matter what Dilke believed, the difference existed and was irreconcilable.

Chamberlain's reply of 6 May was a half-hearted attempt to heal the breach. Although he began with an excuse about the strain and tension under which he had last written, he was still unable to muster anything more than a 'Yours ever sincerely' at the end. While he said that he did not include Dilke among those 'most intimate associates' who had crossed him and with whom he could never work again 'with the slightest real pleasure or confidence', the tone of the letter suggested that it would not be long before Dilke would join the ranks of the Morleys and Lefevres who had refused to bend to his domineering will. 'You must do what you believe to be right,' Chamberlain condescended, 'even though it sends us for once into opposite lobbies.'[62]

Dilke was 'touched' by Chamberlain's letter and vowed to say no more of the matter and to record a 'silent vote' for the Home Rule Bill. His estimate of Chamberlain's response was coloured by the support he had received from him during his private misfortunes. It was for Emilia and 'a perfect blessedness of daily life' that he had saved him, and for that Dilke would be eternally grateful. 'Nothing', he told Chamberlain, 'could ever come really between us, because it takes two to make a fight, & even if your mind was turned against me it would come back to me when you found as you would find that nothing could ever turn mine against you.' The radical alliance was dead but the friendship survived for a few years simply because, as Dilke admitted in the same letter, he 'counted now for about 1/4th of Tom Potter!'[63]

During May Chamberlain strove to coordinate opposition to the bill, leading dissident radicals alongside diehard Whigs in the very sort of alliance that Dilke had bridled at. The strategy was successful. Gladstone refused to compromise in order to appease Chamberlain, and the Home Rule Bill was, accordingly, defeated on the second reading on 8 June by the combined opposition of Tories, Chamberlainite radicals and renegade Whigs, who finished with an overall majority of thirty. Most radicals had gone into the Home Rule lobby, but a sufficiently sizeable minority had gone with Chamberlain and thereby ensured the measure's defeat. Dilke recorded his silent vote for the bill.

Gladstone's only choice was to put the issue to the country. Dilke, preoccupied as he was with the forthcoming second trial, was narrowly defeated by 176 votes at Chelsea on 5 July 1886. He had anticipated defeat for some time, but his strong support among the working class of Kensal Town had enabled him to hold the seat against the odds in 1880 and 1885. His defeat had little to do with the scandal or the Tory revival and more to do with the increasingly residential character of Chelsea, especially after the boundary changes wrought by his own Redistribution Act. The country's verdict was a decisive rejection of Home Rule. The Liberals lost 143 seats, a reversal without parallel since 1832. The Conservatives, now becoming more clearly identifiable as the party of the middle class, were returned with a majority, but one dependent upon the phalanx of anti-Home Rule Liberals. The split in the Liberal Party was to prove irrevocable and was damaging to its long-term chances of survival. Without the Whigs it could not become the party of property, while its close identification with Irish Home Rule and its loss of effective radical leaders meant that it would struggle to become a broadly-based progressive party.

Chamberlain inevitably found himself aligned with the Conservatives, at a cost to his former radicalism. While Dilke was outside politics, their friendship could survive, but its undulations of intensity gradually decreased. By early 1887 he was confiding to his diary that the 'split' had 'spoilt Chn.', and that he would be 'very difficult for all men to work with in the future'. He and Randolph Churchill were now 'like rogue elephants'. By November 1890 Chamberlain was apologising for having little spare time in which to call on Dilke and expressing a desire for more frequent meetings: 'owing to the changes in our lives and the pressure on both of us, we have been slipping away from one another – and this I do not desire or intend'. He did what he could to assist Dilke's re-election. However, on re-entering the House in 1892, Dilke found 'Chamberlain's debating power marvellous, but, while his method has improved, it is play acting, & no longer carries the conviction of conviction with it, – which, to me, is everything. I admire him immensely, – but he seems to have sold his old true self to the Devil.' Henceforward, political rivalry made friendship more and more impossible. In March 1894 Chamberlain was complaining of a rumour, which had no foundation as it proved, that Dilke was to speak in Birmingham to his 'political opponents'.[64] Their correspondence was already dwindling by this date, and their respective stands on South Africa and, later, the fiscal controversy, showed that intimacy was no longer possible. A thread from the past remained and Chamberlain continued to write occasionally until 1906, when he was incapacitated by a stroke and confined to a wheelchair. When Dilke died in 1911, he sent his son Austen to the funeral on his behalf. Perhaps Dilke's death stirred memories of the unfulfilled dreams and hopes that the two radicals had once shared and which had been shattered in the small space of just twelve months.

Dilke had played little part in Irish questions prior to 1885–86, and he played little part in them thereafter.[65] But he had an appreciation of the depth of nationalist feeling in Ireland towards which Chamberlain, by contrast, was almost totally unsympathetic. In 1883 he had observed that, 'The Irish movement is Nationalist. It is patriotic – not cosmopolitan, and is as detached from French Anarchism and German or American Socialism as is the Polish Nationalist movement.' Whereas Chamberlain believed that Home Rule or independence would put the empire in jeopardy and make war between England and Ireland likely, Dilke was of entirely the opposite opinion. 'Ireland', he said at the time of the Home Rule crisis, 'would behave as other nations had done when granted the privileges which were now demanded by the Nationalists ... A people should be trusted to govern themselves and ... when so trusted the result was the establishment of a firm and good government.'[66] He had always admitted that his understanding of the Irish problem was limited, but in 1885–86 he had firmly held that the time was ripe for a solution. The failure to move forward with any sort of settlement in that year was one further illustration of his own aphorism that the course of Irish history was cursed with tardy remedies.

Chapter 14

Picking up the Pieces

At the time of the second verdict and his election defeat, Dilke was still only forty-three – an age at which politicians were usually beginning not ending their ministerial careers – and he might reasonably have looked forward to another twenty years or so in the higher echelons of the British political establishment. Politics had been his life and his political talents now appeared redundant. He was faced not only with the possibility of having to create a new career for himself but, more immediately, with the problem of how to occupy his unwanted leisure time.

In this last regard, two newly-acquired properties now came into their own. In 1883 he had bought land at Dockett Eddy, a small island on the upper reaches of the Thames near Shepperton, and had built there a cottage to serve as a summer retreat and a place where he could indulge his passion for rowing. It was completed in 1885 and thereafter became a regular summer haunt and the scene of frequent weekend house-parties. A boatman was employed to ferry visitors across the small stretch of water to the house. Here Dilke's social life was as strictly regimented as his political life had been. He would rise at 5 a.m. and swim in the river, breakfast at 6 a.m. and have his guests swimming at 7 a.m. A morning gallop would be followed by rowing and fencing. Much of the afternoon would be spent in reading, writing or conversation. During moments of relaxation, he would indulge his liking for large cigars and frequent cups of tea. This regime moderated only slightly with Dilke's advancing years. He began to spend some of the time on the river in a more leisurely fashion – punting, or taking Lady Dilke out in a dinghy. More time was spent in the garden, and breakfast was sometimes taken later with his guests at around 8.45 a.m. But, aside from this, there was little discernible abatement of his passion for exercise. Indeed, on his fifty-third birthday he began sculling, and he continued to fence and ride until the last months of his life.

The second retreat was a winter cottage at Pyrford Rough, Woking, just six miles from Dockett, which Dilke purchased from Lord Onslow; it was here, in 1885, that he and his new wife spent their first Christmas together. The house was architecturally ugly and, unlike Dockett, had no formal garden. Dilke surrounded the property with pine trees, which added to its privacy. It had the advantage over Dockett of being away from the winter dampness of the river and over Sloane Street of providing greater solitude and a more relaxed atmosphere. It was at Pyrford that, from the 1890s, he spent the weekends dictating his Memoir to his secretary. It was here, too, that he indulged his love of cats. There were always numerous beautiful tailless white or ginger Persians in his Pyrford cattery.

The Dilkes' principal residence remained 76 Sloane Street. This large, fashionable, London terraced house contained two drawing-rooms, two dining-rooms (one of which led out on to the back terrace where Dilke fenced), and the 'Blue Room' where visitors were normally received. In addition, there were rooms on the first floor for Dilke's private secretary and the secretary's clerk; a suite of three rooms on the second floor which were used by Wentie when he was at home; a sitting-room on the next half-landing; the master bedroom was on the third floor; and the servants' quarters at the top of the house. Lady Dilke's influence could be seen in the groaning shelves of art books that now lined its walls, which were hung too with her paintings and drawings. The furniture was adorned with her porcelain and her own valuable works of art joined those that Dilke had himself assembled over many years: paintings by Dutch and Flemish masters, drawings by Blake, miniatures and portraits of family-members past and present, and Dilke's favourite commissioned portraits – of Gambetta by Legros, of Chamberlain by Holl, of Fawcett by Ford Madox Brown, of Mill by Watts, and of Dilke himself, also by Watts. Sloane Street was the storehouse too for Dilke's unrivalled collection of Keats memorabilia, and for personally-prized possessions (such as his section of the Trinity Hall boat which had finished head of the river in 1864).

Dilke was certainly rich enough not to have to worry about finding employment, but he was not the sort of man to slide quietly into a leisurely obscurity. The trial had left him in a state of despondency and had affected Lady Dilke's health. Their social circle inevitably shrank. The ostracism which they suffered was particularly painful when it came from long-standing friends and associates. Dilke was expelled from societies with which he had had a long association, such as the Ad Eundem Club, founded in 1864 to bring together liberal intellectuals from Oxford and Cambridge and which he had joined while still at university.[1] After the trial, the couple went to Royat to recuperate. They returned to Dockett in

September. Winter was spent at Pyrford. During 1887 Dilke kept only a desultory eye on domestic politics. Chamberlain relayed to him details of the Round Table talks on Liberal reunion, the major political event of that year. But he wished to avoid controversy for the time being and preferred, therefore, to begin the patient recovery of his shattered political career by concentrating, as he had told Chamberlain he would, on foreign affairs and defence policy.

He turned once again, as in 1874, to his pen as the instrument by which to achieve rehabilitation. His first thought was to enter journalism and to edit an evening newspaper, but he soon abandoned that idea.[2] Instead, he wrote a series of six erudite articles for the *Fortnightly Review* on the relations of the European powers, which appeared anonymously, but which were shortly afterwards collected together under his name as *The Present Position of European Politics*. Germany, France, Russia, Austria-Hungary, Italy and the United Kingdom were considered in turn, the theme of the book being set in its blunt opening sentence: 'The present position of the European world is one in which sheer force holds a larger place than it has held in modern times since the fall of Napoleon.' Tension had been created by Germany's annexation of Alsace-Lorraine in 1871, but was unlikely to erupt into war providing that Russia, 'the one power which is a comet of eccentric orbit rather than a planet in the European system', was kept in check. Unfortunately, Russia was the very power with which Britain had to reckon. From this perspective, Constantinople was more important to Britain's future interests than Suez. A visit to Constantinople and Athens in the autumn had convinced Dilke that Russia must be kept out of the Turkish capital and her influence in the Mediterranean checked by the creation of a large Greek state incorporating Albania. She must be discouraged also from invading India by strengthening the defence of the North-West Frontier.

Dilke's views on Russia were not especially novel and were not, therefore, the cause of the short-lived furore that greeted the publication of his articles. Rather, critical attention focused on one particular question which he had posed. In the event of a war between Germany and France, he had asked, would Britain guarantee Belgian neutrality under the terms of the treaty of 1839? He thought it unlikely. The treaty was out-of-date and Britain's army was not up to the task. This issue became, of course, crucial a generation later, but even in 1887 any suggestion that Britain might stand aloof from a European entanglement was a source of concern in both Belgium and France, where his opinions were castigated in some sections of the press. His argument, however, had been distorted in translation. He had not said unequivocally that Britain would not come to the aid of Belgium, only that Britain was not *militarily prepared* to come to her assistance.[3]

The question of Belgian neutrality was just one small part of a broader homily that Dilke was now beginning to preach on the need for extensive military reform. A series of articles, quickly brought out in hardcovers as *The British Army*, appeared in the *Fortnightly Review* shortly after his survey of power politics in Europe, and took up where it had left off. He began with the melodramatic claim that Britain was not 'in a position to fight even France alone'.[4] A maritime power needed an army to protect its coaling-stations and garrisons, to deliver counter-attacks to an enemy and to stand surety against the danger of invasion inherent in any temporary loss of naval supremacy. It was also a necessary line of defence in India against Russia until such time as a native Indian army was sufficiently trained and equipped for the task.

In the most important essay, which became the fifth chapter of the book, Dilke outlined his 'ideal army'. The four essentials for national defence were, in his opinion, a fleet strong enough in fast cruisers to secure communications and in armed ships to act as the first line of defence by shutting in, where possible, the enemy's fleet; a separate long-service army for India untrammelled by home requirements; an expeditionary force to deliver a counter-attack; and a short-service home army to act as the second line of defence in the event of any setback to the navy. To achieve these ends, mobilisation would have to be speeded up; the shortage of cavalry-horses made good; officers trained and promoted according to merit not birth; and the soldiers themselves given adequate practical training with modern weaponry, and dressed for fighting rather than, as one evening newspaper observed in summarising Dilke's views, 'to the tastes of kitchen-maids and the model of scarlet pin-cushions'.[5] Conscription would not be necessary provided there was an improvement in conditions, especially with regard to discipline and opportunities for promotion. Dilke, unlike many Liberals, had no theoretical objection to conscription as such and thought it might be necessary in the event of a major war. The militia would become a second army of partially-trained men, providing a great increase in fighting strength and relieving the regular army of such duties as garrisoning. The volunteers would be called to arms whenever the militia was forced by dire emergency to leave the country, and the yeomanry would be trained as auxiliary cavalry and field artillery. Decentralisation was the 'mother principle' of the whole plan. This would be possible, however, only if the 'linked battalion' system, introduced by Cardwell in 1871 during the last major reform of the army, was abandoned and an entirely separate army for India established. Other aspects of Cardwell's system would be retained. For example, regiments would continue to be associated with particular districts drawing, as far as possible, recruits from their localities. Of the two army corps, one would be based at Aldershot and the other somewhere in the north of England. The whole army, which with imperial troops could total one million men, would have a general staff as its 'brain and nervous system'. Dilke concluded his survey by stating that his object in writing had been to draw attention to the shortcomings in Britain's military strength despite the huge expenditure upon it; and to show that the remedy lay not in a costly increase in the regular army but in making the best possible use of existing materials by proper organisation and utilisation of the voluntary principle.

By displaying in these writings his informed grasp of foreign and defence issues, Dilke hoped to regain some of his former respect and influence within the broader community and to deflate those critics who were waiting to attack any intimation on his part of a possible return to the political stage. During 1887 he had, for the most part, succeeded in maintaining his calculated silence on national domestic matters. He was aware that, for a while, he must be patient and allow time to work a change in public opinion. He looked first, therefore, to resuming political activity at the local level. He became an active figure in Chelsea affairs, a vestryman and chairman of the board of guardians. In April 1887 he told Joseph Reinach, the French historian, that he was happy in his marriage and in this local work, and that he was not prepared to reopen the divorce case just yet.[6] Reinach had been Gambetta's secretary until the latter's death, and had afterwards replaced him as Dilke's closest friend in France.

In the event, it was the debates on the Local Government Bill during 1888 which drew Dilke back into national politics. Chamberlain has sometimes been credited with the achievement of this legislation. He pressed for the bill and aligned his followers, the Liberal Unionists, behind it. However, it was only a shadow of the scheme prepared for him by Dilke in 1886. The latter remarked that the Conservatives proposed two-thirds of it and carried one-third. They were able to abandon large parts of the 1886 draft precisely because Chamberlain never had the influence that has been attributed to him. During the bill's preparation he was in Washington, and he was 'furious' when Salisbury outflanked the attempts by Churchill, his scheming Chancellor of the Exchequer, to secure a more radical reform. He would, he told Dilke, seek to defeat the government if the bill was 'not altered back again to suit his policy'.[7] But he did no such thing. He lent his support to the truncated measure and was able to do so because he had no very deep commitment to the scheme of 1886, which had been his in name only.

Dilke, by contrast, had just such a commitment, one sufficiently strong to lead him to abandon his Trappist silence on national domestic issues. When the bill was introduced into parliament in March 1888, he immediately published his main criticisms of it in T. P. O'Connor's new radical London evening newspaper, the *Star*, without waiting to learn all the details. He next produced, in association with a group of county MPs, two pamphlets advising radical members how to vote on the various clauses and amendments.[8]

The bill went nowhere near far enough in the direction of greater decentralisation for Dilke, but from outside parliament he felt impotent to mount a serious opposition. However, his fellow pamphleteers, the MPs Francis Stevenson and Herbert Gardner, tabled amendments on his behalf. One of these sought to include democratised parish councils in the legislation, a proposal that, by holding out a better prospect for participation to the working class, was likely to appeal to them more than the Tory focus upon county councils. The bill's critics were also against the subordination of the district to the county councils, but their opposition served only to persuade ministers to drop the former from the measure altogether in order to facilitate its passage. The act of 1888 set the pattern for future local government reform. The Liberals in 1894 worked within its hierarchical framework, introducing district and parish councils into it, but without altering the emphasis upon the county as the most important unit.

With encouragement from Chamberlain, Dilke was momentarily tempted by an invitation to stand for Fulham in the first election to the newly-created London County Council, on the grounds that it would be a stepping-stone back to national politics. But his wife persuaded him to decline the offer.[9] Such was his attachment to devolved local government by this stage that, when the LCC attempted to use its powers to reform London government in the centralising direction that he had once favoured, he now came out as a staunch defender of the second-tier authorities, organising a defence of the Chelsea vestry that helped to ensure its survival as a separate authority.[10]

Publication of *The British Army* had, meanwhile, attracted a great deal of attention and put Dilke at the forefront of military reformers. In preparing it, he had exchanged views with several distinguished officers, most notably Sir Frederick Roberts, Lord Wolseley and the brothers Charles and Henry Brackenbury.[11] Roberts had first written to him at the time of the Penjdeh crisis in support of his proposal for demarcation of the Afghan frontier. He now invited Dilke to come to India to examine at first hand the problem of defending the North-West Frontier. Accordingly, the

Dilkes spent the winter of 1888 there. Dilke described his visit and his somewhat hazardous tour of the Baluch and Afghan borders in two articles for the *Fortnightly* which have some of the sparkle of *Greater Britain*. For example, he observed: 'The first requisites in this country are a large hat and a small nose, and the officer commanding the cavalry who was out with us ... who has a large nose and a small helmet, suffered according to this rule.' He concluded that India was deficient in white troops, particularly officers; that to partition Afghanistan with Russia would be to invite invasion and alienate the Afghans (an opinion which led him into a controversy with George Curzon, later to become Viceroy of India, who favoured partition); and that, in the event of war, Britain's only possible offensive would be to attack Vladivostok, which would stretch Russian defences though in itself would probably be insufficient to bring her to her knees.[12]

The experience had confirmed and strengthened opinions which Dilke already held, especially with regard to the desirability of preserving Afghan independence with minimal British interference, and the differences on military planning that persisted between the home and Indian armies. He turned next in his writings, therefore, to demonstrating the need for coordinated imperial defence. He discussed this at some length in the *Problems of Greater Britain*, a book which he dedicated to Roberts. It was published in two volumes in January 1890 and was generally well-received. It was not, like *Greater Britain*, a work of travel, but rather one of reflection and analysis. In addition to the chapters on defence, Dilke examined social experiments in 'Greater Britain' of interest to policy-makers in England. He provided a British audience with an informed survey of colonial politics and with pen-portraits of colonial politicians, many of whom he had met on his travels and with whom he had kept up a correspondence on social, political and imperial questions.

His purpose in writing the book was in part to render *Greater Britain* obsolete. The latter was 'so much out of date' that he found its continuing success somewhat embarrassing.[13] The world had moved on since 1868 and he was not slow to recognise that many points in the earlier book were 'wholly inapplicable to existing circumstances'.[14] Above all, there was a much greater interest in imperial questions and especially on ways of establishing closer links between the mother country and the colonies. He now accepted the need for retaining the empire, especially if Britain was to compete with the emerging giants of Russia and the United States. Characteristically, he did not find much to admire in the conventional arguments of the imperial federalists for closer political and economic ties. He was one of very few to appreciate the strength of colonial nationalism, and to recognise therefore that attempts to force forward imperial union were more likely to damage rather than to strengthen the fabric of the empire. He preferred instead to emphasise the common institutions and common interests that were shared throughout Greater Britain – his book is pervaded with the sense that cooperation on such subjects was much the most effective means of retaining imperial sentiment and preserving the empire.

Dilke's prolific output of books and articles was combined with a great deal of travelling. Following his trips to Turkey and Greece in 1887 and India in 1888, he paid a visit to the German Chancellor Bismarck at his Friedrichsruh estate in 1889. He learnt from the Iron Chancellor of his bad relations with the new Emperor, and of his belief that William would not dismiss him – a misplaced optimism, for he was to survive for only a few more months. Their conversation ranged over European history and they found each other's knowledge and grasp of foreign affairs mutually stimulating. Curiously, from Dilke's account of their meeting, it seems that what struck him most was the standard of the cuisine at Friedrichsruh which, consisting as it did mainly of fish and game washed down with 'a most extraordinary mixture' of wines and beers, signally failed to impress him.[15] The annual visits to France were also kept up. The Dilkes invariably spent Christmas in Paris where, over a number of years, they acquired many friends – artists and writers, as well as politicians, including Rodin, Cambon, Jusserand, Jaurès and Ollivier. In September 1891 Dilke attended the French army manoeuvres where he encountered many of the military men later involved in the Dreyfus affair. His observations were recounted once again in the pages of the *Fortnightly*.

At the turn of the year, the same journal carried a trenchant critique by him of Conservative foreign policy, the most interesting feature of which was his perceptive assessment of the strategic importance of Heligoland, an island whose situation at the entrance to the Weser and Elbe rivers afforded Britain 'mastery' over Germany's trade routes, but which Salisbury had foolishly ceded to Germany in return for recognition of British interests in East Africa.[16] Underpinning Dilke's argument was his concern at the extent to which British policy remained constrained by the continuing occupation of Egypt, which fuelled French 'jealousy' and left Britain overly dependent upon German support. In an article in the *Speaker*, he recommended immediate withdrawal.[17] He tried to enlist Chamberlain's assistance by reminding him of his support for evacuation in 1884. The latter was already too far down the imperialist path and advised Dilke to follow him: 'Be as Radical as you like – Be Home Ruler if you must – but be a little Jingo if you can.'[18]

At the time of writing *The British Army*, Dilke had been resigned to the fact that, while the navy was the first line of defence, its superiority might be negated by new technological developments, imperial commitments or the combined strength of two or more hostile naval powers. However, a body of opinion known as the 'Blue-Water School' argued that British naval supremacy should be maintained at all times. There had been a comparative decline in British naval power since the 1870s, and H. O. Arnold-Forster (the adopted son of W. E. Forster) had attacked its shortcomings in the pages of the *Pall Mall Gazette* in the mid eighties. The first success of the school was the Naval Defence Act of 1889 which established the principle of building to a two-power standard. Dilke was converted to their position by Spenser Wilkinson, the military correspondent of the *Manchester Guardian*, who later became the first Chichele Professor of Military History at Oxford.

The two had first met in 1887 when Dilke was researching his book on the army. Wilkinson had loaned him the manuscript of his own book on the workings of a general staff entitled *The Brain of an Army*. Thereafter, they became friends. Dilke was invited to spend the Whitsuntide of 1891 at Aldershot barracks with Wilkinson's old regiment. Shortly afterwards, he suggested that they should cooperate to produce a book on imperial defence. He 'jibbed' at first at the Blue-Water School arguments which Wilkinson's draft chapters contained, and suggested that they dissolve the partnership, but he was won over.[19] This conversion was of no little significance, for Dilke was to become one of the school's major spokesmen in the House of Commons in the coming years.

The first priority, according to the authors of *Imperial Defence*, was to secure command of the sea, to all intents 'a British possession'. To this end the navy required sufficient battleships to keep the enemy in its ports and sufficient cruisers of superior speed to pursue and destroy enemy cruisers parasitic on British trade and commerce. To perform these tactics successfully, a battleship superiority of five to three and a cruiser superiority of two to one were essential, supported if possible by a reserve fleet. If adopted, the Blue-Water policy would mean that neither Britain nor the empire, with the exceptions of Canada and India, need fear invasion.[20]

Dilke's patient rebuilding of his career through this battery of publications and the occasional interventions in domestic politics had kept the scandal-mongers active, not least of all the ever-vigilant Stead, who attacked any move he made in the direction of renewed political activity. In his letter informing Chamberlain of his intention not to run in the county council elections, Dilke had written:

> I saw a curious letter from Stead last week about me in which he said he was forced to keep attacking me because there was no one else who would, & that he mistrusted the English people on such a point. This seems to shew that even he knows that if I was to fight him right out I shd. beat him pretty easily, but I don't think County Councils good enough for the purpose, while Parliament is a hopeless business till I have a clear political line. National defence & so forth being as much swamped by Ireland as is Local Government, & I not being able to make violent speeches about Ireland I had best keep still, I feel sure.[21]

As an amusing aside to the methods employed to defame him, he told of how, in 1887, Stead had asked *Pall Mall Gazette* readers to name candidates for heaven and hell with the innuendo that Dilke was the principal contender for the latter, 'but was disconcerted to find when the answers came in that Mr Gladstone was at the head of the poll for both ... .'[22]

The 'clear political line' for which Dilke was searching was soon to present itself, and was partly shaped by and partly determined his eventual choice of constituency. He received numerous offers as seats fell vacant – from the Forest of Dean as early as 1887, and later from Glasgow, Fulham, Leicester and North Kensington.[23] Certain obstacles had to be overcome before he could even contemplate acceptance. First, he needed at least the tacit approval of the Liberal leadership. In June 1889 he learnt, through the mediation of James, that Gladstone was 'most anxious' to see him back, but that the necessary steps should not be 'too quickly taken'.[24] Three weeks later, the Liberal leader called at Sloane Street to discuss the matter, but Dilke was out, and Gladstone therefore wrote instead. After a long-winded discourse on the precept 'Judge not', his letter continued:

> I deeply feel the loss we sustain in your absence from public life after you had given such varied and conclusive proofs of high capacity to serve your country. And I have almost taken for granted that with the end of this parliament, after anything approaching the full term, the ostracism would die a kind of natural death. And I heartily wish and hope that you may have lying before you in the future a long and happy time of *public* usefulness.[25]

This kindly letter, largely in tune with Dilke's own feelings about his situation, encouraged him to begin to take more seriously the invitations from the constituencies. There was still the animosity of a number of church leaders and of certain sections of the press to overcome but, if he was to have any realistic chance of standing at the next general election, the time was rapidly approaching when he must declare his candidature.

By November 1890 he was nearing the point of decision. He told Chamberlain that he was sorting his private papers for the Memoir but that:

By March at latest I shall have finished ... & then shall undoubtedly become restless, & be less indisposed than I have been to accept the good offers made to me. In fact I shall soon after that decide whether I will stand or whether I shall travel – for another book. One of the chief difficulties is the Times.[26]

Chamberlain did what he could to smooth Dilke's return. He saw Buckle, the editor of *The Times*, which was boycotting him and had ignored the *Problems*, but found him unsympathetic.

By March 1891 Dilke had made up his mind. He was now ready to abandon the caution that had hitherto restricted his interventions in national political debate. He had settled upon the programme on which he would fight, a programme that represented an advanced position on social questions and one which he had been maturing since 1885, but which had been constrained by his personal circumstances. This new social radicalism was to be an integral part of his politics for the remainder of his life.

Chapter 15

Towards a Social Radicalism

The Liberal Party in 1886 stood at a major crossroads in its history. The individualist political radicalism that had sustained it for a generation was no longer sufficient, especially in the face of the social unrest created by the depressed economic climate of the 1880s. Contemporary liberal political theorists recognised the need to engage with issues of social reform, or, in the language of the time, to embrace collectivism. This new spirit was described by a self-styled 'radical parson', the Rev. W. Tuckwell, the father of Lady Dilke's niece: 'everywhere public interest and private effort were being directed towards the problems of poverty and the possibilities of social reform. Socialism was in the air; an economic revolution seemed at hand'.[1] The parliamentary diarist, Henry Lucy, put the matter more bluntly. 'The shadow of the Working Man lies darkly over the House of Commons', he wrote in the late eighties. 'The horny hand is at its throat.'[2]

The Home Rule crisis, by depriving the Liberal Party of its Chamberlainite radicals, had apparently weakened its capacity to respond to the new circumstances. For this reason, the beginnings of Liberal decline have sometimes been traced to these years. Dilke was disappointed when Chamberlain did not remain within the party to take it in a new and more radical direction, having sacrificed the opportunity to do so for the sake of an issue which aroused in him very little enthusiasm. But Dilke, like many historians since, overestimated Chamberlain's radicalism. The latter was contemptuous of the working-class leaders of labour, regarding them as mere 'fetchers and carriers for the Gladstonian party', and hindering rather than advancing social legislation.[3] Later, in refusing a request from Dilke for support on the eight-hours' question, Chamberlain wrote: 'I am ... impatient of their [the labour leaders'] extremely unpractical policy, & ... I believe their real influence is immensely exaggerated. A political leader having genuine sympathy with the working classes and a practical programme could, in my opinion, afford to set them aside.'[4] Patronising attitudes of this sort go a long way towards explaining the gradual emergence within the working class of a desire for independent political representation. Chamberlain was content to legislate on behalf of the working classes, but could never quite bring himself to work with them or accept their right to legislate on his behalf.

Not so Dilke; from 1885 he began to revise the radical programme to embrace social and collectivist goals and, more importantly, to encourage the working class to use the reformed political system to press actively their own claims rather than to await passively upon the benefactions of a middle-class legislature. A number of factors influenced his intellectual development at this time: his analysis of the significance of the democratic reforms; his experiences at the LGB and particularly his chairmanship of the housing commission; his participation in the Industrial Remuneration Conference; and his marriage to Emilia Pattison.

Dilke believed that the democratic reforms of the 1880s would end the dominance of Whiggism within the Liberal Party and transform English politics. At the City Liberal Club, following the triumph of redistribution, he hailed the recent legislation as 'the great democratic reform, the great democratic revolution' which 'lay at the very root of English politics of the future'.[5] On a number of occasions he emphasised the *social* importance of the political changes. He had pressed for the Reform Act, he said, precisely because it was 'not an end, but a means to an end. The Franchise Act is a revolution; not a revolution in the bad sense of the word; not so much a strictly political as a social revolution.' He meant by this that there would be greater class harmony, greater power to the mass of the people and, above all, improvements in the conditions of the poor. For, 'political reform lay at the very base of social reform'. In conformity with the old radicalism, he believed that the newly-enfranchised agricultural community would be a chief beneficiary of the democratic changes and that pauperism would recede from the countryside. Also, and this was indicative of the new direction that radicalism would now have to take, the extended franchise and new constituencies would facilitate the return of labour representatives interested in social amelioration.[6] In sum, the reforms had placed 'political power in the hands of the masses of the people, so that if a majority ... did not obtain from Parliament the kind of legislation which they desired it was their own fault'.[7]

Dilke's supervision of the poor law department while at the LGB had impressed upon him forcibly the deplorable conditions of many labourers during the depression. In his 1885 memorandum on the condition of the poor, in which he had criticised Childers' budget, he had drawn attention

A RADICAL PROGRAMME

BY

THE RIGHT HON.

SIR CHARLES W. DILKE, BART.

———

Reprinted by permission from the NEW REVIEW, *and carefully revised.*

———

𝔚ith 𝔓ortrait.

PRINTED AND PUBLISHED BY THE

NATIONAL PRESS AGENCY, LIMITED,

13, Whitefriars Street, Fleet Street, E.C.

———

1890.

Title-page of *A Radical Programme* (1890)

to the heavy and disproportionate burden of taxes borne by the working classes, and particularly the regressive nature of indirect taxes. His tour of the slums of London's East End for the housing commission had opened his eyes to the extent of urban poverty. Despite the limited recommendations of the commission, housing and its attendant problems were increasingly perceived as epitomising the failure of a *laissez-faire* social policy, and as demonstrating the need for greater state intervention. The housing question was at the centre of the assault on the traditional Victorian assumptions about the causes and control of poverty.[8] Dilke's experiences led directly to his chairmanship of the Industrial Remuneration Conference, and explain why he was receptive to the collectivist arguments he heard there. From that point on he was converted to the need for state intervention to limit hours of work. Within a short period, he was contemplating intervention to control prices and protect wages.[9] However, his backwardness still on unemployment throws into relief the considerable influence of his new wife in encouraging him towards a social radicalism after 1885.[10]

Emilia Pattison's deeply religious views and her conviction that public service was an essential part of Christian morality helped to rekindle the Christian impulses behind Dilke's own radicalism. After their marriage and during the great crisis of his life, he found that the Holy Sacrament was once again 'a profound blessing' to him.[11] His periods of greatest faith coincided with the influence of two women on him – his mother in his early years, and his second wife from 1885 to 1904.

Still more inspirational were Emilia's trade union and feminist politics. During her marriage to Mark Pattison, she had joined the Women's Suffrage Society at Oxford. In 1876 she became a member of the Women's Protective and Provident League, founded by Emma Paterson, and helped to establish a branch at Oxford. By this time she was coming into ever-closer contact with Dilke, a fact reflected in her election in 1878 as one of the twenty non-MPs of the Radical Club. Her own radical agenda embraced female suffrage, women's education and improvements in the working conditions of women. With regard to this last, her influence on Dilke can be detected as early as 1879, when he spoke out against a reduction in wages at the Royal Army Clothing Factory at Pimlico, a government firm employing women, many of them the wives of disabled soldiers. Six months later, he attended a meeting on the Pimlico dispute called by the WPPL. A parliamentary enquiry was launched, perhaps the first ever in direct response to a demand from women workers themselves.[12] His uncompromising stand on the women's suffrage amendment of 1884 is perhaps also symptomatic of Emilia's strong influence upon him.

Emma Paterson's death in 1886 pushed Lady Dilke to the forefront of the Women's League, and from 1889 she served as its representative at the annual Trades Union Congress. The league was in financial difficulty and she contributed approximately £100 annually to it until her death, helping thereby to keep it solvent. She was joined in her trade union work by her niece, Gertrude Tuckwell, who came to London in 1883 to work as an elementary school teacher in a poor part of Chelsea.[13] Her championship of women's trade unionism, especially among textile workers, and her activism in the cause of non-unionised female labour, particularly employed in dangerous trades (such as the match-workers), was taken up by Dilke and became a main component of his social radicalism.

Under Lady Dilke the WPPL changed its name to the Women's Trade Union League, emphasising a reversal in its hitherto hostile attitude towards intervention in the labour market, and now strongly pressed for government regulation of working conditions. Her shift from self-help and *laissez-faire* was in tandem with the evolving position of many labour women, whose new-found commitment to state protection alienated those feminists who believed that regulation would rob women of employment or limit their capacity to earn a living. Female labour activists like Lady Dilke derided these arguments as the rantings of upper- and middle-class women who denied the reality of women's working- conditions. She referred to such feminist opponents of protective legislation as the 'shrieking sisterhood', and stressed the importance of cooperation between the sexes.[14] The progress of the Dilkes towards an acceptance of the need for greater state intervention was no doubt a reciprocal process, but it is difficult to believe that Dilke would have gone quite as far down the collectivist road had he not been married to a committed feminist and trade unionist.

After 1886 he adapted and expanded his radicalism to include social issues. His own evolution anticipated the politics of the Labour Party; but he was never tempted to abandon radical Liberalism. He augmented his radicalism by his support for trade union, feminist and labour issues, but regarded them as only part, albeit an important one, of a broader politics. The inveterate radical attention to the importance of political participation was not displaced. The focus from 1885 upon the extension of local democracy was perceived as a means of confronting the challenge of socialism. Dilke's new radical programme therefore included many of the traditional demands – local government, education, land reform, adult suffrage and so on – as well as new ones, like the eight-hour day. His aim was to retain the support of the working classes for the Liberal Party by extending their civil rights and responding to their demands.

Following the failure of the Round Table Conference to heal the schism over Home Rule, Dilke predicted that the leading Liberal Unionists, Hartington and Chamberlain, would join Salisbury's government before the next election, and would 'gradually come to call themselves Tories'. In the meantime, 'the Liberal party will become more and more an extreme party'.[15] In 1889, in tune with arguments that were just beginning to be used by proponents of the new liberalism, he warned that the party must move forward and adopt more advanced reforms or else it would fall 'between two stools – between the party of stagnation or of the party in the towns who were likely to supplant and drive out the great Liberal Party'.[16]

By 1890 Dilke's new thinking had crystallised into a concrete agenda of reform which appeared first in the *New Review* and then in pamphlet form as *A Radical Programme*. In it the centrality of social reform was made explicit. The purpose of the Liberal Party must be to create a more egalitarian society by a 'gradualist evolution ... from an individualist to a collectivist state, and one accomplished without danger'. Dilke looked to the future and to the changes in society that his proposed reforms would bring:

> While the interest on the capital of the rich, the rents of land, trade profits, and returns from manufacturing, on the whole, decrease, and while the rich save less, the poor will become more and more educated and more able to make use of every advantage they obtain. Great fortunes will be divided, new ones will become hard to found, and only a few who personally minister to the wants of the democracy – inventors, engineers, newspaper proprietors and journalists, highly-skilled surgeons, actors, singers, and so forth – will grow very rich; a handful as compared with the numbers of human beings in an organised society.[17]

The pamphlet defined his position in relation to the development of socialist ideas. British socialism was, he said, empirical rather than theoretical:

> The English people know no rule but rule of thumb. It is possible to believe that we are moving towards a more socialistic state of society without on that account holding Socialist opinions. It is possible to see that the whole drift of modern change is in the Socialist direction, without helping on the steps which would have to be yet taken to bring about a social revolution. The practical politician is concerned with the matter, because it is his duty to make the change as little harmful and as greatly beneficial as may be, both to the individual and to the state.[18]

Among the reforms that would assist this change were adult suffrage, taxation of the unearned increment on land, taxation reform (including the introduction of progressive death duties), housing legislation, and the limitation of hours in certain industries. These last two, in particular, demonstrate his progress towards a collectivist politics. With regard to housing, and in contrast to his rather tame proposals at the time of the royal commission, he was now prepared to give towns the power to destroy filthy dwellings without compensation and to buy up sites cheaply for rebuilding. On state intervention to regulate working-hours, he wrote unequivocally in favour of the eight-hour day for coal-miners. Above all, the best answer to socialism would be the progressive democratisation of local government. Smaller units of local government were likely to be more representative of popular opinion. For this reason, it was essential to democratise and empower the parishes, for it was at this level that the lives of the poor were most affected – through the guardians, the vestry, and the magistracy: 'the Radical ideal', Dilke wrote, 'will be the municipally-socialist State in which each community will manage its own concerns.'[19] The fact that local government remained within the pattern stamped upon it by the creation of the county councils makes it impossible to determine whether a genuine participative local democracy would, as he hoped, have been sufficient to counter socialist ideas and retain for the Liberal Party the allegiance of the working class.[20]

The development by Dilke of a social radical politics raises questions about the significance of his downfall for the survival of the Liberal Party. If he had succeeded Gladstone as Liberal leader, would his policies have obviated the need for a separate working-class party and would the future of the Liberal Party have thereby been more secure than it subsequently proved to be? Although answers to such questions must inevitably be speculative, it is necessary to broach them in order to reach any sort of assessment of Dilke's later radicalism or any conclusions concerning the repercussions for Liberalism of his fall.

The decline of the Liberal Party has been a source of endless fascination for historians. They have been intrigued in particular by two interrelated questions concerning its potential for survival. What impact did the Home Rule crisis of 1886 and its aftermath have upon its composition and its overall doctrinal position? Secondly, how capable was it of keeping working-class support in the face of changing economic (industrial unrest) and political (the extended franchise) circumstances? Both questions have been subsumed within the general debate on the importance of new liberal thinking within the party after 1886.

The Home Rule crisis had paradoxical consequences for the radicalism of the Liberal Party. The issue led to the departure of many moderates, leaving the party more cohesive and receptive to radical reforms than it had been hitherto, but at the same time there were qualifications to this radicalism which acted as impediments upon the transformation of the party into a broad-based organisation capable of holding the allegiance of the working class. In the first place, the commitment to Home Rule acted as a drag upon the party's capacity to enact social reforms. Progressive Liberals wanted to clear Ireland out of the way in order to focus on the social question but were unable to do so. Home Rule too easily became a *sine qua non* and an excuse for the failure to make progress. Moreover, when the Liberals were returned to office in 1892, their dependence on Irish support made it difficult to avoid prioritising Home Rule.

It was not the commitment to Home Rule as such that accounted for the failure of the Liberal Party to address social issues but rather the nature of Liberal radicalism itself, which was very much the radicalism of the 1870s rather than a radicalism attuned to the new realities of the 1890s.[21] Old radicalism had by now become Liberal orthodoxy, a factor explained by the composition of the post-1886 parliamentary party. While there had been an unusually large turnover of Liberal MPs, most of the new men had been weaned on radical Liberalism and were drawn from broadly the same social groups as before – principally landed gentlemen, business interests and the professional middle class.[22] These interrelated factors (the traditional social composition of the Liberal Party and its political attachment to the old radicalism) were in large part responsible for the faltering progress of the new liberalism – above all, its patchy regional uptake, the general malaise within the party during the twenty years of Unionist hegemony especially among those who would normally have been more active,[23] the resistance of the party rank and file to some of the industrial demands of the working class,[24] the dilemma of reconciling the need for middle-class money and working-class votes,[25] and the continued Gladstonian cast of the Liberal leadership.

The last of these – the restamping of Gladstone's authority on the Liberal Party and the effect on its potential for modernisation – has sometimes been seen as the most crucial consequence of the Home Rule crisis. Despite some genuflection on Gladstone's part to radicalism, it was primarily to the old radicalism.[26] Moreover, his mission to pacify Ireland was, as yet, unfulfilled. He told Andrew Reid, when the latter invited him in October 1886 to contribute to a symposium on 'The New Liberal Programme', that he wished to settle the Irish question and preferred to leave the new issues to others.[27] He remained acceptable to the party as Liberal leader precisely because its general complexion was still old radical. There was also no prominent social radical in the leadership to succeed him and to try to steer the party in a new direction. Instead, it was weakened after his retirement by the internecine rivalries of Rosebery and Harcourt.

With the loss to the radical cause of the talents of Chamberlain and Dilke, the torch of parliamentary radicalism passed after 1886 to Labouchere who, despite his legitimate concerns about the timidity of the leadership, was a political maverick, distrusted by, and lacking sufficient support within, the party. In 1889 he created a 'Fourth Party' with Philip Stanhope and Alfred Jacoby as its Whips, the latter's name inevitably prompting wits to dub its members the 'Jacobyns'. It was said to embrace about seventy MPs but was divided over social questions, and Labby and the other leaders lacked the organisational skills of a Dilke or a Chamberlain. It therefore proved largely ineffective. One of its members – L. A. Atherley-Jones (the son of the Chartist Ernest Jones) – contributed an article to the *Nineteenth Century* in August 1889 whose title, 'The New Liberalism', was soon adopted by social radicals as a term which encapsulated the philosophy and the social agenda which they deemed necessary to secure the party's future. Atherley-Jones later claimed that his purpose in writing it had been to 'demonstrate to the electorate that we were not indifferent to the needs and aspirations of the English working man'.[28] He recognised that the Liberal Party could not long survive on the support of the middle class and a programme largely devoted to satisfying Nonconformity. Yet it was hamstrung in broadening its appeal by Gladstone's continuing dominance and by radicalism's 'want of leadership'.[29] The article prompted a debate in the pages of the *Nineteenth Century* to which other young radicals like G. W. E. Russell (who had been Dilke's secretary at the LGB) and J. Guinness Rogers contributed.

The Jacobyns were not the only reforming element within the Liberal Party in the late 1880s. A number of talented, up-and-coming Liberal MPs, drawn mainly from the professions and including Haldane, Buxton, Acland and Grey, coalesced in a search for what one of their number, Henry Asquith, called 'the better kind of Radicalism',[30] a phrase which reflected their suspicion of Jacobynism. One thing which distinguished them from radicals like Labouchere was their belief in the importance of empire. Curiously, they sought inspiration and leadership from John Morley, a dry old stick who had little appetite for political manoeuvring, and a fervent anti-imperialist to boot who was far too close to Gladstone to contemplate abandoning the emphasis in official Liberal policy upon the priority of Home Rule. In any case, as Russell observed, men like Morley were too hidebound by their attachment to political economy to offer a lead on social issues.

The lawyer R. B. Haldane sought to remedy this by establishing a *rapprochement* with the Fabians. In August 1888 Sidney Webb responded to Haldane's approach by privately circulating among Liberal politicians a pamphlet entitled *Wanted a Programme: An Appeal to the Liberal Party*. He recommended to the Liberals the 'London Programme' which had appeared in the *Star* evening newspaper on 8 August and which embodied the ideals of the progressivist alliance then being forged on the new London County Council between a reforming middle class and labour.[31] Similarly, the authors of the *Fabian Essays* of December 1889 urged the Liberals to adopt a social radicalism and pressed Morley to declare for the eight-hour day. Unlike Haldane, Morley was decidedly lukewarm towards a Liberal-Fabian alliance.

The Newcastle Programme, adopted by the National Liberal Federation in 1891 and upon which the Liberal Party fought and won the general election of the following year, revealed the limits of the progress made by the social radicals. It contained some concessions designed to appeal to the working class – principally one man one vote, payment for MPs and the eight-hour day for miners – but, in its focus on such issues as Home Rule, temperance, disestablishment and further instalments of political and economic reform, it was overwhelmingly a statement of the old radicalism rather than the new. It failed to address labour's main demand for the shorter working day.

The slow and piecemeal adoption of social measures by the Liberal leadership led to disappointment among many radicals with the administration of 1892–95. It was in these years that a genuinely new liberalism began to be articulated and propagandised. The lead in this was taken by the Rainbow Circle, set up in 1894 to bring social radicals together through regular meetings and through its journal, the *Progressive Review*, edited by Ramsay MacDonald, which appeared from 1896 onwards. Dilke's prominence as a social radical was acknowledged in the invitation to him to contribute to the inaugural issue of the *Review*.[32] Among the more notable intellectuals and writers (many of them journalists) in the Circle were Herbert Samuel, C. F. G. Masterman, H. W. Nevinson, H. W. Massingham, A. G. Gardiner, C. P. Scott and, above all, J. A. Hobson and L. T. Hobhouse. The thinking of these men was new in the sense that they provided an ideological rationale for the social reform proposals that had thus far been advocated primarily on pragmatic grounds. Their revision of liberal ideology was aimed at demonstrating that the evils of the market economy could be mitigated by state intervention without at the same time threatening individual freedom. They thereby prepared the Liberal Party as a whole for the measures that collectively laid the foundations of the welfare state. In the older radical tradition, the focus had been on the international (peace), economic (retrenchment), and political (reform) domains. A series of *ad hoc* measures had been brought forward for several decades past to advance this tripartite programme. The new liberals now added an extra dimension, the social, which supplemented but did not displace the others, together with an organicist theory of liberalism that justified a more complete programme of reform.

New liberalism, or social radicalism, must not be confused with socialism. It was a development of liberalism not an abandonment of it, an ideological response to the economic recession and the rise of organised labour. In the last two decades of the nineteenth century, the Liberal Party was buffeted by the twin forces of socialism and imperialism, the products of a capitalist crisis that extended beyond the shores of Britain. The economic depression was met by internal and external strategies to maintain profitability – for example, internally by a reduction of labour costs through increased mechanisation, economies of scale, lower wages or unemployment; and externally by capital export and the search for cheap raw materials overseas. The social cost of such strategies was industrial unrest and the emergence of organised labour for economic (new unionism) and political (independent working-class representation) ends. New liberalism was one attempt to absorb the class conflict engendered by this capitalist crisis by way of a restructuring of capital-labour relations. At the heart of new liberal thinking was an emphasis upon conciliation, arbitration and class cooperation. But it was not the only ideological response to the crisis. Some imperialists, for example, made a connection between the external and internal strategies by looking to the empire to provide a solvent for domestic social problems. At its simplest level, as a form of 'bread-and-circuses' propaganda, the empire offered a distraction from social concerns. Social imperialists ranged from, on the extreme right, proto-fascists who wished to sterilise the poor or ship them overseas to labour colonies, to those who emphasised national efficiency as a prerequisite for imperial efficiency and therefore saw social policy as driven by imperial requirements. This latter category included individuals normally thought of as being on the political left, such as the Fabians. In fact, social imperialism had many nuances and was evident even in the thought of some radicals, including Dilke, who looked to colonial practices as a guide to domestic policy. Responses to the economic crisis formed part of a continuum taking on different inflexions across the political spectrum, embracing Cobdenites, new liberals, social imperialists and outright imperialists. The die-hard Cobdenites and out-and-out imperialists were on the fringes of the Liberal Party. The mainstream response was a more sophisticated and complex amalgam of social and imperial positions than that associated with either of these two extremes, while most Liberal politicians were of a kind in seeking to demonstrate that it was not class considerations that motivated them – neither working-class pressure nor middle-class self-interest – but rather the general good of the community and the nation and the empire.

The question at issue among historians has concerned the extent to which the reformers within the Liberal Party succeeded in converting it into a viable political vehicle that, on a social democratic platform, was able to retain the allegiance of middle and working classes alike. The 'Accidentalist' school maintains that the Edwardian Liberal Party was decidedly not moribund, as George Dangerfield had so famously claimed in his classic account of *The Strange Death of Liberal England* (1935), and that its terminal crisis only came about as a result of the 'accident' of the First World War and the Asquith–Lloyd George split of 1916. The 'Inevitabilists', by contrast, contend that the Liberal Party was essentially a middle-class party doomed to decline when faced with the emergence of a politicised working class.[33]

According to the Accidentalists, the new liberalism injected ideological vitality into the party and led to the adoption of a social reform programme that prepared the way for the pre-war victories and the introduction of welfare capitalism, which, by promoting class harmony over conflict, helped reconcile labour to the Liberal Party.[34] By 1910 the new liberal programme had been absorbed by leading Liberal politicians, especially with regard to the promotion of land and fiscal policies as instruments for the redistribution of wealth and the means of paying for social reform. They had displaced the old radical policies, whose limitations in this latter regard had been exposed by Chamberlain's ambitious scheme to finance social reform from tariff revenues. New liberalism, in effect, tried to adjust the old radical emphasis on class cooperation to the new economic and political circumstances of the depressed years of the late nineteenth century. Its success in doing so was registered in the party's electoral performance in the decade before the great split. To the Accidentalists at least it appears that, but for the war, it would have been only a matter of time before the Labour Party was borne to its grave by a rejuvenated Liberalism.

It is undoubtedly the case that many Liberal radicals of the late 1880s and early 1890s, including Dilke, held views that were at least as advanced as those of most labour leaders.[35] It is also the case that the regeneration of liberalism came from within the liberal tradition, though the catalytic influence of socialism should not be discounted.[36] There were, of course, socialist policies and strategies that even the most advanced radicals balked at – nationalisation, for example, or revolutionary as opposed to gradual change – but these were issues that had not as yet penetrated very far into working-class politics.

Whether new liberalism ever succeeded in capturing the mainstream of the Liberal Party is doubtful. Old radicalism survived and formed the kernel of the policies supported by Liberal candidates in many areas, not least of all the Celtic fringe, the support of which was essential to Liberal success and where issues like Home Rule, disestablishment and temperance remained ahead of labour issues.[37] It was, after all, the defence of free trade that largely accounted for the Liberal landslide in 1906. The upper echelons of the party – in the cabinet and in the leadership of men like Rosebery, Campbell-Bannerman and Asquith – remained, with the notable exception of Lloyd George, in the grip of traditionalists.[38] The new liberals themselves certainly did not believe that they had succeeded in transforming the party. Siren warnings of the persistent dangers that threatened its survival appeared from the pens of Hobson in 1909 (*The Crisis of Liberalism*), and Hobhouse (*Liberalism*) two years later, that is precisely at a time when, according to the Accidentalists, the new liberalism was supposed already to have worked its magic.[39]

The fact that the new liberalism had made only spotty progress does not resolve the question of the party's viability in the face of the emergence of a politicised labour movement. Perhaps its very catholicity, embracing *both* old and new forms of radicalism and attuned thereby to the many different political levels that persisted across the country, was the real key to its strength and continued viability. The Inevitabilists, however, maintain that the Liberal Party was intrinsically incapable of surviving the rise of class politics. The mechanics of the democratised constitution created a perilous position for any party that was not a natural home for either capital or labour, partly because of the effects of an extended franchise upon the disposition of political power, partly because the combination of single-member constituencies (for which Dilke had in large part been responsible) with a first-past-the-post voting system made electoral survival difficult for third parties and effectively created a duopoly. The Liberal Party was in a cleft stick after 1885. If it devised an advanced programme targeted at the broader working-class electorate it would risk quickening the loss of middle-class support, which was already haemorrhaging to the Conservatives. If it did not, it would be faced with working-class defection to an independent party. There were signs before 1914 that this dilemma would prove fatal. Labour was steadily increasing its share of the parliamentary vote and making gains in local elections. Moreover, the 'natural' alignment of the working class with Labour may have been masked and delayed by widespread disfranchisement under the registration system that prevailed down to 1918, though the evidence on this point is equivocal.[40]

At the root of the Inevitabilist case is the conviction that the Liberal Party was in essence a middle-class party incapable of accommodating some of the most central demands of labour. Led by the middle class, dependent for survival upon middle-class money and, most important of all, responsive to a middle-class rank and file, the Liberal Party was unable to meet working-class needs quickly enough or completely enough in the one area that was of immediate importance to their everyday lives – their working conditions – and in the defence of which, during the recession, they turned first to trade unionism and then to independent labour representation. The *timing* and the *extent* of reform were therefore crucial in explaining the defection of the working class. While the middle-class Nonconformists who formed the grassroots of the Liberal Party may have sympathised with the new liberal arguments, acknowledging the need for a programme that would appeal to members of the working class, they had difficulty satisfying them sufficently on the questions that pressed them most closely, such as the right to strike, a statutory reduction in working hours, and unemployment. When working-class candidates came forward as Liberals in an attempt to redress these grievances, they met with hostility or at best a distinct lack of enthusiasm from the constituency associations. Local political questions such as the selection of candidates, and local economic issues such as trade disputes, sharpened the class consciousness of working and middle classes alike, towards which the national programme of class reconciliation advanced by the new liberals provided no real answer.[41] The very approaches developed by the new liberals to address working-class grievances may, ironically, have served only to heighten working-class consciousness. In the face of a transparently class-based assault by the courts upon the rights of trade unions in the 1890s, and the organisation of anti-labour employers' associations, the new liberal emphasis upon neutrality, even-handedness, arbitration, conciliation and class harmony had a hollow ring. Neutrality in these circumstances was not enough. Organised labour expected a much more committed political support for its cause.[42]

Furthermore, state interventionist policies may have had an ambiguous effect in terms of retaining working-class allegiance to the Liberal Party. 'Social reform' is not an unproblematic concept. It was perceived by new liberals as a basis for a 'progressive' alliance with the working class. But the working class had reason, especially in the 1890s, to be extremely distrustful of the state. Experience taught them that social *reform* was often only a mechanism of social *control*, designed to preserve the status quo. As

Balfour admitted to a Manchester audience in January 1895: 'Social legislation ... is not merely to be distinguished from socialist legislation, but it is its most direct opposite and its most effective antidote.'[43] Hence, even when the Liberal Party began to grapple with some of the key working-class demands, especially after 1906, it did not automatically win favour with the labour movement, which not unnaturally remained suspicious of attempts to tie the trade unions more closely to the state and which continued to regard wages and employment issues as more important than social welfare legislation.[44] Liberal intervention on labour questions not infrequently provoked a divided response from within the working class.

The new liberalism was a logical progression for middle-class radicalism, which had traditionally been presented as a non-class and non-ideological programme of reform, but which in reality was an ideological and class strategy for securing and maintaining the hegemony of the middle class.[45] This is not to claim that the Labour Party emerged on the back of an alternative socialist ideology that had finally succeeded in casting aside the mask of radicalism and exposing its class face. Rather, the labour movement emerged because it articulated the class and sectional interests of working people better than the Liberals. The class conflict of the 1890s and early 1900s produced first the Independent Labour Party and then the Labour Party proper. Support for them varied enormously from region to region.[46] Each step in the emergence of a separate labour movement was a faltering one and was complicated by the sympathy of social radicals for the labour cause. There was nonetheless a gradual accretion of support for independent working-class representation. At the same time as the structure of British capitalism changed and industrial capital gave way to finance capital, the increasingly interlocking interests of landowners, monopoly industrialists and financiers and their shared commitment to imperialism found political representation through a reconstituted Conservative Party. The mechanics of the constitution effectively predicated a two-party system which meant that, in the long term, labour through the trade unions would finance its own party in opposition to the party of capital. This was a protracted process in which class and political realignments only slowly fell into place in the face of other persistent but weakening forms of solidarity, such as religion, occupation and region, and which was influenced by the defensive responses of those Liberals who saw decline written on the walls. In this transitional phase the Liberals were successful. However, electoral success was a mirage that may have deluded the party into underestimating the seriousness of Labour's arrival on the political stage, something its hesitant radicalism had failed to forestall. It might have done so had it given priority to working-class issues – but this was probably an impossible task for a middle-class party. It certainly went beyond the ambition or desire of the great majority of Liberals, who increasingly came from professional backgrounds and whose 'organic intellectuals' continued to express their objection to the promotion of particularist 'class' interests.

The fact of the matter was that by 1914 the Labour Party *existed*, and was able to take advantage of the Liberal split brought on by the war. The Accidentalists have failed to grasp that the war and the concomitant split were not 'accidents' but were part of the problem: of a Liberal Party fatally riven by the imperialist rivalries that stemmed from the late nineteenth-century changes in capitalism. The 'Accident' of 1916 was therefore the conjunctural moment in a long-term organic ('Inevitable') crisis for liberalism. In that crisis, liberal ideology had been reconstructed and, in the dialectic of class conflict and ideological negotiation, had been compelled to incorporate labour issues that it had earlier eschewed.[47] So, although the intellectual contributions of the new liberals and the practical contributions of the social radicals were not sufficient to save the Liberal Party, they helped, paradoxically, to make the Labour Party into a vehicle of welfare capitalism and social democracy. In sum, the rise of a party of the working class *was* inevitable – nothing in the end could overcome, despite similarities of policy, the desire by Labour to be independent of the Liberals – but its character was determined by the evolution of the new liberalism.

This review of the historiographical debate upon the decline of the Liberal Party establishes the context within which to assess Dilke's elaboration of a social radicalism and the political implications of his downfall. Had Dilke not been ruined by the scandal, he would have helped shape the political programme of the Liberal Party from a position at or near its top. Of course, it may be that it was only his changed circumstances that led him to a more advanced radicalism and that as a Liberal leader he would have pursued an altogether different politics. The influences that were beginning to shape his political thought from the mid eighties, however, were turning him towards a social radical position even before his ruin. They point to the likelihood that he would have continued along the same path, regardless of the position he occupied in the party after 1886. It seems probable therefore that, but for the scandal, he would have injected a social radicalism into the *leadership* earlier and made it more dynamic and attractive to the working class than it was destined to be under the aristocratic tutelage of the Fifth Earl of Rosebery. The emergence of an alternative party during the years when the Liberal Party was marking time was an important factor in explaining its eventual demise; something which Dilke, from a position of authority, might have been able to forestall. The fact that the ILP wanted him as leader goes some way to support this contention.

If the preceding analysis is correct, the decline of Liberalism owed less to the absence of a sympathetic and appropriate response to working-class demands at the national and leadership levels and much more to the inbred and antagonistic attitudes that persisted at the local and grassroots levels. Here day-to-day 'class' experience overrode the elaboration of a new liberal theory. In this respect, 'saving' the Liberal Party was an impossible task and certainly beyond the capabilities of one man. Yet the decline of the Liberal Party should not be seen as evidence that the new liberalism was an intellectual dead-end. On the contrary, in its transformed state, liberalism found a new host. Middle-class radicals like Dilke contributed to reconstructing liberalism in the form in which it was carried over into the Labour Party. When, after the war, many of them deserted the Liberals and joined Labour, primarily because of its unsullied foreign policy, they brought their radical baggage with them and continued to shape it into the social democratic rather than socialist body that it has remained to this day.

Chapter 16

The Forest of Dean

By March 1891 Dilke felt that the time had arrived when he could announce his intention to return to political life. The animus of his critics and certain sections of the press had not entirely disappeared, but it had subsided. The Liberal leadership was sympathetic to his return. Above all, whenever he spoke at meetings in the country he was greeted with a support that drove out any lingering fears that the scandal had turned public opinion irrevocably against him. Now was the moment to publish his new radical programme, which spelled out the platform on which he would re-enter the political arena and which, by its elaboration of a social dimension would, he believed, not only secure his own re-election, but would, if adopted, guarantee the future of the Liberal Party.

The inclusion in it of the miners' eight-hour day, more than any other issue, determined his eventual choice of constituency. The Miners' Federation of Great Britain had been set up in 1888 to agitate for the eight-hour day. It had drafted a bill which was introduced into parliament for the first time the following year by R. B. Cunninghame Graham, the president of the recently-formed Scottish Labour Party. In August 1890 Dilke addressed his first miners' meeting, at Cannock Chase. Within a year he had spoken in most of the major mining areas of the country.[1] His popularity with the miners was unquestionable and he was overwhelmed with requests to attend their rallies.[2] Despite a reputation for rigid Nonconformity, the miners were not stirred into boycotting him by the fulminations of the puritan press. When, for example, he was due to speak at Wakefield in the summer of 1892, the local newspaper published disapproving letters, notably from the bishop and several local clergymen, and afterwards declined to report his speech. Nevertheless, 56,000 miners turned out to welcome him.[3]

In February 1891 G. B. Samuelson, MP for the Forest of Dean, announced that he was not prepared to be bound by a resolution of the MFGB in favour of the Eight-Hours Bill, and had accordingly decided to stand down at the next election. The local association, known as the Liberal Four Hundred, immediately offered the vacancy to Dilke. He had spoken on the eight-hour question in the constituency two years earlier, when he had been reproved by John Morley, an arch opponent of state regulation of hours, for 'putting out an ultra programme' likely to divide the Liberals and endanger the seat. Dilke denied that he had gone to the Forest with any such intention: 'I am an 8 Hours man but I do not say so. When I spoke on the 8 hrs. I advised only ....'[4] Nevertheless, the advice had obviously been welcomed by the Foresters and had earned him many friends – he was now undoubtedly very keen to accept their invitation.

He was conscious of the need to proceed cautiously. News of the offer had alerted Stead into renewing his anti-Dilke crusade. Along with Annie Besant, the theosophist, and several clergymen, he had written to *The Times* to remind its readers that Dilke had not yet 'taken any practical steps to fulfil his pledge to clear his character'.[5] Dilke responded by presenting the evidence amassed by the Chesson Committee to a meeting at Cinderford on 9 March. Stead next issued a pamphlet entitled *Has Sir Charles Dilke Cleared his Character? An Examination of the Report of the Alleged Commission*, which challenged the credibility of the new evidence, particularly that relating to the part played by Fanny Grey in the affair, and which he distributed widely.[6] He also orchestrated the protest of a group of church leaders and a number of prominent ladies, including Josephine Butler and Mrs Fawcett. He tried to get Morley to block Dilke's nomination, but Morley was non-commital.[7] Gladstone, despite his encouraging letter of August 1889, was beginning, in the wake of the Parnell scandal, to have misgivings, and he asked a friend of Dilke's to tell him that his candidature at that moment would be 'most prejudicial'.[8]

Any reservations that Dilke had were dispelled by the encouragement that came from Highbury and, above all, by the unanimity of support displayed upon his tour of the Forest in the early summer.[9] At an electrifying meeting in Lydney on 11 June, he gave his affirmative reply to the invitation in a speech that was, by his standards, emotional and lyrical, and which he afterwards described as 'the best' of his life.[10] His announcement was greeted with hostility in several sections of the press, and he asked Chamberlain to use his influence to silence some of the reports. However, his friend advised him that a '*mauvais quart d'heure*' was only to be expected, though he did what he could.[11]

The Forest of Dean was a strong centre of Nonconformity. It was also an agricultural as well as a mining area, a fact which explains why it was exceptional among coal-mining constituencies in opting for representation by a non-miner. Whereas Dilke's campaign for the eight-hour day was guaranteed to secure him the backing of the coal-miners, who made up a quarter of the electorate, his appeal to the agricultural labourers rested upon his support for agricultural trade unionism and for the municipalisation of the land through the empowerment of local councils to provide allotments. As a bourgeois property-owner himself, he shrank from nationalisation. He believed that land already owned by the state should be retained and not sold into private hands, but that wholesale takeover was nothing less than robbery. The break-up of the large estates could be achieved gradually, especially by taxing unearned increment and using the revenue for social reform.[12] He would have been horrified by any scheme to socialise the means of production, even one confined to the land. The base of his radicalism had been broadened to include social reform, not socialism, but judging from his popularity, this was more than enough to satisfy the working classes of Dean Forest.

With his nomination secured, Dilke was invited to address the next annual conference of the MFGB, to be held at Stoke in January 1892. The failure of the Eight-Hours Bill to make progress had hardened the federation's rank and file members in support of an international coal strike, but in his speech he persuaded them to reconsider.[13] They would, he said, be going into battle with weakened ranks. On the one hand, the continental miners were not as well organised as their British counterparts. In any international industrial war, therefore, the MFGB would bear the brunt of the struggle. On the other, the British movement was itself divided by the differences which existed between the federation and the non-federation areas of South Wales, Northumberland and Durham, where the skilled hewers already worked less than eight hours a day. Dilke advised the miners to cooperate with other trades, particularly the railwaymen, and to lobby MPs in favour of their bill. The conference voted down the strike. Dilke had the gratification of being present at the miners' international congress six months later to see the more moderate strategy adopted.[14]

By then he was back in the Commons, following his success in the general election held in July. The excitement surrounding the contest in the Forest of Dean had been fanned, as Dilke had predicted, by Stead's uncompromising opposition, in the face of which he was characteristically phlegmatic. 'He'll end', he told Labouchere, 'by making me a "popular force".'[15] In May Stead tried once more to induce Gladstone to intervene, but the Liberal leader refused.[16] He hinted that he would stand himself as an independent candidate; and he raked over the coals of the scandal yet again in a lengthy pamphlet entitled *Deliverance or Doom? or The Choice of Sir Charles Dilke*, which was circulated gratis to many influential figures. However, when he tried to speak in the constituency, the Foresters, according to Lady Dilke, forced him 'to fly for his life'. His effigy was conveyed through Lydney in a coach drawn by six donkeys and then burnt on a pyre of his pamphlets.[17] In the event, Dilke had to face only the conventional opposition of a local Tory squire, Colchester Wemyss, who refused to bring personal questions into the campaign. This did not deter some of his supporters from behaving rather less honourably, though their attempts to make political capital out of the scandal met with little success. The result was an overwhelming victory for Dilke, by 5,360 votes to 2,942.[18] The Forest was unashamedly Liberal and provided him with a safe seat for the rest of his life. Henceforward, he usually went there three times a year: for a holiday at Whitsun; to work on the parliamentary register when the Revision Courts were in session in the autumn (thereby making it one of the most complete); and to attend political meetings and the miners' rallies in winter. Apart from the annual Christmas holiday in Paris and a trip to Stockholm in 1897, he now travelled less abroad (a passion in any case not shared by Lady Dilke), and he sold his cottage near Toulon.

The Liberals, in alliance with the Irish Nationalists, had a slight majority in the new parliament over the combined forces of the Conservatives and Liberal Unionists, and Gladstone proceeded to form his fourth and last administration. There was never any prospect that Dilke would be asked to join it. The Queen had made her opposition to such a possibility quite plain.[19] Nor did he expect to be asked. For the moment, he was happy just to be back. He was still only forty-eight and had a wealth of experience behind him, and a disposition which would soon regain him the respect of the House. Ten years' hard work might erase past memories. In May 1893 he wrote: 'From this time forward I shall not name my speeches & ordinary action in the House as I had now gained the position which I had held up to 1878, though not my position of 1879–80, nor that of 1884–5.'[20] Beyond the position of an independent member, however, he was never to proceed.

After six years of Tory government, the Liberal rank and file expected their leaders to press ahead with a reforming programme. The return of a number of Lib-Lab representatives – most notably John Burns, Keir Hardie, Havelock Wilson and Sam Woods – was a signal to many radicals that the party would ignore labour issues at its peril. The attitude of MPs to the eight-hour day was regarded as a litmus test of their (and the Liberal Party's) willingness or otherwise to countenance state intervention in the affairs of industry. Gladstone, however, had other plans and was preparing once more to lead his party into the Home Rule quagmire.

This course of action was in large part unavoidable in view of the government's dependence on Nationalist support. Despite Parnell's fall in 1890, Home Rule could not be shelved and, in fact, dominated the first session of the new parliament. The parliamentary time of the Liberal administration of 1892–95 was largely taken up by three traditional issues: Home Rule; the Parish Councils Bill; and Harcourt's fiscal reforms of 1894. All the same, some important social measures were brought forward – most notably the Employers' Liability Bill, the Mines' Eight-Hour Bill and the Factory and Workshops Bill – while the introduction of death duties in Harcourt's budget was a significant departure in raising revenue for social reform and more than just an orthodox financial measure.

Dilke's first full-dress debate was on immigration, on which he took a heroic stand: one unjustly and unaccountably ignored by his previous biographers.[21] According to the historian of the aliens legislation, he was 'the acknowledged leader' of its opponents in 1893 and his speech a 'brilliant ... defence of immigration'.[22]

The East End of London was home to the great sweated tailoring trade, employing many Jewish immigrants, who were held, even by many on the left, to be responsible for the long hours and low rates of pay which characterised the industry. Chamberlain was among those who thought that it was in the interests of native English workers to exclude immigrants. Dilke, whose work on the housing commission had taken him to some of the worst areas where immigration contributed to overcrowding, did not accept this as a solution. He had long been a critic of interference with the free movement of peoples and, in this particular instance, his classic liberalism remained inflexible.[23]

His opposition to immigration restrictions at first brought him into conflict with many trade unionists. The TUC had responded to rising unemployment in the depression by demanding, in 1892, a ban on the entry of destitute peoples. There is no doubt that immigrant labour did compete for jobs in certain trades and that the unions were right to be concerned about the effects in terms of unemployment, blacklegging and sweating through the undercutting of wage rates. Some Conservatives were not slow to exploit this as a potential vote-winning issue. When, in 1893, a Tory protectionist moved an amendment to the Queen's Speech calling for legislation to prohibit alien immigration, it provided a stern test for the traditional Liberal defence of individual liberty.

In his finely-argued speech responding to the amendment, Dilke pointed out that many immigrants were not destitute and were often highly skilled.

The evils of the tailoring trade lay in the sweating system not in the employment of cheap foreign labour, and prohibition was therefore a 'sham remedy for very grave evils in the labour market'. The proposed restrictions were a challenge to free trade theory, the advantages of which were greater than its drawbacks. More destitute people were leaving the country than entering it. Above all, the proposal was a challenge to British liberty and the tradition of giving asylum to persecuted peoples. The amendment was rejected. Dilke believed that his speech had turned votes and led to his regaining influence 'of a quiet sort'.[24] By 1895 the TUC had swung round dramatically and thereafter opposed restrictions. How much this owed to Dilke it is impossible to say.

Coincidentally, some of the leading military and naval reformers with whom he was otherwise cooperating were at the forefront of the anti-alien movement: Lord Charles Beresford for one, and Sir John Colomb, the Blue-Water theorist, who represented an East End constituency and who supported his attempts to introduce the reforms outlined in *Imperial Defence*. Dilke's association with men like these, together with his informed interest in imperial questions, have led some historians to bracket him, wrongly, with the Liberal Imperialists.[25] He sometimes worked with them, particularly on naval questions, but only spasmodically and never closely. Many of the leading Liberal Imperialists distrusted him, especially because of his connection with radical cabals and radical programmes. Their main source of conflict with the Liberal leadership concerned their desire to ditch Home Rule, something which Dilke never espoused. Moreover, on a number of occasions he swam against the popular imperialist tide that was gathering momentum in the nineties, especially over African questions.

Dilke was increasingly concerned that the occupation of Egypt was damaging Anglo-French relations and dragging Britain into a partition of Africa from which no advantage was to be derived, and which was weakening British influence in more important and lucrative spheres. Shortly after the general election, he wrote informing Gladstone of his intention to raise the matter in the House. Gladstone sent for him four days later, but the Prime Minister's only memorable contribution to a long interview was an epigram on the gathering force of jingoism: 'It is no longer war-fever, but earth hunger.' When Dilke went ahead with his resolution, Gladstone, fettered by the hostility of Rosebery, his Foreign Secretary, was compelled to state that his government did not regard evacuation as timely.[26]

Dilke's anxieties were heightened by the crisis in Uganda, where the collapse of the British East Africa Company and with it indirect British influence, had led first Salisbury and then Rosebery to contemplate intervention to secure control of the headwaters of the Nile and thereby safeguard the Suez Canal. His warnings against such a forward policy were not heeded, and in June 1894 he condemned British intervention as 'bad from beginning to end'. He could not think of anywhere in the whole world that was 'a more undesirable region for us to hold'. Randolph Churchill, who followed him in the debate, thought him long-winded, and his speech won only 52 supporters to the government's 218.[27]

At the same time, Dilke helped put the need for a permanent body to coordinate defence planning upon the national agenda. He alluded to the idea during the navy debate of December 1893, and was afterwards approached by Balfour who suggested that he circulate details to the party leaders. This was done on 12 February 1894 in a letter drafted by Wilkinson and addressed to Gladstone for the Liberals, Salisbury and Balfour for the Conservatives, and Chamberlain and Hartington (who had recently succeeded to the family title as the Eighth Duke of Devonshire) for the Liberal Unionists. It was signed by Dilke, George Chesney, an army general and back-bench Liberal Unionist, H. O. Arnold-Forster, a Unionist who had become a close friend of Dilke's through their common interest in army reform, and Wilkinson himself. It urged the coordination of defence questions under one minister responsible for the working of the system, and the appointment by the cabinet of an officer from each service to act as professional and accountable advisers.[28]

Chamberlain's response was non-committal. He was 'favourably inclined' to the idea of closer co-operation between the two services, but differences of opinion among military experts made him reluctant to declare himself for this particular plan. Gladstone, who was on the point of resigning as Prime Minister but had not yet announced the fact, replied somewhat opaquely that he had taken care to bring the letter to the attention of his colleagues. Balfour expressed polite interest but declared his preference for a defence committee.[29]

Wilkinson, who disliked Balfour, told the following story of these exchanges:

> I had no faith in that [Balfour's] scheme, and said so. 'What am I to say to Arthur Balfour?' said Dilke. 'When you see him tomorrow,' I said, 'just refer to the subject again, and he will repeat the opinion he has already given you. You then say: "What you tell me is very interesting, but there is something you have forgotten." "What is that?" he will ask, and you will answer: "War! How will your scheme work in the event of war?" Arthur Balfour has never in his life thought about war, and he cannot answer you. He will take out his watch, look at the time, and say, "I am very sorry but I have an appointment", and he will run for his life. That will be tomorrow, Tuesday. I will meet you on Wednesday at half-past two in the lobby and you will then report this conversation.'

> On Wednesday, at 2.30, I went to the House, and in the lobby came Dilke to meet
> me and said: 'My dear fellow, it went off word for word as you said; as soon as I
> mentioned war he looked at his watch, said he had a man to meet, and was off.'[30]

This is Wilkinson at his journalistic best, but his anecdote nevertheless makes an important point. He and Dilke favoured a system akin to the American one where the president is commander-in-chief of the armed forces and bears the burden of responsibility in wartime. They believed that a committee would be unable to operate as quickly or as effectively, and would be less accountable. Balfour's objection was that a presidential-type of system placed too much store upon the capabilities and leadership of one individual.

In the interests of some improvement, Dilke was prepared to be flexible. On 16 March he put the proposals of the circular letter before the House, indicating his willingness to support any reasonable scheme. He received assurances from Balfour and Campbell-Bannerman that the principle had the backing of their respective parties. With Arnold-Forster, he raised the matter again the following year, but nothing was done until late summer, when the Conservatives came in and Balfour proceeded to establish an informal committee as a basis for improving communication between the two services. Dilke thought this totally inadequate.[31] The mismanagement of the South African War did much to confirm his judgement.

His approach to defence planning was symptomatic not just of his independence on returning to the House but also of a commitment to cross-party cooperation, which had been burned into his political consciousness by the success of the redistribution negotiations and which he now held should be applied to a range of issues. These included not just grand constitutional adjustments (like parliamentary reform or Irish Home Rule), or questions of national defence, but more mundane matters as well, like the Mines' Eight-Hours Bill. In March 1893 a large deputation on behalf of the MFGB, which included Dilke, had failed to persuade Gladstone and Asquith to commit the Liberal Party to it, and it therefore remained a private member's measure. In these circumstances, he tried to get the names of reformers from all parties on the back of the bill, and he approached Churchill and Chamberlain for their support. The latter thought that the miners ought to accept local option for reasons of 'tactics more than of principle', while Churchill appears to have been of much the same opinion.[32] Local option, however, was not acceptable to the employers in the federation area, who feared the competition it would entail. Nor was it acceptable to Dilke, who correctly perceived that the shorter shift system of the skilled miners in the non-federation areas rested on the backs of the unskilled labour of boys employed for ten hours a day. He made this point when the bill was debated on 3 May. His speech winding up the case for the eight-hours men and attacking local option was described as a masterpiece by Thomas Ashton, the secretary of the MFGB.[33] The bill passed its second reading but failed to progress through lack of time. The most prolonged industrial dispute of the decade, the great miners' lock-out, ensued, and was only resolved by government intervention after winter had begun to bite deep into the short supplies of coal. This unprecedented act of conciliation raised expectations when the Eight-Hours Bill was reintroduced in the new session but, although the second reading was again carried, the bill was wrecked in committee by a local option amendment.

76 Sloane Street was by now becoming a regular port-of-call for many of labour's leaders. During his time in office, Dilke had entertained the parliamentary committee of the TUC to lunch at the start of each new parliamentary session in order to discuss labour questions with them. In 1892 he had attended his first Trades Union Congress at Glasgow. Among his new acquaintances were William Abraham ('Mabon'), the Welsh miners' leader and MP; H. M. Hyndman, founder of the Marxist-inspired Social Democratic Federation, who introduced him to Jean Jaurès, the French socialist; Cunninghame Graham, the Scottish laird and South American adventurer, who had been arrested on 'Bloody Sunday' in 1887; and, of course, the many female trade unionists who were associates of Lady Dilke. His reputation in labour circles was such that, if we are to believe his testimony in the Memoir, in August 1894 Keir Hardie, Ben Tillett and Tom Mann offered him the leadership of the Independent Labour Party, formed at Bradford in the previous year. This is quite credible given the deference of many working-class leaders at the time. 'But my willingness', he observed, 'to sink home questions & join the Tories in a strong policy in the event of war, & my wish to increase the white army in India, & the fleet – even as matters stand, – are a fatal bar, & I cannot accept.'[34] Foreign and defence policies were not the only impediments. His perception that labour questions were only one part of the radical programme, and that the Liberal Party could be persuaded to respond itself to labour's demands, made his acceptance improbable, if not impossible. The ILP, he wrote in a contemporary magazine, would not pose a threat to the Liberal Party provided the latter was 'democratized'. Elsewhere, he pointed to the fate of the Belgian Liberal Party as a warning of what might happen if British Liberalism became 'suffocated between the two opposing forces of Toryism and Socialism'.[35]

His strategy therefore was to create a pressure-group to galvanise the

Liberal Party on radical issues. Under the rules of the Radical Club, he had ceased to be a member upon taking office in 1880 and his brother had succeeded him as its secretary. Upon Ashton's death, the club had been replaced by a loosely-organised committee elected by all radicals who wished to attend. Dilke joined the committee on his return to the House, despite vehement opposition from one member who claimed that it would be contaminated by the inclusion on it of an adulterer.[36] Perhaps because of this unpleasant incident, but also because of an attempt by the party whips to pack the meeting, open elections were abandoned in 1893. Dilke now turned the Radical Committee into a close body 'chiefly composed of those who would attend and work', and without a formal 'party' constitution. Its purpose, as he defined it, was to keep 'Governments up to the mark and for current work, such as making the best use of private members' time, ballotting [*sic*] for Bills and motions, etc.'. Its members supported the Eight-Hours Bill, payment of MPs and 'drastic action' regarding the House of Lords. A majority of them were adult suffragists and Home Rulers. All of them took part in balloting for labour measures.[37] Dilke worked most closely with Labouchere, the atheist MP for Northampton and editor of *Truth*, whose radical apostasy in part owed something to having been passed over for office in 1892. But he was never able to form a partnership with him to match that with Chamberlain. The two occupied the bench in the House below the gangway, Dilke reserving the corner-seat for Labouchere by slipping a card into the back of it during prayers, which the latter did not attend. They differed, however, on defence and foreign policy, while on social questions and issues such as women's rights Labouchere was far less radical than Dilke. In this regard, he was not unlike Chamberlain, but he lacked altogether the latter's political talents and stature.

Despite his increased commitment to labour questions, Dilke maintained his interest in traditional Liberal issues. He persuaded the Lord Chancellor, Herschell, to broaden the composition of the magistracy and thereby end the packing of the bench in some counties with Tories nominated by the lords lieutenant.[38] He also introduced two bills to amend the system of voting at local elections and to abolish property qualifications with the aim of making local authorities popular and representative.[39] These objectives were overtaken by, but incorporated into, the Liberals' Parish Councils Bill. In drafting it, H. H. Fowler had consulted his predecessor at the Local Government Board on a number of details. He was also attentive to Dilke's comments in the House and was prepared to accept his amendments on several key points. Dilke immodestly remarked in his Memoir that his interventions 'carried a great deal of weight', and that he 'was able greatly to improve the measure'. He succeeded in modifying some of the clauses governing the powers of the urban parishes and in improving its electoral provisions, especially those relating to the enfranchisement of women.[40] With the passing of this act, the basic restructuring of local government, begun in 1888, was completed and remained largely unchanged for eighty years.

Dilke had by this date become an uncompromising supporter of the simple franchise. He opposed any measure which would add to the existing morass of electoral law, such as the proposed service franchise, even though this would increase the electorate, or John Morley's Period of Qualifications and Elections Bill of 1894, even though this would have substantially reduced the residence qualification.[41] He applied the same principle to the disfranchisement of women. He introduced an Adult Suffrage Bill but found difficulty in enlisting support for it. The merging of women's suffrage with the broader democratic demand of adult suffrage did not win favour with many feminists, who saw the simultaneous enfranchisement of men as a dilution of their purist emphasis upon the priority of female enfranchisement.[42] The opposition of these feminists may have tempered the support of some labour men. Keir Hardie, the socialist member for West Ham South, had told Dilke that he would vote for the bill even if he, and the ILP, did not actively back it. Just before it was due to be debated, he became even less supportive. 'I am more than ever convinced', he wrote to Dilke, 'of the necessity of concentrating all our energies on measures of Social Reform, which are sadly neglected and overlooked at present.'[43]

Dilke also proposed to update the redistribution scheme by disfranchising thirty-one constituencies (including seven university seats), reassigning eleven of these and reducing the House by twenty. He shortly afterwards abandoned this plan in favour of 'a self-acting scheme which would automatically redistribute all the seats'. He had sought Chamberlain's support,[44] but their differences over Home Rule made any agreement on this issue unlikely. The disproportion between Irish and English constituencies was increasing yearly: if Ireland was to lose the thirty seats which equal electoral districts would entail, Home Rule would indeed be a burning issue. So, during Dilke's lifetime, the one question was shelved with the other.

Home Rule had also thrust the question of reform of the House of Lords back to the top of the political agenda. Lords reform, like Home Rule, became another 'obstacle' that would have to be removed before progress could be made on social questions. For some Liberals it served as an excuse for paralysis. In an essay published shortly before his re-election, Dilke had repeated his objection to 'reform' and indicated his support for outright abolition.[45] When, in March 1894, a dispirited and weary Gladstone, his Irish mission thwarted by the recalcitrant peers, finally stepped down over the navy estimates, Dilke favoured Rosebery rather than Harcourt as his successor largely because he believed that the former was more likely to deal with the Lords.[46] In the event, Rosebery gave birth to a mouse – a moderate reform proposal, which would have had the effect of strengthening the bicameral system, the very thing which Dilke was against and which therefore left him and many other Liberals bitterly disappointed. As Salisbury observed, Rosebery's proposal was as much a declaration of war on the radicals as on the peers.[47] Chamberlain sought to exploit the simmering discontent by moving an amendment to the Queen's Speech in February 1895 that ridiculed the government's incapacity to get its programme through the Lords. In the debate that followed, Labouchere and Dilke were barbed in their criticism of Rosebery's handling of the whole affair. Dilke was especially effective. The government, he argued, had lost the support of advanced radicals in the constituencies by its failure to give a clear lead. If it was to avoid disaster then 'the Prime Minister's trumpet would have to give forth a much more certain sound'. Hamilton wrote in his diary: 'Dilke made a very nasty speech with all kinds of disagreeable innuendoes about Rosebery; and no one on the ministerial bench got up to defend R. – an omission which produced a bad impression.' At the next cabinet, Rosebery criticised his colleagues for failing to speak out and, taking this as a sign of lack of confidence in his leadership, intimated that he intended to resign. Harcourt argued instead that they had been wise to ignore Dilke's recriminations.[48] In the event, the crisis passed and Rosebery did not resign, but his reputation had been dented and the incident was indicative of the moribundity of his administration.

The government limped on for four more months during which time it produced only one measure of any significance: Asquith's Factory Bill, which sought to extend inspection to laundries, wharves and docks, and dangerous trades, and to regulate the working hours of women and young people. Dilke was a member of the grand committee which considered the bill. He was, he unabashedly recalled, of 'essential service'. 'I was entrusted', he added, 'with the case of the Tailors, of the West Riding Woollen operatives, of the women trades unionists and others, and got much for them of what they wanted and deserved.' He flattered himself. The committee was dominated by manufacturers who combined to crush amendments moved on behalf of the trade unions by the radical minority.[49]

On 9 April Dilke wrote to Harcourt to stress the urgency of carrying the bill before the imminent dissolution in order to win votes in the English constituencies. When it was debated, on 22 April, he pressed for a tightening of the clauses governing sweatshops.[50] In the event, the act (which became law shortly after the fall of the government) obliged employers to send a list of places of outwork to the factory inspectorate, with a paltry fine of £10 if the buildings were found to be insanitary. Without a multitude of inspectors it was impossible to enforce and subsequently proved a dead letter.

Rosebery's administration lasted in all only fifteen months. His handling of Lords reform had left the party divided and demoralised. It would have been difficult enough from his position in the Upper House to exercise authority over the Commons, but the task was made doubly difficult by the truculence of Harcourt and by his own temperamental unsuitability for the task. The government fell in June 1895 when its War Secretary, Campbell-Bannerman, suffered a vote of censure for failing to procure sufficient cordite explosive for the army. Dilke was the only Liberal to vote in the majority, though the division was lost more through the absence of Liberals (including six ministers) because of poor organisation by the government whips than from the strength of the Opposition.

The radicals had in any case been disappointed with Rosebery's failure to give a more positive lead and there was little grief among them at the government's collapse: the Factories Act had been the only substantive legislative success of the last session, which had been dominated by Welsh disestablishment, and they felt that the government had not done enough in the social domain. Keir Hardie expressed his 'disgust at the way in which the Liberal Party has broken faith with its supporters'.[51] In his memoirs, Atherley-Jones recorded the following verdict on the administration: 'The working man sought satisfaction for his material wants; they offered him Welsh disestablishment; he asked for bread; they gave him a stone.... The woes which have been the subsequent fate of the Liberal party are traceable to their lamentable failure to read and act by the light of the times.'[52] The new liberals of the Rainbow Circle had recently begun to articulate this discontent. The parliamentary radicals for their part, led by Dilke, set about drafting a manifesto and reorganising their ranks in an attempt to be more effective in the new parliament.

Chapter 17

'The Most Independent Man in the House'

In the electoral manifesto drafted by the Radical Committee further democratisation was given priority. It was presented as the essential preliminary to other planks in the radical programme. These included Home Rule all round; disestablishment and disendowment of all state churches; licensing reform giving local option; fixity of tenure, free sale, and fair rents for farmers; international arbitration; taxation of land; extension of death-duties; economic use of public revenues; and, lastly, social reforms such as 'the limitation of hours, full rights of combination, compensation for injuries, and direct representation in Parliament', which were included alongside, but given no particular emphasis over, the other proposals.[1]

At the election in July 1895, the Liberal Party was resoundingly defeated, losing further ground in London (where it now held only eight out of sixty-two seats) and Lancashire. With the economy in recession and the leadership divided over whether to focus on Lords reform (Rosebery), local veto (Harcourt) or Home Rule (Morley), it was not the best of times to go to the country. Indeed, the party was dispirited and left many seats uncontested. Harcourt went down at Derby; and Morley, still stubbornly refusing to endorse the eight-hour principle, at Newcastle. The fact that labour candidates fared even worse did not deter progressives from interpreting the electoral disaster for the Liberals, which yielded an overall Conservative and Unionist majority of 152, as evidence of the failure of the old radicalism and the limits of working-class patience.

At the beginning of August, Philip Stanhope invited five of the newly-elected MPs to the first meeting of the Radical Committee in the hope, he told Dilke, that they would 'strengthen the Radical Party which to tell the truth had become rather ragged in the last part of the late Parliament'. He advised making future meetings 'as "impersonal" as possible', especially by electing the chairman at each sitting. Dilke or Labouchere would normally be selected as any other choice 'would lead to personal jealousies'.[2] Despite its somewhat anarchical regard for organisation, the committee was determined to make its presence felt in the new parliament.

The radicals were disappointed with the Liberal leadership over the party's dismal performance in the election and had some success in registering their dissatisfaction. They were concerned about the influence that the National Liberal Federation exercised over the selection of candidates. A deputation led by Dilke, Labouchere and Stanhope complained to Harcourt and Ellis, the Chief Whip, about the overlapping of its functions with the Liberal Central Association, and about the manner in which its executive committee was chosen, which worked against radical and grassroot representation. When they got no satisfaction they called a meeting of the party for the following March, timed to put pressure on the federation which was about to assemble at Huddersfield.

Their manoeuvre stung the leadership. Campbell-Bannerman, who had not forgiven Dilke for his silent vote in the cordite affair, told a friend that he:

> has no following but three in the party (Dalziel, young [C. P.] Allen, and McKenna) – the party *will have none of him* but he is an insatiate intriguer. He dines and otherwise nobbles the press men in the lobby, who sing his praises.
>
> We have had lately the ludicrous cabal got up by him, Labby and Philip Stanhope: each one has his own personal grudge against the late Govt. – and would rather defeat and thwart *us* than help the Lib. party or injure the Govt. Yet the correspondents talk of them as 'the Radicals' and hold them up as patriots. That view is not taken by the honest rank and file here ... I can only say that the whole dirty tissue of intrigue so revolts me (and others) that the temptation is great to chuck the whole affair. You should hear for instance honest John Burns or Tommie Burt giving their minds on those gentlemen.[3]

A sizeable turnout at the Huddersfield meeting, however, convinced the NLF of the wisdom of introducing new rules for the selection of the executive committee, which did much to draw the teeth of the radicals' complaint. Over the next few years radical influence on the committee increased, which perhaps explains why the NLF was eventually (in 1903) to endorse social reform as an integral element in party policy.[4]

The general election inaugurated a decade of Conservative rule which coincided with the persistence of a deep and systemic economic recession marked by falling land prices, industrial stagnation and unemployment. A resolution of the profitability crisis was sought through an extension of imperialist activity in a search for new overseas markets and raw materials and, at home, through a squeeze on wage costs. The political firmament was therefore dominated by a series of overseas confrontations as international competition intensified, and by labour unrest as the trade unions fought to protect hard-won rights and conditions.

In these circumstances, Dilke's efforts on behalf of labour intensified. In 1896 he took up the cause of the shop-workers. Many of them worked for ninety hours a week and were accommodated in unsanitary quarters. Dilke publicised their conditions in a pamphlet, *Shop Life*, in which he advocated state regulation of hours. However, the recently-formed National Union of Shop Assistants was not yet fully united behind this principle and the first bill which he introduced on their behalf was therefore a moderate one. Within a few years, the union had come round to Dilke's position. Accordingly, his next bill proposed to restrict hours to sixty a week inclusive of meal-times. The government adopted instead a permissive measure, sponsored by Lord Avebury, which had the backing of the employers.[5]

Following the publication in 1898 of a report on the so-called 'dangerous trades' (many of which, such as the pottery and match industries, and trades exempted under the Factory Acts because of their seasonal nature, such as fish-curing and fruit-preserving, were great employers of women), Dilke began a campaign to stamp out the worst practices by way of greater inspection and more stringent regulations.[6] He explained his frequent parliamentary interventions on behalf of female labour by reference to their non-unionised and politically disfranchised position. He pressed for legal responsibility for the health and safety of the workforce to be thrown onto the employer, and for better compensation schemes. In 1902 he urged parliament to compel pottery manufacturers to use glazes with a low lead content, and became a leading proponent of their universal adoption. He was the guest-speaker at a London exhibition in 1906 of pottery produced in this way. Within a decade of his taking up the issue, the number of cases of lead poisoning had fallen by 80 per cent.[7] In the case of the match industry, the use of phosphorus produced poisonous fumes that caused necrosis, a gangrene of the jawbone known colloquially as 'phossy jaw'. The development of safety-matches made it possible in 1900 for the government to meet Dilke's demand for restrictions in its use and eventually to ban it completely.

Dilke had appointed women inspectors at the Local Government Board,[8] and in 1893 had persuaded Asquith to employ them at the Home Office. He was also in favour of international agreements to regulate working conditions, cooperating to that end with European labour leaders like Arthur Fontaine of France and Emile Vandervelde of Belgium. He was anxious that the British government should participate in the

International Labour Conference, held in Switzerland in 1905, which included on the agenda proposals to control the use of lead and white phosphorus and to regulate the night-time employment of women.[9]

He sought as well to remedy abuses in the wages system. He wanted a wider application of what was known as the 'particulars clause' of the Factory Act of 1891, which required employers to give employees written particulars of wage rates. It covered only certain groups of textile workers, but was extended in 1895 to all textile workers, and in 1901 to textile outworkers. In 1903 he pressed for it to include also the piecework trades of London and the small hardware trades of Birmingham. A more serious abuse was the practice of imposing fines on workers for offences such as lateness for work or tending dirty machinery. In an 1896 pamphlet on the subject, he described fines and deductions as 'the chief of all the workmen's grievances'.[10]

He continued to act on behalf of the Miners' Federation. In 1896 he achieved some small improvements in mining safety regulations. The following year, he was given charge by the MFGB of a further regulation bill, which on this occasion included a clause to prevent the employment of boys for more than eight hours below ground, a shrewd tactic designed to expose the extent to which the opposition of the north-east coalfields to the eight-hour day rested upon the exploitation of boy-labour.[11] The latter question remained insoluble, though opposition to it was steadily weakening. In 1901 an eight-hour bill was read a second time only to be talked out in committee. It seemed only a matter of time, therefore, before the principle would be adopted.

The problem of state regulation of working conditions was a comparatively small gnat for *laissez-faire* liberals to strain at. Protection of the individual against danger or wrongdoing had, after all, been embodied in common law for centuries. The principle of state intervention to provide an income for individuals faced with injury, illness, unemployment or old age was much more difficult to swallow. Even an advanced radical like Dilke did not come easily to collectivist views on these issues.

He had at first thought that state insurance schemes were 'visionary', preferring instead extension of the existing laws which left compensation for injury to an assessment of employer liability.[12] In 1894, during the debates on the Employers' Liability Bill, he had taken up the TUC's call for adequate cover for workmen employed by subcontractors. However, when three years later Chamberlain proposed to make compensation no longer dependent upon proof of employer liability, Dilke had by now come to the view that only a comprehensive scheme of national insurance would do.[13] He had been converted to this more uncompromising position by shortcomings in the liability scheme, especially the failure to compel employers to insure against bankruptcy.

Dilke's increasingly independent political outlook was not confined to social questions but extended to foreign policy. This was partly occasioned by the continuing drift of the Liberal Party and the lack of effective leadership. The party underwent a phase of internecine struggle following Rosebery's resignation in October 1896 and lacked any strong personality to guide it. Harcourt, victorious at a by-election in 1896, was now the nominal leader, but the party's progressive wing grew steadily more restless as it appeared to mark time on new liberal issues. These discontents were compounded by serious differences over foreign policy where the Liberal Imperialists (the 'Limps') found much to criticise in Harcourt's and Morley's 'Little Englandism'. When the leadership of the party once more became vacant following Harcourt's abdication in 1898, Dilke favoured Asquith against Campbell-Bannerman. 'The matter is important to me', he told Chamberlain, 'as I can get from Asquith & cannot get from Bannerman such a labour policy as would enable me to support & the War Office policy of Campbell-Bannerman must drive me into a position of complete independence.' Besides, he added, Bannerman was a Tory, while Asquith, for a lawyer, was a radical.[14]

The party turmoil coincided with a succession of serious overseas crises prompted by imperialist rivalries. After Rosebery's retirement, the Liberal leadership appeared particularly lacking in the knowledge and experience needed to mount an incisive critique of Conservative foreign policy. Backbenchers who possessed these qualities, like Dilke, felt obliged to compensate for front bench ignorance or inaction. In 1897, following the outbreak of war between Greece and Turkey, he requested a day to debate Crete, which he wished to see independent of Turkish rule and united with Greece. The concession of a day would be tantamount to a vote of censure on the government's foreign policy. Balfour, the Leader of the House, therefore refused the request on the grounds that such a right could only be granted to the 'official' Opposition. He acknowledged, however, 'that no man in the House speaks with greater authority or knowledge on Foreign Affairs than yourself: and that no man has a better right to ask for opportunities for criticising the course pursued in respect to Foreign Affairs by this or any other Government'. In the event, the 'official' Opposition asked for a day, the debate went ahead, and Dilke was able to make his points.[15]

In the following year, imperialist rivalries in both Africa and the Far East reached flashpoint and appeared momentarily to threaten wars in which Britain would be dangerously overstretched and isolated. The government's Egyptian policy, which Dilke had never ceased to attack, culminated in Kitchener's occupation of Khartoum and the Fashoda mission, which brought France and Britain to the brink of conflict. In the Far East, Russia, France and Germany were extracting concessions from a China weakened by defeat in 1895 at the hands of Japan. Here Dilke favoured a more interventionist policy. He attributed Salisbury's supineness to the African entanglements, which distracted attention from those areas of the world like the Far East where economic interests were worth contesting. So critical had international affairs become that he decided to initiate a debate on Conservative foreign policy by moving a reduction in the Foreign Secretary's salary, a course of action that was frowned upon by the party leadership but which he persisted with annually until the Liberals were back in office.[16] Also, during the course of 1898, he wrote a number of newspaper articles on imperial problems which were brought out in hardcover the following year as *The British Empire*.

One of these essays dealt with Newfoundland, where the British government was resisting French demands for certain fishing rights. The point at issue devolved upon the apparently trivial distinction that a lobster was not a fish and therefore France had no rights under the Treaty of Utrecht to land lobster catches on the Newfoundland coast. By describing this as 'the most dangerous of all international questions', Dilke appeared to treat the issue with a sobriety that bordered on the absurd. Yet, according to one contemporary, his opinion was 'cabled to all parts of the world and published as a statement of the greatest consequence' and assisted the process that led to a negotiated settlement.[17]

From the independence of the back benches, Dilke's criticism of the foreign policy of the day was often too destructive to find many supporters in or outside the government. Yet his advice carried authority, even if it was seldom heeded. He was also able to reconcile an active and positive foreign policy with a commitment to social change.

Nowhere was this more evident than in his demand for a more efficient and cost-effective system of imperial defence. Expenditure on defence was a traditional radical concern, but Dilke differed from many of his fellow radicals by wanting savings on the army to be spent on improving the navy. He returned again and again to the need for Britain to maintain a superiority of ships not just over the next two largest naval powers (the so-called two-power standard) but over the next three. He moved annually for statistics on the number of serviceable ships, which soon became known as the 'Dilke Return'. He described himself as 'more extreme than any Jingo in the House of Commons' on naval matters. However, he strenuously denied the accusations of some radical colleagues that he was in any way in favour of 'the position of grab which is commonly associated with the name of Jingo', and he rebuked them for shrinking from the responsibility of facing up to defence questions upon which social progress depended.[18]

Shortly before the outbreak of the Boer War, he warned that the army was in a 'hopeless' state.[19] The reverses in the early campaigns seemed to confirm his analysis. His single-minded attention to the military short-comings of the war left him almost totally isolated in parliament, caught between the Campbell-Bannerman Liberals and radicals who opposed it on Gladstonian principles and the Liberal Imperialists and jingoes who supported the government. At the beginning of 1900, he urged Campbell-Bannerman to move an amendment to the Queen's Speech condemning the government's lack of military preparation. The Liberal leader knew that the government would shrug this off with a simple tu quoque,[20] and decided therefore to confine the Opposition's charge to a censure of the government's failure to foresee that their policy would lead to war. Dilke went ahead alone. Fitzmaurice complained to Campbell-Bannerman that Dilke's tactic had let the government off the hook, and put it down to his desire 'to show off his own knowledge'. By contrast, the radical journalist H. W. Massingham thought Dilke's 'the *finest* speech I have ever heard in the House of Commons!'.[21]

The shortage of trained horses, poor equipment, the inadequate military education of many officers and the inability to cope with Boer guerilla tactics formed the stuffing of Dilke's indictment. The remedy lay in 'revolutionary army reform' and a secret inquiry into the preparation and conduct of the war.[22] In the event, a royal commission of inquiry was appointed and its report confirmed many of Dilke's criticisms. Some of these were met by the reforms set in train by his friend Arnold-Forster, following his promotion to the War Office in October 1903, though a more complete reorganisation of the army had to await the return of a Liberal ministry. Moreover, the war had prompted Balfour to reorganise the defence committee and put it on a permanent footing. Although this new Committee of Imperial Defence was not precisely the arrangement which Dilke had envisaged in 1893, he was satisfied that it would achieve much the same purpose.[23]

Few of Dilke's ideas on national defence were original. In naval matters he was influenced by Wilkinson and Sir John Colomb, and on the army by Roberts, Wolseley and the Brackenburys. Nevertheless, he succeeded in fusing their various proposals into a system which he persistently brought before parliament and the reading public. He helped to popularise the concept of Prime Ministerial responsibility for imperial defence and of naval supremacy backed by a well-organised, cost-effective regular army and an easily deployed expeditionary force. By refusing to relax his criticism of defence arrangements, he paved the way in the aftermath of the South African War for a more ready acceptance of the sweeping reforms of Balfour, Haldane and Fisher. In his combination of advanced social reforming policy secured by thorough and efficient defence, and his mastery of the details of both, he was probably unique among his generation and certainly among fellow radicals.

Many of the latter had in any case been defeated in the famous 'Khaki' election of October 1900, when the government sought to capitalise on jingoistic support for the war. The Conservatives and Unionists were returned with an overall majority of 134 and Salisbury proceeded to form his fourth administration. Within a few months the government had succeeded in alienating large sections of the voting public through a series of unpopular decisions which paved the way for the great Liberal victory of 1906. Popular chauvinism was soon dampened by the military setbacks in South Africa; trade unionists were politicised by the Taff Vale judgement; Nonconformist anger was mobilised against the Education Act; and the Liberal Party generally was reunited in defence of free trade and against the spectre of dear food held out by tariff reform.

Disillusionment with the Liberal leadership's handling of opposition to the war in South Africa encouraged attempts at greater cooperation between radicals, socialists and Irish Nationalists. Meetings were held to this end between Dilke, Hardie and John Redmond, the leader of the Irish party. Hardie appears to have occasionally dreamt of a new and independent radical party embracing these three groups, but he was also extremely wary of labour becoming marginalised in any such political realignment. He therefore blew hot and cold in his relations with the radicals. If such a regrouping had ever been possible, which is doubtful, the revival of the Liberal Party after the end of the war rendered it academic. Nevertheless, informal contacts were maintained. Dilke had suggested to the TUC's parliamentary committee the formation of 'a non-political party to deal with all labour questions of importance',[24] and from 1900 to 1902 acted as its spokesman in the House. He was instrumental, by securing the cooperation of Redmond's Irish group, in getting the government to replace a retrograde Factory Bill in 1900 with a more satisfactory measure. It was also to Dilke that the committee turned when faced with the biggest challenge to the trade unions since their legalisation.

Following a strike by the railwaymen of Taff Vale in South Wales, the railway company successfully sued the union for damages. This decision was reversed in the Court of Appeal, but re-instated by the House of Lords in 1901. Hitherto it had been assumed that trade unions were not corporate bodies. Now, however, they were to be held responsible for the activities of their striking members and, indeed, for the tortious act of any individual acting on their behalf. Henceforth, they were in danger of being mulcted of their accumulated funds in legal cases arising out of industrial disputes. Their response to the judgement proved to be a major turning-point in the history and progress of the labour movement.

The animus of the state towards the unions was confirmed less than a fortnight later in the case of *Quinn* v. *Leathem*, the significance of which was that a union could not boycott the trade of an employer without being open to the charge of 'maliciously conspiring' against him.[25] Its harshness is only evident when judged in the light of an earlier case, that of *Mogul Steamship Company* v. *McGregor, Gow and Company* (1892), in which economic rivalry, including boycotting, was recognised as legitimate between companies. There appeared to be one law for the unions and another for the employers.

The assault on the trade unions has to be understood in the context of the economic recession and the unionisation of the unskilled. The employers responded by attempting to elevate the status of 'free labour', or the rights of individuals not to join unions, which, they claimed, were infringed by intimidatory picketing. The right to picket was vital to unskilled workers. From their point of view, 'free labour' was merely a euphemism for 'blackleg labour'.

Dilke had taken no part in the debates on the great trade union acts of the 1870s, though he had observed at the time that they had been 'spoilt ... by the insertion of obscure definition clauses'. The Webbs, in their standard history of trade unionism, thought that this remark, in its anticipation of the later legal judgements, demonstrated Dilke's 'prescience'.[26]

Although he held that industrial action was extremely damaging and should if possible be avoided, he nevertheless defended the right of the unions to strike and to be organised in such a way as to be powerful enough to win. His commitment contrasted sharply with the general lack of enthusiasm among the Liberal leaders for fighting the legal decisions. It puts into perspective not only the exceptionally advanced nature of his social radicalism, but also explains why, in spite of his belief that such help would obviate the need for it, the unions began to look to creating an independent political organisation of their own.

Dilke had acted as spokesman for the Amalgamated Society of Railway Servants when legislation touching upon its funds and pensions had been introduced into the Commons in 1897 and 1898. He had also in 1897 contributed a short preface to a book by Clement Edwards in which he had endorsed the latter's plan for railway nationalisation. It was probably for these reasons that the union now turned to him for advice. At the same time, the parliamentary committee of the TUC asked him to arrange a conference with the legalists of the Liberal Party. He approached Asquith, who agreed to participate and who suggested that Sir Robert Reid and R. B. Haldane should also attend.[27] He also gave a detailed exposition of his views on the legal situation to Sam Woods, secretary of the parliamentary committee. Further appeals to the Lords, he argued, were useless and the only remedy lay in legislation, though legislation would be difficult. In the Taff Vale decision the Lords had taken 'two inconsistent views, and are evidently prepared to maintain whichever of them suits their prejudice on the particular case that comes before them'. The inconsistency lay in treating the unions both as corporate bodies and as collectivities of individuals. It was not, therefore, sufficient to protect the unions against being sued, as this would leave them open to attack through actions against individuals. Rather, it would be necessary to legislate to protect their funds. In the case of *Quinn* v. *Leathem*, Dilke continued, 'some of our friends have given up the main point too easily'. He believed that 'it ought not to be actionable merely to abstain from work and induce others to abstain from work', and that the unions must reassert this principle. In that event, further legislation would probably not be necessary. With regard to *Lyons* v. *Wilkins*,[28] which had severely weakened the right to picket, Dilke held that the judgement was sufficiently within the terms of the act of 1875 (presumably because of the 'obscure definition clauses') for there to be 'no chance whatever of reversing it'. Nevertheless, the case was contrary to parliament's intention in 1875 and a bill might be necessary to clarify the law. 'These views', Dilke concluded, 'point to a Bill on the Taff Vale and picketing cases, and to leaving alone the peculiar case of *Quinn* v. *Leathem*.'[29]

This was no doubt the course which he urged on his Liberal and labour colleagues when they met on 3 December 1901 – in effect, to restore and safeguard in law the position nominally enjoyed by the unions since 1875. With some of the trade unionists, as well as Asquith and Haldane, prepared to accept parts of the legal judgements, and the parliamentary committee wavering over what action to take, the positive line urged by Dilke was important. He recorded that he converted all except Asquith, who was 'doubtful as to the wisdom of fighting'. It was decided at the conference, upon the suggestion of Haldane, to draft two bills, one dealing with picketing and the other with the protection of trade union funds. Asquith confirmed his support for this course two days later.[30]

Asquith and Haldane saw the separation of the bills as a way round a difficult situation, for neither of them wished for a complete return to the *status quo ante* Taff Vale. Complete immunity for the funds of the trade unions would give them a legal concession not enjoyed by other corporate bodies or individuals and risk making them too powerful. The Liberal leaders could salve their consciences and, hopefully, appease the unions with a bill to legalise picketing, but at the same time, in a second bill, place a check upon the use of union funds by making them subject to the regulations governing companies. Francis Palmer, an authority on company law, was therefore instructed to draft this latter bill, which afterwards became known as the 'subsidiary companies scheme'. Its complex nature stimulated no interest among trade union leaders and it was quietly shelved.[31]

In his letter to Dilke, affirming his opinion in favour of two separate bills, Asquith had stressed that they should be introduced by someone who represented the trade unions or (like Dilke) could speak on their behalf. For his part, he would support but not lead. Dilke had hoped for more decisive involvement by the Liberal hierarchy than this.[32] He led a deputation to the cabinet which was received by C. T. Ritchie, the President of the Board of Trade, and his old friend, Henry James, now Lord James of Hereford. While the latter was sympathetic, the Tory party as a whole was not. A resolution proposing the restoration of the *status quo ante* Taff Vale was defeated in the Commons in May 1902 by twenty-nine votes.[33] The opposition of the one party and the timid support of the other provided the background to a meeting in a Commons committee room at the beginning of June, presided over by Dilke, between advanced radicals of the Liberal Party, labour members, and representatives of the parliamentary committee of the TUC. They resolved to act together in future upon all labour questions involving parliamentary or public action; and to meet jointly, at the request of any one of the three, whenever occasion arose.[34]

The Taff Vale case had stimulated the affiliation of trade unions to the Labour Representation Committee, founded in 1900 to organise the election of independent labour candidates to parliament. One of the first fruits of this new spirit was the return of David Shackleton, Will Crooks and Arthur Henderson at by-elections in 1902–3. Shackleton was almost immediately given charge of a Trade Disputes Bill. Dilke maintained that it now fell to these men to direct the affairs of labour, though he was willing to advise them.

His aloofness may in part be explained by the temperamental hostility of Hardie and the jealousy of MacDonald towards him, so he kept a discreet distance even though he privately thought Shackleton's bill too moderate. It failed to progress. Instead, a Royal Commission on Trade Disputes was set up but, as it contained no trade unionists, it was anathema to the TUC. The parliamentary committee, instructed by congress in the autumn of 1903 to prepare a new bill restoring the *status quo ante*, approached Dilke for permission to draw upon a far-reaching measure which he had drafted. The unions were still prepared to accept some checks on their funds, and they did not borrow all Dilke's clauses. The two Trade Disputes Bills, Dilke's and the TUC's, appeared on the parliamentary agenda in 1904. Dilke had his printed and read, without debate, in order to emphasise the moderation of the latter. The government fell back upon its royal commission as an excuse for delay and for postponing legislation until after the forthcoming general election.

Cooperation between advanced Liberals and the new labour men had helped to revitalise the Radical Committee, the membership of which was increased in 1903 from twenty-seven to forty-seven. At the same time, MPs from both groups agreed to take joint action over the private members' ballot.[35] Dilke claimed that as a result of this alliance, the group 'invariably [secured] a place for the Miners' Eight-Hours Bill, [and] frequently a place for two miners' bills'. A small core of about ten radicals met weekly to arrange current business, and an emergency committee of four was established in 1904. In this way, they were able to use the ballot to bring a large number of radical measures before the House.

Meanwhile, having alienated the unions, the government next succeeded in raising the hackles of middle-class Nonconfomists by introducing in 1902 an avowedly pro-church Education Bill, which not only abolished the school boards and transferred responsibility for secondary and primary education to the county councils, but also gave the voluntary schools a share of the rates and grants. Dilke fought it tooth and nail, opposing it at every stage. He was one of only twenty-three who bothered to vote against its first reading in March and when, after an autumn session and a ruthless use of the closure, it came before the House for the final time in December, he moved the deferment of the Lords' amendments for three months, a motion in parliamentary practice tantamount to killing the measure. His constituents had asked him to 'obstruct the Bill even to the extent of being sent to the Clock Tower', and though matters never came to that pass, he was certainly one of its most vociferous critics. His numerous and well-informed interventions were satirised by *Punch*:

At this juncture Dilke interposed. Belated Members sat bolt upright. Now they would know all about it; dark places would be made clear. Well-known Parliamentary axiom,

'If when occasion for reference to fact or figure arises and you haven't got a copy of *Encyclopaedia Britannica* in your waistcoat pocket, consult Dilke'.[36]

He damned the bill as 'the first thoroughly reactionary piece of legislation in English-speaking countries in our time'. As its success became certain, he took up one of the few purely factious stands of his political life: his impassioned speech on the third reading on 2 December was the most partisan he ever made. It concluded, in language that was the nearest he ever came to making a peroration, with a call to Liberals to take the fight to every parish and county council election in the country.[37]

It is easy with hindsight to see the benefits which accrued from placing education in the charge of the county councils. Many of the rural school boards were too small to function cheaply and efficiently. The act laid the foundations for a system of state elementary and secondary education and, in retrospect, it is its opponents who appear reactionary. This should not be allowed to disguise the fact that, to contemporaries, the Conservative Party seemed to have one clear-cut and overriding aim in introducing reform, namely to reassert the authority of the established church in the field of education.

Dilke's energetic opposition to the bill once more contrasted sharply with that of the Liberal leadership, which underestimated the animosity of the Nonconformists. In Wales, several county councils and county boroughs refused at first to implement the legislation, while many Dissenters refused to pay the portion of their rates which went to the voluntary schools. The drift of middle-class Nonconformists to the Conservative Party was temporarily reversed and they were galvanised to work for the government's defeat at the next general election.

The government seemed hell-bent on self-destruction when, in the next session, it trumped Taff Vale and education with tariff reform. This was not, of course, the intention of its progenitors. They conceived tariff reform partly as a way of resolving rather than compounding the government's mounting difficulties and of reversing its developing unpopularity. Prior to the Boer War, the Conservative Party had found imperialism rather easier to deliver than the social reform with which it was supposed, according to the Disraelian legacy, to be linked. Imperialism had become too often a distraction from, rather than an accompaniment to, social legislation, and a more agreeable option for a party whose supporters would inevitably have to bear the cost of any redistributive policies. The reversals in South Africa placed a question mark over this strategy. It was the renegade radical, Joseph Chamberlain, who came up with what appeared to be a perfect solution – tariff reform – to the Conservative dilemma. Not the rich but the foreigner would pay for the social measures that would allow the Conservatives to outbid the Liberals in the competition for the burgeoning working-class vote. Chamberlain's espousal of the tariff reform programme is partly explicable in terms of his radical background – his break with the Liberal Party had not dimmed his concern with social issues; and partly in terms of his Birmingham interests – the non-monopoly manufacturing industries of the Midlands were especially feeling the pinch of overseas competition. The connections Chamberlain sought to establish between tariff reform and social issues, such as pensions and unemployment, made this a particularly well-integrated form of social imperialism. The future of Britain in terms of its social development and economic survival was dependent upon the empire; the empire's future was in turn dependent upon solving social and industrial problems in Britain.

The Boer War had driven home these lessons. As Colonial Secretary, Chamberlain had been greatly impressed by the cooperation of the colonies in resisting the rebellious Boer republics. The cost of imperial defence, a perenially sore point between the mother country and the colonies, the economic and social problems raised by the war, and the need to find an alternative to taxing the rich to finance social reform, all pointed, in Chamberlain's mind, to new military and financial arrangements within the British Empire. The key to the system was improved trade based upon preferential tariffs. Such a policy would be the death-knell of free trade, a commercial system which had become almost sacrosanct after more than half a century of economic growth.

Dilke held no illusions about Britain's economic future, recognising that she would eventually be outstripped commercially by countries with more abundant resources. However, he was entirely opposed to any form of imperial federation, except for defence purposes, and he dismissed any notions of closer imperial ties based upon sentiment. The best Britain could hope for was to be relieved of the cost of colonial defence by the granting of independence. Thereafter friendly relations might be cultivated by way of bilateral agreements on such issues as defence, communications, laws and currency.[38] His part in the fiscal controversy has been largely ignored in previous biographies. Yet, he was the first to press for a debate on Chamberlain's proposals and, if John Morley is to be believed, Chamberlain's first doubts about free trade derived from his association with Dilke.[39]

It is certainly the case that the ideas expressed in *Greater Britain* alerted Chamberlain to the possibilities of a new imperial arrangement and they might even have led him to question Britain's attachment to free trade. At the height of the fair trade campaign in 1881, he had written to Dilke: 'I have been occupying my leisure with reading over again a book called *Greater Britain* ... And a very bright & instructive book it is!'[40] Chamberlain did not specify in what ways he found the book instructive, but it may have helped him to resolve some of his doubts during the fair trade debate. His biographer, J. L. Garvin, was quite definite that 'Chamberlain always acknowledged his original debt in Imperial affairs to the author of *Greater Britain*'.[41] He does not substantiate this statement, but it is plausible. It is only necessary to read the first page of the *Problems of Greater Britain*, where Dilke describes the vast natural resources of the empire and concludes that 'we might, if we pleased, be entirely independent of any foreign source',[42] to surmise his influence.

If, indeed, Chamberlain derived some inspiration from Dilke, then there is a certain irony about the parts played by the two men in the tariff campaign, for it was the bitterest of their differences after 1886. When Chamberlain took his campaign to the country, the first public reply came from Asquith at a meeting in Dean Forest chaired by Dilke.[43] Dilke toured the country in 1903–4 denouncing 'fiscalitis', the Chamberlain disease. He spoke at Salford, Liverpool, Wakefield, Normanton, Hull and Derby in the autumn of 1903, and at Cardiff, Chesterfield, Manchester, Swindon, Stroud and Ashton-under-Lyne in January 1904.

Chamberlain had initially gone no further than to press for an inquiry into the existing fiscal system, but this was enough to cause consternation among free trade Unionists. The Liberal leaders were prepared to play for time in order to allow Conservative and Unionist unrest to develop and fester. The radicals, however, refused to go along with this. Dilke and Lloyd George, anxious to exploit potential divisions in the government signalled by an equivocal response on Balfour's part to Chamberlain's announcement, forced the pace by using the motion for the Whitsun adjournment to initiate a debate. It took place on 28 May 1903, with many Liberal frontbenchers absenting themselves through pique at the radical *démarche*.

The debate had been awaited with some excitement, for politicians of all stripes were anxious to discover whether indeed Balfour was in agreement with his Colonial Secretary.[44] The Prime Minister, however, serene to the point of complacency, appeared to believe that by not supporting either wing of the Unionist party he would not, thereby, offend either. In opening the debate, Dilke naturally sought to exploit Balfour's equivocation by pressing him on his views and by mischievously describing Chamberlain as the 'master of the Government'. The radicals succeeded that day in drawing from Chamberlain the admission that his policy would involve a tax on food.

Dilke's case rested on three basic points: that tariff reform would not improve British trade but damage it; that imperial preference would not unite the empire but divide it; and that import duties would not benefit the poorer classes but place heavier burdens upon them.[45] Chamberlain was at first unable to meet much of this criticism. Dilke got him to admit that he was not well-versed upon the subject of Britain's trade with Latin America which, even in the worst periods of depression, took something like £50,000,000 of British exports, and which would be damaged by tariffs. Nor, crucially, had he considered the place of India in any scheme of imperial preference. Australia for her part had her own protectionist policies and showed no enthusiasm for federal union. Of the British Empire's 400,000,000 people, therefore, only 50,000,000, mainly in Canada and New Zealand, would gain by the preference scheme. Finally, Dilke flatly rejected Chamberlain's argument that the working class would benefit by way of an overall reduction in food prices and an expansion of unemployment, or from social measures financed out of the tariff revenues.

Other, more insidious, effects of the tariff campaign on social reform alarmed Dilke. The 'blaze of anti-Chamberlainism' was distracting attention from more pressing problems. He was also disturbed by the possibility that it would drive reactionary elements back into the Liberal fold – a throwback to Whiggism 'as we used to know it in our youth, only worse'.[46] In February 1904, therefore, he once again arranged meetings between representatives of the Irish Nationalists, labour and the radicals, to coordinate opposition to any possible coalition between the Liberal leadership and a rump of Liberal Unionists led by the Duke of Devonshire.[47] In the event, the threat proved evanescent. Devonshire was old and ailing – he died in 1908 – and had lost much of his political appetite, while several of his closest followers were in the House of Lords and isolated from the main fray. Above all, the country was shortly to pronounce decisively against tariff reform.

With an election approaching and Conservative popularity among the working-class voters dented by Taff Vale and the tariff campaign, the government attempted in 1904 to recoup some of this lost support by reviving the anti-immigration legislation abandoned in 1896. Further outbreaks of anti-semitism in eastern Europe, coupled with the pogroms and unrest that preceded the Russian revolution of 1905, had led to a new influx of immigrants. With unemployment rising sharply after the Boer War, the Tories calculated that an Aliens Bill might be one measure of 'protection' that would appeal to the working class and at the same time point the lesson that interference with the free market could be beneficial.

Opposition to it once again centred on Dilke, but he was able this time to speak with the blessing of the labour MPs who no longer supported restrictions. He found two able assistants in C. P. Trevelyan, the son of his old friend George Trevelyan, and Winston Churchill, a renegade from the Tories over tariffs who had turned to Dilke for advice on the immigration question and who now became a prominent opponent of the legislation. In an excellent speech in the Commons on 29 March, which reiterated many of the objections he had made eleven years earlier, Dilke set about destroying the restrictionists' case. He emphasised in particular Britain's reputation as the bastion of liberty and freedom. At one point, he made a statement which is interesting not only because it drew interjections from chauvinistic Tories, but because of its clear divergence from the views on race which he had held thirty years earlier at the time of *Greater Britain*. The immigrants, he said, were 'not of a stock inferior to our own. They are of a stock which, when it mixes with our own ... goes rather to improve than to deteriorate the British race.'[48]

In support of his contention that immigration was 'a mere drop in the ocean', and with his usual meticulous attention to accuracy and detail, he showed that the Board of Trade figures distorted the picture by including transients bound for America who were simply taking advantage of the cheaper fares offered by British shipping lines. The profitability of the shipowners was seriously threatened by the government's proposal. Moreover, the proportion of immigrants in Britain was lower than in Germany, France, Belgium and Switzerland. He also sought to separate the problem of sweating from that of immigration and to safeguard the right of asylum for the victims of persecution, but his amendment to that effect was easily defeated after a lengthy debate. A leading restrictionist sneered that it was alright for Dilke to defend such liberties from 'the sylvan seclusion of the Forest of Dean ... the open door is a very fine thing, so long as it is someone else's.'[49]

The controversy had been heated and the bill was temporarily laid on one side to allow the government time to amend some of its more contentious clauses. When it was reintroduced the following session, an obstructionist campaign was again mounted to it, and the government had to fall back on ruthless use of the closure to get it through. Dilke's amendment to safeguard the right of asylum for those fleeing from persecution was, on this occasion, only narrowly defeated by thirty-four votes in a large House,[50] a margin so close that the government decided a week later to accept it. It was their only significant concession and constitutes a singular achievement by Dilke. His stand had led to his becoming for a time the butt of anti-semites, from whom he received many poisonous letters.

The Aliens Bill finally became law in 1905. It was framed with the express purpose of excluding 'undesirables', who were defined to all intents and purposes as the poor, the sick and those thought likely to commit crime. Its class dimension was very clearly evident in the confinement of the law of inspection only to steerage passengers and not to those who had travelled cabin class. Immigration to Britain was stemmed by this statute, the first of a series of stringent restrictions. In its breaking of the principle of free movement of peoples, in its attempts to construct a sense of national community in opposition to and by exclusion of those defined as 'alien', and in its attenuation of the rights of asylum, the Aliens Act marked, in the words of a recent historian, 'a landmark in the decline of liberal England'.[51]

It was the last significant act of a desperate and moribund administration. During the ten years of Tory rule, Dilke had established an independent position, which he increasingly rationalised in terms of a cynicism and contempt for a system constructed around dogmatic party politics. It is therefore extraordinarily difficult to situate his radicalism within the political spectrum of the late Victorian period. His attachment to traditional radical Liberal policies combined with a concern for labour and feminist issues put him in a category of his own. He had moved beyond orthodox middle-class radicalism but did not embrace socialism. In many respects he was a social democrat at a time when such political creatures were still rare. The problem of classifying his politics is compounded by his stand on foreign, imperial and defence matters where he was neither a conventional radical nor a typical imperialist. His social imperialism was as distinct and independent as his social radicalism. The peculiar and unique character of his politics was well summed up by a writer in the *Labour Leader* calling himself 'Marxian' who, in regretting that he could not call Dilke a socialist, ascribed his position as 'the most independent man in the House of Commons' to 'a strange grafting of complete Socialist tendencies upon a courteous, soldierly, and widely informed gentleman, who has too much brains for Liberalism and too much daring for Toryism'.[52]

Chapter 18

The Last Years

The Conservative government, led first by Salisbury and then from 1902 by his nephew Balfour, had rapidly lost popularity in the wake of a series of political mistakes and policy failures. National pride had been wounded by the defeats in South Africa; trade unionists had been alienated by Taff Vale and the disgraceful employment of cheap Chinese labour in the Rand mines;[1] Nonconformists were outraged by the Education Act; and the Conservative Party itself was riven by tariff reform. In the face of all this, Balfour tried one last gamble. Instead of dissolving, he decided in December 1905 to resign in the hope that attempts at forming a Liberal ministry would expose all the old rivalries and divisions. However, the very political setbacks that had weakened the government had served to unite the Liberal Party under Campbell-Bannerman's ecumenical leadership and to give it a purpose that had previously been lacking. Campbell-Bannerman accepted the challenge, took office in December, and went to the country the following month.

The general election of January 1906 yielded the greatest majority for any party since 1832. The Liberals won 377 seats, a majority of eighty-four over all other parties combined, but the biggest surprise and the most significant outcome for the future was the return of twenty-nine candidates of the Labour Representation Committee, sizeable enough to justify their adopting the title 'Labour Party'. After a twenty-year hiatus, radicalism seemed set fair to resume its forward momentum and expectations among progressives were high.

The preponderance of traditional issues in the election manifestos of Liberal candidates, however, underlined the negative character of the victory and should perhaps have cautioned the reformers against over optimism. Most frequently mentioned were free trade, education, Ireland and licensing reform. By contrast, the Labour candidates had a different set of priorities. At the top of their agenda was the need for increased working-class representation, closely followed by Taff Vale, unemployment and old age pensions.[2] In other words, the Liberal Party as a whole was still some way from embracing the new liberalism.

Dilke, for his part, had not even bothered to produce a manifesto. His grip on the Forest of Dean constituency was such that he could issue an address that was terse even by his standards: 'Gentlemen, I solicit, with confidence, the renewal of your trust. Believe me, Your devoted servant, Charles W. Dilke'.[3]

There had been some speculation before Christmas that he might be included in the new government, possibly at the War Office. One potential obstacle to his promotion had disappeared with the death of Queen Victoria in 1901. She had remained unbending in her opposition to his reappearance at court.[4] In 1897, when he had presented himself as a privy councillor at the Diamond Jubilee celebrations, he had felt a most unwelcome atmosphere. With Edward's coronation in 1901, this ostracism had ceased, and he had resumed regular attendance at court functions. However, Campbell-Bannerman shared the late Queen's intense dislike of Dilke.[5] He therefore needed little excuse to exclude him, pointing to the protests of church leaders as evidence that there would be a split in the party if he were in the cabinet. Reginald McKenna, who obtained a junior post and who was a staunch disciple of Dilke's naval policy, was one of several who expressed disappointment at his omission. Morley pleaded his case with the Prime Minister but left the interview convinced that the exclusion was 'a *chose jugée*' from the start.[6]

Apart from a typically parsimonious regret about missing out on a ministerial salary, Dilke appears not to have been unduly worried. Lady Dilke had been anxious that he should regain some of his former standing. This had helped to sustain his ambition, but it had died with her in 1904. Their marriage had been a happy and successful one. She had continued to write and combine her academic interests with a highly-effective involvement in women's trade unionism. In the last years of her life, her dedication to the women's movement had taken her further to the left than her husband and, a month before her death, she had resigned from the Women's Liberal Association with the intention of devoting herself entirely to the Labour Party.[7] She had become ill following a meeting at Chelsea Town Hall in the autumn of 1904 at which Dilke had addressed his former constituents for the first time in many years. At Pyrford, their winter home, she had rallied briefly but, on 23 October, suffered a relapse and, shortly after midnight, she passed away peacefully in Dilke's arms. He produced a tribute to her in the form of an introductory eulogy to a manuscript of hers entitled *The Book of the Spiritual Life*, which was published in 1905. 'I put my soul into the work of bringing out her posthumous book with a proper memoir', he wrote, 'and it nearly killed me.' But, he added, 'I was never so pleased with anything as with the success of the book.' [8]

There is a poignancy about Dilke's last years. After Emilia's death, he had no immediate family to provide companionship in his old age, and unabated political activity must have been poor recompense for periods of great sadness and loneliness. As he contemplated his own mortality and set about ordering his affairs, a sense of unfulfilled promise bore in on him. He burnt many of his private papers, including the once-prized letters from his grandfather which must have painfully reminded him of the high expectations the latter had held out for him.[9] In 1906 he wrote to a friend, 'I never cared for my Father. My grandfather is my spiritual Father. The two people that I loved – my grandfather and Fussie [i.e. Emilia] – died telling me that I had given them perfect happiness.'[10] He also remade his will. He was a very wealthy man – indeed, when his will was proved the gross value of his estate was put at over £130,000. Among the principal beneficiaries were Gertrude Tuckwell and May Tennant, whom he had come to know through Emilia and whom he wished to continue to assist financially in their trade union endeavours. The *Athenaeum* and *Notes and Queries* were to be managed by a trust under the control of his secretary, Henry Hudson. A large part of his valuable art collection was to be gifted to various libraries and museums.

Much of his property, including holdings in Australia, financial wealth in the form of shares and debentures, and personal effects and family heirlooms were to pass to his son, but a trust fund was to manage this legacy on his behalf. These arrangements were necessary in view of Wentie's deteriorating mental condition. In 1896 he had wanted to marry a half-Jewish girl and had written a pathetic letter from Adelaide seeking his father's advice. Dilke had presumably said no, for seven years later Wentie was to be disappointed in love once more when he was refused permission to marry, this time by the girl's parents, ostensibly on the grounds that she was suffering from advanced heart disease but perhaps because of early manifestations of his approaching insanity. He suffered from a persecution complex and had eventually to be confined in an asylum. His condition was such that, in 1909, Dilke felt compelled to change his will, reducing Wentie's inheritance and making it dependent upon an assessment of his mental condition by his trustees, a course which, predictably, simply fuelled Wentie's paranoia.[11] His health later improved, he left the sanatorium and, in 1915, married Pearl Faithfull. He died in

December 1918 without heir, the baronetcy passing to the descendants of Dilke's brother, Ashton.

Dilke's own health was gradually declining, and he increasingly looked to the new men, particularly within the Labour Party, to carry forward the torch of radicalism and social reform. He did not sour with age or look back nostalgically to some imagined golden era of his past. Rather, he believed that the membership of the House of Commons was in many ways superior to that of his heyday.[12] In Winston Churchill and, more curiously, Loulou Harcourt, he saw greater men than their fathers had been. The new men, for their part, in general found his speeches in the House heavygoing, but they delighted in his conversation when they afterwards met up with him in the smoking-room. He remained optimistic and preferred to spend his remaining years, as he had spent his time since 1892, as an independent critic. These feelings were distilled in a letter to Labouchere in January 1906:

> I never thought C. B. cd. possibly offer me the W[ar] O[ffice], & I cd. not have refused it, or made conditions for that post, & it wd. have killed me. I did not expect him to offer me any place. Had my wife lived that would have hurt her, and through her, me. As it is I prefer to be outside – a thing which, though often true, no one ever believes of others ... The only pleasant thing about office would have been the money ... But when in office ... I was exceptionally powerful and nearly always got my own way in every department. That could never have been repeated – a strong reason why I have all along preferred the present front seat in the house to a less commanding position on the stage.[13]

If Dilke no longer cared much about his own prospects, he did care a great deal about those of the Labour Party. He viewed the electoral success of the working class with the equanimity of one who had always accepted and encouraged such an event, and who regarded it as a beneficial stimulus to a party still in the grip of Whigs and moderates. 'The triumph of the principles to which I have devoted my life' he wrote, 'is now bound up with the future of the Labour Party ... The Labour Party itself was my original scheme for the I. L. P. as developed in my talks at Pyrford, before its formation, with Champion, & with Ben Tillett. To join it or to lead it was never my thought.' To lead it would have been well-nigh impossible in view of the suspicion with which he was regarded by Hardie and MacDonald. When he attended a conference of Labour Party officials on 17 November, he refused to take the chair in MacDonald's absence because of the latter's envy of him.[14] Labouchere later claimed that Dilke had wanted to become the leader of the Labour MPs but that they had made it clear that they would only have a Labour man. 'In the main', he added, 'this was due to jealousy of him.'[15] Dilke, however, had never shown any desire or seen the need to leave the Liberal Party which, he believed, contained 'men of ideas as advanced as are found in the ranks of the Labour party'.[16]

For this reason he continued, perhaps mistakenly, to place his faith in the ability of the Radical Committee to act as an effective parliamentary pressure-group. It had been temporarily weakened by the ennoblement of Stanhope and the retirement of Labouchere, and the elevation to the government of Harcourt and Captain Norton. At the start of the parliament, therefore, a preliminary meeting was arranged which about sixty MPs attended and which set up a new committee. Dilke was one of four members of what he called 'a committee of inquisition' which vetted new MPs to prevent dilution of the group's radicalism through the admission of any too timid to act independently.[17] He prepared a list of topics for the group to consider and upon which they might act, which included shop-hours legislation, South African native rights and the reversal of Taff Vale. The return of Labour representatives had as well made payment of MPs, something which he had supported from early days, now an urgent matter. 'Non-payment', he wrote, 'means deliberate preference for monied oligarchy, – & only rare exceptions can produce a democratic member under such a system. It excludes all poor men of genius unless they can get themselves paid by parties, like the Irish, – which makes them slaves. It throws undue power into the hands of the capital as the seat of the legislative. It leads to poor members selling their souls to rotten companies.' The paramount aim remained the same as it had been in 1895, namely to prioritise further democratisation.

The Radical Committee continued in existence throughout the Liberal parliament, but it was never united, and did not long survive Dilke's death. There was no one among the radical backbenchers who combined his social reform instincts with a sound grasp of foreign and military matters.[18] As one of its members later remarked: 'We agreed on nothing ... save that we loved and respected Dilke, who had been a great man before we were born.'[19]

Dilke's faith in radical Liberalism was quickly to be tested, for the first major business facing the new House was a bill to heal the running-sore opened by Taff Vale. It drew upon the recommendations of the royal commission set up by the outgoing government, and aimed to protect peaceful picketing and union funds. But it stopped short of giving the unions complete legal immunity. While they would almost certainly have been content under Tory rule with a bill which gave them less than they desired, now, buoyant with success, they refused to accept any such thing from the Liberals. The bill was therefore repudiated by the parliamentary committee of the TUC.

The government was forced to bow to Labour demands, in part orchestrated by Dilke, Hardie and Redmond, and withdraw the measure. In May 1906 the TUC asked Dilke to keep a watchful eye on its replacement. This was not an idle task. He scrutinised each clause with great care. Shackleton recalled that he consulted with him 'almost daily. On many occasions he crossed the floor to give me points in answer to speeches that were made in opposition to the Labour position.'[20] This was a measure of Dilke's determination to leave Labour to conduct its own battles, but it was coupled with a recognition that they were too easily satisfied.

Conscious of the fate that had befallen the last union legislation, he was anxious to ensure that the wording of the bill this time would be so unambiguously clear that it would not be tested in the courts. In this regard, the acceptance by the Labour MPs of the picketing clause seemed to confirm his contention that they were too compliant. He tried to get the qualifying words 'peaceably and in a reasonable manner' taken out, but was comfortably defeated. He next attempted to safeguard pickets from prosecution under common law, but his amendment to that effect was rejected by five votes after the Attorney-General had pronounced that the law of nuisance could not be used in that way. Events were to justify Dilke's fears and prove the Attorney-General wrong. Nor did the bill extend absolute protection to trade union funds in the event of any prosecution for breach of contract, as he would have liked. On one point, however, he gained an important victory. He succeeded in carrying an amendment safeguarding union members from prosecution for 'persuading' (as defined in the bill) others to break their contract of employment.[21]

The *Manchester Guardian* later acclaimed Dilke as the man who 'must more than any other... be considered the author' of the Trades Disputes Act, which it quite accurately described as the greatest bill of rights ever granted to the trade unions.[22] Such a sweeping judgement does not do justice to the many union activists who campaigned for the reform, or to the Labour men, like David Shackleton, who helped to steer it through the House. Yet Dilke had acted as the TUC's watchdog in the bleak years at the turn of the century when the judges were the willing agents of a repressive state, and in 1906 he had converted many faint-hearted unionists to his more uncompromising standpoint. His amendment on picketing helped to secure for the trade unions the most liberal position which they ever enjoyed and which was not finally eroded until the legislation of the Thatcher years.

The other major labour measure of the first session was the Workmen's Compensation Act, which opened the way for the extension of Chamberlain's scheme of 1897 to industrial diseases such as lead and phosphorus poisoning. It thereby satisfied one of Dilke's objectives but fell short of his demand for compulsory and universal state insurance. He tried to incorporate into the bill a state-enforced guarantee of payment in the event of employer bankruptcy.[23]

Trade union reform apart, Dilke was critical of the government for not using its mandate and its gigantic majority to carry measures that were, by 1906, no longer 'specially radical'.[24] For example, his bill to enfranchise women was talked out.[25] A similar motion by Hardie met the same fate shortly afterwards and prompted the first demonstration inside the precincts of the House. The women were beginning to lose faith in constitutional methods. Likewise, having secured a royal commission to inquire into the practice of deducting fines from wages, Dilke was disappointed when the government failed to act upon its recommendations. By July 1907 he was complaining that 'Labour legislation was beginning to fall into arrear'. He desired, he told the Forest of Dean Labour Association, 'a more active labour policy than that hitherto pursued within the present Parliament by either the Liberal party as a whole or even by the Labour party'.[26]

Despite these criticisms and his inclination towards independent action, his talents were not completely ignored by the government. It was necessary for the Liberals to show that social reform could be paid for without resorting to tariffs. Accordingly, a select committee on income tax reform was set up shortly after the general election, which Dilke was asked to chair. Characteristically, he tried to make up for his lack of specialised knowledge of the subject by spending the summer reading all the available literature. At sixty-two the strain proved injurious. 'My health now began to fail fast,' he recorded, '& the thankless labour I undertook for the Income Tax committee broke me down.'[27]

The committee, which included Keir Hardie, reported in the autumn. Dilke had found the task of chairing it a thankless one because he was out of tune with the majority of its members. It recommended tax-relief on lower incomes, a super-tax on incomes above £5,000, and differential taxation of earned and unearned income. Dilke thought that differentiation would be difficult to operate, and preferred instead to tax property. While he helped to carry the super-tax provision against the Conservatives on the committee, he personally favoured an extensive scale of graduated income tax, reserving the super-tax for times of national emergency. His minority report making these recommendations was supported only by

Hardie.[28] The committee's central recommendation, differentiation, was accepted by the government and was introduced by the Chancellor, Asquith, in his budget the following spring.

The 1907 session was also taken up with army reform. Haldane recalled that when he first presented his Territorial and Reserve Forces Bill to the cabinet, a number of ministers cited Dilke to the effect that the reforms could be accomplished without the need for legislation. The War Secretary did not, however, attach the same value to Dilke's opinions as his colleagues and pressed ahead with his bill.[29] In brief, it created an expeditionary force comprising six infantry divisions and one cavalry division ready for rapid deployment overseas, and merged the yeomanry and volunteers into a stand-by territorial force, primarily responsible for home defence but including a reserve unit capable of replenishing the regular army overseas in wartime.

Dilke was the bill's most persistent critic during its passage through the House, whereas most radicals and Labour men were either uninterested or uninformed, and were satisfied by the economies that accompanied reorganisation. In particular, he disliked the destruction of the Volunteer system. He believed that the scheme as a whole would divert resources from the navy. Finally, he and J. E. B. Seely were the only two 'experts' to question the retention of Cardwell's linked-battalion system.[30] Although Dilke's objections mirrored the general lack of enthusiasm in the army itself for Haldane's plan, it has to be said that he failed to recognise its considerable merits. His vision was clouded by a somewhat sentimental attachment to the Volunteer system of which he had once been a part. He had been criticising War Secretaries for so long and his own prejudices were so deeply ingrained that he was unable to appreciate anything that fell short of them.

Asquith followed up his taxation reforms with the introduction, in his next budget, of old age pensions. He set aside the small sum of £1,200,000 to provide non-contributory pensions of 5s. per week, or 7s.6d for married couples, for those over seventy whose incomes were less than 10s. per week. Such were the meagre beginnings of a principle that was to extend greatly the financial obligations of the state. Dilke was satisfied that provision was based, for the most part, upon the principle of need not thrift, but he disliked two details in the scheme: the late qualifying age of seventy; and the exclusion of paupers. Lloyd George addressed this last criticism by moving an amendment which limited the number of disqualifications, though Dilke's central objection remained. However, he gave his 'whole Parliamentary time' to the bill and supported it as an interim measure until such time that pensions could be dealt with 'on a broader and more generous scale'.[31]

There were other social achievements in 1908. The miners' eight-hour day was carried at last. Dilke secured a limited improvement in the conditions relating to the factory employment of children. He seized upon the general wording of an earlier statute, the Children Act of 1903, which had not been devised for the purpose, but which he realised could be used to safeguard children against dangerous practices such as the lifting of heavy weights or the cleaning of dirty machinery. He persuaded the Home Office to issue a circular drawing the attention of the inspectors to the relevant clauses. He also reintroduced the Shops Bill. Avebury's act had failed to reduce hours, as Dilke had predicted it would. His central argument, that it was necessary to limit the hours of the assistants as well as of the shops, found its exegesis in a long speech. The second reading was carried, and the government agreed to adopt the bill, but it was delayed by the budget and constitutional crises of 1909–10. It did not become law until after Dilke's death and had in any case been emasculated by the deletion of its most important clause, providing for a maximum sixty-hour week.[32] His services on behalf of the shop assistants were not forgotten by the union which, in 1914, named its new offices in Malet Street, London, after him.

Despite progress in the social domain during 1908, a feeling was nevertheless growing, especially among radical backbenchers, that the first three sessions had been wasted – the first two on abortive Education Bills, the third on the temperance issue. Although obstruction by the Lords was in large part responsible for this, many radicals believed that the government had missed the opportunity to confront the peers immediately, on the back of the great election victory, and that the strategy of 'filling up the cup' with rejected bills was not enough. The initiative was beginning to pass to the more advanced members of the party – a process helped along by the death of Campbell-Bannerman in April 1908 and his replacement as Prime Minister by Asquith, for whom Dilke had a strong admiration; and, above all, by the elevation of Lloyd George to the Exchequer.

The new Chancellor was determined to revive Liberal fortunes and to show that the party had a policy to pay for social reform as well as meet the requirements of national defence. Its kernel was the radically redistributive 'People's Budget', carefully constructed to appeal to the working class through taxation of the rich, without at the same time forfeiting middle-class support.[33] The inclusion in it of the licensing duties, the super-tax, and the land taxes were intended to preserve the progressive coalition by reviving the conventional middle-class radical appeal to middle and working classes alike through an attack on the aristocracy. In sum, the budget was the mainspring of a comprehensive strategy directed at countering the two political threats to Liberalism – from the Conservatives through tariff reform, and from Labour through socialism.

Dilke gave it his 'hearty support', though he was critical of Lloyd George's failure to relax the indirect duties upon tea and tobacco.[34] As well as paying for social reform, the budget would raise revenue for the Dreadnought programme and therefore for the strong navy which Dilke had always supported. Although he thought John Fisher, the First Lord and architect of the Dreadnought programme, a 'Bounder', he also recognised that he was extremely able and 'right in the main'. 'Besides,' he told the same correspondent, 'Nelson was rather of the same sort, & was equally – & with justice – disliked.'[35] Fisher, for his part, had earlier described Dilke as 'the one man in the House of Commons who is invariably right on naval affairs'.[36]

The radicalisation of the government accounted as well for its adoption, in 1909, of one of Dilke's most cherished reforms – the institution of the minimum wage. He traced his interest in this subject to a passage written by John Stuart Mill in the 1840s 'showing that sweated wages depressed all wages in the country'.[37] Boards to regulate wages in the sweated industries had been set up in the Australian state of Victoria in 1896. Dilke had been corresponding for some time on the subject with Alfred Deakin, Victoria's Prime Minister, and in 1900 he unsuccessfully introduced a bill modelled upon the Australian scheme.[38] In 1906 a campaign and exhibition on sweated industries sponsored by the *Daily News* stirred public opinion and led to the formation of the National Anti-Sweating League. A Sweated Industries Bill, whose 'real author' according to Dilke was his niece Gertrude Tuckwell,[39] was introduced by Arthur Henderson of the Labour Party with the backing of the TUC. In October the league organised a three-day conference of trade unionists at the Guildhall to discuss reform. Dilke presided on the first day. The main resolution, demanding the introduction of wages boards, was supported by Sidney Webb, Gertrude Tuckwell, J. A. Hobson and Dilke himself. The conference nearly broke up when a number of delegates (mainly from the Social Democratic Federation) denounced wages boards as middle-class palliatives designed to put off real change, and tried to introduce a counter-proposal proscribing all outwork. It was saved by the judicious intervention of Mary Macarthur, who persuaded the dissidents to separate the two issues, and whose speech led to the carrying of the resolution by acclamation.[40]

The league's agitation prompted a major government investigation. A Select Committee on Home Work was appointed in June 1907 by Herbert Gladstone, the Home Secretary, who had sought Dilke's advice as to its composition and terms of reference. Dilke confessed that he was a 'heretic' in that he supported *both* the licensing of places of outwork (which was favoured by Labour leaders like MacDonald) *and* wages boards, but that as the committee of the Anti-Sweating League and the Home Office Inspectorate were so strongly against licensing, he had hardly dared open his mouth on the subject for many years.[41] One of the members of the select committee, Ernest Aves, was sent to Australia to study the wages-board system. He recommended against it on the grounds that conditions in Australia were completely different to those in England. In his evidence to the committee, Dilke agreed that Australia could not provide conclusive guidance, but he believed, nonetheless, that the boards should be tried on an experimental basis.[42]

In April 1908, while the committee was still hearing evidence, Dilke presided at a meeting of the Anti-Sweating League where Arthur Fontaine, French Director of Labour, and Emile Vandervelde, leader of the Belgian Socialist Party, spoke in favour of coordinated international action.[43] Pressure for reform was kept up by the Women's Trade Union League, most notably by Mary Macarthur, Susan Lawrence and Gertrude Tuckwell. Despite Aves's scepticism, the select committee reported in the summer in favour of a system of boards and against licensing. On 4 December the Prime Minister promised a deputation led by Dilke and the Archbishop of Canterbury that the government would now introduce its own bill. This official measure, in the charge of Winston Churchill at the Board of Trade, fell short of the WTUL's expectations. Dilke and the Conservative MP for Durham City, J. W. Hills, therefore decided to proceed with a private bill.[44] They only agreed to withdraw it when Churchill's bill was altered to accommodate their proposal for introducing wages boards experimentally in four trades. It became law without any further serious opposition. From 1 January 1910 ready-made tailoring, chain-making, paper box-making and machine lace-making were required to establish boards consisting of equal numbers of employers and employed, and a minority of independent government nominees, to arbitrate upon fixing minimum wage rates for their industries.

At one stroke over 200,000 workers (of whom approximately two-thirds were female) were brought under the provisions of the act, a figure which nearly doubled in 1913 when it was extended to five more trades. Its importance can be gauged from the first agreement which emerged under its terms. In March 1910 the chain-makers received an increase in wages which amounted to 'not less than 100 per cent for many of the women',[45] though in other respects the impact of the boards was patchy because of different wage-rates across the country and because of the methods of evasion adopted by some employers. Thereafter the councils were progressively extended to cover a wide range of low-paid occupations and, in the absence of a national minimum wage, were the one safeguard against over-exploitation for countless thousands of workers. On 14 April 1910 a dinner was held at the Westminster Palace Hotel to honour Dilke for his services to sweated workers and his part in the passage of the act. The parliamentary committee of the TUC for its part presented him with a gold match-box inscribed with the badge of the TUC and the word 'Labour'.[46]

In general, the boards appear to have accomplished an improvement in unskilled wages that otherwise would not have occurred, and led to a decline in outwork and the length of the working week. They embodied a corporatist approach to industrial relations, and survived until corporatism went out of fashion. By 1993, on the eve of their abolition, they covered twenty-six sectors of industry providing minimum wage protection for 2,500,000 workers (80 per cent of them women).[47]

J. E. B. Seely considered that 'the mainspring' of all Dilke's actions was his 'intense desire to help those who could not help themselves',[48] and this extended beyond the sweatshops of London's East End to exploited workers in far-flung outposts of the empire. In 1906 he told a meeting that he 'objected to all servile labour anywhere and everywhere where practised',[49] and in his last years was able to secure a degree of amelioration for some of these oppressed groups. He had been a life-long member of the Aborigines Protection Society, and had at various times spoken out against the employment of servile labour in British colonies, such as Fiji, Cyprus and North Borneo, but the opening up of the interior of Africa by the European powers dramatically increased the incidences of exploitation. In 1896 he had condemned the theft, flogging, murder and destruction which the European powers had inflicted upon Africa in the name of 'civilisation'. He was so ashamed of the evil perpetrated by the powers that he declared categorically, and in stark contrast to his youthful confidence in England's 'civilising mission', that 'it would have been far better, in the interests of civilisation and philanthropy, if Africa had been left alone'.[50]

At that time he was campaigning with Joseph Pease, MP for Tyneside, for the abolition of slavery in Zanzibar, and had succeeded, with the help of Alfred Tucker, the Bishop of Uganda, in forcing the government to admit what it had previously attempted to cover up, namely its own part in facilitating the return of fugitive slaves to their owners.[51] In 1907, and very much in response to pressure from Dilke, Churchill announced that the legal status of slavery in Zanzibar would be ended that year.[52] On hearing the news, a delighted Bishop Tucker wrote from Uganda to thank Dilke for his part 'in bringing the Government to this decision. I feel that without your assistance the affair would have dragged on possibly for years'.[53]

More horrific still and more intractable were the problems stemming from maladministration of the Congo. In the eighties Dilke had favoured Portugal's claim to the territory, but had not at first been unduly perturbed by the decision of the great powers at Berlin in 1885 to grant Leopold II of Belgium personal sovereignty over the newly-created Congo Free State, subject to trade concessions. However, he shortly afterwards noted in the margin of his Memoir account of this decision: 'My joy was shortlived, for King Leopold has not kept his promises.'[54]

Having sunk money into the Congo and lost heavily, the Belgian monarch embarked upon its ruthless exploitation. Quotas for raw materials were established and the indigenous population were tortured or massacred if they failed to meet them. Cannibal troops provisioned on human flesh were employed to enforce the regime. These horrors were first revealed by Dilke to the House of Commons on 2 April 1897 and repeated annually, but the Tory government remained deaf to his demand for joint European action to force reform upon the Congo.[55]

In 1901 he joined forces with Edmund Dene Morel, a man who had risen from humble origins to become a successful journalist and who was now prepared to devote his life to the campaign. Whereas Dilke had proceeded from a sense of justice, trusting in the existing humanitarian societies, and treating the Congo question as but one element in a larger programme, Morel brought to the amorphous movement a single-minded dedication to the cause of establishing the right of the aboriginal population to its own land and trade.[56] Morel urged Dilke to 'force the pace' in the House, and inundated him with the information by which he could do so.

Their efforts were partly rewarded in 1903 when parliament instructed the government to act in concert with the other signatories of the Berlin Treaty to protect the rights of natives and traders in the Congo. The following year, Morel took the lead in setting up the Congo Reform Association to coordinate the campaign. Morel thought that Britain was capable of achieving success single-handedly, whereas Dilke favoured coordinated international pressure. During his annual Christmas vacation in Paris in December 1906, he met Clemenceau, the French Prime Minister, and tried, without success, to enlist his support.[57] In 1908 the

Congo was transferred from the personal rule of Leopold to the Belgian state, which a year later came up with a plan of reform that the CRA thought inadequate. In January 1910 Dilke reluctantly agreed, after some urging from Morel, to take the chair of the Commons' Congo Committee in place of Ramsay MacDonald, who was proving to be 'a most unsatisfactory chap'. '... everyone will follow you, on both sides,' Morel added, 'and everyone won't follow MacDonald, and the Tories hate him like poison.'[58] In April a 'Parliamentary Memorial on the Congo Problem', urging action against Belgium, and signed by Dilke as chairman and 161 other MPs, was sent to the Prime Minister.[59] It was pressure of this sort that compelled the Congo State to mitigate the worst evils, though Dilke did not live quite long enough to see the day, in 1913, when Morel felt at last able to disband the CRA.

In South Africa, too, the rights of the indigenous black majority were far from secure in the uncertain aftermath of the war. In February 1906 Dilke urged the government to clarify its policy towards the coloured population, and to make provisions to safeguard tribal institutions, grant independence to Basutoland and Northern Bechuanaland, and set apart tribal reserves in Swaziland and the Northern Transvaal. These proposals formed the substance of a joint letter to the Prime Minister and a Commons' resolution that was carried unanimously.[60]

Dilke was, in this particular instance, pushing against an open door. Campbell-Bannerman needed no encouragement to set in train the process which led to the adoption of a constitution for South Africa, though he died before it was completed. The draft constitution, setting up the Union, was generally welcomed when it came before the House for ratification. While MPs on both sides were concerned about the inclusion in the legislation of a colour bar, preventing the election of non-whites to the Union parliament and empowering it to withdraw the franchise from non-whites who held it, most were prepared to accept the government's argument that interference on this point would antagonise the Boers and jeopardise the bill. Dilke was one of only a handful of Liberals determined to make a stand against this racially-divisive arrangement which stored up all sorts of problems for the long-term future of the South African state. The institution of a colour bar, he told the Commons, was the 'most momentous' imperial decision ever taken by parliament. It was incumbent upon them to ensure that clear stipulations were made to prevent permanent supremacy for the white minority. He believed that the 'whole fabric' of the empire would collapse if the principle of permanent white supremacy was constitutionally enshrined.[61] His misgivings were well-founded. Never before had Britain made race a criterion for political participation.

He also prepared the ground for the visit to England of W. P. Schreiner, the South African champion of black rights, who came to pressurise parliament to amend the bill. In May 1909 he led a deputation of Liberal and Labour MPs to Lord Crewe, the Colonial Secretary, to protest against the colour bar, and moved a resolution at the annual meeting of the Aborigines Protection Society urging the government to safeguard the existing native franchise.[62] But the Commons, preoccupied with Lloyd George's budget and with the German navy scare, showed an almost total disregard for such principled objections. Indeed, the government issued a whip instructing Liberal MPs not to press amendments to a division.

Dilke became despondent. 'We shall not carry anything', he wrote to Schreiner, 'and therefore what we move (if anything) depends on how it looks....' Of the fifty-three amendments tabled, only one went to a division and that was overwhelmingly defeated in a thin House. In his speech on the second reading on 16 August, Dilke's words were full of foreboding. They were ignoring, he warned, the fate of 6,250,000 people who were to be governed 'by an absolute and permanent oligarchy of a million people'. Such an unprecedented act did not augur well for the '360 millions of coloured people under our rule' or, therefore, for the future of the empire. His sole achievement was to persuade the government to alter the bill to protect the rights of the indigenous populations in the British protectorates of Basutoland, Bechuanaland and Swaziland. Schreiner wrote: 'I am very greatly indebted to you for your splendid stand in the House, and constant labours for the cause I am advocating & obsessed by.'[63]

The friendship of South Africa was gained at the expense of the permanent alienation of the black majority. In the short term the success of the policy was undeniable, but for a handful of more far-sighted politicians it was a disaster. The heir to the colour bar was apartheid and the maintenance of white minority rule by brutal oppression.

Meanwhile, Lloyd George's budget had prompted the most serious constitutional crisis since 1832, in which the very survival of the House of Lords was once again called into question. Dilke had thought the abolition of the Lords a priority in 1906 while radical enthusiasm in the country was still strong. He cynically predicted that this enthusiasm would be allowed to dissipate. 'The really weak point', he told Labouchere, 'is that the Govt. is damned unless it fights the Lords in 1907 and that the promise of "5 years of power" will prevent the hacks from fighting.'[64] When the showdown finally came, Dilke's energies were directed to preventing

Asquith from backing down and accepting proposals for reforming the Lords. To that end he led a deputation of radicals to the Prime Minister shortly after the state opening of parliament in February 1910.[65]

In May, in the middle of the crisis, Edward VII died. At the funeral Dilke, as senior privy councillor, was ranked third among the commoners behind the Prime Minister and Speaker. He was appointed to the civil list committee to provide for the next reign. It limited the number of occasional grants, but rejected his recommendation of a fixed grant. He therefore opposed its report.[66]

His own health was now very poor and, like the King, he did not live to see the outcome of the constitutional crisis. The Parliament Act, which limited the Lords' powers to the delaying of non-financial measures, was passed in August 1911. It had taken two general elections, in January and December 1910, to force the issue. They had taken Dilke twice to the Forest of Dean in the midst of winter, journeys he would rather have avoided because of his deteriorating health, and which severely sapped his strength. Two years earlier, in 1908, he had been indisposed for much of the year through illness. He had lost a great deal of weight 'from fever caused by lung trouble ... '.[67] Travel abroad, which he had resumed to a moderate degree after Lady Dilke's death, assisted his recuperation. He visited the Italian lakes and, in 1909 and again in 1910, returned to his beloved Provence. These interludes of convalescence enabled him to continue his political activity. In May 1910 he told his former secretary, Bodley, that he was 'a "happy" person, and always at *work* with *interest*'.[68] In September 1910 he was invited to attend the twenty-fifth Indian National Congress at Allahabad, in recognition of his long interest in furthering 'the progress of good administration in India'.[69] He had never departed from the view, first expressed over forty years earlier in *Greater Britain*, that India should be progressively prepared for self-government. The state of his health made such a long journey impossible and he was therefore obliged to decline. He nevertheless travelled to Lugano to attend a meeting of the International Association for Labour Legislation. By October he sensed that the end was not far off. In sending Morel his best wishes for the latter's planned visit to West Africa, he told him that he was 'much more likely to come back alive ... than I am to be alive to welcome you. Yet, I *hope*, that the less likely survival *may* be, & of the other I feel pretty sure.'[70]

But the 'less likely survival' was not to be. The campaigning in Dean Forest in December 1910 left him exhausted. A Christmas visit to Provence was not enough this time to revive him and, when he returned to London in mid January, he was confined to his bed. Still, he continued to see friends, prepare speeches and write reviews for the *Athenaeum*. Hesketh Pearson summed up 'his main characteristic in a phrase: he read blue-books on his death-bed'.[71] On the afternoon of 25 January he completed and despatched several papers for the Women's Trade Union League. During the night he suffered a relapse, his heart failed, and he died in the early hours of the following morning. His last wish was to be cremated, despite the fact that this method of disposal had still not gained general social acceptance.[72] Dilke was a radical to the end.

The funeral service was held at Holy Trinity Church, Sloane Street, on 30 January. The cortège then proceeded to the crematorium at Golders Green. Among the chief mourners were Gertrude Tuckwell, Mrs H. J. Tennant and Harry Hudson. Wentie, who was in the sanatorium at Virginia Water, did not attend. Joseph Chamberlain sent his son Austen. The Prime Minister was represented by Vaughan Nash. Two members of the cabinet and many of Dilke's closest parliamentary colleagues were also present. The King of Greece sent a letter of condolence and members of the Greek government and the Greek community in London paid their last respects. Professor Stephen Bauer, the secretary of the International Association for Labour Legislation, came from Switzerland. There were representatives too of the diverse causes with which Dilke had been closely associated: naval reformers like Spenser Wilkinson, trade union leaders like Ben Tillett, and members of the National Anti-Sweating League, the Congo Reform Association, the Women's Trade Union League and the Commons Preservation Society. Perhaps the most poignant moment of the ceremony was the laying of wreaths by women workers who had benefited from the establishment of Wages Boards.

Dilke's obituarists were not altogether unkind to him. They acknowledged his achievements and his extraordinary grasp of almost all the political topics of the day. Inevitably, his death provided as well some newspapers with the opportunity to recount once again the sordid details of the divorce case. With the passage of time, however, his achievements have been forgotten and it is as the hapless victim of a sensational scandal that he is now largely remembered. Yet recent debates – for example, over the abolition of wages boards, the deregulation of shop hours, the dismantling of apartheid in South Africa, or the desirability of replacing single-member seats with a system of proportional representation – have demonstrated the continuing relevance of much of his politics. The time has come to redress the balance, to restore his achievements as a reformer, and to remember him for his radicalism rather than for the private misfortune that has blighted his reputation for over a century.

In summing up his life, then, it is important to avoid judging it too negatively, in terms of its unfulfilled promise. His contribution to late nineteenth-century radical politics should not be underestimated. He played a leading part in the reorganisation of radicalism in the 1870s which prepared the way for the democratising legislation of 1883–85. The divorce case and the Home Rule crisis forestalled radical plans for capturing control of the Liberal Party, but these events did not halt the evolution of Dilke's own politics. His development of a social radicalism after 1886 was manifest in significant gains made on behalf of women and labour. He was also an accomplished and prolific author with a wide readership and the temptation to quit politics entirely in the hostile atmosphere of 1886 for a career devoted entirely to writing must have been great. Had he done so, the early feminist and labour movements would have been the losers. His determination to continue to make a contribution to public life in the face of difficult circumstances is therefore a quality which we should acknowledge and it was certainly one for which Dilke himself wished to be remembered. This is illustrated by the epigram taken from Henrik Ibsen's play *John Gabriel Borkman* which he chose for inclusion at the head of his unpublished Memoir. It serves as a testimony not just to his resilience but as a fitting conclusion to his biography:

> We are all of us run over, sometime or other in life. The thing is to jump up again, and let no one see you are hurt.

Notes

In the notes throughout this book, the place of publication is London unless otherwise stated.

Notes to Preface

1. Quoted in S. Lowndes (ed.), *Diaries and Letters of Marie Belloc Lowndes, 1911–1947* (1971), pp. 255–56.
2. J. O. Baylen and N. J. Gossman (eds), *Biographical Dictionary of Modern British Radicals*, iii, *1870–1914, A-K* (Hemel Hempstead, 1988), pp. 273–76. The entry was contributed by James B. Brown.
3. To Reinach, 10 Dec. 1892 (DP, Add. MS 43884, f. 287). Dilke began writing and dictating this to his secretary in the 1890s and, though it was never published, his official biographers relied heavily upon it. All references to the folios in the Dilke Papers, Add. MSS 43930–41 are taken from the Memoir.
4. C. A. Law to Dilke, 15 Oct. 1883 (REND, 4/1). For his distortion of the truth about Keats and Fanny, see J. Richardson, *The Everlasting Spell: A Study of Keats and his Friends* (1963), pp. 152–53, 163–64. During his lifetime, he built up an unrivalled collection of Keats memorabilia (most of which is now at Keats House, Hampstead) but, as with his own papers, destroyed anything which *in his opinion* was not worth preserving.
5. DP, Add. MS 43929, f. 105.

Notes to Introduction

1. *Daily Express*, 2 June 1994.
2. See D. Nicholls, 'The English Middle Class and the Ideological Significance of Radicalism', *Journal of British Studies*, 24 (1985), p. 415.
3. E. Royle and J. Walvin, *English Radicals and Reformers, 1760–1848* (Brighton, 1982), p. 9.
4. As I have tried to show in D. Nicholls, 'The Personnel, Methods and Policies of English Middle-Class Radicalism, 1760–1924', *International Journal of Social Education*, 3 (1988), pp. 73–85.
5. Quoted in D. Read, *Cobden and Bright* (1967), p. 30.
6. Quoted in H. Jephson, *The Platform: Its Rise and Progress* (2 vols, 1892; repr. 1968), ii, p. 195.

7 Quoted in D. Jones, *Chartism and the Chartists* (1975), p. 125.
8 For further details, see D. Nicholls, 'Richard Cobden and the International Peace Congress Movement, 1848–1853', *Journal of British Studies*, 30 (1991), pp. 351–76.
9 M. C. Finn, *After Chartism: Class and Nation in English Radical Politics, 1848–1874* (Cambridge, 1993), ch. 5.
10 For one corrective to the traditional emphasis on Chamberlain's centrality, see R. Quinault, 'Joseph Chamberlain: A Reassessment', in T. R. Gourvish and A. O'Day (eds), *Later Victorian Britain, 1867–1900* (1988), ch. 4. The continuing fascination with Chamberlain derives, of course, from his leading part in splitting for a time the two major parties. He was a man of conviction but of flawed political judgement – a fact further illustrated by his failure to register any significant legislative achievement despite occupying the political centre-stage for much longer than Dilke.
11 For example, even Terence Jenkins, in his recent and otherwise admirable account of the political resilience of the Whigs, fails to appreciate the significance of Dilke's downfall for radical fortunes. See T. A. Jenkins, *Gladstone, Whiggery and the Liberal Party, 1874–1886* (Oxford, 1988).
12 R. Jenkins, *Sir Charles Dilke: A Victorian Tragedy* (1965; 1st edn, 1958), p. 411. The observation is really only true of licensing.
13 *Manchester Guardian*, 27 Jan. 1911.
14 L. T. Hobhouse, *Liberalism* (1911), p. 214.

Notes to Chapter 1

1 Dilke accumulated many notebooks about his family tree; see REND, 10/10. These early origins are reflected in the retention of Ashton as a family name.
2 Charles was nicknamed 'the Great Mogul' and 'the Tzar' (or 'Zz' for short), and he was sometimes addressed by his grandfather as 'Numero 3'.
3 DP, Add. MS 43930, ff. 57–58.
4 Granville to Ponsonby, 30 April 1880, quoted in G. E. Buckle (ed.), *The Letters of Queen Victoria 1879–85*, second series, *iii* (1928), pp. 91–92.
5 DP, Add. MS 43930, ff. 13, 52, 58, 67, 81, 118–20, 163.
6 Ibid., ff. 82–83, 91. Dilke was eighteen when the Civil War broke out, but he was probably thinking of his part in a Union debate at Cambridge when he was nineteen.
7 Ibid., f. 108.
8 24 Oct. 1862 (DP, Add. MS 43900, f. 9).
9 DP, Add. MSS 43909, f. 102; 43929, f. 20; 43930, f. 129.
10 DP, Add. MS 43950, f. 191.
11 DP, Add. MS 43899, ff. 43, 58.
12 Ibid., f. 119; DP, Add. MS 43943, f. 11.
13 DP, Add. MS 43930, ff. 136, 138. Dilke had met the seventy-eight year old Palmerston at the exhibition of 1862 and found him 'still bright and lively in walk and talk'. Quoted in G. & T., i, 23. He kept a photograph of Bismarck on a wall in his college rooms.
14 DP, Add. MSS 43930, ff. 163, 166–70; 43943, ff. 19–24.
15 DP, Add. MS 43930, f. 158. It was owing to his influence that Waterhouse was chosen as architect.
16 N.d., but *c.* 1863 (DP, Add. MS 43899, f. 93).
17 Ibid., f. 253.
18 DP, Add. MS 43930, ff. 19, 181–84.
19 Ibid., ff. 91–92.
20 DP, Add. MSS 43904, ff. 7–8; 43909, f. 225.
21 T. P. O'Connor, *Memoirs of an Old Parliamentarian* (2 vols, 1929), i, p. 318.

22 26 Aug. 1866 (DP, Add. MS 43902, ff. 34–37). His official biographers somehow imagined that Dilke had later scrawled 'what a prig he was' across this letter. G. & T., i, p. 64. No such comment exists, but it is an apt description nonetheless.

23 DP, Add. MSS 43902, ff. 17–19; 43930, ff. 85–86.

24 DP, Add. MSS 43930, ff. 164–5; 43931, f. 9. The system required *bona fide* declarations of membership of the Church of England.

25 DP, Add. MS 43930, f. 134; *DFM*, 13 June 1890.

26 JC, 5/24/118.

Notes to Chapter 2

1 DP, Add. MS 43901, f. 2.
2 DP, Add. MS 43930, ff. 174–81.
3 Ibid., f. 185.
4 C. W. Dilke, *Greater Britain* (1869; 1st edn, 1868), p. 58.
5 26 Aug. 1866 (DP, Add. MS 43900, ff. 157–58).
6 Dilke, *Greater Britain*, pp. 69, 76, 81.
7 Ibid., p. 93; Dilke to Mrs Chatfield, 5 Sept. 1866 (DP, Add. MS 43902, f. 216).
8 Dilke sensed from the look in their eyes that they were 'unhappy without knowing it'.
   Dilke, *Greater Britain*, p. 105.
9 Ibid., p. 141.
10 DP, Add. MS 43930, f. 201.
11 To Hepworth Dixon, 29 Nov. 1866 (MP, Add. MS 38794F, ff. 124–25).
12 Dilke, *Greater Britain*, p. 287.
13 Ibid., p. 304.
14 20 Jan. 1867 (DP, Add. MS 43901, ff. 7–9).
15 Dilke, *Greater Britain*, p. 389.
16 Ibid., p. 432.
17 Ibid., p. 440.
18 Ibid., pp. 529, 568–69.
19 DP, Add. MS 43901, f. 2.
20 An exception is C. A. Bodelsen, *Studies in Mid-Victorian Imperialism* (New York, 1968; 1st
   edn, 1924), pp. 60–75.
21 Dilke, *Greater Britain*, p. 574.
22 Ibid., p. 346. Unlike Marx, however, Dilke idealistically believed that society was
   progressing to a point where the distinction between labourer and capitalist would
   disappear and harmony in production relations would prevail.
23 Ibid., p. 384. Transportation was already on the decline and the last convict ship sailed
   for Australia shortly after Dilke's visit and before his words appeared in print.
24 Bodelsen, *Studies*, pp. 62, 65–66.
25 Dilke, *Greater Britain*, p. 395.
26 Ibid., p. 342.
27 Ibid., pp. 398–99.
28 Ibid., p. 397.
29 Ibid., p. 556.
30 Ibid., pp. 563–64.
31 Bodelsen, *Studies*, pp. 67–68.
32 Dilke, *Greater Britain*, p. 237.
33 See, e.g., his comments on China, ibid., pp. 561–62.
34 Ibid., pp. 124, 198.
35 DP, Add. MS 43930, f. 206.
36 Dilke, *Greater Britain*, pp. 223, 230, 573. A glance at a map of the world would show that
   'freedom exists only in the homes of the English race'. Ibid., p. 555.
37 Ibid., pp. 32, 46, 48, 86, 192, 407, 413, 503, 543.
38 Ibid., pp. 281–82.
39 3 March 1867 (DP, Add. MS 43901, ff. 33–34); Dilke, *Greater Britain*, pp. 186, 445, 572.
40 Ibid., pp. 31, 92, 202, 334, 392, 572–73.
41 N. Stepan, *The Idea of Race in Science: Great Britain, 1800–1960* (1982), p. xvi.

42 'Love of race, among the English', he had written in the concluding pages of his book, 'rests upon a firmer base than either love of mankind or love of Britain'. Dilke, *Greater Britain*, p. 570.
43 DP, Add. MS 43900, f. 134.
44 9 Feb. 1869 (DP, Add. MS 43897, ff. 2–4).
45 Ibid., f. 7.
46 26 March 1867 (DP, Add. MS 43901, f. 49).
47 30 May 1867 (ibid., f. 119).
48 Ibid., f. 121.
49 DP, Add. MS 43931, f. 1.
50 16 Dec. 1867 (DP, Add. MS 43901, ff. 134–35).
51 DP, Add. MS 43933, f. 262.
52 The minority clause was intended to allow the minority party to secure at least some representation in the large towns, but the Birmingham Liberals circumvented it by dividing the constituencies into wards where their followers were advised as to which candidates to vote for.
53 *Chelsea News*, 21 Nov. 1868, 3 Nov. 1883; H. J. Hanham, *Elections and Party Management* (1959), pp. 138–39; P. Thompson, *Socialists, Liberals and Labour: The Struggle for London 1885–1914* (1967), p. 92 and n.; Dilke to Chamberlain, 6 May 1886 (JC, 5/24/179); J. Davis, 'Radical Clubs and London Politics, 1870–1900', in D. Feldman and G. Steadman Jones (eds), *Metropolis London: Histories and Representations since 1800* (1989), pp. 106–8.

Notes to Chapter 3

1 To his father, 1 Dec. 1868 (DP, Add. MS 43901, f. 140).
2 DP, Add. MS 43929, f. 43.
3 To his father, Apr. 1869 (DP, Add. MS 43901, f. 144).
4 N. Blewett, 'The Franchise in the United Kingdom, 1885–1918', *Past and Present*, 32 (1965), pp. 27–56. In 1872 Dilke estimated that, of the two to three hundred thousand lodgers in the London boroughs, only about 4,000 were on the registers.
5 *PD*(3), 194, cols 981–82; DP, Add. MS 43931, ff. 7–8.
6 Select Committee on Parliamentary and Municipal Elections, *PP*, 1868–69, viii, pp. 402–16; DP, Add. MS 43931, ff. 168–69.
7 DP, Add. MSS 43909, f. 116; 43931, ff. 33–35; 43932, f. 35. The first meeting of all had been held in Manchester the previous year.
8 Dilke to Dixon, 23 July and 3 Aug. 1869 (MP, Add. MS 38794F, ff. 132–35).
9 The MS for 'The Russian Power' is at Churchill College, along with Charles Dilke's notes. See especially REND, 6/28 from which the points in the next paragraph have been taken.
10 Jenkins, *Dilke*, pp. 52, 113–15; DP, Add. MS 43931, f. 262.
11 DP, Add. MSS 43931, ff. 32, 260; 43932, f. 245; 43948, passim; *Notes and Queries*, 4 Feb. 1911.
12 Gladstone to Dilke, 15 Jan. 1870, quoted in H. C. G. Matthew (ed.), *The Gladstone Diaries*, vii, *Jan. 1869 – June 1871* (Oxford, 1982), p. 221; *PD*(3), 199, cols 64–70.
13 Quoted in B. Simon, *Education and the Labour Movement, 1870–1920* (1965), p. 118.
14 *The Times*, 6 Jan. 1874; Jenkins, *Dilke*, pp. 56–57.
15 DP, Add. MSS 43909, ff. 137–43; 43931, ff. 50–51.
16 Ibid., f. 57. For a while, he flirted with the idea of financing education from the confiscated endowments of a disestablished church.
17 *PD*(3), 202, cols 510–18, 1398–99; 203, cols 271–317 et seq; speech at Birmingham, 17 Dec. 1883 (*Daily News*, 18 Dec. 1883). His ratepayer amendment was defeated by five votes but subsequently adopted by the government.
18 JC, 5/24/278.
19 JC, 5/24/2.
20 A. G. Gardiner, *Life of Sir William Harcourt* (2 vols, 1923), i, pp. 228–29. When Goschen told the cabinet in April 1884 that he would not swim with the stream, Harcourt murmured, 'No, but you are pissing against the wind.' DP, Add. MS 43926, f. 7.
21 D. Rubinstein, 'Victorian Feminists: Henry and Millicent Garrett Fawcett', in L. Goldman (ed.), *The Blind Victorian: Henry Fawcett and British Liberalism* (Cambridge, 1989), p. 77.
22 C. W. Dilke, 'John Stuart Mill, 1869–73', *Cosmopolis*, 5 (1897), pp. 629–41; DP, Add. MS 43931, ff. 12–13.
23 DP, Add. MSS 43918, f. 46; 43919, f. 14; 43929, f. 98; 43931, f. 13.
24 DP, Add. MSS 43931, ff. 246–47; 43932, f. 170. A copy of the rules of the club, as at January 1881, is among Ashton Dilke's papers; REND, 6/23.
25 To Morley, 20 Feb. 1871, quoted in C. Harvie, *The Lights of Liberalism: University Liberals and the Challenge of Democracy 1860–86* (1976), p. 188.
26 4 May 1870, *PD*(3), 201, cols 216–22.
27 Quoted in C. Rover, *Women's Suffrage and Party Politics, 1866–1914* (1967), p. 34.
28 28 May 1870 (DP, Add. MS 43897, f. 17).
29 Dilke had worked hard but unsuccessfully to get Odger returned for Southwark at a by-

election in 1869. The campaign had caused quite a political stir as Odger was a former president of the First International of Working Men's Associations, which Karl Marx had helped to set up in 1866.

30 DP, Add. MS 43931, f. 170; G. & T., i, p. 100.

31 B. English and J. Saville, *Strict Settlement: A Guide for Historians* (Hull, 1983), ch. iii; U. Vogel, 'The Land-Question: A Liberal Theory of Communal Property', *History Workshop*, 27 (1989), pp. 106–35; Finn, *After Chartism*, pp. 267–71.

32 DP, Add. MSS 43931, ff. 59, 167–68; 43932, f. 23; 43933, ff. 187–88; Lord Eversley, *Commons, Forests and Footpaths* (1910; 1st published as G. Shaw Lefevre, *English Commons and Forests*, 1894), passim. After the Commons Act of 1876, the CPS lost much of its impetus.

Notes to Chapter 4

1 DP, Add. MS 43929, ff. 70–71.
2 DP, Add. MS 43931, f. 65.
3 G. & T., i, p. 107.
4 DP, Add. MS 43929, ff. 72–73. In 1871 Dilke attended the autumn army manoeuvres for the first time. Earlier that year Trevelyan had organised a group of radical army reformers. Dilke was assigned the task of criticising the ornamental and wasteful maintenance of the household cavalry. Rather more bizarre was his brief flirtation with a movement to promote universal instruction in arms. It attracted the support of around fifty MPs who, according to Dilke, 'all lived to know better'. *PD*(3), 205, cols 535–38; DP, Add. MS 43931, ff. 132–33.
5 *PD*(3), 205, cols 894–916.
6 DP, Add. MS 43931, ff. 132–33.
7 Ibid., f. 138.
8 O'Connor, *Memoirs*, i, p. 46. For a number of years, *Punch* depicted Dilke adorned with the Phrygian cap of liberty; see, e.g., the illustration below, p. 46.
9 *Chelsea News*, 3 Feb. 1911. Republicanism was not confined to the paternal blood-line. Dilke's mother was descended from the regicide, William Cawley. REND, 10/10.
10 DP, Add. MS 43931, ff. 193–94.
11 It was published under the pseudonymn 'Solomon Temple'. Dilke believed its author to be either G. O. Trevelyan or his father.
12 For details, see Finn, *After Chartism*, pp. 293–95; N. Todd, *The Militant Democracy: Joseph Cowen and Victorian Radicalism* (Whitley Bay, 1991), pp. 86, 94.
13 *The Times*, 9 Nov. 1871. The speech was rushed out as a pamphlet with the title *The Cost of the Crown* (1871).
14 DP, Add. MS 43929, f. 95.
15 REND, 6/1.
16 DP, Add. MS 43931, ff. 175–77.
17 *Daily News*, 21 Nov. 1871.
18 Ibid., 23 Nov. 1871.
19 P. Guedalla (ed.), *The Queen and Mr Gladstone* (2 vols, 1933), i, pp. 308–15.
20 DP, Add. MS 43931, f. 274.
21 *The Times*, 24 Nov. 1871.
22 *Manchester Guardian*, 1 Dec. 1871; G. & T., i, p. 143n.; DP, Add. MS 43931, f. 185.
23 *The Times*, 23 Nov. 1871; DP, Add. MS 43943, ff. 90–91. Ignorance of royal finances was not unpardonable given the secrecy with which they were surrounded. Moreover, Dilke was remarkably prescient, for twentieth-century monarchs were gradually to withdraw from paying income tax. See P. Hall, *Royal Fortune: Tax, Money and the Monarchy* (1992).
24 DP, Add. MS 43931, ff. 186–87. J. L. Garvin, *The Life of Joseph Chamberlain* (6 vols, completed by L. S. Amery, 1932–69), i, p. 153 and nn., claimed that Chamberlain was not at the meeting, but see *Birmingham Daily Post*, 7 Dec. 1871.
25 DP, Add. MS 43931, ff. 187–88; *The Times*, 17 Jan. 1872.
26 *Chelsea News*, 24 Feb. 1872.
27 The councillors of Newcastle, where Dilke had made his most publicised attack on the monarchy, issued a Loyal Address which referred to him as 'scum'. Todd, *The Militant Democracy*, p. 95.
28 *PD*(3), 210, cols 251–91.

29 DP, Add. MS 43931, f. 216. Dilke had told Kate Field: 'I shall make a *statistical*, which means DRY – which means DULL speech.' DP, Add. MS 43909, f. 262.

30 *Punch*, 30 March 1872.

31 *Manchester Guardian*, 21 March 1872.

32 DP, Add. MS 43931, f. 212.

33 S. Shipley, *Club Life and Socialism in Mid-Victorian London* (1971), pp. 72–74.

34 See W.M Kuhn, 'Ceremony and Politics: The British Monarchy, 1871–1872', *Journal of British Studies*, 26 (1987), pp. 133–62. Dilke did not attend the ceremony, and the invitations reside in his official papers with the note, 'The famous tickets wh. we were reported to have used'. DP, Add. MS 43909, ff. 256–57.

35 W. Bagehot, 'Sir Charles Dilke on the Civil List', *Economist*, 10 Jan. 1874, repr. in N. St John Stevas (ed.), *The Collected Works of Walter Bagehot*, v (1974), pp. 414–17.

36 W. Bagehot, 'The Illness of the Prince of Wales', *Economist*, 16 Dec. 1871, repr. ibid., pp. 435–38.

37 *Contra* T. Nairn, *The Enchanted Glass: Britain and its Monarchy* (1988). It will be seen as well that my assessment is markedly different from that of Margot Finn (*After Chartism*, ch. 7), who sees middle-class support for republicanism as evidence of the emergence of a new liberalism responsive to working-class demands and attentive to the need for constructive state intervention. Her analysis, in my view, exaggerates the social content of middle-class radicalism at this date.

38 See W. Bagehot, 'Mr Bright on Republicanism', *Economist*, 17 May 1873, repr. in Stevas (ed.), *Collected Works*, v, pp. 427–30.

39 DP, Add. MS 43930, f. 69.

40 *The Dilkiad: or The Dream of Dilke*, by a Jackdaw (1872). For further examples, see Anon., '*What is the Use of Kings?*' '*Chelsea Buns*', and '*Chant de la Commune*' (1872).

41 DP, Add. MS 43930, ff. 118–20.

42 DP, Add. MSS 43931, f. 190; 43932, f. 35. Only three guests were present and only a handful of people knew of the event.

43 30 Jan. 1872 (DP, Add. MS 43909, f. 250).

44 Quoted in Jenkins, *Dilke*, p. 78.

45 JC, 5/24/3. This was the occasion of Chamberlain's first major speech in London and repaid a visit made by Dilke to Birmingham in October when he had spoken on free schools.

46 W. A. Hayes, *The Background and Passage of the Third Reform Act* (1982), pp. 21–26; E. F. Biagini, *Liberty, Retrenchment and Reform: Popular Liberalism in the Age of Gladstone, 1860–1880* (Cambridge, 1992), p. 316.

47 DP, Add. MS 43932, ff. 6–7. The conflict between the middle- and working-class delegates resurfaced at the annual conference of the association in November 1874. Hayes, *Background and Passage*, p. 27.

48 DP, Add. MS 43923, f. 4.

49 *PD*(3), 215, cols 1561–70; 238, cols 169–78.

50 *The Times*, 14 Jan. 1873; Garvin, *Life of Chamberlain*, i, p. 150n.; DP, Add. MS 43932, f. 4. Lawson asked jokingly: 'Why, oh why, did not a logical man like you add free drink to your programme?' Ibid., f. 6. Dilke never took a serious interest in the licensing question. His approach to drinking and gambling was a broadly libertarian one.

51 Dilke followed Chamberlain with a piece on 'Free Schools': *Fortnightly Review*, new series, 14 (1873), pp. 789–96.

52 Florestan goes on to say, 'As a republican, I had a cordial aversion for Sir Charles Dilke, a clever writer, but an awfully dull speaker, who imagines that his forte is public speaking, and who, having been brought up in a set of strong prejudices, positively makes a merit to himself of never having got over them. This he calls "never changing his opinions".' *The Fall of Prince Florestan of Monaco*, by Himself (1874), pp. 8–11.

53 Ibid., p. 61.

54 DP, Add. MS 43931, f. 193.
55 *The Fall of Prince Florestan*, pp. 78–79.
56 DP, Add. MS 43932, ff. 57–60, 66. A French edition was published simultaneously.
57 DP, Add. MS 43898, f. 165. Sidney Colvin guessed at Dilke's wife '& when she assured him on her honour that he was wrong – he did *not* guess *me*'. Dilke to Harrison, n.d. (FHP, box 4, C, file 34). The secretary who copied out the book was 'stone deaf – & much out of the world'. Ibid.
58 See O. W. Hewett, *Strawberry Fair: A Biography of Frances, Countess Waldegrave, 1821–1879* (1956).
59 H. W. Lucy, *A Diary of Two Parliaments* (2 vols, 1885–86), i, pp. 307–10.
60 *PD*(3), 217, cols 709–14; DP, Add. MS 43932, f. 28; Hall, *Royal Fortune*, pp. 120–21.
61 To the editor of *Reynolds's News*, 23 June 1894; DP, Add. MS 43915, f. 187. He also came to recognise the imperial value of the monarchy: 'the fabric of the British Empire must be kept together by full use of the sentiment which attaches to the person of the King'. C. W. Dilke, 'The King of England', *North American Review*, 162 (1901), p. 416.
62 K. Marx and F. Engels, *Selected Correspondence, 1846–1895* (trans. D. Torr, 1934), p. 391.
63 L. Stephen, *Life of Henry Fawcett* (1885), p. 287; for Bradlaugh, see *The Times*, 12 May 1873.
64 See F. Harcourt, 'Gladstone, Monarchism and the "New" Imperialism, 1868–74', *Journal of Imperial and Commonwealth History*, 14 (1985), pp. 20–51.

Notes to Chapter 5

1 J. P. Parry, 'Religion and the Collapse of Gladstone's First Government, 1870–1874', *Historical Journal*, 25 (1982), pp. 71–101; idem, *Democracy and Religion: Gladstone and the Liberal Party, 1867–1875* (Cambridge, 1986), esp. pp. 396–407.

2 Henry Fawcett was defeated at Brighton but Dilke used his organisational skills to secure his return for Hackney at a by-election two months later. He set up a fund-raising committee of which he was the treasurer and again used voluntary canvassers, so that his old tutor was re-elected at very little expense to himself. Dilke was now renting premises at 17 Sloane Street to use as an office from which to conduct his political campaigns.

3 P. Jalland, *Women, Marriage and Politics, 1860–1914* (Oxford, 1986), p. 171.

4 She had left 76 Sloane Street when Dilke married, but now returned and lived there until her death in 1880.

5 Cremation was not available in England until 1885. It took a long time to become socially acceptable. Dilke suffered some opprobrium for allowing his wife's body to be burnt. See below, p. 343 n. 41.

6 DP, Add. MS 43932, ff. 74–75, 81–84, 93–102; Ashton Dilke to Dilke, n.d. (REND, 6/1).

7 DP, Add. MS 43890, ff. 43–44; WHP, dep. 80, ff. 3–4.

8 Ibid., dep. adds. 8, f. 2.

9 DP, Add. MS 43890, ff. 64, 71.

10 DP, Add. MS 43932, ff. 129–30.

11 DP, Add. MS 43905, f. 213. Cf. also, LHJ, 6, 7 and 9 Nov. 1881 (LHP, dep. 349).

12 'Emilia' appears to have been an affectation. Her birth certificate is at REND, 10/14, where her Christian name is recorded simply as 'Emily'.

13 DP, Add. MS 43932, f. 142.

14 Dilke also received long letters of advice on reforming the Academy from the Pre-Raphaelite painter William Holman Hunt, and he raised the matter in the House in 1875. DP, Add. MSS 43912, f. 149; 43932, ff. 204–5; 43933, f. 15; *PD*(3), 229, cols 265–81.

15 It proposed improvements in the form of the ballot-paper and the scrutiny of votes, and recommended the universal adoption of the Leeds procedure for checking and counting. Select Committee on Parliamentary and Municipal Elections, *PP*, 1876, xii, pp. 359–538. The Leeds procedure was both quick and efficient – for details of how it worked, see C. O'Leary, *The Elimination of Corrupt Practices in British Elections, 1868–1911* (Oxford, 1962), pp. 91–92, 106–8.

16 DP, Add. MS 43932, ff. 161–62; *PD*(3), 224, cols 1009–25.

17 He also wrote an account of 'English Influence in China' for *Macmillan's Magazine*, 24 (1876), pp. 557–68.

18 C. W. Dilke, *Two Recess Speeches* (1876).

19 DP, Add. MS 43933, ff. 109–10.

20 *PD*(3), 227, cols 1126–52; DP, Add. MS 43932, f. 201.

21 JC, 5/24/8; DP, Add. MSS 43885, ff. 33–38; 43932, ff.192–93. A few months earlier, he had been invited by the Liberation Society to lead the disestablishment bloc in the House, but had declined. Ibid., f. 136.

22 Quoted in G. & T., i, p. 197.

23 *PD*(3), 230, cols 1056–66; 234, cols 285–87; DP, Add. MS 43933, ff. 41–46.

24 12 Aug. 1873, quoted in Garvin, *Life of Chamberlain*, i, p. 161. Cf. Dilke's letter to his father, quoted above, p. 31.

25 DP, Add. MSS 43885, f. 24; 43932, f. 46; JC, 5/24/4.
26 *The Times*, 16 Aug. 1876.
27 WHP, dep. adds. 8, ff. 13–14.
28 DP, Add. MS 43933, ff. 16–17.
29 P. Hayes, 'British Foreign Policy, 1867–1900: Continuity and Conflict', in Gourvish & O'Day (eds), *Later Victorian Britain*, p. 157.
30 JC, 5/24/11; DP, Add. MS 43885, f. 49.
31 Harcourt to Dilke, 10 Oct. 1876 (DP, Add. MS 43890, f. 84); Dilke to Harcourt, 16 Oct. 1876 (WHP, dep. 80, ff. 5–6).
32 R. T. Shannon, *Gladstone and the Bulgarian Agitation, 1876* (1963), pp. 272–74.
33 To Granville, 21 Jan. 1875, quoted in B. Holland, *The Life of Spencer Compton: 8th Duke of Devonshire* (2 vols, 1911), i, pp. 143–44. Hartington would also have had a separate leader for the Irish. Ibid.
34 DP, Add. MS 43885, f. 41.
35 *Chelsea News*, 13 Jan. 1877.
36 DP, Add. MSS 43932, ff. 248–49; 43933, ff. 9–10. Dilke had contributed to Burt's election expenses.
37 D. A. Hamer, *John Morley: Liberal Intellectual in Politics* (Oxford, 1968), p. 120.
38 P. Auspos, 'Radicalism, Pressure Groups and Party Politics: From the National Education League to the National Liberal Federation', *Journal of British Studies*, 20 (1980), pp. 184–204.
39 This did not stop him repeating the mistake in 1885; see below, p. 218.
40 DP, Add. MS 43933, ff. 6–7; *The Times*, 10 Jan. 1877.
41 DP, Add. MSS 43903, ff. 51, 119; 43933, f. 34.
42 DP, Add. MSS 43903, f. 68; 43933, ff. 31–33, 58–59; *PD*(3), 233, cols 1145–53.
43 DP, Add. MS 43903, ff. 69–71.
44 DP, Add. MSS 43903, ff. 72–73; 43933, f. 91.
45 See T. A. Jenkins, *Gladstone, Whiggery and the Liberal Party*, p. 88; J. P. Rossi, 'The Transformation of the British Liberal Party: A Study of the Tactics of the Liberal Opposition, 1874–1880', *Transactions of the American Philosophical Society*, 68 (1978), p. 51; Shannon, *Gladstone and the Bulgarian Agitation*, p. 268.
46 C. W. Dilke, *The Eastern Question* (1878), pp. 1–59.
47 DP, Add. MS 43933, ff. 147–48.
48 5 Feb. 1878, *PD*(3), 238, cols 1100–9.
49 DP, Add. MSS 43893, ff. 52–59, 67–70; 43933, ff. 160, 166–67, 173.
50 DP, Add. MS 43934, f. 66.
51 *PD*(3), 242, cols 559–69; DP, Add. MS 43933, ff. 255–56.
52 DP, Add. MS 43934, ff. 48–49, 75–76; *PD*(3), 248, cols 1027–37. In June he helped found the Hellenic Society and in July was given the freedom of the city of Athens. He had the rare distinction for an Englishman of having an Athens street named after him.
53 Quoted in D. A. Hamer, *Liberal Politics in the Age of Gladstone and Rosebery* (1972), p. 55. Cf. also, D. Judd, *Radical Joe: A Life of Joseph Chamberlain* (1977), pp. 78–79; T. A. Jenkins, *Gladstone, Whiggery and the Liberal Party*, p. 91.
54 C. Seymour, *Electoral Reform in England and Wales* (New Haven, 1915), p. 380; Select Committee on the Parliamentary and Municipal Registration Bill, *PP*, 1878, xiii, pp. 573–604; DP, Add. MS 43931, f. 169.
55 DP, Add. MS 43934, f. 4.
56 DP, Add. MS 43933, ff. 111–12; Select Committee on Parliamentary and Municipal Elections (Hours of Polling), *PP*, 1877, xv, pp. 1–93; *PD*(3), 246, cols 1665–68.
57 DP, Add. MS 43933, ff. 180–81; Select Committee on Public Business, *PP*, 1878, xviii.
58 DP, Add. MS 43932, ff. 197, 220. His admission to the ranks of the freemasons in April 1877 provides further evidence of his acceptance back into 'society'. DP, Add. MS 43933, f. 59.

59 DP, Add. MSS 43903, f. 265; 43934, ff. 15, 91, 192. Although Disraeli had not yet joined the saints in heaven, he had in 1876 entered what a later Prime Minister called heaven's waiting-room, the Upper House, as the Earl of Beaconsfield.

60 *PD*(3), 244, cols 1865–86.

61 DP, Add. MSS 43878, f. 26; 43903, f. 186; 43910, ff. 270–71; 43929, f. 118; 43934, f. 26.

62 See Rossi, 'The Transformation of the British Liberal Party', pp. 92–93.

63 See T. A. Jenkins, *Gladstone, Whiggery and the Liberal Party*, p. 97.

Notes to Chapter 6

1 They had been independently valued in 1880 at £12,000,000, but Cross proposed to pay £33,000,000. J. F. B. Firth, *Reform of London Government and of City Guilds* (1888), pp. 80–82.

2 DP, Add. MS 43934, ff. 82, 127.

3 DP, Add. MS 43885, f. 66.

4 DP, Add. MSS 43903, f. 266; 43934, ff. 80–81; T. A. Jenkins, *Gladstone, Whiggery and the Liberal Party*, p. 94.

5 DP, Add. MS 43934, ff. 138–39.

6 5 Apr. 1880 (JC, 5/24/13).

7 19 Apr. 1880 (DP, Add. MS 43885, f. 70).

8 24 Apr. 1880 (JC, 5/24/14).

9 24 Apr. 1880 (JC, 5/24/15).

10 DP, Add. MS 43934, ff. 146–49.

11 JC, 8/1/1.

12 T. Brassey to Dilke, 28 Apr. 1880 (DP, Add. MS 43911, f. 17); Auberon Herbert to Dilke, 28 Apr. 1880 (DP, Add. MS 43898, f. 247).

13 DP, Add. MS 43935, ff. 135–37. He had hoped to get the Admiralty.

14 Buckle (ed.), *Letters of Queen Victoria*, pp. 91–92.

15 Ibid., p. 48; Guedalla (ed.), *The Queen and Mr Gladstone*, ii, pp. 89–90. Cf. Frederic Harrison's prophecy to Dilke: 'It will take a tremendous pull yet to force the poor old lady to let you kiss her hand. Harcourt, Fawcett, Chamberlain she might swallow with a wry face, but she will strain at you unless you are made absolutely inevitable and undeniable.' 5 Apr. 1880 (DP, Add. MS 43898, ff. 179–80).

16 GP, PRO 30/29/121; DP, Add. MS 43878, ff. 38, 41, 48; Buckle (ed.), *Letters of Queen Victoria*, pp. 95–97.

17 DP, Add. MS 43924, f. 59. Dilke added later: 'I afterw[ar]ds sat w[ith] Ky. in Cabt. & changed my opinion of him. He *talks* like a chattering idiot, but *is* a wise man.' Ibid.

18 DP, Add. MS 43880, ff. 65, 69, 72.

19 DP, Add. MSS 43878, f. 120; 43904, ff. 164–65.

20 DP, Add. MSS 43879, ff. 233–36; 43882, ff. 221–24; 43885, ff. 195–97; 43934, ff. 313–14; 43936, ff. 22–24; A. Ramm (ed.), *Political Correspondence of Mr Gladstone and Lord Granville* (2 vols, Oxford, 1962), i, pp. 329, 333; *PD*(3), 267, cols 1218–23.

21 DP, Add. MS 43891, f. 292.

22 DP, Add. MSS 43936, ff. 25–26, 250–51; 43937, ff. 33–34; 43939, f. 91. He also succeeded in getting reinforcements sent to strengthen the British China squadron to warn Russia off from the treaty ports. DP, Add. MSS 43882, ff. 178–79; 43934, f. 249.

23 26 Sept. 1884 (DP Add. MS 43894, ff. 146–47).

24 RP, Add. MS 43528, ff. 103–4; DP, Add. MS 43924, ff. 33–35, 45–46, 246–47.

25 26 March 1881 (ibid., f. 45). Dilke had opposed the prosecution and it was afterwards claimed that he had subscribed to *Freiheit*'s expenses. When Randolph Churchill repeated the accusation in the House, Dilke strenuously denied it. The incident led to a breach with Churchill which lasted for some time. DP, Add. MS 43933, ff. 19–20; *PD*(3), 260, cols 874–77. Gossip had it that this was Churchill's revenge for advances made by Dilke to his wife. See LHJ, 8 March 1882 (LHP, dep. 350); and below, p. 343 n. 25.

26 DP, Add. MS 43885, ff. 158–59; JC, 5/24/19. On 3 Nov. 1881 Dilke wrote to Granville: 'I, as you know, delight in his [Chamberlain's] triumphs more than he does

himself. It is absurd that this should be so between politicians, but so it is. Our friendship only grows closer & my admiration for him stronger day by day.' GP, PRO 30/29/121.

27 To Granville, 4 May 1880 (DP, Add. MS 43878, ff. 42–43). For the stimulus given to the fair trade movement by the French treaty negotiations, see B. H. Brown, *The Tariff Reform Movement in Great Britain, 1881–1895* (New York, 1966), pp. 23–25.

28 DP, Add. MSS 43875, ff. 7–8; 43884, ff. 58–60; 43924, f. 10; 43934, ff. 168, 178, 189, 207–10, 228–29.

29 See, e.g., his letter to Chamberlain, 25 Nov. 1881 (JC, 5/24/21). London government and detestation of Churchill were apparently the only subjects on which he and the Prince could agree.

30 11 June 1880 (RP, Add. MS 43528, ff. 107–8).

31 DP, Add. MSS 43874, ff. 17–20, 23–24; 43904, ff. 106–7; 43934, ff. 214–16, 242–43; *PD*(3), 252, col. 1902 et seq.

32 DP, Add. MS 43934, ff. 240–41.

33 DP, Add. MSS 43875, ff. 44–45; 43935, ff. 144–45.

34 DP, Add. MSS 43911, ff. 208–9; 43924, f. 54; 43935, ff. 77–78.

35 9 June 1881 (RP, Add. MS 43528, f. 137).

36 DP, Add. MSS 43875, ff. 60–61; 43883, ff. 94–95; 43935, ff. 119–23.

37 From Nov. 1881 to Feb. 1882 (DP, Add. MS 43924, f. 59). Dilke was again present at the start of a cabinet four days later. Carlingford thought him so 'very able & striking' that he found it 'strange that he shd. leave the room' when the formal cabinet commenced. Carlingford's diary, 6 Aug. 1881 (CP, Add. MS 63689, f. 170).

38 DP, Add. MSS 43875, f. 66; 43935, ff. 149–50, 154–60.

39 Dilke to Gladstone, 30 Sept. 1881 (WEG, Add. MS 44149, ff. 40–42); DP, Add. MS 43935, ff. 172–73.

40 WEG, Add. MS 44149, f. 44.

41 25 Sept. 1881 (DP, Add. MS 43879, ff. 172–73).

42 DP, Add. MSS 43879, ff. 251, 256; 43935, f. 183; WEG, Add. MS 44149, f. 65; RP, Add. MS 43528, f. 164.

43 DP, Add. MS 43936, ff. 16–18; speech at Paisley on receiving the freedom of the borough for his services to the textile industry, 1 Nov. 1883 (*The Times*, 2 Nov. 1883).

44 DP, Add. MSS 43875, ff. 81–82; 43937, f. 167; GP, PRO 30/29/122.

45 30–31 May 1882 (WEG, Add. MS 44149, ff. 77–78); DP, Add. MS 43875, f. 101.

46 DP, Add. MSS 43924, f. 41; 43935, ff. 33–36, 55–56.

47 Ibid., f. 86.

48 *PD*(3), 228, col. 1573; DP, Add. MS 43933, f. 105.

49 See A. G. Hopkins, 'The Victorians and Africa: A Reconsideration of the Occupation of Egypt, 1882', *Journal of African History*, 27 (1986), pp. 363–91.

50 DP, Add. MS 43919, ff. 238–40. The argument that Dilke was the driving force behind the intervention was most thoroughly rehearsed by Wilfrid Scawen Blunt in his *A Secret History of the British Occupation of Egypt* (1907), but similar claims had been made at the time by some who, like George Russell, knew Dilke quite well. See, e.g., BP, Add. MS 47911, ff. 102–3.

51 M. E. Chamberlain, 'Sir Charles Dilke and the British Intervention in Egypt, 1882: Decision-Making in a Nineteenth-Century Cabinet', *British Journal of International Studies*, 2 (1976), pp. 231–45.

52 DP, Add. MS 43936, ff. 28–30, 45.

53 17–18 May 1882 (DP, Add. MS 43894, ff. 80–81).

54 DP, Add. MS 43925, ff. 1–2.

55 DP, Add. MSS 43880, ff. 228–29; 43936, ff. 135–38. Dilke's list of 'Reparations' is in the Devonshire Papers, 340.1248.

56 Chamberlain, 'Sir Charles Dilke and the British Intervention in Egypt', p. 236.

57 DP, Add. MS 43936, ff. 124–25.

58 DP, Add. MSS 43925, ff. 6–8; 43936, ff. 144–50.

59 DP, Add. MS 43925, ff. 14–15.

60 13 July 1882 (RP, Add. MS 43528, ff. 204–5).

61 Chamberlain, 'Sir Charles Dilke and the British Intervention in Egypt', pp. 238–39.

62 Devonshire Papers, 340.1390; DP, Add. MS 43925, f. 16. 'I never was more wonder struck at anything than at the refusal', Dilke recorded. 'My blunder shews how very easy it is to go wrong in foreign affairs.' Ibid., ff. 51–52.

63 *PD*(3), 272, cols 1710–25; G. & T., i, pp. 474–75.

64 DP, Add. MSS 43890, ff. 178–79; 43925, f. 29.

65 Ibid., ff. 25–26.

66 To Grant Duff, 20 Oct. 1882 (DP, Add. MS 43894, ff. 91–92).

67 When the location of his imprisonment was under consideration, Dilke had noted that any island would be alright except 'St Helena, which would be ridiculous'. DP, Add. MS 43936, f. 249.

Notes to Chapter 7

1 Quoted in Ramm (ed.), *Political Correspondence*, i, p. 311.
2 Barrington to Dilke, 25 Dec. 1882 (DP, Add. MS 43912, f. 109).
3 26 Nov. 1880 (DP, Add. MS 43924, f. 27); R. Blake, *Disraeli* (1969; 1st edn, 1966), p. 736.
4 DP, Add. MS 43936, f. 295. He had, for example, registered a silent vote for Butt's Home Rule scheme in 1874.
5 Dilke claimed that Forster had at first contemplated a measure of repression but that he had outflanked him by getting the *Daily News* to print an article which effectively scuppered it. Allen Warren has argued that Forster had no such plan and that Dilke's account is incorrect. See A. Warren, 'Forster, the Liberals and New Directions in Irish Policy 1880–1882', *Parliamentary History*, 6, (1987), p. 98 and n.
6 DP, Add. MSS 43904, ff. 164–65; 43924, ff. 6, 15, 18–19.
7 23 Nov. 1880 (ibid., f. 167).
8 DP, Add. MSS 43924, ff. 26–30; 43934, ff. 324–25.
9 DP, Add. MS 43935, ff. 3–4, 9, 21. He wanted to resign if the terms of the bill were not improved but could not, on this occasion, persuade Chamberlain and Bright to join him.
10 G. & T., i, pp. 364–65. Dilke walked out when the division on the secret service vote was taken, as he had done the previous May. DP, Add. MSS 43924, f. 38; 43934, ff. 213–14.
11 DP, Add. MS 43935, ff. 39, 42–43.
12 DP, Add. MSS 43924, ff. 39–40; 43935, ff. 50–51. Bright and Courtney had joined Dilke and Chamberlain in absenting themselves from a division on the Transvaal on 21 January in protest at the government's military policy.
13 *Chelsea News*, 4 Feb. 1882; DP, Add. MS 43890, f. 163.
14 Dilke to Ripon, 3 May 1882 (RP, Add. MS 43528, ff. 192–93).
15 Ibid., f. 194; DP, Add. MSS 43924, ff. 81, 83; 43936, ff. 101–2; G. & T., i, p. 441n. – quoting McCarthy. Derby (diary, 6 May 1882) believed that Forster's resignation had been engineered by Chamberlain in order to give the radicals control of Irish affairs. However, they appear to have been more annoyed at not being offered the post than by not actually getting it.
16 Dilke to Chamberlain, 21 Nov. 1890 (JC, 5/24/220). Dilke noted in the margin of his Memoir that he was still angry at Chamberlain's action – in 1890, 1903, '& still 1906'. DP, Add. MS 43936, f. 105.
17 See LHJ, 8 May 1882 (LHP, dep. 351); and Bodley MS, Eng. Lett. d.174, ff. 57–58.
18 DP, Add. MS 43894, ff. 78–79.
19 9 June 1882 (RP, Add. MS 43528, f. 199).
20 Buckle (ed.), *Letters of Queen Victoria*, pp. 290–92. Chamberlain had been prepared to make 'common cause' (DP, Add. MS 43885, f. 229), so that Dilke was able to tell Granville that their relations were now so close that they would resign together if they thought 'Forster did not have his hair cut sufficiently often'. GP, PRO 30/29/122.
21 DP Add. MSS 43880, f. 162; 43885, f. 237.
22 Correspondence, 17–26 Aug. 1882 (DP, Add. MS 43875, ff. 107–9; WEG, Add. MS 44149, f. 87). The Prince too was sympathetic to Dilke's proposal; see DP, Add. MS 43874, f. 44.
23 S. Lee, *King Edward the Seventh* (2 vols, 1925–27), i, p. 519.
24 Buckle (ed.), *Letters of Queen Victoria*, pp. 370–72, 378, 382; Ramm (ed.), *Political Correspondence*, i, p. 467nn.; Guedalla (ed.), *The Queen and Mr Gladstone*, ii, p. 220.

25 Jenkins, *Dilke*, p. 158. Dilke had replied, 'I have your letters which are exactly what I expected & exactly what (I hope) I should have written if the places had been changed'. JC, 5/24/41.
26 DP, Add. MS 43885, ff. 297–98.
27 WEG, Add. MS 44149, ff. 98–99.
28 Dilke to Harcourt, 14 Dec. 1882 (WHP, dep. 80, f. 31).
29 Bodley MS, Eng. Lett. d.174, ff. 57–58.
30 Knollys to Dilke, 15 and 17 Dec. 1882 (DP, Add. MS 43874, ff. 51, 53). Chamberlain had also suggested this in his letter of 13 Dec. (cited above, n. 26).
31 To Dilke, 19 Dec. 1882 (DP, Add. MS 43875, f. 118).
32 To Gladstone, 16, 18, and 21 Dec. 1882 (WEG, Add. MS 44149, ff. 101, 104, 107–8).
33 Ramm (ed.), *Political Correspondence*, i, p. 477.
34 Guedalla (ed.), *The Queen and Mr Gladstone*, ii, p. 225; DP, Add. MS 43875, ff. 122–23.
35 *The Times*, 30 Dec. 1882.
36 WEG, Add. MS 44149, ff. 115–16; Ramm (ed.), *Political Correspondence*, ii, p. 3; Guedalla (ed.), *The Queen and Mr Gladstone*, ii, pp. 225–27.
37 *Standard*, 6 Jan. 1883.
38 Ramm (ed.), *Political Correspondence*, ii, pp. 3–4. In accordance with contemporary practice regarding appointment to cabinet office, Dilke sought re-election at Chelsea. He was returned unopposed on 8 January. His first visit to Windsor as a minister came in November 1883. Hamilton 'asked Ponsonby what sort of effect Dilke had produced at Windsor. He says "Dilke did very fairly well. He himself was very agreeable, but I think H. M. thought his conversation a little too loud. We subdue our voices considerably here while eating the royal beef".' EHP, Add. MS 48635, f. 6.
39 DP, Add. MSS 43929, f. 123; 43938, f. 113; WEG, Add. MS 44646, ff. 123–26.
40 C. Petrie, *The Life and Letters of Austen Chamberlain* (2 vols, 1939–40), ii, pp. 95–96; H. H. Asquith, *Memories and Reflections* (2 vols, 1928), i, pp. 90, 154–55.
41 Lucy, *Diary*, i, pp. 307–10; *DFM*, 7 June 1907.
42 DP, Add. MS 43938, f. 62.
43 Hamilton's diary, 7 Apr. 1884 (EHP, Add. MS 48636, f. 26).
44 *Manchester Guardian*, 27 Jan. 1911; *DFM*, 7 June 1907; *Daily News*, 27 Jan. 1911.
45 T. P. O'Connor, 'The Story of a Memorable Session', quoted in *DFM*, 3 Nov. 1893.
46 *Manchester Guardian*, 27 Jan. 1911.
47 DP, Add. MSS 43886, f. 157; 43898, f. 194; Lucy, *Diary*, ii, p. 149.
48 DP, Add. MS 43909, f. 344.
49 DP, Add. MS 43894, f. 62; 43895, f. 135.
50 EHP, Add. MS 48632, ff. 84–85.
51 Dilke had steered clear of the Bradlaugh affair. Bradlaugh had intimated to him that he would like to be elected to the Radical Club, but not if there was any danger that he would be blackballed. His nomination caused great embarrassment among the club's members, who were frightened of the effect that his election would have on their Nonconformist constituents. See Bradlaugh to Dilke, 7 May 1880 (REND, 4/1); Dilke to Ashton Dilke, n.d. (REND, 6/1).
52 Derby diary, 6 and 24 Feb. 1883.
53 31 Dec. 1882 (JC, 5/24/343). Dilke duly complied – see his speech at Chelsea, 1 Jan. 1883 (*The Times*, 2 Jan. 1883).
54 DP, Add. MS 43886, ff. 12–13.
55 *Fortnightly Review*, second series, 34 (1883), pp. 1–11.
56 They made great use of Morley and Escott. DP, Add. MSS 43895, f. 150; 43934, f. 217. For examples of Hamilton's outrage at leaks by Dilke, see WEG, Add. MS 44644, f. 7; EHP, Add. MSS 48633, ff. 56–57, 67; 48638, f. 49. A cabinet committee was set up in January 1882 to inquire into leaking. In the end, the practice had to be 'institutionalised' through the establishment in 1884 of the lobby system. See H. C. G. Matthew

(ed.), *The Gladstone Diaries*, x, *Jan. 1881 – June 1883* (Oxford, 1990), pp. lvi-lvii. The press in any case was becoming increasingly less compliant by this date, especially after William Stead replaced Morley as editor at the *Pall Mall Gazette*.

57 RP, Add. MS 43528, ff. 121–22, 137–38. At the end of two years in the cabinet, Derby recorded in his diary (27 Nov. 1884) that it had been 'harmonious, though not very businesslike'.

58 Derby diary, 1 and 2 Dec. 1882 and 1 Jan. 1883. Derby had an acute sense of the importance of class. After satisfying himself that Dilke and Chamberlain were the only members of the middle class in the cabinet, he added: 'I do not think these details unimportant: since the social faction which a man holds is apt to affect his conduct more than the opinions which he supposes himself to hold.' Diary, 1 Dec. 1882.

Notes to Chapter 8

1 DP, Add. MS 43886, ff. 46, 120, 126.
2 O'Connor, *Memoirs*, i, p. 322.
3 Quoted in Jenkins, *Dilke*, p. 163. In fact, he urged the inclusion of county government, but was no more conspicuous in his contribution than other members of the cabinet. See Carlingford's diary, 6 Feb. 1883 (CP, Add. MS 63691, ff. 108–9).
4 DP, Add. MSS 43936, f. 296; 43938, ff. 189–90.
5 H. Preston-Thomas, *The Work and Play of a Government Inspector* (Edinburgh, 1909), p. 195; DP, Add. MS 43937, f. 4.
6 Dilke, *Greater Britain*, p. 206. Cf. his lecture to the Statistical Society on 'Local Government among Different Nations' (*The Times*, 17 June 1874); and his Cobden Club essay in J. W. Probyn (ed.), *Local Government and Taxation* (1875).
7 DP, Add. MSS 43876, f. 118; 43935, f. 69.
8 WEG, Add. MS 44252, ff. 122–24, 168; EHP, Add. MS 48631, ff. 82, 118; DP, Add. MS 43936, f. 51; G. & T., i, p. 514.
9 WEG, Add. MS 44235, ff. 128–36.
10 3 Feb. 1883 (JC, 5/24/49).
11 3 March 1883 (DP, Add. MS 43905, f. 195).
12 Cabinet notes in WEG, Add. MS 44644, f. 25.
13 DP, Add. MSS 43923, ff. 49–126; 43937, ff. 90–91.
14 DP, Add. MSS 43894, f. 111; 43937, f. 147; EHP, Add. MS 48634, f. 50.
15 DP, Add. MS 43937, f. 167.
16 WEG, Add. MS 44149, f. 186; DP, Add. MSS 43937, f. 188; 43938, ff. 3–4.
17 DP, Add. MSS 43923, ff. 49–171; 43938, ff. 3–4.
18 WEG, Add. MS 44149, f. 198.
19 3 Jan. 1882 (DP, Add. MS 43924, f. 69). His Memoir account was less egotistical and rather more honest in acknowledging the contribution of his colleagues: 'I found that he [Harcourt] had adopted all the ideas of Beal and Firth and of myself.' DP, Add. MS 43936, f. 8. Dilke had earlier promised Harcourt that he would 'slave & devil' for him over London government. WHP, dep. adds. 8, f. 25.
20 DP, Add. MS 43936, ff. 14, 18–19.
21 DP, Add. MSS 43923, ff. 36–41; 43937, f. 50.
22 DP, Add. MSS 43886, f. 39; 43905, ff. 198–200; EHP, Add. MS 48633, f. 71. Chamberlain backed Dilke on London government without entirely agreeing with him. DP, Add. MS 43887, f. 180. The two radicals were also the strongest supporters of stringent measures to deal with the bombers. See Carlingford's diary, 7 Apr. 1883 (CP, Add. MS 63691, f.138).
23 WEG, Add. MS 44149, ff. 138–39; DP, Add. MS 43875, f. 136; EHP, Add. MS 48633, f. 85.
24 DP, Add. MS 43937, ff. 100, 116–17, 120, 179–80; 43938, ff. 2–3; WEG, Add. MS 44645, f. 8; W. A. Robson, *The Government and Misgovernment of London* (1939), pp. 73–75.
25 21 May 1884 (DP, Add. MS 43886, ff. 158–59).
26 Firth, *Reform of London Government*, pp. 15–17; Robson, *Government and Misgovernment*, pp. 76–79; J. Davis, *Reforming London: The London Government Problem, 1855–1900* (Oxford, 1988), pp. 94–95. The activities of the anti-reformers were examined by the Select Committee on the London Corporation (Charges of Malversation), *PP*, 1887, x. See also, J. Lloyd, *London Municipal Government: History of a Great Reform, 1880–88* (1910),

p. 57 for a description of the disruption of one of Dilke's meetings on the bill by a City-hired gang.

27 DP, Add. MSS 43938, f. 343; 43935, f. 30; G. & T., ii, p. 11.

28 Robson, *Government and Misgovernment*, pp. 74–75.

29 Dilke said that Mearns gave him more assistance during his housing inquiry than anyone; see A. S. Wohl, *The Eternal Slum: Housing and Social Policy in Victorian London* (1977), p. 236.

30 Buckle (ed.), *Letters of Queen Victoria*, pp. 451–52.

31 Dilke, *Two Recess Speeches*, pp. 47–48; speeches at Hammersmith, 4 Sept. 1878 (*The Times*, 5 Sept. 1878); and Chelsea, 19 Aug. 1879 (*Chelsea News*, 23 Aug. 1879).

32 DP, Add. MS 43937, ff. 174–75, 205–6; speech in Commons, 4 March 1884, *PD*(3), 285, cols 530–40. Clerkenwell's churchwarden sprang to the defence of the vestry; see W. Robson, *Sir Charles Dilke and the Clerkenwell Vestry* (1884).

33 DP, Add. MSS 43890, f. 259; 43938, ff. 2–3. He had attached to the second circular a set of model regulations to guide the vestries that had not yet produced bye-laws of their own. Davis has argued that these were so complex that their prime aim must have been to provoke the vestries, and that the general attack on them created an unjust impression that influenced the eventual shape of London reform. Davis, *Reforming London*, pp. 91–92.

34 DP, Add. MSS 43874, f. 9; 43938, ff. 53, 68–69, 82.

35 Ponsonby to Dilke, 17 Feb. 1884 (DP, Add. MS 43874, f. 5).

36 DP, Add. MSS 43896, ff. 29, 33–35, 41; 43938, ff. 61, 144; V. A. McClelland, *Cardinal Manning* (1962), pp. 137–38.

37 DP, Add. MS 43876, ff. 4–6, 9.

38 DP, Add. MS 43938, ff. 126–27, 136–38.

39 *Reynolds's Newspaper*, 17 May 1885.

40 See Wohl, *Eternal Slum*, ch. 9.

41 *Manchester Guardian*, 18 July 1885.

42 Royal Commission on the Housing of the Working Classes, *PP*, 1884–85, xxx. Dilke also favoured giving the leaseholder a statutory right to the renewal of a lease, or even changing his tenure into a perpetual holding at a fixed rent. C. W. Dilke and F. W. Procter, *Papers on the Leasehold System* (1886).

43 *Manchester Guardian*, 18 July 1885; *PD*(3), 300, cols 1597–1606. Experienced social reformers like Sir Edwin Chadwick were disappointed at the bill's lack of teeth; see Chadwick to Dilke, 3 Aug. 1885 (Chadwick Papers, file 628, ff. 57–61).

44 R. C. K. Ensor, *England, 1870–1914* (Oxford, 1936), p. 301. A. S. Wohl's assessment of the commission's achievements and of the legislation that followed, which he sees as marking the beginnings of municipal socialism and state intervention (Wohl, *Eternal Slum*, pp. 248–49) is more positive than my own.

45 2 Dec. 1884 (DP, Add. MS 43898, f. 198).

46 *Report of the Industrial Remuneration Conference* (1885; reissued, New York, 1968, with an introduction by J. Saville), esp. pp. 2–3.

47 Speech at Cinderford, 9 June 1890 (*DFM*, 13 June 1890).

48 George Russell was dismayed by Dilke's refusal to budge on unemployment, his strong attachment to political economy making him think 'any assistance of the State whether in money or otherwise to be almost a crime'. LHJ, 20 and 25 March 1885 (LHP, dep. 366). Dilke had been prepared to prosecute Hyndman for his inflammatory speech at the demonstration. LHJ, 17 Feb. 1885 (LHP, dep. 364).

49 WEG, Add. MS 44149, f. 146; DP, Add. MSS 43875, ff. 140–41; 43890, f. 244; 43925, f. 68; 43937, ff. 147–49; 43942, f. 60.

50 *PD*(3), 280, cols 1030–40; 282, cols 1441–46; DP, Add. MSS 43938, f. 235; 43939, f. 197. For a polemical statement by a libertarian opponent, see W. White, *Speeches of Playfair and Dilke on Vaccination Taken to Pieces and Disposed of* (1884).

Notes to Chapter 9

1 From 439,970 in 1831 to 2,225,692 in 1869. H. J. Hanham, *The Reformed Electoral System in Great Britain, 1832–1914* (1968), p. 35.

2 Dilke himself held votes in nine constituencies returning twenty MPs. *PD* (3), 207, cols 775–82.

3 30 Oct. 1883 (*Daily News*, 31 Oct. 1883).

4 Dilke's own expenses in 1880 amounted to £3,200. O'Leary, *The Elimination of Corrupt Practices*, p. 166.

5 Ibid., p. 118; *PD*(3), 244, cols 1371–74.

6 8 March 1880 (ibid., 250, cols 114–17).

7 It included Selborne, Northbrook, Harcourt, Chamberlain, Bright and James. DP, Add. MSS 43924, f. 23; 43934, ff. 307–9.

8 See, e.g., DP, Add. MSS 43905, f. 89; 43925, f. 18.

9 DP, Add. MSS 43891, ff. 253–55; 43925, f. 69; 43937, f. 16.

10 Hayes, *Background and Passage*, pp. 100–1.

11 To Chamberlain, 10 Jan. 1884, quoted ibid., p. 119.

12 DP, Add. MS 43937, ff. 199–200.

13 Hayes, *Background and Passage*, p. 120; A. Jones, *The Politics of Reform, 1884* (Cambridge, 1972), pp. 86–88. Dilke appears to have kept this promise by basing the redistribution scheme on the 1881 census rather than upon more up-to-date population statistics which would have entailed a reduction in Irish representation. Ibid., p. 183.

14 WEG, Add. MS 44149, ff. 211–12; DP, Add. MSS 43875, f. 165; 43938, f. 154. He told the cabinet on 24 May that he would resign over the issue if Courtney did so. Derby diary, 24 May 1883.

15 Hayes, *Background and Passage*, pp. 146–47.

16 DP, Add. MSS 43886, ff. 176–77; 43938, ff. 174–85; H. J. Hanham (ed.), *The Nineteenth-Century Constitution* (Cambridge, 1969), pp. 87–88.

17 Rover, *Women's Suffrage*, pp. 136–37.

18 16 June 1885 (DP, Add. MS 43906, ff. 94–95). He was also opposed to any measure which excluded married women from the vote. Ibid., ff. 28–29. He withdrew from the London branch of the Women's Suffrage Society when it compromised on this. DP, Add. MS 43931, ff. 58–59.

19 Lord Salisbury, 'The Value of Redistribution: A Note on Electoral Statistics', *National Review*, 20 (1884), pp. 145–62.

20 Dilke certainly believed that this was the 'Tory game'. To J. Loader, 21 May 1884 (DP, Add. MS 43886, ff. 158–59).

21 DP, Add. MS 43926, ff. 20–21; WEG, Add. MS 44149, f. 219; *The Times*, 10 July 1884; Guedalla (ed.), *The Queen and Mr Gladstone*, ii, p. 282.

22 LHJ, 21 July 1884 (LHP, dep. 359).

23 DP, Add. MS 43938, ff. 192–99, 224.

24 21 Aug. 1884, quoted in Holland, *Life of Spencer Compton*, ii, p. 52.

25 To Dilke, 2 Sept. 1884 (DP, Add. MS 43891, f. 264). The irony of this was not lost on Dilke for many radicals had seen redistribution as the means of burying the Conservatives once and for all. E.g. Frederic Harrison to Dilke, 5 April 1880: the Tory must be 'not only killed – but put in his coffin, & not only put in his coffin, but screwed down, & a brass plate nailed on the top. The only way to screw him down is re-distribution.' DP, Add. MS 43898, ff. 179–88.

26 12 Sept. 1884 (DP, Add. MS 43886, ff. 198–99).

27 'District boroughs' were those areas that were rural in all but name and could be quite conveniently merged in the counties.
28 DP, Add. MSS 43923, ff. 179–86; 43938, ff. 237–39; WEG, Add. MS 44149, f. 247.
29 Ibid., ff. 223–39; DP, Add. MS 43923, ff. 179–86.
30 DP, Add. MS 43942, f. 90.
31 29 Sept. 1884 (DP, Add. MS 43875, ff. 177–78).
32 30 Sept. 1884 (WEG, Add. MS 44149, ff. 243–44).
33 Dilke to Gladstone, 1 Oct. 1884 (ibid., f. 245).
34 DP, Add. MS 43886, f. 220.
35 EHP, Add. MS 48637, f. 122; DP, Add. MS 43886, ff. 227, 232. For the argument that Dilke may have been behind the leak, see Jones, *Politics of Reform*, pp. 180–82.
36 LHJ, 22 Oct. 1884 (LHP, dep. 360).
37 DP, Add. MS 43926, f. 21.
38 DP, Add. MS 43886, f. 240.
39 DP, Add. MSS 43875, ff. 187–88; 43886, f. 249.
40 G. & T., ii, p. 70; DP, Add. MS 43926, f. 37.
41 DP, Add. MS 43894, f. 154.
42 Quoted in Hayes, *Background and Passage*, p. 221 and n.
43 *PD*(3), 293, cols 1235–47.
44 Dodson cabinet notes, 22 Oct. 1884 (MBP, dep. 62).
45 To Frank Hill, 7 Nov. 1884 (DP, Add. MS 43898, f. 79).
46 Quoted in G. & T., ii, p. 74.
47 DP, Add. MSS 43875, ff. 195–96; 43891, f. 83; WEG, Add. MS 44149, f. 262.
48 EHP, Add. MS 48638, ff. 50–51.
49 Ibid., f. 55.
50 To Gladstone's displeasure. Ibid., f. 61.
51 DP, Add. MS 43938, ff. 310, 313.
52 DP, Add. MS 43898, f. 93.
53 See IP, Add. MS 50042, ff. 76–79.
54 DP, Add. MSS 43876, ff. 23, 29–31, 36–39; 43938, ff. 315–19.
55 Jones, *Politics of Reform*, p. 210. Dilke was not as gullible as Jones's account suggests. He had told Hartington at the start of the month that he would be prepared to accept grouping, despite hating it, provided the Tories abandoned the cumulative vote. He, Lambert and Lefevre went on to examine the implications of grouping for the South of England and were 'terrified at the unpopularity which will be incurred by any government which carries' it. Devonshire Papers, 340.1564A, 1566A, and 1571A. As a result he told the cabinet on 20 Nov. that 'grouping wd. not bear examination', and that the Tories would therefore give it up. CP, Add. MS 63692, ff. 246–47. It suited his own purpose to be 'tricked' whenever Salisbury raised the stakes.
56 DP, Add. MS 43938, ff. 319–28.
57 DP, Add. MS 43886, ff. 272–76.
58 DP, Add. MS 43938, ff. 327–28; CP, Add. MS 63692, f. 250; L. Masterman (ed.), *Mary Gladstone: Her Diaries and Letters* (2nd edn, 1930), pp. 336–37.
59 DP, Add. MSS 43875, f. 218; 43876, ff. 42–46, 48, 55.
60 DP, Add. MS 43938, ff. 334–36, 345–48. Their correspondence on the subject is in the Althorp Papers, K 12 (provisional).
61 IP, Add. MS 50042, ff. 80–81; Hayes, *Background and Passage*, p. 263; M. E. J. Chadwick, 'The Role of Redistribution in the Making of the Third Reform Act', *Historical Journal*, 19 (1976), pp. 665–83. Crawford's wife, Virginia, was Ashton Dilke's sister-in-law.
62 *Manchester Guardian*, 11 Dec. 1884.
63 17 Dec. 1884 (WEG, Add. MS 44149, f. 298).
64 Devonshire Papers, 340.1606; DP, Add. MS 43891, ff. 89–90.

65 DP, Add. MS 43934, ff. 317–18. This remark leads one to doubt whether Dilke was entirely honest when he denied responsibility for the contents of a leader in the *Daily News* which compared Hartington's contribution to the conduct of the bill adversely with his own. See Dilke to Hartington, 14 Jan. 1885 (Devonshire Papers, 340.1625).

66 13 Jan. 1885 (DP, Add. MS 43875, f. 225).

67 DP, Add. MS 43939, f. 85. Dilke was engaged at this moment in a petty wrangle with Gladstone over a privy councillorship for Lambert. The Prime Minister would not grant the honour until the Redistribution Bill had become law. DP, Add. MS 43875, ff. 233–34; WEG, Add. MS 44235, f. 202.

68 *PD*(3), 294–96, passim; IP, Add. MS 50042, ff. 88–93; DP, Add. MS 43939, ff. 96–102, 135, 189.

69 *The Times*, 13 May 1885; Hamilton's diary, 25 March 1885 (EHP, Add. MS 48639, f. 108).

70 DP, Add. MSS 43887, f. 51; 43939, f. 61.

71 8 May 1885 (DP, Add. MS 43906, f. 70).

72 18 May 1885 (Broadhurst Papers, ii, p. 49).

73 R. Rhodes James, *Lord Randolph Churchill* (1969), p. 182.

74 *PD*(3), 295, cols 725–28. The total number of county seats in England, Scotland and Wales rose from 219 to 292 while the number of borough seats decreased from 323 to 268.

75 C. W. Dilke, *Electoral Reform* (1909), p. 9.

76 The more generous interpretation is quite feasible. After all, the Liberals were quite prepared to carry a scheme which in England and Wales alone abolished fifty-eight of their own, but only thirty-seven Conservative, constituencies. H. W. Stephens and D. W. Brady, 'The Parliamentary Parties and the Electoral Reforms of 1884–85 in Britain', *Legisislative Studies Quarterly*, 1, (1976), p. 496.

Notes to Chapter 10

1 See Granville to Dilke, 20 Jan. 1884 (DP, Add. MS 43881, ff. 146–49).
2 Ibid., f. 150; DP, Add. MS 43938, ff. 6, 8–9.
3 Ibid., ff. 9–11, 42–43.
4 Ibid., ff. 47–48, 63–66, 73–76; DP, Add. MS 43894, f. 121.
5 *PD*, 284, cols 947–68.
6 DP, Add. MSS 43886, ff. 126, 129; 43938, ff. 77–78.
7 DP, Add. MS 43891, ff. 301–2.
8 DP, Add. MS 43894, f. 124.
9 Wolseley to Dilke, 14 March 1884 (DP, Add. MS 43912, ff. 236–37).
10 25 March 1884 (DP, Add. MS 43926, f. 3).
11 DP, Add. MS 43938, ff. 94–134.
12 *PD*(3), 288, cols 277–93; DP, Add. MSS 43926, f. 20; 43938, f. 139. Chamberlain had been against allowing the debate, saying that there was little interest in the country and that the clamour came from 'the London press, which was in the hands of Jews chiefly, & in the interest of the bondholders'. Derby diary, 2 Apr. 1884.
13 DP, Add. MS 43938, ff. 154–66, 208–9.
14 DP, Add. MS 43926, ff. 5–6.
15 To Mrs Pattison, 3 Dec. 1880 (DP, Add. MS 43904, f. 182).
16 DP, Add. MS 43886, f. 190.
17 DP, Add. MS 43938, ff. 221–22.
18 DP, Add. MSS 43886, ff. 205–8; 43913, ff. 59–60; 43938, ff. 306–7, 337–38.
19 LHJ, 4 Jan. 1885 (LHP, dep. 363).
20 A. B. Cooke and J. Vincent, *The Governing Passion: Cabinet Government and Party Politics in Britain, 1885–86* (1974), pp. 26–30.
21 To Grant Duff, 9 Jan. 1885 (DP, Add. MS 43894, f. 163); to Chamberlain, 5 Jan. 1885 (JC, 5/24/94).
22 DP, Add. MSS 43887, ff. 2, 7–10, 14–16; 43939, ff. 27–28, 39; Cooke and Vincent, *Governing Passion*, pp. 180–82.
23 DP, Add. MS 43887, ff. 40–41.
24 DP, Add. MSS 43875, ff. 230–31; 43939, ff. 53–54.
25 3 Feb. 1885 (JC, 5/24/109–10).
26 JC, 5/34/76.
27 DP, Add. MS 43926, f. 30.
28 DP, Add. MS 43894, f. 168.
29 *PD*(3), 294, cols 1484–1504.
30 Quoted in R. Rhodes James, *Rosebery* (1963), p. 165.
31 DP, Add. MS 43882, f. 119.
32 *PD*(3), 205, col. 1684; 239, cols 1181–84; *PD*(4), 57, col. 726; DP, Add. MS 43936, f. 40.
33 DP, Add. MS 43887, ff. 95–103.
34 DP, Add. MSS 43875, ff. 244–47; 43939, ff. 119, 132, 184.
35 Ibid., ff. 121–26.
36 DP, Add. MSS 43936, ff. 54–55; 43939, ff. 127–29.
37 Ibid., ff. 129–32.
38 DP, Add. MS 43894, f. 178.
39 DP, Add. MS 43939, ff. 148–56. Dilke had strongly resisted the purchase amendment to the Land Bill in May of the previous year, and had found for supporters 'a scratch

lot' consisting of Carlingford, Northbrook, Selborne, Hartington and Dodson. 'Will you let the Tories do it?' Chamberlain had yelled at him. 'Certainly', Dilke had yelled back. DP, Add. MSS 43926, ff. 13–14; 43938, ff. 148–49.

40 LHJ, 15 May 1885 (LHP, dep. 368). Derby recorded almost exactly the same view in his diary on 19 May.

41 WHP, dep. 80, ff. 39–40.

42 Jenkins, *Dilke*, p. 202; Cooke and Vincent, *Governing Passion*, p. 239.

43 DP, Add. MS 43875, ff. 255, 258; H. C. G. Matthew (ed.), *The Gladstone Diaries*, xi, *July 1883-Dec. 1886* (Oxford, 1990), pp. 343–44.

44 EHP, Add. MS 48640, f. 73.

45 DP, Add. MS 43907, ff. 232–35.

46 DP, Add. MS 43939, f. 157. Jenkins (*Dilke*, p. 203) baldly states that this was the only visit Dilke ever paid to Ireland. He made at least two others – in 1882 and 1903; see DP, Add. MS 43936, ff. 208–9; *DFM*, 6 Nov. 1903.

47 DP, Add. MS 43939, ff. 168–73.

48 27 May 1885 (DP, Add. MS 43894, f. 180).

49 3 June 1885 (ibid., f. 181). Stead was attacking Chamberlain in the *Pall Mall Gazette*.

50 DP, Add. MS 43886, f. 181.

51 Jenkins, *Dilke*, pp. 204–5. Cf. Gladstone's sardonic comment: 'A very fair cabinet today – only three resignations.' Quoted in J. Morley, *Life of W. E. Gladstone* (3 vols, 1903), iii, p. 185.

52 *PD*(3), 298, cols 1437–45.

53 Quoted in S. H. Harris, *Auberon Herbert: Crusader for Liberty* (1943), p. 276n. Cowper's comment is echoed by Lewis Harcourt, who noted that many Liberals regarded the defeat as a blessing as the Tories would have to come in for six months and face very difficult problems, and this would assist the Liberals to victory at the general election. LHJ, 11 June 1885 (LHP, dep. 369). Derby described (diary, 9 June 1885) the relief on the faces of his cabinet colleagues when they met after the defeat: 'we were far more pleased with our defeat than our opponents can have been with their victory'.

54 WEG, Add. MS 44646, f. 140.

55 *The Times*, 10 June 1885. 'Your speech was admirable to read', wrote Chamberlain on 11 June, '& I have heard from one who was present that the effect was electrical. You never did better in yr. life.' DP, Add. MS 43887, f. 140.

56 JC, 5/24/120.

57 DP, Add. MS 43935, f. 55.

58 DP, Add. MS 43906, ff. 94–95. In 1891 Chamberlain admitted that he had only voted for women's suffrage in the late 1870s out of friendship for Dilke. E. E. Gulley, *Joseph Chamberlain and English Social Politics* (New York, 1926), p. 81.

59 DP, Add. MS 43894, f. 184.

60 They had shared the platform at the Cobden Club on 13 June and had both stressed the importance of local government reform, especially for Ireland.

61 WEG, Add. MS 44149, ff. 183–85; DP, Add. MS 43939, f. 198.

62 A. O'Day, *Parnell and the First Home Rule Episode, 1884–87* (Dublin, 1986), pp. 56–73.

63 DP, Add. MS 43906, f. 99; WEG, Add. MS 44149, ff. 361–62; JC, 5/24/123.

64 DP, Add. MS 43887, f. 158. In mid July they also attempted to capture control of the Liberal Central Association by pressing Schnadhorst's nomination to its standing committee; see M. Barker, *Gladstone and Radicalism: The Reconstruction of Liberal Policy in Britain, 1885–94* (1975), p. 112.

65 DP, Add. MS 43906, f. 103.

66 14 July 1885 (GP, PRO 30/29/29A).

67 17 May 1885 (DP, Add. MS 43907, ff. 232–35).

68 EHP, Add. MSS 48633, f. 76; 48639, f. 5. When the scandal broke, Hamilton reflected that Dilke was 'the only man' on whom the mantle of Hartington and Gladstone could

properly fall, and prophesied that, if he was ruined, Rosebery would be Prime Minister within seven years. EHP, Add. MS 48641, f. 57.

69 To Malcolm MacColl, 15 Jan. 1884, quoted in G. W. E. Russell (ed.), *Malcolm MacColl: Memoirs and Correspondence* (1914), p. 352.

70 Derby diary, 27 Nov. 1884.

71 Granville to Spencer, 14 Aug. 1885, quoted in P. Gordon (ed.), *The Red Earl: The Papers of the Fifth Earl Spencer* (2 vols, Northampton, 1981–86), ii, p. 69.

72 See W. C. Lubenow, *Parliamentary Politics and the Home Rule Crisis in 1886* (Oxford, 1988), p. 174. According to Derby (diary, 2 Nov. 1884), 'A Whig lady said of the two radical members "Chamberlain is not a gentleman, & does not try to be one: Dilke tries & does not succeed." Unjust, yet with a certain approach to truth in it.' Likewise, Granville described a speech made by Chamberlain at a celebration for Bright as in bad taste and 'not the act of a gentleman'. Carlingford, too, noted that 'Chamberlain ignores the gentlemanlike understandings & traditions of the Cabinet & fights for his own hand'. Carlingford's diary, 15 June and 28 Nov. 1883 (CP, Add. MS 63691, ff. 173, 256).

73 See below, p. 178. Earlier in the year, Lewis Harcourt had recorded that the two radicals appeared to have agreed that Chamberlain would be the eventual leader. LHJ, 13 Feb. 1885 (LHP, dep. 364). In May, however, he added that Chamberlain's friends had advised him that it was impossible for him to be Prime Minister just yet and that Dilke would have a better chance of succeeding. LHJ, 19 May 1885 (LHP, dep. 369). Perhaps it was his awareness of these opinions of him that persuaded Chamberlain to recognise that Dilke would be a more popular choice.

74 Carlingford recorded in his diary a conversation with the Queen, 2 Nov. 1883, in which 'She spoke of Dilke favourably – thought he had got rid of his violent opinions.' CP, Add. MS 63691, f. 243.

75 Gladstone's son had been impressed by Dilke's 'devout and most attentive behaviour' in church, while his private secretary had recorded 'on good authority' a rumour that he had become 'a strict High Churchman'. Masterman (ed.), *Mary Gladstone*, p. 278; Hamilton's diary, 1 Oct. 1884 (EHP, Add. MS 48637, f. 104). Dilke's piety was sufficiently well known for it to be a subject of gossip at the time of the scandal; see A. B. Cooke and J. R. Vincent (eds), *Lord Carlingford's Journal* (Oxford, 1971), p. 142.

76 O'Connor, *Memoirs*, i, p. 314.

77 30 Dec. 1884 (DP, Add. MS 43906, ff. 21–22). Dilke pointed out his mistake as to the year in his next letter. Ibid., f. 23. Nicknames were frequently employed in the love letters that passed between Dilke and Mrs Pattison during their engagement. 'Hoya' was perhaps a complimentary allusion to the translucence of Emilia's complexion. The plant *Hoya Carnosa*, also known as 'Porcelain Flower', is noted for the smooth, pure quality of its flowers. For 'Zz', see above, p. 313 n. 2.

Notes to Chapter 11

1 Dilke's diary, 19 July 1885 (DP, Add. MS 43927, f. 4). Crawford, despite his wife's confession of the previous night, had attended the dinner to 'honour' Dilke and had been quite amicable towards him. This suggests either that he did not believe his wife or that he had other reasons for not displaying any animosity towards Dilke; cf. below, pp. 205 and 343 n. 45. I do not intend to repeat here the many details available in Roy Jenkins's very full account of the scandal, which occupies six chapters of his biography of Dilke, and to which I am indebted for those points in the following narrative not otherwise attributed. I have concentrated instead on introducing new information, correcting points of fact and offering my own interpretation of the evidence.

2 Quoted in G. & T., ii, p. 168. His next letter to her was the product of an extremely distraught mind. He believed that the conspirators were planning to accuse him also of homosexuality 'with the brother' (presumably either William or Eustace Smith see n. 26 below), and that Mrs Crawford had 'got up' his bedroom from Mrs Chatfield (a very curious observation as the latter had died in 1880 when Virginia was only seventeen). 76 Sloane Street would have to be 'burnt down' as he did not want to see it again once the scandal became public. The reference to homosexuality was shortly afterwards crossed through and replaced with the sentence: 'This they have already abandoned as a lie.' Likewise, 'burnt down' was changed to 'got rid of'. The letter appears to have been begun on 23 July and added to and altered over the next few days before being sent on 5 August. DP, Add. MS 43906, ff. 113–14.

3 DP, Add. MS 43927, f. 5.

4 See Dilke to Hill, 13 Sept. 1885 (DP, Add. MS 43898, f. 135); and Mrs Crawford to Charles Stewart, 22 July 1885 (DP, Add. MS 49432, f. 39). Right from the outset it appears that Dilke was confident that he could disprove Mrs Crawford's accusation but that he was, as he told Harcourt on 24 July, afraid that other things would come out. LHJ, 24 July 1885 (LHP, dep. 371).

5 Quoted in Petrie, *Life and Letters of Austen Chamberlain*, ii, pp. 95–96. Dilke also taught Austen to shoot, and even succeeded in getting 'Joe *himself*' to play tennis each day. 'I have converted this house where exercise was unknown...', he told Harcourt, 29 Aug. 1885 (WHP, dep. 80, ff. 44–45).

6 Dilke to Maye Dilke, n.d., but from Highbury, summer 1885 (REND, 7/1).

7 DP, Add. MS 43940, f. 25. Chamberlain had written to Mrs Pattison what was, according to Dilke, 'the best letter' of his life, congratulating her on her engagement. In it he had described Dilke's friendship as 'the best gift of my public life', adding that he rejoiced 'unfeignedly that he will have a companion so well able to share his noblest ambitions and to brighten his life'. DP, Add. MS 43907, ff. 226–27; Jenkins, *Dilke*, p. 196.

8 B. Askwith, *Lady Dilke* (1969), p. 114.

9 Gladstone to Dilke, 2 Feb. 1886 (WEG, Add. MS 44149, f. 367). The political events of 1885–86 are considered in more detail in Chapter 13.

10 *The Times*, 13 Feb. 1886.

11 See Dilke to Harcourt, n.d. (WHP, dep. 80, ff. 37–38). Indeed, Dilke's initial judgement was that the trial had not been damaging and that all would be well; but this was not the reaction of London society and Chamberlain had to disillusion him. On 18 Feb. he was advised by friends to leave a meeting of the National Liberal Club and to absent himself from the House. LHJ, 12, 15, and 18 Feb. 1886 (LHP, dep. 377).

12 But see p. 344 n. 48. for differing judicial interpretations of this point of law.

13 O. F. Christie, *The Transition to Democracy, 1867–1914* (1934), pp. 109–10.

14 Lady Dilke had a series of tearful interviews with Stead imploring his help. W. T. Stead, *Deliverance or Doom? or, The Choice of Sir Charles Dilke* (1892); LHJ, 26 Feb. 1886 (LHP, dep. 377). Harcourt adds that Dilke had confessed his intimacy with Mrs Smith but that Stead thought nothing of this because he regarded her as little more than 'a common whore'.

15 See J. W. Robertson Scott, *The Life and Death of a Newspaper* (1952), pp. 72–259. Earlier in the year, Dilke had had a spat with Stead over the attacks on Chamberlain in the *Pall Mall Gazette*. See his letter to Stead, 24 Apr. 1885, saying that as Chamberlain had now forgiven him, 'it is not for me to hold out'. STED, 1/20.

16 DP, Add. MSS 43888, f. 17; 43907, f. 258.

17 Jenkins, *Dilke*, p. 245; W. T. Stead, 'The Sin of Ananias and Sapphira', *Welsh Review*, 1 (1892), pp. 321–38. Stead's claim is supported by an entry in LHJ, 26 Feb. 1886 (LHP, dep. 377).

18 Note by Dodson, 24 July 1886 (MBP, dep. 67). Dilke told Stead that he did not expect to return to politics but wished to prove his innocence for the sake of his wife and son. Stead, *Deliverance or Doom?*

19 The evidence is not clear. Jenkins's only reference is a brief one that states that Mrs Harrison 'first gave him [Dilke] the Hill Street address' in the autumn of 1886. Jenkins, *Dilke*, p. 332. But this cannot be right because, at the July trial, Forster admitted meeting Mrs Crawford there. J. Juxon, *Lewis and Lewis* (1983), pp. 212–14, and Askwith, *Lady Dilke*, p. 154, argue that Mrs Harrison probably gave Dilke much more information in September 1885 than seems likely – of the way in which she and her sister hunted together for men; of the fact that Forster had been Virginia's lover for far longer than Dilke had hitherto known. If this had been the case it would surely have been used at the second trial. These details were only collected later by the Chesson Committee; see below, p. 192.

20 JC, 5/24/189.

21 Quoted in Jenkins, *Dilke*, p. 259. Mrs Crawford too was now only a private party to the case and therefore unable to call on legal representation in court – a fact usually ignored by Dilke's champions.

22 He wrote later of his firm belief in Dilke's innocence; see E. Marjoribanks, *The Life of Sir Edward Marshall Hall* (1929), p. 67.

23 The innuendo was that this could only be the product of guilty behaviour. In fact it was an inveterate habit of Dilke's and was applied to all manner of documents. Part of his obsession was not just, as he explained at the trial, to remove appointments that had been cancelled, it was also to cut down on the amount of paper that was stored in his letter-boxes. To this end, he frequently cut off the letter-heads from notepaper. He also destroyed information that in his opinion was not worth preserving; see above, p. 114. All this was no doubt a convenient habit for an adulterer, but it was an obsessive and idiosyncratic habit for all that and one which he continued to the end of his life.

24 Askwith, *Lady Dilke*, pp. 144–48.

25 But one that weighed heavily with Lady Dilke in convincing her of her husband's innocence. It was also the date of the Pheonix Park murders and was therefore clearly fixed in Dilke's mind.

26 William (b. 11/9/56); Margaret Maye (b. 4/9/57) who married Ashton Dilke; Helen (b. 26/10/58); Olive (b. 22/2/60); Eustace (b. 31/5/61); Virginia (b. 20/11/62); Ida (b. 29/2/64); Rosalind (b. 22/5/66), who married Ernest Enthoven; Clarence (b. 16/5/68); Launcelot (b. 16/5/68). REND, 7/1.

27 See REND, 13/3.

28 See 'Notes on a Talk about Virginia Crawford and the Case of *Crawford* v. *Crawford and Dilke* (1886) held on 8 July 1973' by several of Mrs Crawford's relatives, REND 13/1. The same source also claims that, while conclusive proof is lacking, Donald Crawford

was probably impotent: 'Virginia always wanted a child and told Mrs Marion Rawson [her niece] that if she had had children "nothing that happened would have happened".' See also, Askwith, *Lady Dilke*, p. 139.

29 Eight letters from Liddon to Virginia Crawford, 5 March 1888 to 2 Feb. 1889 (REND, 12/3).

30 See Marya Cheliza to Virginia Crawford, 18 June 1903, expressing sadness at her decision to enter the convent; and Stead to Virginia Crawford, 2 Sept. 1903, expressing pleasure that she was 'once more available for the service of mankind' and asking her to act as his interpreter on a mission to Rome to interview the Pope. REND, 12/3.

31 Marion Rawson related the story of an occasion when, on a Hellenic cruise, she was forbidden by the police from landing at Palermo. REND, 13/3.

32 Some of which are available at REND, 12/4.

33 Biographical details have been taken from her obituary in the *Catholic Citizen*, 15 Nov. 1948, and from F. Bywater, 'Manning, Dilke and Virginia Crawford', *Tablet*, 14 March 1959, pp. 249–50.

34 Askwith, *Lady Dilke*, pp. 154–55; DP, Add. MS 43902, f. 150. Dilke replied on 8 January saying that Lady Dilke had found particularly abhorrent Maye's insinuations that she herself had doubts as to his innocence. He would, he said, continue to perform to the full his duties as a guardian and would always retain a 'kind personal feeling' towards her. '... I am not sure', he added, 'that sacrifice of anything that you may fancy to be truth was ever asked of you'. REND, 7/1.

35 Stead interviewed one of the jurors who told him that the most damning evidence against Dilke came not from Mrs Crawford but from Mrs Rogerson and Maye Dilke. Stead, 'The Sin of Ananias and Sapphira'.

36 See Matthew, *Gladstone Diaries*, xi, pp. 598–601. On 7 July, following news of Dilke's defeat at Chelsea, Gladstone had asked James if there was anything more that could be done to help him for 'he is a great Parliamentary loss & it is impossible not to feel for him'. On 23 July he noted in his diary: 'The terrible cant of the Dilke verdict sadly & deeply marks this day.' Ibid., pp. 584, 598. Gladstone had resigned three days earlier; Salisbury agreed to form a government on 25 July.

37 A popular ditty performed at the old Alhambra was the 'Schoolboy's Song' which began: 'Charlie Dilke he spilt the milk ....' Of the many cartoons of the scandal, one showed a large double bed with three pillows above the caption: 'Sir Charles Dilke's Bedroom in Chelsea.' See REND, 13/1.

38 DP, Add. MS 49610, ff. 35–42; JC, 5/24/191.

39 George Lewis, Mrs Crawford's solicitor, had visited Hill Street to persuade (by threats or bribery) the housekeeper, Mrs Harvey, not to testify about the meetings there of the two sisters and their lovers. Juxon, *Lewis and Lewis*, pp. 214–16; Jenkins, *Dilke*, p. 330.

Notes to Chapter 12

1 An exception is Francis Bywater who, in an unpublished article, argued that Dilke was not put in the box at the first trial because he would have had to deny under oath adultery with Mrs Crawford and would thereby have committed perjury and risked prosecution; see REND 13/6. I am not convinced by this. Dilke does not seem to have been at all perturbed about denying the accusation under oath, and told the Queen's Proctor that that was precisely the reason he wanted him to intervene; see Dilke to Sir Augustus Stephenson, 10 Apr. 1886 (REND, 13/8).

2 Jenkins, *Dilke*, pp. 366–67.

3 Askwith, *Lady Dilke*, p. 171.

4 Shane Leslie, 'Virginia Crawford, Sir Charles Dilke, and Cardinal Manning', *Dublin Review*, 241 (1951), pp. 177–205. Lady Dilke also believed that Mrs Smith was the author of the anonymous letters. Jenkins, *Dilke*, pp. 356–57. See also, Shane Leslie, 'Dilke in His Own Defence', *Daily Telegraph*, 8 Dec. 1960.

5 For the general delight in both the Dilke and Smith families at the engagement of Ashton and Maye, see Helen Smith to her sister Olive, Jan. 1876. Father and mother were 'so enchanted with the marriage that no one ever gets scolded ....' REND, 12/2.

6 Askwith, *Lady Dilke*, p. 142. The local Liberal Association used the scandal as grounds for replacing Smith at Tynemouth with a more acceptable candidate. See Todd, *The Militant Democracy*, p. 157.

7 Juxon, *Lewis and Lewis*, esp. pp. 219–21. There is also an account of the case in H. Montgomery Hyde, *A Tangled Web: Sex Scandals in British Politics and Society* (1986), esp. pp. 112–26. He, too, believes that the weight of the evidence points to Dilke's innocence, but his account is wholly derivative and does not proffer any speculation as to Mrs Crawford's motive.

8 See REND, 13/2.

9 'Notes on a Talk...', REND, 13/1. Cf. Dilke's cryptic hint of homosexual charges in the letter cited above, p. 339. n. 2.

10 See his letter of 25 March 1974 (REND, 13/2).

11 REND, 12/10.

12 REND, 12/3.

13 Ibid.

14 23 July 1885 (EHP, Add. MS 48641, f. 34).

15 The description is Viscountess Waverley's, quoted in Askwith, *Lady Dilke*, pp. 65–67. Bodley's wife, according to her son, said that Dilke had 'the most unbelievable charm and was highly attractive to women', and that she would not have felt safe from 'improper proposals' had she been left alone with him; see R. V. C. Bodley, 'The Man who Insulted King Edward', *Sunday Times*, 5 Jan. 1969. Cf. also, Masterman (ed.), *Mary Gladstone*, p. 337.

16 O'Connor, *Memoirs*, i, pp. 320–21.

17 LHJ, 7 Aug. 1885 (LHP, dep. 371).

18 According to Marie Belloc Lowndes, quoted in Lowndes (ed.), *Diaries*, pp. 114–16, though this story appears, as with so many others, to have originated with Stead; see his *Deliverance or Doom*?

19 DP, Add. MS 49455, ff. 254–57.

20 See the diary entry quoted above, p. 178.

21 7 Sept. 1916 (DP, Add. MS 43967, ff. 287–88), my emphasis. Cf. also, Chamberlain to Morley, 22 Oct. 1885: '... I am *certain* Dilke is innocent of the charge brought against

him. I do not answer for his whole life – nor for my own – nor for any man's – but the particular charge and its accompaniments are false.' Quoted in Garvin, *Life of Chamberlain*, ii, p. 45.

22 Stead, 'The Sin of Ananias and Sapphira'.

23 See his rather unclear letter to R. B. Hithersay, 28 Aug. 1892 (REND, 4/2).

24 Quoted in Shane Leslie, *Memoir of J. E. C. Bodley* (1930), p. 45. Bodley believed that the scandal ruined his own chance of a great career in politics but, despite this, he remained convinced of Dilke's innocence; see Bodley, 'The Man who Insulted King Edward'.

25 M. Asquith, *Autobiography* (2 vols, 1920–22), i, pp. 146–47. Apart, that is, from the gossip about his 'amours' with society ladies like Lady Randolph Churchill and Mrs Sands.

26 T. H. Ford, 'A. V. Dicey and the Destruction of Sir Charles Dilke', *Eire-Ireland*, 11, (1977), pp. 27–50; and *Albert Venn Dicey: The Man and his Times* (Chichester, 1985), pp. 157–58.

27 Jenkins, *Dilke*, pp. 347–53; Rhodes James, *Rosebery*, pp. 182–88. Stead repeated the rumour in his 'The Sin of Ananias and Sapphira'.

28 DP, Add. MSS 43941, ff. 147–48; 49454, ff. 4, 33; 49610, ff. 253–56, 260–61.

29 For early 'threatening letters', see DP, Add. MSS 43924, f. 77; 43936, ff. 66–67; 43938, ff. 198–99, 353–54; 49433, f. 1; and Dilke's letter to Granville, 27 July 1885, to the effect that Chamberlain, 'who knows the motives', knew also that the plot had been 'long hatching'. GP, PRO 30/29/29A.

30 JC, 5/24/122.

31 REND, 12/1.

32 REND, 7/1.

33 Note by Roskill dated 21 Jan. 1979 (ibid.).

34 This is the view also of Francis Bywater in an unpublished article entitled 'Joseph Chamberlain and the Dilke Case', an extract of which is lodged at REND, 13/6.

35 See report in *The Times*, 13 Feb. 1886. The leader in *The Times* was also not unfavourable to Dilke; it re-emphasised the points made by Butt.

36 Marion Rawson claimed that John Roskill, Maye Dilke's son-in-law, told her that Chamberlain had even visited Maye to beg her not to give evidence against Dilke. REND, 13/3. As with other of Mrs Rawson's claims, there is no evidence to support this.

37 Chamberlain's later support for Matthews' candidature can likewise be explained in terms of his political realism.

38 Askwith, *Lady Dilke*, pp. 172–74.

39 Quoted in ibid., p. 174.

40 Taylor introduced yet another prime mover in the conspiracy against Dilke – his sister-in-law Maye – suggesting that the two had had an affair after Ashton's death. I am grateful to Granada Television for loaning me a video-recording of this play.

41 James had a low opinion of Dilke. They had met at a Cambridge dinner in 1878, and James had found him wanting in either 'genius or inspiration'. He added that Dilke's reputation was only just recovering from attacking the Queen and having his first wife cremated. See L. Edel, *Henry James*, ii, *The Conquest of London, 1870–1883* (1962), pp. 335, 337, 356; iii, *The Middle Years, 1884–1894* (1963), p. 106.

42 Quoted in Jenkins, *Dilke*, pp. 218–19.

43 Ibid., p. 356. There is no doubt that Mrs Rogerson's brother and Crawford's solicitor, Charles Stewart, disliked Dilke intensely and wanted to see him ruined.

44 See Dilke to Mrs Pattison, 6 March 1885 (DP, Add. MS 43906, f. 39).

45 So much so that, at the second trial, Crawford testified that her earnest denial had made him suspicious. Also, at the first trial Crawford had told the court that the exchange leading to the confession had been prompted and initiated by Virginia, who was in bed when he got home and clearly wanted to discuss the letter that was waiting for him.

46 Quoted in Jenkins, *Dilke*, p. 262. Her expectation that the case would not be contested might explain why she named Fanny in her confession – it was useful to choose someone who had left Dilke's employ and might be difficult to trace, and yet added a touch of authenticity.

47 Quoted ibid., p. 351.

48 Lord Simon of Glaisdale to Lord Eustace Roskill, 4 Dec. 1976 (REND, 13/7). Simon had advised Jenkins that evidence about Dilke's adultery with Mrs Eustace Smith would have been inadmissable. Roskill had questioned this in a review of Jenkins's book. In their correspondence of 1976 they were still unable to agree on this particular point of law.

49 See below, p. 230.

Notes to Chapter 13

1 *The Times*, 22 July 1885.
2 DP, Add. MS 43875, ff. 266–69.
3 G. & T., ii, p. 159.
4 Its publication has frequently been placed in July, but see Jenkins, *Gladstone, Whiggery and the Liberal Party*, p. 202.
5 P. Fraser, *Joseph Chamberlain: Radicalism and Empire, 1868–1914* (1966), pp. 45–46, 51.
6 Hamer, *Liberal Politics*, p. 103; Barker, *Gladstone and Radicalism*, pp. 37–39.
7 2 Sept. 1885 (DP, Add. MS 43892, f. 59).
8 3 Sept. 1885 (ibid., f. 60). Chamberlain responded in a speech at Warrington on 8 September by referring to Hartington as Rip Van Winkle.
9 This is argued by Jenkins, *Gladstone, Whiggery and the Liberal Party*, pp. 214–15.
10 JC, 5/34/77–78.
11 DP, Add. MS 43887, f. 168.
12 20 Sept. 1885, quoted in Hamer, *Liberal Politics*, p. 107.
13 20 Sept. 1885 (JC, 5/34/79).
14 JC, 5/24/32. He went on to complain of Lefevre's weakness at a critical moment, adding: 'I shall be awfully glad when you can do your share.'
15 7 Oct. 1885 (DP, Add. MS 43887, f. 180).
16 JC, 5/24/434.
17 JC, 5/38/151.
18 *The Times*, 14 Oct. 1885. The speech was reprinted by the National Liberal Federation: C. W. Dilke, *Local Government* (1885).
19 Chamberlain to Dilke, 13, 17, 20 and 26 Oct. 1885 (DP, Add. MS 43887, ff. 187–91, 194).
20 DP, Add. MS 43940, ff. 69–73.
21 A. Simon, 'Church Disestablishment as a Factor in the General Election of 1885', *Historical Journal*, 18 (1975), pp. 791–820.
22 A. Simon, 'Joseph Chamberlain and Free Education in the Election of 1885', *History of Education*, 2 (1973), pp. 56–78.
23 N. Blewett, *The Peers, the Parties and the People* (1972), p. 6.
24 JC, 5/24/145.
25 To Chamberlain, 30 Nov. 1885, quoted in Simon, 'Church Disestablishment', p. 807.
26 T. W. Heyck, *The Dimensions of British Radicalism: The Case of Ireland, 1874–95* (1974), pp. 115–16, claims that radical membership rose from *c.* 33 percent to *c.* 48 percent. This is undoubtedly an overestimate as it does not take into account the changing nature of radicalism, the degree of commitment among 'radicals' to a full range of radical issues, or more pertinently, the differences that persisted over questions of foreign and imperial policy. Cf. Grosvenor's contemporary estimate of radical strength at about one-third of the party. Interpenetration of economic interests makes precise calculations difficult. See Jenkins, *Gladstone, Whiggery and Liberalism*, pp. 225–27; Lubenow, *Parliamentary Politics*, pp. 50, 55–59.
27 Garvin, *Life of Chamberlain*, ii, p. 130; JC, 5/24/157 and 450.
28 Quoted in Lubenow, *Parliamentary Politics*, p. 209.
29 *Daily News*, 10 Dec. 1885.
30 M. Balfour, *Britain and Joseph Chamberlain* (1985), p. 173. Dilke was aware that his action would be interpreted in this way. See his letter to Chamberlain below, pp. 222–23.
31 Hamer, *Morley*, p. 169.
32 13 Dec. 1885, quoted in Rhodes James, *Rosebery*, p. 175.

33 4 Jan. 1886 (JC, 5/38/41).
34 HGP, Add. MS 46051, ff. 226–31.
35 Quoted in Garvin, *Life of Chamberlain*, ii, pp. 133–34.
36 16 Dec. 1885 (DP, Add. MS 43887, f. 211).
37 See, e.g., Chamberlain to his brother Arthur, spring 1886: 'Either Mr Gladstone will succeed and get the Irish question out of the way, or he will fail. In either case he will retire from politics and I do not suppose the Liberal party will accept Childers or even John Morley as its permanent leader.' Quoted in J. W. Derry, *The Radical Tradition: Tom Paine to Lloyd George* (1967), p. 336.
38 JC, 5/24/162–63. It was not the scandal that led him to anticipate defeat, but rather that Chelsea was becoming more residential and that it would be impossible to win back voters on the Irish programme. Ibid.
39 17 Dec. 1885 (DP, Add. MS 43887, ff. 213–15).
40 Ibid., f. 216; JC, 5/24/164.
41 26 Dec. 1885 (DP, Add. MS 43887, ff. 223–26).
42 Ibid., ff. 227–28, 231–32; JC, 5/24/166; *Rugby Advertiser*, 2 Jan. 1886.
43 JC, 5/24/169–70.
44 LHJ, 26 Jan. 1886 (LHP, dep. 377).
45 DP, Add. MS 43940, f. 106. Chamberlain, however, recalled that it was drafted by him and Harcourt at the latter's house. Garvin, *Life of Chamberlain*, ii, p. 165 and n.
46 See Matthew (ed.), *Gladstone Diaries*, xi, p. 488 and n. Harcourt wanted the office of Postmaster-General kept open for Dilke until the outcome of the trial was known. LHJ, 2 and 3 Feb. 1886 (LHP, dep. 377).
47 DP, Add. MSS 43940, ff. 110–11; 49610, f. 160. Albeit, Rosebery's immediate ambition was, oddly, to become Governor of Victoria or New South Wales. On the subject of ambition, Dilke later added: 'I have since known Winston Churchill.' DP, Add. MS 43934, ff. 195–97.
48 DP, Add. MSS 43937, f. 16; 43940, ff. 119–29.
49 Quoted in Hamer, *Morley*, p. 174.
50 JC, 5/24/171.
51 DP, Add. MS 43927, f. 26.
52 DP, Add. MSS 43888, f. 30; 43940, ff. 130–32.
53 Quoted in Judd, *Radical Joe*, p. 149.
54 DP, Add. MS 43888, f. 32.
55 7 Apr. 1886 (JC, 5/24/175–76).
56 See, e.g., Labouchere to Chamberlain, 31 March 1886: 'Ireland is but a pawn in the game.' Quoted in P. Adelman, *Victorian Radicalism: The Middle-Class Experience, 1830–1914* (1984), p. 126.
57 DP, Add. MS 43888, f. 43.
58 JC, 5/24/177.
59 DP, Add. MS 43888, ff. 45–46.
60 Ibid., f. 48.
61 JC, 5/24/178 (my emphasis).
62 DP, Add. MS 43888, f. 50. Chamberlain's ruthlessness to former allies was well illustrated by his break with Morley: 'If you go into the Cabinet without me', he told him, 'you will have me against you, and I shall smash you.' Quoted in Christie, *Transition to Democracy*, p. 81. Dilke was not blind to this trait of Chamberlain's, telling Mrs Pattison in October 1881 of 'the unforgiving ferocity he displays when people don't do as he & I wish'. DP, Add. MS 43904, ff. 63–64.
63 6 May 1886 (JC, 5/24/179).
64 DP, Add. MSS 43889, ff. 30–31; 43927, f. 34; 43941, ff. 116–19, 259.
65 He continued to favour the devolutionary national boards scheme, and remained silent during the debates on the Second Home Rule Bill in 1893.
66 G. & T. i, p. 520n.; speech at Queen's Park, 21 June 1886 (*The Times*, 22 June 1886).

Notes to Chapter 14

1 Harvie, *The Lights of Liberalism*, p. 323n.
2 DP, Add. MS 43940, ff. 160–61; Thursfield MS, Eng. Letts. e.93, f. 35. However, he wrote occasional pieces for American and Australian newspapers for which he was well paid, and he hoped for a while that *The Times* might engage him as an adviser on foreign news. Ibid., ff. 47–48.
3 C. W. Dilke, *The Present Position of European Politics* (1887), esp. pp. 1, 42–47, 276. The articles appeared in France in the *Nouvelle Revue*.
4 C. W. Dilke, *The British Army* (1888), p. 3.
5 *Star*, 27 Feb. 1888.
6 Apr. 1887 (DP, Add. MS 43884, ff. 221–23). Notes from his engagement books reveal the extent of his involvement with Chelsea affairs at this time, serving on such bizarre bodies as the Laundry Committee and the Inmates Examination Committee; see DP, Add. MS 49405, passim.
7 DP, Add. MS 43940, ff. 84, 164; J. P. D. Dunbabin, 'The Politics of the Establishment of County Councils', *Historical Journal*, 8 (1965), pp. 226–52.
8 *Star*, 21 March 1888; C. W. Dilke and H. P. Cobb, *Notes on the Local Government Bills* (1888); C. W. Dilke, H. P. Cobb, H. Gardner, W. A. McArthur and F. S. Stevenson, *Local Government Bills: Notes on the Chief Amendments* (1888); DP, Add. MS 43941, ff. 75–77.
9 Ibid., f. 84.
10 Davis, *Reforming London*, pp. 129–31.
11 Dilke described the chapters on Indian defence as 'undiluted Roberts'. To Thursfield, 25 Nov. 1888 (Thursfield MS, Eng. Letts. e.93, ff. 59–60).
12 DP, Add. MS 43893, ff. 138–39; C. W. Dilke, 'The Baluch and Afghan Frontiers of India', *Fortnightly Review*, 45 (1889), pp. 293–324, 445–80; Lord Roberts Papers, 7101–23–23–1 and 3.
13 To Macmillan, 12 June 1907; Macmillan (Publishers) Papers, Add. MS 55242, f. 120.
14 *Problems*, i, p. vii.
15 DP, Add. MS 43941, ff. 132–35.
16 C. W. Dilke, 'The Conservative Foreign Policy', *Fortnightly Review*, 51 (1892), pp. 1–9.
17 C. W. Dilke, 'Egypt: Now, and After?', *Speaker*, 4 (1891), pp. 730–33.
18 ?18 Feb. 1892 (DP, Add. MS 43889, f. 83).
19 H. S. Wilkinson, *Thirty-Five Years, 1874–1909* (1933), pp. 119–28; SWP, 9011–42–13/11/12. Wilkinson also favoured an alliance with Germany and Italy, but Dilke was dead against that: 'In a sort of way I can swallow [naval] blockade, & I never *absolutely* rejected it. Alliances I can't swallow at all, as they are, to us, impossible.' Ibid., 13/11/13. He was not against alliances *per se*, but thought that the House of Commons was unlikely to enter into any such commitments, especially as Britain would gain little advantage thereby. Ibid., 13/11/20.
20 C. W. Dilke and H. S. Wilkinson, *Imperial Defence* (1892), p. 14 and passim. Dilke was always generous in acknowledging Wilkinson's preponderant part in writing this. See, e.g., SWP, 9011–42–13/10. He admonished Macmillan (19 Apr. 1892) for not giving it, a 'much better' book than *Problems*, the publicity it deserved. Macmillan (Publishers) Papers, Add. MS 55242, ff. 114–15.
21 3 Oct. 1888 (JC, 5/24/206).
22 DP, Add. MS 43941, f. 14.
23 Dilke found the Glasgow offer particularly interesting as Crawford represented the county. JC, 5/24/219.

24 17 June 1889 (DP, Add. MS 43892, ff. 77–78).
25 10 Aug. 1889 (DP, Add. MS 43875, ff. 276–78).
26 JC, 5/24/220. He had contemplated travelling to the Cape in the autumn of 1890 at the invitation of Cecil Rhodes, whom he had met in spring 1889 and liked. South Africa was one of the few parts of the globe that he never visited. Dilke to Roberts, 4 June 1889 (Lord Roberts Papers, 7101–23–23–22).

Notes to Chapter 15

1 W. Tuckwell, *Reminiscences of a Radical Parson* (1905), pp. 12–13.
2 Quoted in H. M. Lynd, *England in the Eighteen-Eighties* (1968; 1st edn, 1945), p. 7.
3 Quoted in Gulley, *Joseph Chamberlain and English Social Politics*, pp. 254–55 and n.
4 21 Apr. 1893 (DP, Add. MS 43889, ff. 88–89). For the intriguing argument that Chamberlain may, instead, have radicalised the Conservative Party by pushing it in a corporate direction, see Alan Hooper, 'From Liberal-Radicalism to Conservative Corporatism: The Pursuit of "Radical Business" in "Tory Livery"', in R. Bellamy (ed.), *Victorian Liberalism: Nineteenth-Century Political Thought and Practice* (1990), ch. 11. Hooper sees radicalism as 'an incubator of corporatism', and argues that Chamberlain used it, albeit with only limited success, to forge a new partnership between large-scale capital and well-paid workers.
5 9 June 1885 (*Manchester Guardian*, 10 June 1885).
6 Speeches at Aylesbury, 10 Dec. 1884; Chiswick, 17 Jan. 1884; and Kensington, 13 Jan. 1885 (*The Times*, 11 Dec. 1884; 18 Jan. 1884; 14 Jan. 1885). He had said half-jokingly to Harcourt that, after the first election under the new constitution, the radicals would be opposed by 'such violent men' that they would henceforward be the moderates. LHJ, 1 Dec. 1884 (LHP, dep. 362).
7 Speech at Clerkenwell, 26 May 1891 (*DFM*, 29 May 1891).
8 See R. Rodger, 'Political Economy, Ideology and the Persistence of Working-Class Housing Problems in Britain, 1850–1914', *International Review of Social History*, 32 (1987), pp. 109–43; and above, p. 132.
9 For an early sign of the tendency of his thought on this question, see Dilke, *Problems*, ii, pp. 289–90.
10 See above, p. 135. He never, even in later life, had much to say on unemployment issues. He supported plans to abolish the poor law and introduce unemployment insurance, and regarded the establishment of labour exchanges and public works schemes such as reafforestation as 'palliatives'. See, e.g., *DFM*, 11 June 1909; *PD*(5), 1, cols 129–33; 4, cols 951–56; 13, cols 433–36. Unemployment was a vital interest to labour and the fact that a Liberal as advanced as Dilke did not include it among his priorities goes some way towards explaining why the working class would be destined to form their own party.
11 DP, Add. MS 43930, f. 134. In 1890 he described the New Testament as the inspiration for 'the whole of the movement in the present century for the improvement in the condition of the people... Modern socialism itself... has been born in and inspired by Christianity.' C. W. Dilke, *A Radical Programme* (1890), pp. 20–21.
12 *Chelsea News*, 23 Aug. 1879; DP, Add. MS 43934, ff. 119–20; N. C. Soldon, *Women in British Trade Unions, 1874–1976* (1978), pp. 16–17.
13 Ibid., pp. 27–28.
14 R. Feurer, 'The Meaning of "Sisterhood": The British Women's Movement and Protective Labor Legislation, 1870–1900', *Victorian Studies*, 31 (1988), pp. 233–60; E. F. Dilke, *The Book of the Spiritual Life* (1905), pp. 44, 115–16. Cf. below, p. 273 for the opposition of some female suffragists to Dilke's adult suffrage strategy.
15 Dilke to Reinach, 25 Aug. 1888 (DP, Add. MS 43884, f. 243).
16 Speech at Lydbrook, 10 May 1889 (*DFM*, 17 May 1889). Cf. Hobhouse, quoted above, p. xxviii.
17 Dilke, *A Radical Programme*, pp. 53–55.
18 Ibid., pp. 23–24.

19 Ibid., pp. 31, 50–51, 54.
20 The success of Progessivism in London suggests that his expectations may not have been without some foundation. Cf. P. Thane, 'Labour and Local Politics: Radicalism, Democracy and Social Reform, 1880–1914', in E. F. Biagini and A. J. Reid (eds), *Currents of Radicalism: Popular Radicalism, Organised Labour and Party Politics in Britain, 1850–1914* (Cambridge, 1991), ch. 11.
21 Heyck, *Dimensions*, p. 167.
22 Lubenow, *Parliamentary Politics*, pp. 220–25, 263, 284. Lubenow, however, interprets his findings rather differently to the account presented here. He argues that because the cleavage of 1886 was political rather than social, a proposition that his own statistics do not conclusively bear out, it did not profoundly threaten the future vitality of the party. Likewise, G. R. Searle, 'The Edwardian Liberal Party and Business', *English Historical Review*, 98 (1983), pp. 28–60, contests the view that the party was losing its support among business interests to the Conservatives and becoming increasingly a party of professional men.
23 Blewett, *The Peers*, pp. 22–23.
24 The fact that many industrial capitalists continued to support the Liberal Party, and were encouraged to do so by the tariff reform campaign, hampered its capacity to deal with social and labour issues.
25 J. P. D. Dunbabin, 'Parliamentary Elections in Great Britain, 1868–1900: A Psephological Note', *English Historical Review*, 81 (1966), pp.95–96.
26 *Pace* Barker, *Gladstone and Radicalism*, who has attempted to show that Gladstone was responsive to radical ideas within the party and to such a degree that by 1892 he had embraced much of the new liberal thinking, making his fourth and last administration one of the most successful reforming governments of the nineteenth century. It has to be said that this is not how he was perceived by the new liberal thinkers themselves, who regarded him as too old and outmoded and saw his obsession with Ireland as an obstacle to the modernisation of the party.
27 A. Reid (ed.), *The New Liberal Programme: Contributed by Representatives of the Liberal Party* (1886). Reid's new Liberal programme, a purely pragmatic response to political circumstances and centred on the desirability of implementing conventional policies like Home Rule and land reform, should not be confused with the new liberalism of the 1890s, which was a refinement of ideology.
28 L. A. Atherley-Jones, *Looking Back: Reminiscences of a Political Career* (1925), p. 54.
29 Quoted in Hamer, *Liberal Politics*, p. 151.
30 Quoted in Barker, *Gladstone and Radicalism*, p. 185.
31 S. Maccoby, *English Radicalism, 1886–1914* (1953), pp. 58–62.
32 Curiously, his piece, a review of the 1896 session, focused on procedural matters, and had nothing to say about social reform. C. W. Dilke, 'The Late Session', *Progressive Review*, 1 (1896), pp. 53–62.
33 There is a massive literature on the subject, some of which is cited in subsequent footnotes – but for useful summaries of the historiographical debate, see K. Laybourn, *The Rise of Labour: The British Labour Party 1890–1979* (1988), pp. 9–31; J. A. Thompson, 'The Historians and the Decline of the Liberal Party', *Albion*, 22 (1990), pp. 65–83; and the editors' introductory chapter in Biagini and Reid (eds), *Currents of Radicalism*. See also G. Hosking and A. King, 'Radicals and Whigs in the British Liberal Party, 1906–14', in W. O. Aydelotte (ed.), *The History of Parliamentary Behavior* (Princeton, NJ, 1977), pp. 136–58, who, in addition to summarising the two positions, come down on the side of the Accidentalists by showing that there were no discernible divisions of any significance in the Liberal Party of 1906–14 that presaged the post-1916 split. It was therefore, they conclude, occasioned by the war and would not otherwise have taken place.
34 See especially, P. F. Clarke, *Lancashire and the New Liberalism* (1971). Clarke's is a subtle

analysis that does not seek to deny the rise of class politics but which shows rather how the new liberalism helped the Liberal Party to adapt to it.

35 Cf. the radical programme with the TUC manifestos of 1880, 1885, 1886 and 1905, in B. C. Roberts, *The Trades Union Congress* (1958), pp. 106, 114–15, 192.

36 *Contra* M. Freeden, *The New Liberalism* (Oxford, 1978), esp. p. 145.

37 Lancashire, the focus of Clarke's study, was perhaps atypical in its espousal of new liberalism. Cf. K. O. Morgan, 'The New Liberalism and the Challenge of Labour: The Welsh Experience, 1885–1929', in K. D. Brown (ed.), *Essays in Anti-Labour History* (1974), ch. 7, on Wales; and K. Laybourn and J. Reynolds, *Liberalism and the Rise of Labour, 1890–1918* (1984), on West Yorkshire.

38 This resilience on the part of the old liberalism has led one historian to suggest that progressivism may have been more of a disruptive than a rejuvenating influence. See M. Bentley, *The Climax of Liberal Politics: British Liberalism in Theory and Practice, 1868–1918* (1987), p. 145.

39 Cf. also the less well-known indictment of Liberal failures by A. Fenner Brockway, *Labour and Liberalism* (Manchester, n.d. but 1913 or early 1914).

40 For the two sides of the argument, see H. C. G. Matthew, R.I McKibbin and J. A. Kay, 'The Franchise Factor in the Rise of the Labour Party', *English Historical Review*, 91 (1976), pp. 723–52; and D. Tanner, 'The Parliamentary Electoral System, the "Fourth Reform Act" and the Rise of Labour in England and Wales', *Bulletin of the Institute of Historical Research*, 56 (1983), pp. 205–19. The debate on voting patterns does not, however, resolve imponderable questions concerning voting behaviour, especially the tactical considerations that came into play under the post-1885 electoral system whenever more than two parties were in contention. The Liberals, as the established party, may well have benefited for much of the pre-war period from *negative* votes cast primarily with the intention of keeping the Conservatives out and until such time as Labour, the party trying to break into the system, was perceived to be a more serious electoral force.

41 A. Howkins, 'Edwardian Liberalism and Industrial Unrest: A Class View of the Decline of Liberalism', *History Workshop*, 4 (1977), pp. 143–61; G. L. Bernstein, *Liberalism and Liberal Politics in Edwardian England* (1986); J. F. Glaser, 'English Nonconformity and the Decline of Liberalism', *American Historical Review*, 63 (1958), pp. 352–63.

42 D. Powell, 'The New Liberalism and the Rise of Labour, 1886–1906', *Historical Journal*, 29 (1986), pp. 369–93. He observes that 'in the struggle between capital and labour the Liberals were always likely to be referees rather than committed protagonists'.

43 Quoted in E. Halévy, *Imperialism and the Rise of Labour (1895–1905)* (1961; 1st edn, 1926), p. 231n.

44 Though working-class suspicions may have diminished over time. See P. Thane, 'The Working Class and State "Welfare" in Britain, 1880–1914', *Historical Journal*, 27 (1984), pp. 877–900; and idem, 'The Labour Party and State "Welfare"', in K. D. Brown (ed.), *The First Labour Party, 1906–1914* (1985), ch. 8.

45 Nicholls, 'The English Middle Class'.

46 See D. Tanner, *Political Change and the Labour Party, 1900–1918* (Cambridge, 1990).

47 As Powell has argued, the character of new liberalism was quickly compromised once the Labour Party came into existence – for example, by the electoral pact of 1903, and by the special protection granted to the trade unions under the Trade Disputes Act. Powell, 'The New Liberalism'.

Notes to Chapter 16

1 His speech in Cumberland on 31 July 1893 completed his attendance at every district within the MFGB. When speaking outside the federation area, he encouraged the miners to affiliate.

2 E.g., he was the Yorkshire miners' first choice as speaker for three years in succession (1891–93). *DFM*, 23 June 1893.

3 *Wakefield Express*, 25 June, 2 July 1892.

4 DP, Add. MS 43895, ff. 175–77.

5 *The Times*, 6 March 1891.

6 Dilke calculated that he sent out at least 25,000 copies. To Bodley, 21 [March 1891?] (Bodley MS, Eng. Lett. d.174, ff. 80–81).

7 STED, 1/20.

8 Copy of note by Gladstone marked 'Secret', 13 March 1891 (BP, Add. MS 47911, ff. 107–8).

9 JC, 5/24/230. Between 9 March and 11 June he spoke at forty meetings in the Forest.

10 DP, Add. MS 43941, ff. 214–15; *DFM*, 12 June 1891.

11 JC, 5/24/234; DP, Add. MS 43889, ff. 62, 225, 242, 249.

12 Speeches at Yorkley, 11 June 1890; Lydney, 11 June 1891; Huntley, 2 June 1892 (*DFM*, 13 June 1890; 12 June 1891; 3 June 1892).

13 Of the federation areas balloted, only the Forest of Dean was opposed to striking. This may have been due to Dilke's moderating influence, but it was more likely because the Forest miners already had a system approaching eight hours. See R. Page Arnot, *The Miners* (1949), p. 135; DP, Add. MS 43941, f. 113; B. McCormick and J. W. Williams, 'The Miners and the Eight-Hour Day, 1863–1901', *Economic History Review*, second series, 12 (1959–60), p. 227.

14 Page Arnot, *The Miners*, pp. 167–70, 178.

15 15 Feb. 1892 (DP, Add. MS 43892, f. 167).

16 DP, Add. MS 43941, ff. 215, 232, 247; Jenkins, *Dilke*, pp. 380–81.

17 To Charles Pearson, 30 Aug. [1892?] (Pearson MS, Eng. Letts. d.187, ff. 104–5). Lady Dilke was a popular figure in the Forest and a good vote-winner.

18 *DFM*, 14 July 1892. The registered electorate was 10,782.

19 Gordon, *The Red Earl*, ii, pp. 212–13.

20 DP, Add. MS 43941, f. 271.

21 It is dealt with cursorily in G. & T., ii, pp. 286, 347.

22 B. Gainer, *The Aliens Invasion: The Origins of the Aliens Act of 1905* (1972), p. 146.

23 He had always opposed state-assisted emigration schemes, preferring to find effective domestic remedies for pauperism rather than to export the problem. See, e.g., C. W. Dilke, *Colonies* (1869), p. 20; *Chelsea News*, 3 Apr., 24 July 1869; DP, Add. MS 43931, f. 54; *PD*(3), 199, cols 1054–59. At the LGB his 'chief new departure' had been to relax the restrictions on the emigration of pauper children. DP, Add. MS 43938, ff. 189–90. He had opposed aid for Irish emigration arguing that it would only lead next to pressure 'to give public money for emigration from East End of London'. Carlingford's diary, 25 July 1883 (CP, Add. MS 63691, f. 193).

24 11 Feb. 1893, *PD*(4), 8, cols 1182–94; Gainer, *The Aliens Invasion*, p. 146.

25 E.g., B. Semmel, *Imperialism and Social Reform* (1960), p. 57.

26 DP, Add. MSS 43875, ff. 287–96; 43941, f. 270; *PD*(4), 9, cols 1634–49.

27 C. W. Dilke, 'The Uganda Problem', *Fortnightly Review*, 53 (1893), pp. 145–61; *PD*(4), 25, cols 194–208.

28 DP, Add. MSS 43877, ff. 2–3; 43941, ff. 275–82; 43945, ff. 13–29; Sandars MS, Eng. Hist. c.725, ff. 94–99. Dilke preferred to cooperate with Balfour rather than Chamberlain on this particular question because the latter was 'oddly enough, a much stronger party man'. Ibid. The correspondence in which the various signatories of the letter hammered out a basis for agreement is at SWP, 9011–42–13/9. Dilke had, for a moment, wanted to stop the letter following a speech by Balfour at Manchester in which he had indicated his sympathy for the idea. Ibid.

29 DP, Add. MSS 43877, ff. 5–6; 43889, f. 114; G. & T., ii, p. 457.

30 Wilkinson, *Thirty-Five Years*, pp. 182–83.

31 *PD*(4), 22, cols 462–76; 31, cols 800–8; 36, cols 1381–85.

32 Chamberlain to Dilke, 21 Apr. 1893 (JC, 5/24/555). Cf. Churchill to Dilke, 16 March 1894 (DP, Add. MS 43833, f. 88) in which he suggested excluding Northumberland and Durham from the bill of 1894.

33 Page Arnot, *The Miners*, p. 197; *PD*(4), 11, cols 1887–95.

34 DP, Add. MS43941, f. 290. Tillett repeated the offer in November, but Dilke again declined: 'I prefer real independence.' Ibid., f. 291.

35 C. W. Dilke, 'Lord Rosebery's Administration', *North American Review*, 158 (1894), p. 534; G. & T., ii, p. 291.

36 H. E. Kearley (Viscount Devonport), *The Travelled Road: Some Memories of a Busy Life* (Rochester, n.d., 1935?), pp. 54–55.

37 DP, Add. MS 43919, ff. 16–17.

38 *PD*(4), 12, cols 258–64; Royal Commission on the Selection of Justices of the Peace, *PP*, 1910, xxxviii, pp. 647–967.

39 *PD*(4), 8, cols 502, 504, 1522–25; 10, cols 1712–16.

40 DP, Add. MS 43941, f. 274; *PD*(4), 10, cols 712–16; 17, 19–21, passim.

41 Ibid., 23, cols 388–89; 24, cols 74–88.

42 B. Harrison, 'Women's Suffrage at Westminster, 1866–1928', in M. Bentley and J. Stevenson (eds), *High and Low Politics in Modern Britain: Ten Studies* (Oxford, 1983), pp. 98–100.

43 26 July 1894 (DP, Add. MS 43915, ff. 194–95).

44 *PD*(4), 9, cols 73–79; 24, cols 74–88; JC, 5/24/261 and 264.

45 C. W. Dilke, 'Against Reformed Upper Houses', *Subjects of the Day*, 4 (1891), pp. 96–103.

46 Dilke, 'Lord Rosebery's Administration'.

47 H. C. G. Matthew, *The Liberal Imperialists: The Ideas and Politics of a Post-Gladstonian Elite* (1973), p. 261.

48 D. Brooks (ed.), *The Destruction of Lord Rosebery: From the Diary of Sir Edward Hamilton 1894–1895* (1986), pp. 58–59, 218–19. Rosebery later claimed that his threat was a tactical one aimed at restoring party discipline; see P. Stansky, *Ambitions and Strategies: The Struggle for the Leadership of the Liberal Party in the 1890s* (Oxford, 1964), p. 153. At this moment as well, Dilke was making it clear to the Conservative whips that the radicals would be prepared to support a Tory candidate for the vacant Speakership (Sandars MS, Eng. Hist. c.726, ff. 47–50), which no doubt compounded Campbell-Bannerman's opinion of him as an 'insatiate intriguer' (see below, p. 278), for the War Secretary badly wanted the job himself.

49 DP, Add. MS 43941, f. 294; Standing Committee on Trade, *PP*, 1895, x.

50 WHP, dep. 80, ff. 70–71; *PD*(4), 32, cols 1464–70.

51 Quoted in P. Weiler, *The New Liberalism: Liberal Social Theory in Great Britain, 1889–1914* (1982), p. 64.

52 Atherley-Jones, *Looking Back*, p. 67.

Notes to Chapter 17

1 DP, Add. MS 43915, f. 237. Dilke, Labouchere, Sir James Carmichael and Philip Stanhope were the authors of the manifesto. Its fourteen other signatories provide a clue to the membership of the Radical Committee at this time: W. Allen, J. Bayley, W. P. Byles, G. B. Clark, J. H. Dalziel, H. Hoare, H. S. Leon, J. A. Murray Macdonald, J. H. Maden, A. C. Morton, S. Norton, W. Wedderburn, T. P. Whittaker and A. G. Symonds.

2 Ibid., ff. 244, 246.

3 To D. H. Saunders, 24 March 1896, quoted in H. V. Emy, *Liberals, Radicals, and Social Politics, 1892–1914* (1973), pp. 64–65.

4 For the criticisms raised by the radicals at the Huddersfield meeting, 26–27 March 1896, and its president's reply, see R. Spence Watson, *The National Liberal Federation* (1907), pp. 191–96. In May the Radical Committee was reconstituted (notable new members included Lloyd George, Atherley-Jones and Ben Pickard), but Dilke did not like its new determination to formulate a statement of policy and remained aloof from its activities for a time. Emy, *Liberals, Radicals*, pp. 65, 76–78.

5 P. C. Hoffman, *They Also Serve: The Story of the Shop-Worker* (1949), pp. 4–5, 8; *PD*(4), 132, cols 794–99; 135, cols 577–78.

6 To give just one example, the exemptions to the Factory Acts, which allowed the fish-curing trade to employ women for long hours for a specified number of days in the year, were abused by the practice of moving the workers around the coast with the seasonal migration of the fish. In his annual speeches Dilke condemned similar abuses in a whole range of trades. His parliamentary interventions are too numerous to list in full here, but can be found by reference to the index of *PD*, 1898–1910.

7 *DFM*, 23 Nov. 1906; G. & T., ii, p. 355.

8 This was not, *contra* Gwynn and Tuckwell, a precedent, for Mrs Nassau Senior had been appointed for a short period as a poor law inspector in 1871. However, Dilke's was certainly the more significant departure. He had also offered inspectorships to working-class leaders like Burt and Broadhurst.

9 DP, Add. MS 43918, ff. 26–27.

10 C. W. Dilke, *Fines and Deductions* (Huddersfield, 1896), pp. 4, 6. This pamphlet gives numerous examples of trivial offences for which fines were exacted. A similar abuse was that of 'time-cribbing' whereby an employer would add a couple of minutes on to the working day, perhaps thereby gaining an extra hour's work from each employee per week.

11 *PD*(4), 37, col. 360; 40, col. 592; 43, col. 760; *DFM*, 16 July 1897. Thereafter, he tabled a regulation bill annually.

12 *DFM*, 14 Aug. 1891, 28 Oct. 1892.

13 *PD*(4), 18, cols 478–80; 48, cols 1451–54; 49, cols 658–65, 1274–77; *DFM*, 27 Aug. 1897.

14 18 Dec. 1898 (JC, 5/24/274).

15 DP, Add. MS 43877, f. 11; *PD*(4), 50, cols 187–89.

16 Ibid., 58, cols 686–89, 1317–40.

17 The essay had originally appeared as C. W. Dilke, 'Newfoundland', *Pall Mall Magazine*, 17 (1899), pp. 211–16. See also, 'Men, Women and Events', *Cosmopolitan*, 37 (1904), pp. 241–42. This same article claimed that Dilke was still considered 'a strong possibility for the premiership'.

18 *DFM*, 25 Jan. 1901; G. & T., ii, p. 494.

19 A. H. Lawrence, 'Great Britain as a Military Power: An Interview with Sir Charles

Dilke', *Idler*, 13 (1898), pp. 273–79. He had privately disliked the Chamberlain-Milner policy leading up to the war but had remained silent, probably to avoid embarrassing his former friend who had large financial interests in South Africa; see DP, Add. MS 43925, f. 52.

20 Bannerman to Bryce, 11 Jan. 1900, quoted in J. A. Spender, *Life of Sir Henry Campbell-Bannerman* (2 vols, 1923), i, p. 270.

21 W. S. Hamer, *The British Army: Civil-Military Relations, 1885–1905* (Oxford, 1970), pp. 177–78; Lady Dilke to Dilke, Feb. 1900 (DP, Add. MS 43906, f. 162).

22 DP, Add. MS 43945, ff. 37–45; *PD*(4), 78, cols 296–316; 80, cols 625–32; 89, cols 131–41; *DFM*, 19 July 1901; C. W. Dilke, 'Guerilla and Counter-Guerilla', *Fortnightly Review*, 70 (1901), pp. 927–33; idem, 'The Army and South Africa', *Speaker*, new series, 1 (1899), pp. 91–92.

23 *PD*(4), 118, cols 1602–9; C. W. Dilke, 'The Command-in-Chief', *Empire Review*, 1 (1901), pp. 240–46.

24 10 May 1899, quoted in H. A. Clegg, A. Fox and A. F. Thompson, *A History of British Trade Unions*, i (Oxford, 1964), p. 267.

25 Leathem was a Belfast butcher who, because he employed non-union labour, was boycotted by the Belfast Journeymen Butchers' Association, of which Quinn was the treasurer. Leathem won an action for damages. J. Saville, 'Trade Unions and Free Labour: The Background to the Taff Vale Decision', in A. Briggs and J. Saville (eds), *Essays in Labour History* (1967; 1st edn, 1960), pp. 317–50, is still the best account of the anti-union atmosphere in which these legal decisions were made.

26 *Daily News*, 5 Sept. 1877; S. and B. Webb, *The History of Trade Unionism, 1666–1920* (1920; 1st edn, 1894), p. 617n.

27 DP, Add. MS 43877, ff. 23–25.

28 Wilkins was the secretary of the Amalgamated Society of Fancy Leather Workers which, during a strike, had picketed not only the leather goods firm of Lyons but also one which worked for Lyons on subcontract. An injunction brought by Lyons against the union was upheld, and the right to picket jeopardised by being narrowly confined to 'communicating information'.

29 9 Nov. 1901 (DP, Add. MS 43917, ff. 70–73).

30 Ibid., f. 73; Asquith to Dilke, 5 Dec. 1901 (DP, Add. MS 43877, ff. 27–28).

31 F. Bealey and H. Pelling, *Labour and Politics 1900–1906* (1958), pp. 80–81.

32 The TUC's parliamentary committee met with several Liberals – notably Dilke, McKenna, Reid and John Burns – at the House on 5 Feb. Burns, with typical egoism, recorded that he suggested that a bill to reverse Taff Vale was at that moment useless, and that the only sensible approach was to kick out the government, adding laconically that, 'Most agreed'. JBP, Add. MS 46320, f. 6.

33 Evidence of Mary Macarthur, quoted in G. & T., ii, pp. 365–66.

34 *DFM*, 6 June 1902.

35 Emy, *Liberals, Radicals*, pp. 135–36. Hardie was at this moment refusing to participate.

36 *Punch*, 26 Nov. 1902.

37 *PD*(4), 105, cols 963–66; 110, cols 1269–72; 114, cols 939–40, 1146–48; 115, cols 518–20, 540–42, 956–67; 116, cols 1346–49; 117, cols 681–92.

38 Ibid.,(5), 16, cols 1896–98; Dilke, *Problems*, ii, pp. 468–84.

39 L. S. Amery, *Joseph Chamberlain and the Tariff Reform Campaign* (1969; vols v and vi completing Garvin's *Life of Chamberlain*), v, p. 213.

40 DP, Add. MS 43885, ff. 154–55.

41 Garvin, *Life of Chamberlain*, i, p. 434.

42 Dilke, *Problems*, i, p. 1.

43 8 Oct. 1903 (*DFM*, 16 Oct. 1903).

44 Chamberlain referred to the premature motion as 'an affair of spies'. Amery, *Joseph Chamberlain*, v, pp. 227, 231.

45 *PD*(4), 123, cols 141–45, 457–61; 129, cols 855–66; 147, cols 990–94.

46 *The Times*, 11 July 1904; *DFM*, 29 Jan. 1904, 10 Nov. 1905.

47 DP, Add. MSS 43918, f. 17; 43941, f. 317.

48 *PD*(4), 132, cols 991–95; 133, cols 1062–75.

49 Quoted in Gainer, *The Aliens Invasion*, p. 163.

50 *PD*(4), 145, cols 468–72, 688–99; 148, cols 1184–87; 149, cols 150–52, 943–44.

51 D. Feldman, 'The Importance of Being English', in Feldman and Stedman Jones (eds), *Metropolis London*, p. 79. It has to be said, however, that the act was administered half-heartedly by the incoming Liberal government.

52 Quoted in *DFM*, 27 Aug. 1897. In his last years he became acutely conscious of his independence from the two main parties. He told the Royal Commission on Electoral Systems in 1910 that the country was wedded to a system that he was 'perhaps in a minority of one in not believing in'. *PP*, 1910, xxvi, pp. 458–59. In his will, he instructed Gertrude Tuckwell not to seek assistance in editing his papers from anyone closely connected to the Liberal or Conservative parties to avoid importing 'into the publications any of the conventional attitudes of "the old parties". The same objection would not apply to members of the other parties.'

Notes to Chapter 18

1 Curiously, Dilke had said little about Chinese labour, focusing his criticism instead on the importation of black labour, primarily from Portuguese East Africa.

2 A. K. Russell, *Liberal Landslide: The General Election of 1906* (Newton Abbot, 1973), pp. 65 and 79.

3 *DFM*, 5 Jan. 1906.

4 DP, Add. MS 43915, f. 258. He emulated his father by serving on the Paris exhibition commission in 1900, but without thereby appeasing the Queen. DP, Add. MS 43876, f. 103.

5 See, e.g., C-BP, Add. MS 41246, f. 53; Campbell-Bannerman to Herbert Gladstone, 5 Jan. 1900, quoted in Spender, *Life of Campbell-Bannerman* , i, p. 269.

6 *Manchester Guardian*, 27 Jan. 1911; Labouchere to Lord Channing, 18 Feb. 1911, quoted in A. Thorold, *Life of Henry Labouchere* (1913), pp. 483–84; Morley to Dilke, 10 Dec. 1905 (DP, Add. MS 43895, ff. 259–60). From markings on this letter, Dilke appears to have attributed his exclusion more to Stead's baleful influence than to Campbell-Bannerman's antipathy.

7 S. Hutton and B. Nield, 'Emily Dilke', in J. M. Bellamy and J. Saville (eds), *Dictionary of Labour Biography*, iii (1976), pp. 63–67.

8 Quoted in G. & T., ii, p. 463.

9 See Richardson, *The Everlasting Spell*, pp. 182–83 – though she exaggerates the amount of material destroyed.

10 DP, Add. MS 49446, f. 71.

11 See CWD, Add. MS 58277, unfoliated.

12 'There has probably never sat so interesting a House of Commons in the history of this country.' C. W. Dilke, 'Finance in the New Parliament', *Financial Review of Reviews*, Apr. 1906.

13 6 Jan. 1906 (DP, Add. MS 43892, ff. 242–44).

14 DP, Add. MS 43941, f. 326.

15 18 Feb. 1911, quoted in Thorold, *Life of Labouchere*, pp. 483–84.

16 Dilke, 'Finance in the New Parliament'.

17 To Lewis Harcourt, 16 Feb. 1906 (LHP, dep. 439, ff. 28–31).

18 DP, Add. MSS 43919, ff. 16–27; 43929, ff. 159–60. A. J. A. Morris, *Radicalism against War, 1906–14* (1972), pp. 263–64n. quotes the following extract from the *Labour Leader*, 15 Nov. 1911: 'The Radical element in Liberalism has practically ceased to count since the death of Sir Charles Dilke. He was the last of the great Radicals, and though the Dilke tradition remains, no one has arisen to take his place. A Radical group still meets from time to time, but they are leaderless, timid and ineffective.'

19 Quoted in Hosking and King, 'Radicals and Whigs', p. 145.

20 Quoted in G. & T., ii, p. 345.

21 *PD*(4), 162, passim.

22 *Manchester Guardian*, 27 Jan. 1911.

23 *PD*(4), 154, cols 906–8; 166, cols 988–92; 167, cols 704–5. The TUC took up Dilke's call for safeguards against insolvency.

24 DP, Add. MS 43929, f. 159.

25 *PD*(4), 152, cols 1448–50. His last contribution on the subject was the pamphlet *Woman Suffrage and Electoral Reform* (1910).

26 *PD*(4), 179, cols 261–62; *The Times*, 15 July 1907.

27 DP, Add. MS 43941, f. 326; G. & T., ii, p. 472.

28 Select Committee on Income Tax, *PP*, 1906, ix. Afterwards, he was elected President

of the Royal Statistical Society, of which he had been a member for forty years. His presidential address (19 Nov. 1907) was an indictment of government backwardness in the provision of statistical information. *Journal of the Royal Statistical Society*, 70 (1907), pp. 553–82.

29 R. B. Haldane, *An Autobiography* (1929), p. 194.

30 *PD*(4), 172, cols 110–22; 174, cols 1660–70; 176, cols 503–12; 179, cols 889–93; 190, cols 1093–97; Morris, *Radicalism against War*, pp. 92, 95n. Although isolated from fellow radicals on this question, he was at one with them in opposing the major foreign policy *démarche* of 1907, the *entente* with Russia.

31 *DFM*, 17 July 1908; *PD*(4), 191, cols 430–33, 809–11.

32 Ibid., 187, cols. 1534–49; Hoffman, *They Also Serve*, p. 12. Compulsory closing was not introduced until 1928.

33 B. K. Murray, *The People's Budget, 1909–10: Lloyd George and Liberal Politics* (Oxford, 1980), pp. 4–5 and passim.

34 *DFM*, 11 June 1909, 24 Sept. 1909; *PD*(5), 4, cols 951–60; 5, cols 83–91; 6, cols 362–69, 1777–81; 18, cols 1657–64.

35 To J. R. Thursfield, 24 Jan. 1907 (Thursfield MS, Eng. Letts. e.93, ff. 104–5).

36 6 Aug. 1902, quoted in R. H. Bacon, *Life of Lord Fisher of Kilverstone* (2 vols, 1929), i, p. 159.

37 Speech at the Westminster Palace Hotel, 14 Apr. 1910 (*Daily News*, 15 Apr. 1910).

38 DP, Add. MS 43877, ff. 79–81. He was also influenced in formulating his opinions on wages boards by Beatrice Webb; see his letters to her of 7 Feb. and 7 March 1900 (Passfield Papers, ii, 4, B, 4 and 6).

39 To Herbert Gladstone, 15 Feb. 1908 (HGP, Add. MS 46065, f. 133).

40 M. A. Hamilton, *Mary Macarthur: A Biographical Sketch* (1925), pp. 65–69; J. A. Schmiechen, *Sweated Industries and Sweated Labor: The London Clothing Trades, 1860–1914* (1984), pp. 166–67.

41 23 May 1907 (HGP, Add. MS 46064, ff. 189–90).

42 Select Committee on Home Work, *PP*, 1908, viii, pp. 173–85; C. W. Dilke, 'Prospects of Wages Boards', *Woman Worker*, Apr. 1908.

43 DP, Add. MS 43920, f. 87; *DFM*, 17 Apr. 1908.

44 G. & T., ii, p. 361; *PD*(5), 2, cols 2062–65; Schmiechen, *Sweated Industries*, p. 171.

45 B. L. Hutchins and A. Harrison, *A History of Factory Legislation* (1966; 1st edn, 1903), p. 268. It was because it mainly benefited women that the measure attracted so little attention from the TUC.

46 DP, Add. MS 43921, f. 11.

47 Schmiechen, *Sweated Industries*, pp. 174–79; *Guardian*, 10 Feb. 1993.

48 Quoted in G. & T., ii, pp. 378–79.

49 *DFM*, 19 Jan. 1906.

50 C. W. Dilke, 'Civilisation in Africa', *Cosmopolis*, 3 (1896), pp. 18–35; *PD*(4), 45, cols 1458–62. He told a Paris conference in 1907 that Britain would never 'get back the blood and treasure' squandered in Africa. DP, Add. MS 43944, f. 206.

51 DP, Add. MS 43916, ff. 32–38; *PD*(4), 50, cols 511–15; 64, cols 380–85.

52 Ibid., 177, col. 1155; copy from Churchill Papers of Tucker to Dilke, 16 Nov. 1906, forwarded to Churchill with marginal notes (REND, 9/3).

53 17 Aug. 1907 (DP, Add. MS 43919, ff. 258–59).

54 DP, Add. MSS 43936, ff. 231–32; 43938, f. 115; 43939, ff. 3–4.

55 *PD*(4), 47, cols 425–32.

56 Address of the Aborigines Protection Society to the Belgian Chamber of Representatives, 29 Apr. 1901 (DP, Add. MS 43917, ff. 33–34); W. R. Louis and J. Stengers (ed.), *E. D. Morel's History of the Congo Reform Movement* (Oxford, 1968), p. 67. Cf. Dilke to Morel, 26 Jan. 1910: 'I cannot isolate "Congo" from "Foreign Affairs".' DP, Add. MS 43897, f. 236.

57 Hudson to Morel, 4 Dec. 1906 (Morel Papers, F8, file 41). Dilke at times felt badgered by Morel, particularly in 1908 when he was ill, and their relationship was never more than cordial.

58 24 Jan. 1910 (ibid., file 43).

59 Ibid., file 44.

60 DP, Add. MS 43919, ff. 50–51.

61 *PD*(4), 98, cols 1481–86; 120, cols 67–72; 138, cols 813–22; 162, cols 764–73; 167, cols 1090–98.

62 G. B. Pyrah, *Imperial Policy and South Africa* (Oxford, 1955), p. 118; *The Times*, 20 May 1909.

63 E. A. Walker, *W. P. Schreiner: A South African* (Oxford, 1937), pp. 330–31; *PD*(5), 9, cols 973–81, 1534–37, 1566–67, 1610–11; DP, Add. MS 43921, f. 223.

64 6 Jan. 1906 (DP, Add. MS 43892, ff. 242–44).

65 J. A. Spender and C. Asquith, *The Life of Lord Oxford and Asquith* (2 vols, 1932), i, p. 272.

66 Select Committee on the Civil List, *PP*, 1910, vi, pp. 315–36; DP, Add. MS 43923, ff. 203–13.

67 Hudson to Morel, 10 and 13 July 1908 (Morel Papers, F8, file 42).

68 24 May 1910, quoted in Leslie, *Bodley*, pp. 50–51.

69 DP, Add. MS 43922, ff. 149–51.

70 18 Oct. 1910 (Morel Papers, F8, file 44).

71 H. Pearson, *Labby: The Life of Henry Labouchere* (1936), p. 188.

72 In 1910 there were only 840 cremations across the whole country. *Transactions of the Cremation Society of England* (1922), 33, p. 10.

Bibliography

1. PRIVATE PAPERS

Birmingham University Library

Chamberlain, Joseph

Bodleian Library, Oxford

Bodley, J. E. C.
Crook, William M.
Harcourt, Sir William
Harcourt, Lord
Lee, Sir Sidney
Monk Bretton, Lord (Dodson)
Oxford and Asquith, Earl of
Pearson, Charles H. and Edith
Ponsonby, Arthur (1st Baron Ponsonby of Shulbrede)
Sandars, J. S.
Selborne, 2nd Earl of
Thursfield, Sir James

British Library

Althorp (5th Earl Spencer)
Battersea (Cyril Flower)
Burns, John
Campbell-Bannerman, Sir Henry
Carlingford, Lord
Dilke, Sir Charles Wentworth, 2nd baronet
Dilke, Sir Charles Wentworth, 3rd baronet
Dixon, William Hepworth
Gladstone, Herbert (Viscount)
Gladstone, William Ewart
Hamilton, Sir Edward W.
Iddesleigh, 1st Earl of (Stafford Northcote)
Macmillan (Publishers)
Ripon, Marquis of

British Library of Political and Economic Science

Broadhurst, Henry
Harrison, Frederic
Morel, Edmund Dene
Passfield Papers (Beatrice and Sidney Webb)

Chatsworth House

Devonshire, 8th Duke of, second series

Churchill College Archives Centre, Cambridge

Roskill-Enthoven-Dilke Papers
Stead, William T.

Cooperative Union Library, Manchester

Holyoake, George Jacob

Liverpool Public Record Office

Derby, 15th Earl of – 920 DER (15)

Museum of Labour History, Manchester

Labour Representation Committee – Letters

National Army Museum, London

Roberts, Lord Frederick
Wilkinson, Spenser

Public Record Office

Granville, 2nd Earl

University College, London

Chadwick, Sir Edwin

2. *PARLIAMENTARY PAPERS*

Hansard:

Parliamentary Debates, 3rd, 4th and 5th series.

Special Reports etc.:

Select Committee on Parliamentary and Municipal Elections, *Parliamentary Papers*, 1868–69, viii.
Select Committee on Parliamentary and Municipal Elections, *Parliamentary Papers*, 1876, xii.
Select Committee on Parliamentary and Municipal Elections (Hours of Polling), *Parliamentary Papers*, 1877, xv.
Select Committee on the Parliamentary and Municipal Registration Bill, *Parliamentary Papers*, 1878, xiii.
Select Committee on Public Business, *Parliamentary Papers*, 1878, xviii.
Royal Commission on the Housing of the Working Classes, *Parliamentary Papers*, 1884–85, xxx.
Select Committee on the London Corporation (Charges of Malversation), *Parliamentary Papers*, 1887, x.
Standing Committee on Trade, *Parliamentary Papers*, 1895, x.
Select Committee on Income Tax, *Parliamentary Papers*, 1906, ix.
Select Committee on Home Work, *Parliamentary Papers*, 1908, viii.
Select Committee on the Civil List, *Parliamentary Papers*, 1910, vi.
Royal Commission on the Selection of Justices of the Peace, *Parliamentary Papers*, 1910, xxxviii.
Royal Commission on Electoral Systems, *Parliamentary Papers*, 1910, xxvi.

3. *CONTEMPORARY NEWSPAPERS AND PERIODICALS*

Annual Register
Athenaeum
Birmingham Daily Post
Bristol Evening News
Chelsea News
Daily News
Daily Telegraph
Dean Forest Guardian
Dean Forest Mercury
Fortnightly Review
Graphic
Illustrated London News
Journal of the Royal Statistical Society
Leigh Chronicle
Manchester Guardian
Mumbles Observer
Nineteenth Century
North American Review
Notes and Queries
Political Quarterly
Punch
Republican
Reynolds's News
Rugby Advertiser
Sheffield Daily Telegraph
Speaker
Standard
Star
The Times
Wakefield Express
Wiltshire's Magazine

4. *WRITINGS BY SIR CHARLES DILKE IN ORDER OF PUBLICATION*
(Place of publication is London unless otherwise stated)

Mr Disraeli's Manifesto (pamphlet, 1868).
Colonies (pamphlet, 1869).
Greater Britain (1st edn, 1868; 5th edn, 1870).
Education (pamphlet, 1870).
The Cost of the Crown (pamphlet, 1871).
'Free Schools', *Fortnightly Review*, new series, 14 (1873), pp. 789–96.
The Fall of Prince Florestan of Monaco (1874).
Two Recess Speeches (pamphlet, 1876).
'English Influence in China', *Macmillan's Magazine*, 34 (1876), pp. 557–68.
The Eastern Question (1878).
Parliamentary Reform (pamphlet, 1879).
Local Government (pamphlet, 1885).
[with F. W. Procter], *Papers on the Leasehold System* (pamphlet, 1886).
The Present Position of European Politics (1887).
'The State of Europe and the Present Position of England', *Universal Review*, 1 (1888), pp.
    5–26.
The British Army (1888).
[with H. P. Cobb], *Notes on the Local Government Bills* (pamphlet, 1888).
[with H. P. Cobb, H. Gardner, W. A. McArthur and F. S. Stevenson], *Local Government
    Bills: Notes on the Chief Amendments* (pamphlet, 1888).
'The Baluch and Afghan Frontiers of India', *Fortnightly Review*, 45 (1889), pp. 293–324,
    445–80.
A Radical Programme (pamphlet, 1890).
Problems of Greater Britain (2 vols, 1890).
'On Defence Expenditure', *Saturday Review*, 70 (1890), p. 734.
'Statistics of the Defence Expenditure of the Chief Military and Naval Powers' (lecture, 16
    Dec. 1890, to the Royal Statistical Society), *Journal of the Royal Statistical Society*, March
    1891.
'The Commonwealth of Australia', *Forum*, 45 (1891), p. 379.
'The British Army in 1891', *Fortnightly Review*, 49 (1891), pp. 857–76.
'The French Armies', *Fortnightly Review*, 50 (1891), pp. 597–635.
'Egypt, Now and After', *Speaker*, 4 (1891), pp. 730–33.
'Against Reformed Upper Houses', *Subjects of the Day*, 4 (1891), pp. 96–103.
'The Position of the Party', *Speaker*, 4 (1891), p. 280.
'Conservative Foreign Policy', *Fortnightly Review*, 51 (1892), pp. 1–9.
'Foreign Affairs and Home Defence: An Interview with Sir Charles Dilke', *Albemarle*, Jan.
    1892, p. 1.
'The Pope, Friendly Societies, and Masons', *Speaker*, 5 (1892), pp. 310–11.
[with S. Wilkinson], *Imperial Defence* (1892).
'The Uganda Problem', *Fortnightly Review*, 52 (1893), pp. 145–61.
'Lord Rosebery's Administration', *North American Review*, 158 (1894), p. 534.
'The Navy', *New Review*, 12 (1895), p. 22.
Fines and Deductions (pamphlet, Huddersfield, 1896).
Shop Life (pamphlet, Cardiff, 1896).
'Civilization in Africa', *Cosmopolis*, 3 (1896), pp. 18–35.
'The Late Session', *Progressive Review*, 1 (1896), pp. 53–62.
'John Stuart Mill, 1869–1873', *Cosmopolis*, 5 (1897), pp. 629–41.
'Great Britain as a Military Power: An Interview with Sir Charles Dilke', *Idler*, 13 (1898),
    pp. 273–79.

The British Empire (1899).
'Newfoundland', *Pall Mall Magazine*, 17 (1899), pp. 211–16.
'The Army and South Africa', *Speaker*, new series, 1 (1899), pp. 91–92.
'The British Army', *Weekly Sun*, 27 Jan. 1900, p. 10.
'The Case against the War Office', *Weekly Sun*, 3 Feb. 1900, p. 1.
'Armaments of the United Kingdom', *Daily Express*, 2 June (p. 4) and 4 June (p. 5) 1900.
'United Kingdom, United States and the Ship Canals', *Forum*, June 1900, p. 449.
'Imperial Reserves', *Empire Review*, 1 (1901), pp. 61–65.
'The Command-in-Chief', *Empire Review*, 1 (1901), pp. 240–46.
'The King of England', *North American Review*, 162 (1901), p. 416.
'Guerilla and Counter-Guerilla', *Fortnightly Review*, 70 (1901), pp. 927–33.
'The Naval Strength of Nations', *Cosmopolitan Magazine*, 32 (1902), pp. 349–57.
'The Armies of the Powers', *Munsey Magazine*, April 1902, pp. 17–21.
'The Boy, What will he Become: An Interview with Sir Charles Dilke', *Tatler*, 9 (1904).
'War in the Far East', *North American Review*, 178 (1902), p. 481.
'Trade Unions and the Law', *Independent Review*, 3 (1904).
'The British Frontier Towards Russia', *Monthly Review*, 21 (1905), pp. 9–16.
'South African Problems', *Aborigines' Friend*, March 1906, pp. 481–89.
'Finance in the New Parliament', *Financial Review of Reviews*, April 1906.
'Presidential Address', *Journal of the Royal Statistical Society*, 70 (1907), pp. 553–82.
'Prospects of Wages Boards', *Woman Worker*, April 1908.
'Lord Kitchener's Scheme of Redistribution', letter to the editor, *Morning Post*, 9 Dec.
    1908, p. 6.
'Dreadnoughts in the North Sea', letter to the editor, *Morning Post*, 25 March 1909, p. 7.
'Address to the Royal Economic Society on the Poor Law, March 30th 1909', *Economic
    Journal*, 19 (1909), pp. 308–12.
'Foreign Affairs', *English Review*, 3 (1909), pp. 495–500.
Electoral Reform (pamphlet, 1909).
Woman Suffrage and Electoral Reform (pamphlet, 1910).
'Indentured and Forced Labour', in Universal Races Congress, *Papers on Inter-Racial
    Problems* (1911), pp. 312–22.

Publications which include contributions by Dilke

J. W. Probyn (ed.), *Local Government and Taxation* (Cobden Club Essays, 1875).
C. W. Dilke, *Papers of a Critic* (edited, with an introduction by Sir Charles Dilke; 2 vols,
    1875).
C. Edwards, *Railway Nationalization* (with an introduction by Sir Charles Dilke, 1897).
J. A. Cockburn, *Australian Federation* (with a preface by Sir Charles Dilke, 1901).
E. F. (Lady) Dilke, *Book of the Spiritual Life* (with a memoir of the author by Sir Charles
    Dilke, 1905).

5. *OTHER CONTEMPORARY SOURCES*
(Place of publication is London unless otherwise stated)

Anon., *What is the Use of Kings?* (pamphlet, 1872).
A. Fenner Brockway, *Labour and Liberalism* (Manchester, n.d.).
B. Disraeli, *Endymion* (1881).
T. H. S. Escott, *England, its People, Polity, and Pursuits* (2 vols, 1879).
—, (ed.), *The Radical Programme* (1885).
J. F. B. Firth, *Reform of London Government and of City Guilds* (1888).
L. T. Hobhouse, *Liberalism* (1911).
'Jackdaw', *The Dilkiad: or, The Dream of Dilke* (pamphlet, 1872).
J. Lloyd, *London Municipal Government: History of a Great Reform, 1880–88* (1910).
H. W. Lucy, *A Diary of Two Parliaments* (2 vols, 1885–86).
A. Macmorran, *The Local Government Act, 1888* (1888).
A. Macmorran and T. R. C. Dill, *The Local Government Act, 1894* (1894).
C. F. G. Masterman, *The Condition of England* (1909).
A. Reid (ed.), *The New Liberal Programme. Contributed by Representatives of the Liberal Party* (1886).
J. Renwick-Seager, *The Representation of the People Act* (1884).
Report of the Industrial Remuneration Conference (1885; reissued, New York, 1968, with an introduction by J. Saville).
W. Robson, *Sir Charles Dilke and the Clerkenwell Vestry* (1884).
Lord Salisbury, 'The Value of Redistribution: A Note on Electoral Statistics', *National Review*, 20 (1884), pp. 145–62.
W. T. Stead, *Has Sir Charles Dilke Cleared his Character? An Examination of the Report of the Alleged Commission* (pamphlet, 1891).
—, 'The Sin of Ananias and Sapphira', *Welsh Review*, 1 (1892), pp. 321–38.
—, *Deliverance or Doom? or, The Choice of Sir Charles Dilke* (pamphlet, 1892).
TUC *Annual Reports* (1890–1911).
R. Spence Watson, *The National Liberal Federation* (1907).
W. White, *Speeches of Playfair and Dilke on Vaccination Taken to Pieces and Disposed of* (1884).

6. *SECONDARY SOURCES*

A complete list of secondary sources would run to many pages. The following has therefore been confined to those which have been cited in the footnotes. Place of publication is London unless otherwise stated.

P. Adelman, *Victorian Radicalism: The Middle-Class Experience, 1830–1914* (1984).
R. Page Arnot, *The Miners* (1949).
B. Askwith, *Lady Dilke* (1969).
H. H. Asquith, *Memories and Reflections* (2 vols, 1928).
M. Asquith, *Autobiography* (2 vols, 1920–22).
L. Atherley-Jones, *Looking Back: Reminiscences of a Political Career* (1925).
P. Auspos, 'Radicalism, Pressure Groups and Party Politics: From the National Education League to the National Liberal Federation', *Journal of British Studies*, 20 (1980), pp. 184–204.
W. O. Aydelotte (ed.), *The History of Parliamentary Behavior* (Princeton, NJ, 1977).
R. H. Bacon, *Life of Lord Fisher of Kilverstone* (2 vols, 1929).
M. Balfour, *Britain and Joseph Chamberlain* (1985).
M. Barker, *Gladstone and Radicalism: The Reconstruction of Liberal Policy in Britain, 1885–94* (1975).
J. O. Baylen and N. J. Gossman (eds), *Biographical Dictionary of Modern British Radicals*, iii, *1870–1914, A–K* (Hemel Hempstead, 1988).
F. Bealey and H. Pelling, *Labour and Politics, 1900–06* (1958).
J. M. Bellamy and J. Saville (eds), *Dictionary of Labour Biography*, iii (1976).
R. Bellamy (ed.), *Victorian Liberalism: Nineteenth-Century Political Thought and Practice* (1990).
M. Bentley, *The Climax of Liberal Politics: British Liberalism in Theory and Practice, 1868–1918* (1987).
M. Bentley and J. Stevenson (eds), *High and Low Politics in Modern Britain: Ten Studies* (Oxford, 1983).
G. L. Bernstein, *Liberalism and Liberal Politics in Edwardian England* (1986).
E. F. Biagini, *Liberty, Retrenchment and Reform: Popular Liberalism in the Age of Gladstone, 1860–1880* (Cambridge, 1992).
E. F. Biagini and A. J. Reid (eds), *Currents of Radicalism: Popular Radicalism, Organised Labour and Party Politics in Britain, 1850–1914* (Cambridge, 1991).
R. Blake, *Disraeli* (1969; 1st edn, 1966).
N. Blewett, 'The Franchise in the United Kingdom, 1885–1918', *Past and Present*, 32 (1965), pp. 27–56.
—, *The Peers, the Parties and the People: The General Elections of 1910* (1972).
W. S. Blunt, *A Secret History of the British Occupation of Egypt* (1907).
C. A. Bodelsen, *Studies in Mid-Victorian Imperialism* (New York, 1968; 1st edn, 1924).
R. V. C. Bodley, 'The Man Who Insulted King Edward', *Sunday Times*, 5 Jan. 1969.
A. Briggs and J. Saville (eds), *Essays in Labour History* (1967; 1st edn, 1960).
D. Brooks (ed.), *The Destruction of Lord Rosebery: From the Diary of Sir Edward Hamilton, 1894–1895* (1986).
B. H. Brown, *The Tariff Reform Movement in Great Britain, 1881–1895* (New York, 1966).
K. D. Brown (ed.), *Essays in Anti-Labour History* (1974).
G. E. Buckle (ed.), *The Letters of Queen Victoria*, 2nd series, iii, *1879–85* (1928).
M. E. J. Chadwick, 'The Role of Redistribution in the Making of the Third Reform Act', *Historical Journal*, 19, (1976), pp. 665–83.
M. E. Chamberlain, 'Sir Charles Dilke and the British Intervention in Egypt, 1882', *British Journal of International Studies*, 2 (1976), pp. 231–45.
O. F. Christie, *The Transition to Democracy, 1867–1914* (1934).

P. F. Clarke, *Lancashire and the New Liberalism* (1971).

H. A. Clegg, A. Fox and A. F. Thompson, *A History of British Trade Unions*, i (Oxford, 1964).

A. B. Cooke and J. Vincent, *The Governing Passion: Cabinet Government and Party Politics in Britain, 1885–86* (1974).

A. B. Cooke and J. Vincent (eds), *Lord Carlingford's Journal* (Oxford, 1971).

J. Davis, *Reforming London: The London Government Problem, 1855–1900* (Oxford, 1988).

J. W. Derry, *The Radical Tradition: Tom Paine to Lloyd George* (1967).

J. P. D. Dunbabin, 'The Politics of the Establishment of County Councils', *Historical Journal*, 8 (1965), pp. 226–52.

—, 'Parliamentary Elections in Great Britain, 1868–1900: A Psephological Note', *English Historical Review*, 81 (1966), pp. 82–99.

L. Edel, *Henry James*, ii, *The Conquest of London, 1870–1883* (1962).

—, *Henry James*, iii, *The Middle Years, 1884–1894* (1963).

H. V. Emy, *Liberals, Radicals, and Social Politics, 1892–1914* (1973).

B. English and J. Saville, *Strict Settlement: A Guide for Historians* (Hull, 1983).

R. C. K. Ensor, *England, 1870–1914* (Oxford, 1936).

Lord Eversley, *Commons, Forests and Footpaths* (1910; 1st edn, G. Shaw Lefevre, *English Commons and Forests*, 1894).

D. Feldman and G. Stedman Jones (eds), *Metropolis London: Histories and Representations since 1800* (1989).

R. Feurer, 'The Meaning of "Sisterhood": The British Women's Movement and Protective Labor Legislation, 1870–1900', *Victorian Studies*, 31 (1988), pp. 233–60.

M. C. Finn, *After Chartism: Class and Nation in English Radical Politics, 1848–1874* (Cambridge, 1993).

T. H. Ford, *Albert Venn Dicey: The Man and his Times* (Chichester, 1985).

—, 'A. V. Dicey and the Destruction of Sir Charles Dilke', *Eire–Ireland*, 11, (1977), pp. 27–50.

P. Fraser, *Joseph Chamberlain: Radicalism and Empire, 1868–1914* (1966).

M. Freeden, *The New Liberalism* (Oxford, 1978).

B. Gainer, *The Aliens Invasion: The Origins of the Aliens Act of 1905* (1972).

A. G. Gardiner, *Life of Sir William Harcourt* (2 vols, 1923).

J. L. Garvin and L. S. Amery, *The Life of Joseph Chamberlain* (6 vols, 1932–69).

J. F. Glaser, 'English Nonconformity and the Decline of Liberalism', *American Historical Review*, 63 (1958), pp. 352–63.

L. Goldman (ed.), *The Blind Victorian: Henry Fawcett and British Liberalism* (Cambridge, 1989).

P. Gordon, *The Red Earl: The Papers of the Fifth Earl Spencer, 1835–1910* (2 vols, Northampton, 1981–86).

T. R. Gourvish and A. O'Day (eds), *Later Victorian Britain, 1867–1900* (1988).

P. Guedalla (ed.), *The Queen and Mr Gladstone* (2 vols, 1933).

E. E. Gulley, *Joseph Chamberlain and English Social Politics* (New York, 1926).

S. Gwynn and G. M. Tuckwell, *The Life of Sir Charles W. Dilke* (2 vols, 1917).

R. B. Haldane, *An Autobiography* (1929).

E. Halévy, *Imperialism and the Rise of Labour, 1895–1905* (1961; 1st edn, 1926).

P. Hall, *Royal Fortune: Tax, Money and the Monarchy* (1992).

D. A. Hamer, *John Morley: Liberal Intellectual in Politics* (Oxford, 1968).

—, *Liberal Politics in the Age of Gladstone and Rosebery* (1972).

W. S. Hamer, *The British Army: Civil-Military Relations, 1885–1905* (Oxford, 1970).

M. A. Hamilton, *Mary Macarthur: A Biographical Sketch* (1925).

H. J. Hanham, *Elections and Party Management* (1959).

—, *The Reformed Electoral System in Great Britain, 1832–1914* (1968).

— (ed.), *The Nineteenth-Century Constitution* (Cambridge, 1969).

F. Harcourt, 'Gladstone, Monarchism and the "New" Imperialism, 1868–74', *Journal of Imperial and Commonwealth History*, 14 (1985), pp. 20–51.

S. H. Harris, *Auberon Herbert: Crusader for Liberty* (1943).

C. Harvie, *The Lights of Liberalism: University Liberals and the Challenge of Democracy, 1860–86* (1976).

W. A. Hayes, *The Background and Passage of the Third Reform Act* (1982).

O. W. Hewett, *Strawberry Fair: A Biography of Frances, Countess Waldegrave, 1821–1879* (1956).

T. W. Heyck, *The Dimensions of British Radicalism: The Case of Ireland, 1874–95* (1974).

P. C. Hoffman, *They Also Serve: The Story of the Shop-Worker* (1949).

B. Holland, *The Life of Spencer Compton, 8th Duke of Devonshire* (2 vols, 1911).

A. G. Hopkins, 'The Victorians and Africa: A Reconsideration of the Occupation of Egypt, 1882', *Journal of African History*, 27 (1986), pp. 363–91.

A. Howkins, 'Edwardian Liberalism and Industrial Unrest: A Class View of the Decline of Liberalism', *History Workshop*, 4 (1977), pp. 143–61.

B. L. Hutchins and A. Harrison, *A History of Factory Legislation* (1966; 1st edn, 1903).

P. Jalland, *Women, Marriage and Politics, 1860–1914* (Oxford, 1986).

R. Jenkins, *Sir Charles Dilke: A Victorian Tragedy* (1965; 1st edn, 1958).

T. A. Jenkins, *Gladstone, Whiggery and the Liberal Party, 1874–1886* (Oxford, 1988).

H. Jephson, *The Platform: Its Rise and Progress* (2 vols, 1892; repr. 1968).

A. Jones, *The Politics of Reform, 1884* (Cambridge, 1972).

D. Jones, *Chartism and the Chartists* (1975).

D. Judd, *Radical Joe: A Life of Joseph Chamberlain* (1977).

J. Juxon, *Lewis and Lewis* (1983).

H. E. Kearley [Viscount Devonport], *The Travelled Road: Some Memories of a Busy Life* (Rochester, n.d., 1935?).

W. M. Kuhn, 'Ceremony and Politics: The British Monarchy, 1871–1872', *Journal of British Studies*, 26 (1987), pp. 133–62.

K. Laybourn, *The Rise of Labour: The British Labour Party, 1890–1979* (1988).

K. Laybourn and J. Reynolds, *Liberalism and the Rise of Labour, 1890–1918* (1984).

S. Lee, *King Edward the Seventh* (2 vols, 1925–27).

S. Leslie, *Memoir of J. E. C. Bodley* (1930).

—, 'Virginia Crawford, Sir Charles Dilke, and Cardinal Manning', *Dublin Review*, 241 (1951), pp. 177–205.

—, 'Dilke in his own Defence', *Daily Telegraph*, 8 Dec. 1960.

W. R. Louis and J. Stengers (eds), *E. D. Morel's History of the Congo Reform Movement* (Oxford, 1968).

S. Lowndes (ed.), *Diaries and Letters of Marie Belloc Lowndes, 1911–1947* (1971).

W. C. Lubenow, *Parliamentary Politics and the Home Rule Crisis in 1886* (Oxford, 1988).

H. M. Lynd, *England in the Eighteen-Eighties* (1968; 1st edn, 1945).

V. A. McClelland, *Cardinal Manning* (1962).

S. Maccoby, *English Radicalism, 1886–1914* (1953).

B. McCormick and J. W. Williams, 'The Miners and the Eight-Hour Day, 1863–1901', *Economic History Review*, 2nd series, 12 (1959–60), pp. 222–38.

E. Marjoribanks, *The Life of Sir Edward Marshall Hall* (1929).

K. Marx and F. Engels, *Selected Correspondence, 1846–1895* (trans. D. Torr, 1934).

L. Masterman (ed.), *Mary Gladstone: Her Diaries and Letters* (2nd edn, 1930).

H. C. G. Matthew, *The Liberal Imperialists: The Ideas and Politics of a Post-Gladstonian Elite* (1973).

— (ed.), *The Gladstone Diaries*, vii, *Jan. 1869–June 1871* (Oxford, 1982).

— (ed.), *The Gladstone Diaries*, x, *Jan. 1881–June 1883* (Oxford, 1990).

— (ed.), *The Gladstone Diaries*, xi, *July 1883–Dec. 1886* (Oxford, 1990).

H. C. G. Matthew, R. I. McKibbin and J. A. Kay, 'The Franchise Factor in the Rise of the Labour Party', *English Historical Review*, 91 (1976), pp. 723–52.

H. Montgomery Hyde, *A Tangled Web: Sex Scandals in British Politics and Society* (1986).

J. Morley, *Life of W. E. Gladstone* (3 vols, 1903).

A. J. A. Morris, *Radicalism against War, 1906–14* (1972).

B. K. Murray, *The People's Budget, 1909–10: Lloyd George and Liberal Politics* (Oxford, 1980).

T. Nairn, *The Enchanted Glass. Britain and its Monarchy* (1988)

D. Nicholls, 'The English Middle Class and the Ideological Significance of Radicalism', *Journal of British Studies*, 24 (1985), pp. 415–33.

–, 'The Personnel, Methods, and Policies of English Middle-Class Radicalism, 1760–1924', *International Journal of Social Education*, 3 (1988), pp. 73–85.

—, 'Richard Cobden and the International Peace Congress Movement, 1848–1853', *Journal of British Studies*, 30 (1991), pp. 351–76.

T. P. O'Connor, *Memoirs of an Old Parliamentarian* (2 vols, 1929).

A. O'Day, *Parnell and the First Home Rule Episode, 1884–87* (Dublin, 1986).

C. O'Leary, *The Elimination of Corrupt Practices in British Elections, 1868–1911* (Oxford, 1962).

J. P. Parry, *Democracy and Religion: Gladstone and the Liberal Party, 1867–1875* (Cambridge, 1986).

—, 'Religion and the Collapse of Gladstone's First Government, 1870–1874', *Historical Journal*, 25 (1982), pp. 71–101.

H. Pearson, *Labby: The Life of Henry Labouchere* (1936).

C. Petrie, *The Life and Letters of Austen Chamberlain* (2 vols, 1939–40).

D. Powell, 'The New Liberalism and the Rise of Labour, 1886–1906, *Historical Journal*, 29 (1986), pp. 369–93.

H. Preston-Thomas, *The Work and Play of a Government Inspector* (Edinburgh, 1909).

G. B. Pyrah, *Imperial Policy and South Africa* (Oxford, 1955).

A. Ramm (ed.), *Political Correspondence of Mr Gladstone and Lord Granville* (2 vols, Oxford, 1962).

D. Read, *Cobden and Bright* (1967).

R. Rhodes James, *Rosebery* (1963).

—, *Lord Randolph Churchill* (1969).

J. Richardson, *The Everlasting Spell: A Study of Keats and His Friends* (1963).

B. C. Roberts, *The Trades Union Congress* (1958).

J. W. Robertson Scott, *The Life and Death of a Newspaper* (1952).

W. A. Robson, *The Government and Misgovernment of London* (1939).

R. Rodger, 'Political Economy, Ideology and the Persistence of Working-Class Housing Problems in Britain, 1850–1914', *International Review of Social History*, 32 (1987), pp. 109–43.

J. P. Rossi, 'The Transformation of the British Liberal Party: A Study of the Tactics of the Liberal Opposition, 1874–1880', *Transactions of the American Philosophical Society*, 68 (1978), pp. 1–133.

C. Rover, *Women's Suffrage and Party Politics, 1866–1914* (1967).

E. Royle and J. Walvin, *English Radicals and Reformers, 1760–1848* (Brighton, 1982).

G. W. E. Russell (ed.), *Malcolm MacColl: Memoirs and Correspondence* (1914).

J. A. Schmiechen, *Sweated Industries and Sweated Labor: The London Clothing Trades, 1860–1914* (1984).

G. R. Searle, 'The Edwardian Liberal Party and Business', *English Historical Review*, 98 (1983), pp. 28–60.

B. Semmel, *Imperialism and Social Reform* (1960).

C. Seymour, *Electoral Reform in England and Wales* (New Haven, 1915).

R. T. Shannon, *Gladstone and the Bulgarian Agitation, 1876* (1963).

S. Shipley, *Club Life and Socialism in Mid-Victorian London* (1971).

A. Simon, 'Church Disestablishment as a Factor in the General Election of 1885', *Historical Journal*, 18 (1975), pp. 791–820.

—, 'Joseph Chamberlain and Free Education in the Election of 1885', *History of Education*, 2 (1973), pp. 56–78.

B. Simon, *Education and the Labour Movement, 1870–1920* (1965).

N. C. Soldon, *Women in British Trade Unions, 1874–1976* (1978).

J. A. Spender, *Life of Sir Henry Campbell-Bannerman* (2 vols, 1923).

J. A. Spender and C. Asquith, *The Life of Lord Oxford and Asquith* (2 vols, 1932).

P. Stansky, *Ambitions and Strategies: The Struggle for the Leadership of the Liberal Party in the 1890s* (Oxford, 1964).

N. Stepan, *The Idea of Race in Science: Great Britain, 1800–1960* (1982).

L. Stephen, *Life of Henry Fawcett* (1885).

H. W. Stephens and D. W. Brady, 'The Parliamentary Parties and the Electoral Reforms of 1884–85 in Britain', *Legislative Studies Quarterly*, 1 (1976), pp. 491–510.

N. St John Stevas (ed.), *The Collected Works of Walter Bagehot*, v (1974).

D. Tanner, *Political Change and the Labour Party, 1900–1918* (Cambridge, 1990).

—, 'The Parliamentary Electoral System, the "Fourth Reform Act" and the Rise of Labour in England and Wales', *Bulletin of the Institute of Historical Research*, 56 (1983), pp. 205–19.

P. Thane, 'The Working Class and State "Welfare" in Britain, 1880–1914', *Historical Journal*, 27 (1984), pp. 877–900.

J. A. Thompson, 'The Historians and the Decline of the Liberal Party', *Albion*, 22 (1990), pp. 65–83.

P. Thompson, *Socialists, Liberals and Labour: The Struggle for London, 1885–1914* (1967).

A. Thorold, *Life of Henry Labouchere* (1913).

N. Todd, *The Militant Democracy: Joseph Cowen and Victorian Radicalism* (Whitley Bay, 1991). *Transactions of the Cremation Society of England* (1922), 33.

W. Tuckwell, *Reminiscences of a Radical Parson* (1905).

U. Vogel, 'The Land-Question: A Liberal Theory of Communal Property', *History Workshop*, 27 (1989), pp. 106–35.

E. A. Walker, *W. P. Schreiner: A South African* (Oxford, 1937).

A. Warren, 'Forster, the Liberals and New Directions in Irish Policy 1880–1882', *Parliamentary History*, 6 (1987), pp. 95–126.

S. and B. Webb, *The History of Trade Unionism, 1666–1920* (1920; 1st edn, 1894).

P. Weiler, *The New Liberalism: Liberal Social Theory in Great Britain, 1889–1914* (1982).

H. S. Wilkinson, *Thirty-Five Years, 1874–1909* (1933).

A. S. Wohl, *The Eternal Slum: Housing and Social Policy in Victorian London* (1977).

Index

(Plate numbers in bold)